INSIDERS, OUTSIDERS, INJURIES, & LAW

A central theme of law and society is that people's ideas about law and the decisions they make to mobilize law are shaped by community norms and cultural context. But this was not always an established concept. Among the first empirical pieces to articulate this theory was David Engel's 1984 article "The Oven Bird's Song: Insiders, Outsiders, and Personal Injuries in an American Community." More than thirty years later, this article is now widely considered to be part of the law and society canon. This book argues that Engel's article succeeds so brilliantly because it integrates a wide variety of issues, such as cultural transformation, attitudes about law, dispute processing, legal consciousness, rights mobilization, inclusion and exclusion, and inequality. Contributors to this volume explore the influence of Engel's important work, engaging with the possibilities in its challenging hypotheses and provocative omissions related to the legal system and legal process, class conflict and difference, and law in other cultures.

Mary Nell Trautner is Associate Professor of Sociology at the University at Buffalo, SUNY. She earned her Ph.D. in Sociology from the University of Arizona. She is currently working on a National Science Foundation–funded study of how families cope and make decisions about their child's birth injuries. Her research appears in *Gender & Society*, *American Sociological Review*, *Law & Policy*, and other outlets.

Cambridge Studies in Law and Society

Cambridge Studies in Law and Society aims to publish the best scholarly work on legal discourse and practice in its social and institutional contexts, combining theoretical insights and empirical research.

The fields that it covers are: studies of law in action; the sociology of law; the anthropology of law; cultural studies of law, including the role of legal discourses in social formations; law and economics; law and politics; and studies of governance. The books consider all forms of legal discourse across societies, rather than being limited to lawyers' discourses alone.

The series editors come from a range of disciplines: academic law; socio-legal studies; sociology; and anthropology. All have been actively involved in teaching and writing about law in context.

Series editors

Chris Arup *Monash University, Victoria*
Sally Engle Merry *New York University*
Susan Silbey *Massachusetts Institute of Technology*

A list of books in the series can be found at the back of this book.

Insiders, Outsiders, Injuries, & Law

REVISITING "THE OVEN BIRD'S SONG"

Edited by
MARY NELL TRAUTNER
University at Buffalo, State University of New York

CAMBRIDGE
UNIVERSITY PRESS

CAMBRIDGE
UNIVERSITY PRESS

University Printing House, Cambridge CB2 8BS, United Kingdom

One Liberty Plaza, 20th Floor, New York, NY 10006, USA

477 Williamstown Road, Port Melbourne, VIC 3207, Australia

314–321, 3rd Floor, Plot 3, Splendor Forum, Jasola District Centre, New Delhi – 110025, India

79 Anson Road, #06–04/06, Singapore 079906

Cambridge University Press is part of the University of Cambridge.

It furthers the University's mission by disseminating knowledge in the pursuit of education, learning, and research at the highest international levels of excellence.

www.cambridge.org
Information on this title: www.cambridge.org/9781316638484
DOI: 10.1017/9781316979716

© Cambridge University Press 2018

First published 2018

Printed in the United States of America by Sheridan Books, Inc.

A *catalogue record for this publication is available from the British Library.*

Library of Congress Cataloging-in-Publication Data
NAMES: Celebrating David Engel's "The Oven Bird's Song" (Conference) (2015 :
    Baldy Center for Law and Social Policy (Buffalo, N.Y.) | Trautner, Mary Nell, 1974- |
    Baldy Center for Law and Social Policy (Buffalo, N.Y.), sponsoring body.
TITLE: Insiders, outsiders, injuries, & law : revisiting "the oven bird's song" /
    edited by Mary Nell Trautner, University of Buffalo.
DESCRIPTION: New York, NY, USA : Cambridge University Press, 2018. |
    Series: Cambridge studies in law and society | Includes papers presented at the conference
    "Celebrating David Engel's "The Oven Bird's Song" held on October 23, 2015 at the
    Baldy Center for Law & Social Policy at the University at Buffalo. | "David M. Engel.
    The Oven Bird's Song: Insiders, Outsiders, and Personal Injuries in an American
    Community, 18 Law & Society Review 551-582 (1984)" | Includes bibliographical references and index.
IDENTIFIERS: LCCN 2017028893 | ISBN 9781107188402 (alk. paper) |
    ISBN 9781316638484 (alk. paper)
SUBJECTS: LCSH: Personal injuries–Social aspects–United States–Congresses. |
    Personal injuries–Social aspects–Illinois–Case studies–Congresses. | Engel,
    David M. Oven bird's song–Congresses.
CLASSIFICATION: LCC KF1257.A5 C45 2015 | DDC 346.7303/23–dc23 LC record
    available at https://lccn.loc.gov/2017028893

ISBN 978-1-107-18840-2 Hardback
ISBN 978-1-316-63848-4 Paperback

Contents

Notes on the Contributors   *page* vii

Acknowledgments   xiii

PART I INTRODUCTION AND CONTEXTUALIZATION   1

1   Insiders, Outsiders, Injuries, and Law   3
     Mary Nell Trautner

2   The Oven Bird's Song: Insiders, Outsiders, and Personal Injuries
     in an American Community   8
     David M. Engel

3   Emulating Sherlock Holmes: The Dog That Didn't Bark,
     the Victim Who Didn't Sue, and Other Contradictions of the
     "Hyper-Litigious" Society   38
     Barbara Yngvesson

4   Karl's Law School, or The Oven Bird in Buffalo   56
     Alfred S. Konefsky

PART II THE OVEN BIRD'S INSIGHTS INTO THE LEGAL SYSTEM
AND LEGAL PROCESS   69

5   Challenging Legal Consciousness: Practice, Institutions, and
     Varieties of Resistance   71
     Anna-Maria Marshall

6   Client Selection: How Lawyers Reflect and Influence
     Community Values   82
     Lynn Mather

7   Do Jurors Hear the Oven Bird's Song?   98
     Valerie P. Hans

8　Having a Right but Using It Too: "The Oven Bird's Song"
　　about Contracts　　　　　113
　　Stewart Macaulay

PART III INSIDERS, OUTSIDERS, CLASS CONFLICT,
AND DIFFERENCE　　　　　121

9　Indigenous Litigiousness: The Oven Bird's Song and the
　　Miner's Canary　　　　　123
　　Eve Darian-Smith

10　Listening for the Songs of Others: Insiders, Outsiders, and the
　　Legal Marginalization of the Working Underclass in America　　139
　　Michael McCann

11　Racing the Oven Bird: Criminalization, Rightlessness, and the
　　Politics of Immigration　　　　　161
　　Jamie Longazel

12　Irresponsible Matter: Sublunar Dreams of Injury and Identity　　181
　　Anne Bloom

13　Student Perceptions of (Their) Place in Relationship to
　　"The Oven Bird's Song"　　　　　199
　　Renée Ann Cramer

PART IV CONFLICT AND LAW IN OTHER CULTURES　　　　　217

14　The Songs of Other Birds　　　　　219
　　Anya Bernstein

15　Imagined Community and Litigation Behavior: The Meaning
　　of Automobile Compensation Lawsuits in Japan　　　　　237
　　Yoshitaka Wada

16　Can "The Oven Bird" Migrate North of the Border?　　　　　262
　　Annie Bunting

PART V AFTERWORD　　　　　277

17　Looking Backward, Looking Forward: Past and Future Lives
　　of "The Oven Bird's Song"　　　　　279
　　David M. Engel

Index　　　　　295

Notes on the Contributors

Anya Bernstein, Associate Professor at SUNY Buffalo Law School, holds a PhD in Anthropology from the University of Chicago and a JD from Yale Law School. Her research investigates how states constitute themselves as social actors. She has written on how government administrators justify the law and construct democratic identities; how information undercuts knowledge in national security governance; and how courts evaluate non-legal realities and misrecognize their own interpretive practices. Spanning the United States and Taiwan, her current projects aim to illuminate everyday practices of legal interpretation among government actors in those two very different democracies.

Anne Bloom is Executive Director of the Civil Justice Research Institute at the University of California Berkeley and Irvine Schools of Law. She holds a JD and a PhD in political science. Previously, she was Associate Dean for Scholarship and Professor of Law at McGeorge Law School, where she taught courses in litigation, law and politics, and public interest law. She has also served as the Associate Director of the Civil Justice Program at Loyola Law School and the Director of Public Programs at Equal Justice Works. Anne has significant experience as a public interest lawyer, primarily with Public Justice, where she worked for more than ten years litigating precedent-setting cases. She has authored many articles on law and society-related subjects and is currently working on an edited collection of essays on injuries in cultural perspective, which will be published by Cambridge University Press.

Annie Bunting is Associate Professor in the Law & Society program at York University in Toronto, teaching in the areas of legal pluralism and human rights. She is currently directing an international research collaboration on forced marriage in conflict situations with historians of slavery and women's human rights scholars. Her books include *Marriage by Force? Contestations* *over Coercion and Consent in Africa* (edited with Benjamin N. Lawrance and Richard L. Roberts, 2016) and *Contemporary Slavery: Popular Rhetoric and Political Practice* (edited with Joel Quirk, 2017).

Renée Ann Cramer PhD is Professor and Chair of Law, Politics, and Society at Drake University. Her second book, *Pregnant with the Stars: Watching and Wanting the Celebrity Baby Bump,* on our obsession with celebrity pregnancy, was published in 2015. Cramer is currently working on a project mapping the regulation of homebirth midwifery, funded by the National Science Foundation. She teaches a wide range of interdisciplinary courses in undergraduate legal studies, and serves as president of the Consortium of Undergraduate Law and Justice Programs.

Eve Darian-Smith is Professor of Anthropology and Law and Director of International Studies at the University of California, Irvine. She is also an adjunct professor in the School of Regulation and Global Governance, Australian National University. Trained as a lawyer, historian, and anthropologist, she is interested in issues of postcolonialism, legal pluralism, and sociolegal theory and has published widely, including ten books and edited volumes. Her first book, *Bridging Divides: The Channel Tunnel and English Legal Identity in the New Europe* (2009), won the Law & Society Association Herbert Jacob Book Prize. Her more recent book *Laws and Societies in Global Contexts* (2013) won the International Book Award in law and the Kevin Boyle Book Award. Her upcoming book is *The Global Turn: Theories, Research Designs and Methods* (2017). She is on various editorial boards, including those of the *Canadian Journal of Law and Society* and *Social & Legal Studies,* and she is a former associate editor of *American Ethnologist* and *Law & Society Review.* She is also currently on the executive committee and board of trustees of the Law & Society Association.

David M. Engel is SUNY Distinguished Service Professor of Law at the State University of New York at Buffalo, a former President of the Law & Society Association, and the recipient of that Association's 2017 Kalven Award for Outstanding Scholarship in Law and Society. He studies law, culture, and society in America and Thailand, where he has lived, worked, and taught for many years. His book *Tort, Custom, and Karma: Globalization and Legal Consciousness in Thailand* (2010) examines the effects of global transformations on Thailand's legal culture, and *The Myth of the Litigious Society: Why We Don't Sue* (2016) explains American injury victims' avoidance of claiming. Engel is a visiting professor at the Chiang Mai University Law School, from which he received an honorary doctorate in 2011. He serves as an editor-in-chief of the *Asian Journal of Law and Society* and is a member of the inaugural Board of Trustees of the Asian Law and Society Association.

Valerie P. Hans is Professor of Law at Cornell Law School, where she teaches courses on law and social science, empirical legal studies, torts, and the contemporary American jury. Trained as a social psychologist, she has conducted extensive research and lectured widely about juries, jury reform, and other law and social science issues. Professor Hans has written more than one hundred scholarly articles and is the author or editor of eight books. Her latest book is *The Psychology of Tort Law* (2016), coauthored with Jennifer Robbennolt. She served as President of the Law & Society Association from 2015 to 2017.

Alfred S. Konefsky, a University at Buffalo Distinguished Professor Emeritus, joined the SUNY Buffalo Law School faculty in 1977 after serving as the Charles Warren Fellow in American Legal History at Harvard Law School and as editor of *The Legal Papers of Daniel Webster at Dartmouth College*. He taught contracts and a variety of courses in American legal history, including the subject areas of the nineteenth century (from the Revolution to the Civil War), the colonial period, law and American labor history, American constitutional history, and Herman Melville and the law.

Jamie Longazel is Associate Professor of Law & Society in the Department of Political Science at John Jay College. His recent book, *Undocumented Fears: Immigration and the Politics of Divide and Conquer in Hazleton, Pennsylvania*, won the North Central Sociological Association's Scholarly Achievement Award. It examines the politics of race and class surrounding Hazleton's 2006 passage of an exclusionary immigration ordinance. He is also the coauthor of *The Pains of Mass Imprisonment* (with Benjamin Fleury-Steiner). His work on race, immigration control, and political economy has appeared in publications such as *Law & Social Inquiry*, *Punishment & Society*, *Theoretical Criminology*, and the *Chicana/o-Latina/o Law Review*.

Stewart Macaulay is the Malcolm Pitman Sharp Professor Emeritus of the University of Wisconsin-Madison. He is a past president of the Law and Society Association and a fellow of the American Academy of Arts and Sciences. He pioneered the study of business practices and the work of lawyers related to contracts. He is the author of the frequently cited "Non-Contractual Relations in Business: A Preliminary Study" (*American Sociological Review*, 1963) and coeditor of *Law in Action: A Socio-Legal Reader* (with Lawrence Friedman and Elizabeth Mertz, 2007) and *Contracts: Law in Action* (with William Whitford, Kathryn Hendley, and Jonathan Lipson; 4th ed., 2017).

Anna-Maria Marshall is Associate Professor in the Sociology Department at the University of Illinois, Urbana-Champaign. She received her JD from the University of Virginia (1985) and her PhD in Political Science from Northwestern University (1999). Her research is broadly focused on studying the relationship between law and social change. Her first book, *Confronting Sexual Harassment: The Law and Politics of Everyday Life* (2005), analyzed the institutional and political foundations of legal consciousness when women navigate problems in the workplace. Her articles have appeared in *Law & Society Review*, *Law & Social Inquiry*, and *Annual Review of Law and Social Science*.

Lynn Mather, SUNY Distinguished Service Professor and Professor of Law and Political Science Emerita, has published widely on lawyers, legal ethics, dispute processing, and trial courts. Her recent books include *Lawyers in Practice: Ethical Decision Making in Context* (2012), *Private Lawyers and the Public Interest: The Evolving Role of Pro Bono in the Legal Profession* (2009), and *Divorce Lawyers at Work: Varieties of Professionalism in Practice* (2001). She has also analyzed litigation against tobacco manufacturers in the United States and in the United Kingdom. A former director of the Baldy Center for Law & Social Policy, Mather has served as President of the Law & Society Association and Chair of the Law and Courts Section of APSA.

Michael McCann is Gordon Hirabayashi Professor for the Advancement of Citizenship at the University of Washington. McCann is the author of more than sixty article-length publications and author, coauthor, editor, or coeditor of eight books, including the monographs *Rights at Work: Pay Equity Reform and the Politics of Legal Mobilization* (1994) and (with William Haltom) *Distorting the Law: Politics, Media, and the Litigation Crisis* (2004). Michael is currently writing a book with George Lovell that documents and analyzes the history of struggles for socioeconomic rights and social justice by Filipino immigrant workers in the western United States over the twentieth century. McCann is a former President of the Law & Society Association (2011–13) and presently is Director of the Harry Bridges Center for Labor Studies at UW and Co-Director of the SeaTac/Seattle Minimum Wage Campaign Project.

Yoshitaka Wada is Professor of Law at Waseda Law School and is engaged in research on law and society, including socio-legal theory, dispute resolution, and legal professions. His books with Japanese publishers include *Process of Dispute Negotiation* (1991), *Dispute Resolution* (1994), *Deconstruction of Sociology of Law: Beyond Postmodern Perspectives* (1996), *Medical Malpractice Dispute Resolution* (2001), *Promise of Sociology of Law* (2004), and *Medical Conflict*

Management (2006). Wada served as a member of the program committee for the 2003 Annual Meeting of Law and Society Association and has been Executive Officer of the Asian Law & Society Association since 2015.

Barbara Yngvesson is Professor Emerita of Anthropology at Hampshire College in Amherst, Massachusetts, where she was Dean of the School of Social Science and founding director of the Culture, Brain, and Development Program. Her publications include *Virtuous Citizens, Disruptive Subjects: Order and Complaint in a New England Court* (1993), *Law and Community in Three American Towns* (coauthored with Carol Greenhouse and David M. Engel, 1994; recipient of the 1996 Law & Society Association Book Award), and *Belonging in an Adopted World: Race, Identity and Transnational Adoption* (2010).

Acknowledgments

The Baldy Center for Law & Social Policy at the University at Buffalo provided substantial financial and logistical support for the October 2015 conference that was the genesis of this volume. The Humanities Institute, the Department of Sociology, and the Law School at the University at Buffalo also provided financial support. We appreciate the assistance provided by Baldy Center Director Errol Meidinger, staff support from Laura Wirth, and the enthusiastic help provided by sociology PhD students Matthew McLeskey and Yaqi (Sam) Yuan.

Lynn Mather, Alfred Konefsky, David Engel, Anya Bernstein, and Samantha Barbas helped organize the conference. This volume is based on the excellent presentations and remarks provided by its participants.

John Berger at Cambridge University Press was unendingly supportive and patient. David Engel, Lynn Mather, and Debra Street gave helpful advice regarding editing and completing this collection of essays. I feel fortunate to have learned from such experienced and smart colleagues. Special thanks go to David, of course, for creating such an inspirational work of legal scholarship in the first place. "The Oven Bird's Song" is such an enduringly influential work that law and society scholars around the world turn to David's work again and again and again for insight and inspiration.

Introduction and Contextualization

Insiders, Outsiders, Injuries, and Law

MARY NELL TRAUTNER

INTRODUCTION

One central theme of law and society scholarship is that people's ideas about law and the decisions they make to mobilize law are shaped by community norms and cultural context. But this has not always been taken for granted. Among the first empirical pieces to articulate what now seems obvious about the contextual expression of law was David Engel's 1984 article in the *Law & Society Review*, "The Oven Bird's Song: Insiders, Outsiders, and Personal Injuries in an American Community." Since its publication, his article has been a core work in the field, so influential and widely cited that it is now commonly considered to be part of the law and society "canon."[1]

Why would an article about personal injury and contract litigation be titled "The Oven Bird's Song"? David Engel's love of literature inspired him to invoke Robert Frost's poem as a metaphor for people's use of the law as a response to their perceptions of social change. The article's memorable title underscores the enduring value of this signature contribution to the law and society movement. The product of intensive fieldwork, Engel's research revealed that residents in a rural Illinois community perceived and behaved in ways that underscored contested cultural issues regarding personal injury, dispute resolution, social change, and law. He spent years interviewing litigants and a wide cross-section of community members, new and established and with varying characteristics, about how they resolved disputes and chose (or did not choose) to use the law in the process. He also carefully mined local court records for instances of personal injury and contract litigation. By linking the first-hand accounts of residents with a careful study of court data,

---

[1] Seron, Carroll, Susan Bibler Coutin, and Pauline White Meeusen. 2013. "Is There a Canon of Law and Society?" *Annual Review of Law and Social Science* 9: 287–306.

Engel created a landmark ethnographic study that revealed the cultural contours of law and rendered individuals' responses to it unavoidable and obvious.

Engel discovered that most longtime majority residents of "Sander County" – the insiders – typically resolved their (many) disputes informally, rather than taking legal action against one another. In contrast, "outsiders" (newcomers and some nonwhite residents), whose community ties and personal relationships were fewer and less robust than those of the "insiders," often turned to law when faced with a grievance or dispute. Such use of law by "outsiders" resulted in a major point of critique and disparagement from "insiders," which Engel reveals was really more about nostalgia and resisting change to the status quo than the use of law per se.

The chapter authors in *Insiders, Outsiders, Injuries, & Law* argue that Engel's article succeeds so brilliantly because it integrates such a wide variety of significant issues and themes. Engel's seminal work addresses cultural anxiety, cultural transformation, attitudes about law, dispute processing, legal consciousness, the rule of law, rights mobilization, inclusion and exclusion, inequality, and the haves and have-nots. Accessible to undergraduate and graduate students alike, even after thirty years, "The Oven Bird's Song" still resonates with new audiences. And in a populist era of American and global politics, Engel's insights about insider nostalgia and outsiders/social change are perhaps even more relevant than ever (a point that several contributors in this volume underscore).

After the thirtieth anniversary of the publication of "The Oven Bird's Song," a diverse committee of legal scholars – Lynn Mather, Alfred Konefsky, Anya Bernstein, Samantha Barbas, and I – organized a symposium to examine the intellectual context within which Engel's article was written, its insights into law and the legal process, the pedagogical opportunities and challenges presented by the work, and the continuing influence of "The Oven Bird's Song" on law and society scholarship. Scholars from across the country and around the world convened in Buffalo for a conference held at the University at Buffalo's Baldy Center for Law & Social Policy in October 2015. Most of the chapters in this volume arose from the conference presentations, supplemented by two additional chapters specifically prepared for this collection.

A central feature of this volume is its interdisciplinary and multi-focal nature. Scholars from law, political science, history, sociology, anthropology, and global studies explore how rights, legal consciousness, immigration, contracts, the legal profession, jury decision-making, and the body are situated not only in legal doctrine and legal practice, but also, as Engel demonstrated, in culture, history, and society. The relationship that Engel explored between the use of law and the cultures and politics of different communities has been extended because of its contemporary salience to a wide range of policy issues. Together, the chapters provide new insights and provide readers a way to see and understand the open-ended possibilities in "The Oven Bird's" challenging hypotheses and provocative omissions.

The following chapter includes the original article as it appeared in *Law & Society Review*. Subsequent chapters share a focus on the insider/outsider dichotomy, the reluctance to make legal claims, and a forward-looking consideration of where the field is headed next.

Part I of the volume contextualizes Engel's article. Barbara Yngvesson begins with an examination of the significance of the interpretive turn in shaping sociolegal studies, and how this turn allowed researchers to focus on lived experiences and explain "non-events" such as the decision not to sue. Alfred Konefsky situates "The Oven Bird's Song" in the intellectual context of the early 1980s Buffalo Law School where, after delivering an early version of the analysis as his job talk, Engel completed writing the manuscript.

Part II features work that uses Engel's article as a window into the legal system and legal process itself. Anna-Maria Marshall demonstrates how "The Oven Bird's Song" laid the foundation for legal consciousness studies while simultaneously anticipating some of the significant debates in that tradition. By analyzing the legal significance of what individuals think and do, Marshall argues, Engel demonstrated that law is a thread that runs through the everyday lives of ordinary people. Lynn Mather turns her focus to the legal profession and considers how the perceptions of law, legal conduct, and changing social context that affected Sander Country residents so profoundly are also reflected in the ways lawyers screen cases and construct legal cases. She gives special attention to the lawyers representing the "outsiders" in Sander County, and compares them to other lawyers in the United States who have sought to use law to promote particular causes or interests in times of social change. Valerie Hans reviews research on jury decision-making in tort cases, exploring whether the hostility to personal injury plaintiffs and the tendency to blame injury victims that Engel discovered decades ago are reflected in contemporary jurors' responses. Hans shows that jurors believe there are many unjustified lawsuits. The jurors she discusses express concern about greedy plaintiffs, a decline in personal responsibility, and exaggeration of injuries – attitudes that lead to over-attribution of plaintiff fault and minimization of injury. Hans closes her chapter by reflecting on the lessons of "The Oven Bird's Song" for jury trial advocacy. Finally, Stewart Macaulay reflects on what Engel's article reveals about contracts and contract law. Sander County residents disapproved of people who sued others for injuries in tort actions, but accepted that contract actions were legitimate because, with few exceptions, "a deal is a deal." Macaulay adds "a footnote" to "The Oven Bird's Song," showing that while there are indeed disincentives to using legal rights in many contexts, there is an imprecise cultural norm in some contexts that calls for one party in a contract not to sue but, rather, to work out an acceptable solution to the other party's problems in performing.

Engel's work challenges the popular notion that justice – and, by extension, law – is somehow blind or neutral to differences in social statuses. Otherwise, why does it matter for law if people are "insiders" or "outsiders" in society? Chapters in Section 3 grapple with this question, exploring how gender, race, immigration status, social class, and other forms of difference influence not only the decisions that people make about law, but also how others respond to those decisions. Eve Darian-Smith draws on fifteen years of research with Native American communities to illustrate how they are perceived as a new group of "outsiders," using law to redress wrongs and fight enduring discrimination. Michael McCann's analysis of the import of Engel's essay focuses on workers and other relatively rights-less outsider groups, opening up a variety of questions about the possibilities as well as the significant obstacles to subaltern mobilization of rights in, and especially, beyond courts, through politics. Jamie Longazel shows how some of the central arguments in "The Oven Bird's Song" align with and are enhanced by developments in Critical Race Theory, focusing on how immigrants as "outsiders" in a small town – Hazelton, Pennsylvania – resemble the outsiders of Engel's Sander County. Longazel's analysis shows how the White majority uses criminalization not simply to stereotype immigrants as crime-prone but rather to draw a "line of demarcation" that validates the personhood of some while stripping it from others. In this way, racialized criminalization troublingly becomes a tool used to construct eligibility for rights and resources that many find especially "valuable" in the context of economic uncertainty. Anne Bloom's chapter speculates on the contributions of Engel's work to deeper understanding how changing conceptions of bodily identity, especially in terms of gender, aging, and disability, might shape the future of tort law. She argues that the desire to adopt "outsider" identities and to become "irresponsible" (or at least less responsible) matter underlies contemporary bodily identity practices, particularly as they relate to gender and disability. Renée Cramer closes out this section by engaging the sense of familiarity students have with the spatial and temporal aspects of Engel's classic article, and takes seriously their stories about places like Sander County. In developing this theme, Cramer's chapter examines the implications this comfort has for students' politics – their willingness to accept a narrative of tort reform as necessary, their acceptance of risk as indeed a "part of life," their deep (and paradoxical) distrust of professionalism, and their articulation of the divide between outsiders and insiders.

Section 4 considers "The Oven Bird's Song" contributions to understanding conflict and law outside the United States. Yoshitaka Wada modifies and develops Engel's perspective to improve understanding of the complex relationships among cultural values, the nature of community and relationships, and the meaning of suing behavior in automobile dispute resolution in Japan. He uses the concept of "imagined communities" to clarify the characteristics of Japanese communities, the structure of the judicial system, and legal consciousness to illustrate the wider possibility of applying Engel's insights beyond American borders. Anya Bernstein draws on "The Oven Bird's Song" to understand government administrators and community activists in Taipei, "insider" groups who are reluctant to use the law to justify – or even to enforce – their positions. Much like the residents of Sander County, she finds that these Taipei insiders saw recourse to the law as a failure of other, more legitimate forms of social ordering such as interpersonal relations and shared values – not dissimilar from the informal dispute resolution typically pursued by Sander County insiders. Annie Bunting questions whether the themes of "The Oven Bird's Song" translate to the Canadian context, given cultural differences in how Canadians and Americans think about insiders and outsiders, and, for that matter, how national cultures might shape perceptions of legitimate uses of the law. She presents us an opportunity to think about legal pluralism and parochialism in law and society research on both sides of the border.

David Engel concludes with a brief social history of his thinking and writing of the work that inspired the 2015 conference and this volume, but gives more attention to new directions that remain to be explored, particularly with regard to the central topic of "The Oven Bird's Song," personal injuries. Engel argues that the comparative and interpretive perspectives that emerged in law and society research thirty years ago can still be usefully deployed in a broader effort to understand why injuries remain such a serious social problem in our country, why injuries are widely misunderstood, and why the law has been so ineffective in redressing the inequalities and hardships that injuries inflict on those who are least able to deal with them.

2

The Oven Bird's Song: Insiders, Outsiders, and Personal Injuries in an American Community*

DAVID M. ENGEL**

In "Sander County" Illinois, concerns about litigiousness in the local population tended to focus on personal injury suits, although such cases were very rarely brought. This article explores the roots of these concerns in the ideology of the rural community and in the reactions of many residents to social, cultural, and economic changes that created a pervasive sense of social disintegration and loss. Personal injury claims are contrasted with contract actions, which were far more numerous yet were generally viewed with approval and did not give rise to perceptions of litigiousness or greed. The distinction is explained in terms of changing conceptions of the community itself and in terms of the problematic relationships between "insiders" and "outsiders" in Sander County.

* The title refers to Robert Frost's poem "The Oven Bird," which describes a response to the perception of disintegration and decay not unlike the response that is the subject of this paper:

> There is a singer everyone has heard,
> Loud, a mid-summer and a mid-wood bird,
> Who makes the solid tree trunks sound again.
> He says that leaves are old and that for flowers
> Mid-summer is to spring as one to ten.
> He says the early petal-fall is past
> When pear and cherry bloom went down in showers
> On sunny days a moment overcast;
> And comes that other fall we name the fall.
> He says the highway dust is over all.
> The bird would cease and be as other birds
> But that he knows in singing not to sing.
> The question that he frames in all but words
> Is what to make of a diminished thing.

From *The Poetry of Robert Frost*, edited by Edward Connery Lathem. Copyright 1916, © 1969 by Holt, Rinehart and Winston. Copyright 1944 by Robert Frost. Reprinted by permission of Holt, Rinehart and Winston, Publishers.

** I am deeply grateful to the residents of "Sander County" for their generous participation in this study.
LAW & SOCIETY REVIEW, Volume 18, Number 4 (1984)

I. INTRODUCTION

Although it is generally acknowledged that law is a vital part of culture and of the social order, there are times when the invocation of formal law is viewed as an anti-social act and as a contravention of established cultural norms. Criticism of what is seen as an overuse of law and legal institutions often reveals less about the quantity of litigation at any given time than about the interests being asserted or protected through litigation and the kinds of individuals or groups involved in cases that the courts are asked to resolve. Periodic concerns over litigation as a "problem" in particular societies or historical eras can thus draw our attention to important underlying conflicts in cultural values and changes or tensions in the structure of social relationships.

In our own society at present, perhaps no category of litigation has produced greater public criticism than personal injuries. The popular culture is full of tales of feigned or exaggerated physical harms, of spurious whiplash suits, ambulance-chasing lawyers, and exorbitant claims for compensation. Scholars, journalists, and legal professionals, voicing concern with crowded dockets and rising insurance costs, have often shared the perception that personal injury litigation is a field dominated by overly litigious plaintiffs and by trigger-happy attorneys interested only in their fee (Seymour, 1973: 177; Tondel, 1976: 547; Perham, 1977; Rosenberg, 1977: 154; Taylor, 1981; Gest et al., 1982; Greene, 1983).

To the mind agitated by such concerns, Sander County (a pseudonym) appears to offer a quiet refuge. In this small, predominantly rural county in Illinois, personal injury litigation rates were low in comparison to other major categories of litigation[1] and were apparently somewhat lower than the personal

I would also like to thank the following friends and colleagues who read and commented on this article at one stage or another in its development: Richard L. Abel, James B. Atleson, Guyora Binder, Donald Black, Marc Galanter, Fred Konefsky, Virginia Leary, Richard O. Lempert, Felice J. Levine, John Henry Schlegel, Eric H. Steele, Robert J. Steinfeld, and Barbara Yngvesson. I am also grateful to Linda Kosinski for her skill and patience in typing and retyping the manuscript.

The research on which this article is based was supported by the National Science Foundation under Grant No. SOC 77-11654 and by the American Bar Foundation. Opinions, findings, and conclusions are those of the author and not of the supporting organizations.

[1] By "litigation" I mean simply the filing of a formal complaint in the civil trial court, even if no further adversarial processes occur. The annual litigation rate for personal injuries was 1.45 cases filed per 1,000 population as compared to 13.7 contract cases (mostly collection matters), 3.62 property-related cases (mostly landlord-tenant matters), and 11.74 family-related cases (mostly divorces). All litigation rates are based on the combined civil filings for 1975 and 1976 in the Sander County Court. Population figures are based on the 1970 census and are therefore somewhat understated. That is, the actual litigation rates for 1975–1976 are probably lower than those given here.

injury rates in other locations as well.[2] Yet Sander County residents displayed a deep concern with and an aversion toward this particular form of "litigious behavior" despite its rarity in their community.[3]

Those who sought to enforce personal injury claims in Sander County were characterized by their fellow residents as "very greedy," as "quick to sue," as "people looking for the easy buck," and as those who just "naturally sue and try to get something [for] ... life's little accidents." One minister describing the local scene told me, "Everybody's going to court. That's the thing to do, because a lot of people see a chance to make money." A social worker, speaking of local perceptions of personal injury litigation, particularly among the older residents of Sander County, observed: "Someone sues every time you turn around. Sue happy, you hear them say. Sue happy." Personal injury plaintiffs were viewed in Sander County as people who made waves and as troublemakers. Even members of the community who occupied positions of prestige or respect could not escape criticism if they brought personal injury

---

[2]   McIntosh reports a rate of approximately 6 tort actions per 1,000 population in the St. Louis Circuit Court in 1970. He does not state what proportion of these involved personal injuries (McIntosh, 1980–81: 832). Friedman and Percival (1976: 281–82) report 2.80 and 1.87 cases filed per 1,000 population in the Alameda and San Benito Superior Courts (respectively) in 1970 under the combined categories of "auto accidents" and "other personal injuries." The two California courts had original jurisdiction only for claims of $5,000 or more, however, while the Sander County figures include personal injury claims of all amounts. Friedman and Percival do not indicate what proportion of the auto accident cases involved personal injuries as opposed to property damage only. Statewide data for California and New York, compiled by the National Center for State Courts (1979: 49, 51) for tort cases filed in 1975, also tend to indicate litigation rates higher than Sander County's. However, these aggregate litigation rates are understated in that they exclude filings from smaller courts of limited jurisdiction in both states and are overstated in that they fail to separate personal injury cases from other tort actions. Litigation rates for tort cases filed per 1,000 population in 1975 are: California, 3.55 and New York, 2.21 (but in 1977, when additional lower court dockets were included in the survey of tort cases filed, the rate reported for New York more than doubled to 4.47; see National Center for State Courts, 1982: 61). In comparing the Sander County litigation rates to those in other cities or states, it should also be remembered that, because Sander County was quite small, the *absolute number* of personal injury actions filed in the county court was also very small compared to more urban areas.

[3]   I use the term "community" somewhat loosely in this discussion to mean the county seat of Sander County and the surrounding farmlands. Since Sander County is rather small, this takes in most of the county. There are a handful of very small towns elsewhere in the county. Although they are not far from the county seat and are linked to it in many ways, it is probably stretching things to consider them part of a single "community." I should add that the problem of defining the term "community" as a subject of empirical study has vexed social scientists for many years, and I aspired to no conceptual breakthrough in this regard. My interest was in finding a research site where the jurisdiction of the court was roughly congruent with a social unit comprising a set of meaningful interactions and relationships.

cases to court. When a minister filed a personal injury suit in Sander County after having slipped and fallen at a school, there were, in the words of one local observer:

> [A] lot of people who are resentful for it, because . . . he chose to sue. There's been, you know, not hard feelings, just some strange intangible things. . . .

How can one explain these troubled perceptions of personal injury litigation in a community where personal injury actions were in fact so seldom brought? The answer lies partly in culturally-conditioned ideas of what constitutes an injury and how conflicts over injuries should be handled. The answer is also found in changes that were occurring in the social structure of Sander County at the time of this study and in challenges to the traditional order that were being raised by newly arrived "outsiders." The local trial court was potentially an important battleground in the clash of cultures, for it could be called on to recognize claims that traditional norms stigmatized in the strongest possible terms.[4]

II. SOCIAL CHANGES AND THE SENSE OF COMMUNITY

Sander County in the late 1970s was a society that was strongly rooted in its rural past yet undergoing economic and social changes of major proportions. It was a small county (between 20,000 and 30,000 population in the 1970s), with more than half its population concentrated in its county seat and the rest in several much smaller towns and rural areas. Agriculture was still central to county life. Sander County had 10 percent more of its land in farms in the mid-1970s than did the state of Illinois as a whole, but the number of farms in Sander County had decreased by more than one-third over the preceding twenty years while their average size had grown by almost half. Rising costs, land values, and taxes had been accompanied by an increase in the mechanization of agriculture in Sander County, and the older, smaller farming operations were being rapidly transformed. At the same time, a few large manufacturing plants had brought blue collar employees from other areas to work (but not always to live) in Sander County. Also, a local canning plant had for many years employed seasonal migrant workers, many of whom

---

[4] Hostility toward personal injury litigation as a form of "hyperlexis" may also have been influenced in Sander County by mass media treatment of this form of legal claim. Yet the attitudes and antagonisms I describe had deep roots in the culture of Sander County itself as well as in the popular culture of the country as a whole. A critical appraisal of the hyperlexis literature, which parallels this discussion in some respects, is found in Galanter (1983).

were Latinos. In recent years, however, a variety of "outsiders" had come to stay permanently in Sander County, and the face of the local society was gradually changing.

To some extent these changes had been deliberately planned by local leaders, for it was thought that the large manufacturing plants would revitalize the local economy. Yet from the beginning there had also been a sense of foreboding. In the words of one older farmer:

> A guy that I used to do business with told me when he saw this plant coming in down here that he felt real bad for the community. He said, that's gonna be the end of your community, he said, because you get too many people in that don't have roots in anything. And I didn't think too much about it at the time, but I can understand what he was talking about now. I know that to some extent, at least, this is true. Not that there haven't been some real good people come in, I don't mean that. But I think you get quite a number of a certain element that you've never had before.

Others were more blunt about the "certain element" that had entered Sander County: union members, southerners and southwesterners, blacks, and Latinos. One long-time rural resident told us, "I think there's too many Commies around. I think this country takes too many people in, don't you? ... That's why this country's going to the dogs." Many Sander County residents referred nostalgically to the days when they could walk down Main Street and see none but familiar faces. Now there were many strangers. An elderly woman from a farming family, who was struggling to preserve her farm in the face of rising taxes and operating costs, spoke in troubled tones of going into the post office and seeing Spanish-speaking workers mailing locally-earned money to families outside the country. "This," she said, "I don't like." Another woman, also a long-time resident, spoke of the changing appearance of the town:

> [It was] lots different than it is right now. For one thing, I think we knew everybody in town. If you walked uptown you could speak to every single person on the street. It just wasn't at all like it is today. Another thing, the stores were different. We have so many places now that are foreign, Mexican, and health spas, which we're not very happy about, most of us. My mother was going uptown here a year ago and didn't feel very well when she got up to State Street. But she just kept going, and I thought it was terrible because the whole north side of town was the kind of place that you wouldn't want to go into for information or for help. Mostly because we've not grown up with an area where there were any foreign people at all.

There was also in the late 1970s a pervasive sense of a breakdown in the traditional relationships and reciprocities that had characterized life in Sander County. As one elderly farmer told me:

It used to be I could tell you any place in Sander County where it was, but I can't now because I don't know who lives on them.... And as I say in the last 20 years people don't change work like they used to— or in the last 30 years. Everybody's got big equipment, they do all their own work so they don't have to change labor. Like years ago ... why you had about 15 or 20 farmers together doing the exchange and all.

Many Sander County residents with farming backgrounds had warm memories of the harvest season, when groups of neighbors got together to share work and food:

When we had the threshing run, the dining room table it stretched a full 17 feet of the dining room, and guys would come in like hungry wolves, you know, at dinner time and supper again the same thing.... And they'd fire the engine up and have it ready to start running by 7:00.... You know, it was quite a sight to see that old steam engine coming down the road. I don't know, while I never want to be doing it again, I still gotta get kind of a kick out of watching a steam engine operate.

And all could remember socializing with other farming families on Saturday evenings during the summertime. In the words of two long-time farmers:

A: Well, on Saturday night they used to come into town, and the farmers would be lined up along the sidewalk with an ice cream cone or maybe a glass of beer or something....
B: If you met one to three people, you'd get all the news in the neighborhood....
A: If you go downtown now, anytime, I doubt if you'll see half a dozen people that you know. I mean to what you say sit down and really, really know them.
B: You practically knew everybody.
A. That's right, but you don't now.
B: No, no, no. If you go down Saturday night ...
A: Everything is dead.

III. THE STUDY

I shall argue in this article that perceptions of personal injury claims in Sander County were strongly influenced by these social changes as local residents experienced them and by the sense that traditional relationships and exchanges in the community were gradually disintegrating.[5] I cannot say that the frequent

---

[5] The sense of social change and disintegration in Sander County helped crystallize a set of values opposed to personal injury litigation. These values were almost certainly rooted in long established norms, but the targets of their expression and the intensity with which they were asserted may have been new. This article focuses on how and why such values came

condemnation of personal injury litigation elsewhere in the United States is linked to a similar set of social processes, but investigation in other settings may disclose some parallels. The sense of community can take many forms in American society, and when members of a community feel threatened by change, their response may be broadly similar to the kind of response I describe here.

My discussion is based on fieldwork conducted from 1978 to 1980. Besides doing background research and immersing myself in the community and in the workings of the Sander County Court, I collected data for the study in three ways: (1) A sample of civil case files opened in 1975 and 1976 was drawn and analyzed.[6] (2) Plaintiffs and defendants in a subsample of these civil cases were contacted and interviewed in broad-ranging, semi-structured conversations.[7] (3) Strategically placed "community observers" were identified and interviewed at length. These were individuals who had particular insights into different groups, settings, occupations, or activities in the community.[8] Discussions with them touched on various aspects of the community, including the ways in which the relationships, situations, and problems that might give rise to litigated cases were handled when the court was not used. The insights derived from the community observer interviews thus provided a broader social and cultural context for the insights derived from the court-based research.

Personal injuries were one of four major substantive topics selected to receive special attention in this study.[9] It soon became apparent, however, that personal injuries were viewed quite differently from the other topics, and

---

to be expressed and acutely felt in the late 1970s by many Sander County residents. See note 19 *infra*.

[6] A 20% sample was taken for the years 1975–1976 within each of 12 civil categories mandated by the Administrative Office of the Illinois Courts: (1) Law (claim over $15,000), (2) Law (claim $15,000 or less), (3) Chancery, (4) Miscellaneous Remedies, (5) Eminent Domain, (6) Estates, (7) Tax, (8) Municipal Corporations, (9) Mental Health, (10) Divorce, (11) Family, (12) Small Claims. After the sample was drawn, the cases were reclassified into the substantive categories referred to throughout this article.

[7] Parties in 66 cases were interviewed. Wherever possible, all parties to each case were included. Particular attention was given to the individuals themselves, the relationship between them, and to the origin, development, and outcome of each case.

[8] Among the 71 community observers were judges, lawyers, teachers, ministers, farmers, a beautician, a barber, city and county officials, a funeral parlor operator, youth workers, social service workers, various "ordinary citizens" from different segments of the community, a union steward, a management representative, agricultural extension workers, doctors, a newspaper reporter, the members of a rescue squad, and others.

[9] The other three substantive areas were injuries to reputation, contracts, and marital problems.

the differences appeared to be related to the fundamental social changes that were taking place in Sander County. Focusing on personal injuries in this article makes it possible to examine the role played by formal law in mediating relationships between different groups in a changing society and to consider why the rare use of formal legal institutions for certain purposes can evoke strong concern and reaction in a community. The answer, I shall suggest, lies in the ideological responses of longtime residents of Sander County whose values and assumptions were subjected to profound challenges by what they saw as the intrusion of newcomers into their close-knit society.

IV. INJURIES AND INDIVIDUALISM

For many of the residents of Sander County, exposure to the risk of physical injury was simply an accepted part of life. In a primarily agricultural community, which depended on hard physical work and the use of dangerous implements and machinery, such risks were unavoidable. Farmers in Sander County told many stories of terrible injuries caused by hazardous farming equipment, vehicles of different kinds, and other dangers that were associated with their means of obtaining a livelihood. There was a feeling among many in Sander County –particularly among those from a farming background – that injuries were an ever-present possibility, although prudent persons could protect themselves much of the time by taking proper precautions.

It would be accurate to characterize the traditional values associated with personal injuries in Sander County as individualistic, but individualism may be of at least two types. A rights-oriented individualism is consistent with an aggressive demand for compensation (or other remedies) when important interests are perceived to have been violated. By contrast, an individualism emphasizing self-sufficiency and personal responsibility rather than rights is consistent with the expectation that people should ordinarily provide their own protection against injuries and should personally absorb the consequences of harms they fail to ward off.[10]

It is not clear why the brand of individualism that developed over the years in Sander County emphasized self-sufficiency rather than rights and remedies, but with respect to personal injuries at least, there can be no doubt that this had occurred. If the values associated with this form of individualism originated in an earlier face-to-face community dominated by economically self-sufficient farmers and merchants, they remained vitally important to many

---

[10] This distinction between the two types of individualism emerged from an ongoing dialogue with Fred Konefsky, whose contribution to this conceptualization I gratefully acknowledge.

of the long-time Sander County residents even at the time of this study. For them, injuries were viewed in relation to the victims, their fate, and their ability to protect themselves. Injuries were not viewed in terms of conflict or potential conflict between victims and other persons, nor was there much sympathy for those who sought to characterize the situation in such terms. To the traditional individualists of Sander County, transforming a personal injury into a claim against someone else was an attempt to escape responsibility for one's own actions. The psychology of contributory negligence and assumption of risk had deep roots in the local culture. The critical fact of personal injuries in most cases was that the victims probably could have prevented them if they had been more careful, even if others were to some degree at fault. This fact alone is an important reason why it was considered inappropriate for injured persons to attempt to transform their misfortune into a demand for compensation or to view it as an occasion for interpersonal conflict.

Attitudes toward money also help explain the feelings of long-time residents of Sander County toward personal injury claimants. While there might be sympathy for those who suffered such injuries, it was considered highly improper to try to "cash in" on them through claims for damages. Money was viewed as something one acquired through long hours of hard work, not by exhibiting one's misfortunes to a judge or jury or other third party, even when the injuries were clearly caused by the wrongful behavior of another. Such attitudes were reinforced by the pervasive sense of living in what had long been a small and close-knit community. In such a community, potential plaintiffs and defendants are likely to know each other, at least by reputation, or to have acquaintances in common. It is probable that they will interact in the future, if not directly then through friends and relatives. In these circumstances it is, at best, awkward to sue or otherwise assert a claim. In addition, in a small community one cannot hide the fact of a suit for damages, and the disapproving attitudes of others are likely to be keenly felt. Thus, I was frequently assured that local residents who were mindful of community pressures generally reacted to cases of personal injury, even those that might give rise to liability in tort, in a "level-headed" and "realistic" way. By this it was meant that they would not sue or even, in most cases, demand compensation extrajudicially from anyone except, perhaps, their own insurance companies.[11]

---

[11] I heard of only a few cases where injured persons negotiated compensatory payments from the liability insurance of the party responsible for their harm. In these cases expectations (or demands) appeared to be modest. One involved a woman who lived on a farm. When visiting a neighbor's house, she fell down the basement stairs because of a negligently installed door,

Given the negative views that local juries adopted toward personal injury cases, terms such as "realistic" for those who avoided litigation were indeed well chosen. Judges, lawyers, and laypersons all told me that civil trial juries in the county reflected – and thus reinforced – the most conservative values and attitudes toward personal injury litigation. Awards were very low and suspicion of personal injury plaintiffs was very high. A local insurance adjuster told me:

> [T]he jury will be people from right around here that are, a good share of them will be farmers, and they've been out there slaving away for every penny they've got and they aren't about to just give it away to make that free gift to anybody.

And one of the leading local trial lawyers observed:

> [T]here's a natural feeling, what's this son of a bitch doing here? Why is he taking our time? Why is he trying to look for something for nothing? . . . So I've got to overcome that. That's a natural prejudice in a small [community], they don't have that natural prejudice in Cook County. But you do have it out here. So first I've got to sell the jury on the fact that this man's tried every way or this woman's tried every way to get justice and she couldn't. And they now come to you for their big day. . . . And then you try like hell to show that they're one of you, they've lived here and this and that.

The prospects for trying a personal injury case before a local jury, he concluded, were so discouraging that, "If I can figure out a way not to try a case in [this] county for injury, I try to."

Where there was no alternative as to venue, potential plaintiffs typically resigned themselves to nonjudicial settlements without any thought of

---

fractured her skull, was unconscious for three days, and was in intensive care for five days. As a result of the accident she suffered a permanent loss of her sense of smell and a substantial (almost total) impairment of her sense of taste. Her husband, a successful young farmer, told me that their own insurance did not cover the injury. Their neighbor had liability insurance, which paid only $1000 (the hospital bills alone were approximately $2500). Nevertheless, they never considered seeking greater compensation from their neighbor or the neighbor's insurance company:

> We were thankful that she recovered as well as she did. . . . We never considered a lawsuit there at all. I don't know what other people would have done in the case. Possibly that insurance company would have paid the total medical if we would have just, well, I have a brother who is an attorney, could have just wrote them a letter maybe. But, I don't know, we just didn't do it, that's all.

Further discussion of the role of insurance in the handling of personal injuries in Sander County appears in the next section.

litigation. And, as I have already suggested, for many in the community the possibility of litigation was not considered in any case. One woman I spoke with had lost her child in an automobile accident. She settled the case for $12,000 without filing a claim, yet she was sure that this amount was much less than she could have obtained through a lawsuit. She told me that since she and her family knew they were going to stay permanently in the community, the pressure of the local value system foreclosed the possibility of taking the matter to court:

> One of the reasons that I was extremely hesitant to sue was because of the community pressure.... Local people in this community are not impressed when you tell them that you're involved in a lawsuit.... That really turns them off.... They're not impressed with people who don't earn their own way. And that's taking money that they're not sure that you deserve.

Others had so internalized this value system that they followed its dictates even when community pressures did not exist. A doctor told me that one of his patients was seriously burned during a trip out of state when an airline stewardess spilled hot coffee on her legs, causing permanent discoloration of her skin. This woman refused to contact a lawyer and instead settled directly with the airline for medical expenses and the cost of the one-week vacation she had missed. Regarding the possibility of taking formal legal action to seek a more substantial award, she said simply, "We don't do that." This same attitude may help to explain the apparent reluctance of local residents to assert claims against other potential defendants from outside Sander County, such as negligent drivers or businesses or manufacturers.

Thus, if we consider the range of traditional responses to personal injuries in Sander County, we find, first of all, a great deal of self-reliant behavior. Injured persons typically responded to injuries without taking any overt action, either because they did not view the problem in terms of a claim against or conflict with another person or because membership in a small, close-knit community inhibited them from asserting a claim that would be socially disapproved. Some sought compensation through direct discussions with the other party, but such behavior was considered atypical. When sympathy or advice was sought, many turned to friends, neighbors, relatives, and physicians. The County Health Department, the mayor, and city council representatives also reported that injured persons occasionally sought them out, particularly when the injuries were caused by hazards that might endanger others. In such cases, the goal was generally to see the hazard removed for the benefit of the public rather than to seek compensation or otherwise advance personal interests.

V. INSURING AGAINST INJURIES

Persons who had been injured often sought compensation from their own health and accident insurance without even considering the possibility of a claim against another party or another insurance company. As a local insurance adjuster told me:

> We have some people that have had their kid injured on our insured's property, and they were not our insured. And we call up and offer to pay their bills, because our insured has called and said my kid Tommy cracked that kid over the head with a shovel and they hauled him off to the hospital. And I called the people and say we have medical coverage and they are absolutely floored, some of them, that it never even crossed their minds. They were just going to turn it in to their own little insurance, their health insurance, and not do anything about it whatsoever, especially if [Tommy's parents] are close friends. . . .

By moving quickly to pay compensation in such cases before claims could arise, this adjuster believed that she prevented disputes and litigation. It helped, too, that the adjuster and the parties to an accident, even an automobile accident, usually knew each other:

> In Chicago, all those people don't know the guy next door to them, much less the guy they had the wreck with. And right here in town, if you don't know the people, you probably know their neighbor or some of their family or you can find out real quick who they are or where they are.

The contrast between injuries in a face-to-face community and in a metropolis like Chicago was drawn in explicit terms:

> I think things are pretty calm and peaceful as, say, compared to Chicago. Now I have talked to some of the adjusters in that area from time to time and I know, well, and we have our own insureds that go in there and get in an accident in Chicago, and we'll have a lawsuit or at least have an attorney ... on the claim within a day or maybe two days of the accident even happening. Sometimes our insured has not any more than called back and said I've had a wreck but I don't even know who it was with. And before you can do anything, even get a police report or anything, why you'll get a letter from the attorney. And that would never, that rarely ever happens around here.

This adjuster estimated that over the past 15 years, her office had been involved in no more than 10 automobile-related lawsuits, an extraordinarily low number compared to the frequency of such cases in other jurisdictions.[12] Of course, once an insurance company has paid compensation to its insured, it may exercise its right of subrogation against the party that caused the accident, and one might expect insurance companies to be unaffected by local values opposing the assertion or litigation of injury claims. It is not entirely clear why insurance companies, like individuals, seldom brought personal injury actions in Sander County, but there are some clues. This particular adjuster, who had grown up in Sander County, shared the local value system. Although she did not decide whether to bring suit as a subrogée, she may well have affected the decisions of her central office by her own perceptions and by her handling of the people and documents in particular cases. Furthermore, her insurance company was connected to the Farm Bureau, a membership organization to which most local farmers belonged. The evident popularity of this insurance carrier in Sander County (over 75 percent of the eligible farm families were estimated to be members of the Farm Bureau; it is not known how many members carried the insurance, but the percentage was apparently high) meant that injuries in many cases may have involved two parties covered by the same insurance company.

Occasionally, an insurance company did bring suit in the name of its insured, but given the unsympathetic attitudes of local juries, such lawsuits seldom met with success in Sander County. The adjuster mentioned above told me of a farm worker from Oklahoma who was harvesting peas for a local cannery. He stopped to lie down and rest in the high grass near the road and was run over by her insured, who was driving a pick-up truck and had swerved slightly off the road to avoid a large combine. When the fieldworker's insurance carrier sought compensation, the local adjuster refused, claiming that the injured man should not have been lying in the grass near the road and could not have been seen by her insured, who, she insisted, was driving carefully. The case went to trial and a jury composed largely of local farmers was drawn:

> I was not even in there because our lawyers that represent us said, how many of those people do you know out there? And I said, I can give you the first name of everybody on the jury. He said, you stay over there in the library . . . don't let them see you. . . . So I stayed out in my little corner and listened to what went on and we won, we didn't pay 5 cents on it.

---

[12] In Sander County as a whole, the litigation rate for automobile-related personal injury cases in 1975–76 was 0.88 cases each year per 1,000 population. For *all* automobile-related tort actions, including those where there was no personal injury claim, the litigation rate was 1.87 cases per 1,000 population. In the absence of reliable or meaningful comparative data, it is difficult to say how low or high these county-wide rates are; but my hunch is that these are rather low for a jurisdiction in which no-fault approaches were *not* used for motor vehicle cases.

Thus, even a lawsuit involving insurance companies on both sides was ultimately resolved in a manner that accorded with traditional values. The insurance companies' knowledge of jury attitudes in Sander County undoubtedly affected their handling of most injury cases.

VI. LAWYERS AND LOCAL VALUES

Sander County attorneys reported that personal injury cases came to them with some regularity, although they also felt that many injury victims never consulted an attorney but settled directly with insurance companies for less than they should have received. When these attorneys were consulted, it was by people who, in the opinion of the attorneys, had real, nonfrivolous grievances, but the result was seldom formal legal action. Most personal injury cases were resolved, as they are elsewhere (Ross, 1970), through informal negotiation. Formal judicial procedures were initiated primarily to prod the other side to negotiate seriously or when it became necessary to preserve a claim before it would be barred by the statute of limitations. The negotiating process was, of course, strongly influenced by the parties' shared knowledge of likely juror reaction if the case actually went to trial. Thus, plaintiffs found negotiated settlements relatively attractive even when the terms were not particularly favorable.

But expectations regarding the outcome of litigation were probably not the only reason that members of the local bar so seldom filed personal injury cases. To some extent Sander County lawyers, many of whom were born and raised in the area, shared the local tendency to censure those who aggressively asserted personal injury claims. One attorney, for example, described client attitudes toward injury claims in the following terms: "A lot of people are more conducive to settlement here just because they're attempting to be fair as opposed to making a fast buck." Yet this same attorney admitted that informal settlements were often for small amounts of money and were usually limited to medical expenses, without any "general" damages whatever.[13] His characterization of such outcomes as "fair" suggests an internalization of local values even on the part of those whose professional role it was to assert claims on behalf of tort plaintiffs.

[13] This is particularly striking since Laurence Ross' observation of insurance company settlement practices in automobile accident cases suggests that general damages are a standard part of the settlement "package" and are rather routinely calculated "for the most part... [by] multiplying the medical bills by a tacitly but generally accepted arbitrary constant" (Ross, 1970: 239).

The local bar was widely perceived as inhospitable to personal injury claimants, not only because there were few tort specialists but because Sander County lawyers were seen as closely linked to the kinds of individuals and businesses against whom tort actions were typically brought. Although plaintiffs hired Sander County attorneys in 72.5 percent of all non-tort actions filed locally in which plaintiffs were represented by counsel, they did so in only 12.5 percent of the tort cases.[14] One lawyer, who was frequently consulted by potential tort plaintiffs, lived across the county line in a small town outside of Sander County. He told me, "I get a lot of cases where people just don't want to be involved with the, they perceive it to be the hierarchy of Sander County. . . . I'm not part of the establishment."

Thus, even from the perspective of insurance company personnel and attorneys, who were most likely to witness the entry of personal injury cases into the formal legal system in Sander County, it is clear that the local culture tended in many ways to deter litigation. And when personal injury cases were formally filed, it usually was no more than another step in an ongoing negotiation process.

Why was the litigation of personal injury cases in Sander County subjected to disapproval so pervasive that it inhibited the assertion of claims at all stages, from the moment injuries occurred and were perceived to the time parties stood at the very threshold of the formal legal system? The answer, I shall argue, lies partly in the role of the Sander County Court in a changing social system and partly in the nature of the personal injury claim itself.

VII. THE USE OF THE COURT

In the recent literature on dispute processing and conflict resolution, various typologies of conflict-handling forums and procedures have been proposed. Such typologies usually include courts, arbitrators, mediators, and ombudsmen, as well as two-party and one-party procedures such as negotiation, self-help, avoidance, and "lumping it" (see, e.g., typologies in Abel, 1973; Felstiner, 1974; Steele, 1975; Nader and Todd, 1978; Black and Baumgartner, 1983;

---

[14] These figures are from a sample of cases for the years 1975-1976. See note 6 *supra*. From these data alone one cannot conclude that Sander County attorneys were less often *approached* by potential personal injury plaintiffs, since the data consist only of cases that were filed and tell us nothing about cases brought to an attorney but not filed. We know that Sander County attorneys were sometimes reluctant to bring such actions even when approached by prospective plaintiffs. Attorneys elsewhere, particularly those who were tort specialists, may not have shared this reluctance and may have filed a higher proportion of the Sander County claims that were brought to them.

Galanter, 1983). Analyses of these alternative approaches incorporate a number of variables that critically affect the ways in which conflict is handled and transformed. Such variables include, among others, procedural formality, the power and authority of the intervenor, the coerciveness of the proceedings, the range and severity of outcomes, role differentiation and specialization of third parties and advocates, cost factors, time required, the scope of the inquiry, language specialization, and the quality of the evidence that will be heard. When variables such as these are used to analyze various approaches to conflict resolution, the result is typically a continuum ranging from the most formal, specialized, functionally differentiated, and costly approaches to the most informal, accessible, undifferentiated, and inexpensive. The court as a forum for dispute processing and conflict resolution is typically placed at the costly, formalistic end of such continua.

Yet common sense and empirical investigations consistently remind us that trial courts rarely employ the adjudicative procedures that make them a symbol of extreme formalism. Very few of the complaints filed in courts are tried and adjudicated. Most are settled through bilateral negotiations of the parties or, occasionally, through the efforts of a judge who encourages the parties to reach an agreement without going to trial. This was true of the Sander County Court, as it is of courts elsewhere, and it applied with particular force to the relatively infrequent personal injury complaints that were filed in Sander County. Adjudication on the merits was extremely rare. In my sample only one of fifteen personal injury cases went to trial, and the judges and lawyers to whom I talked confirmed the generality of this pattern. Yet the court did play a crucial role in the handling of personal injury conflicts. It did so by providing what was perhaps the only setting in which meaningful and effective procedures of any kind could be applied. To understand why this was so, we must examine some distinctive characteristics of the relationships between the parties in the personal injury cases that were litigated in Sander County.

Among the relative handful of personal injury cases filed in the Sander County Court, almost all shared a common feature: the parties were separated by either geographic or social "distance" that could not be bridged by any conflict resolution process short of litigation.[15] In at least half of the fifteen personal injury cases in the sample, the plaintiff and the defendant resided in different counties or states. These cases were evenly split between instances

---

[15] In this discussion of geographic and social distance and their impact on patterns of legal behavior, I draw upon a body of theory that has been developed in several earlier studies. See Black (1976); Perin (1977); Engel (1978); Todd (1978); Greenhouse (1982).

in which the plaintiff, on the one hand, and the defendant, on the other hand, was a local resident. In either situation, geographic distance meant that the parties almost certainly belonged to different communities and different social networks. Informal responses by the injured party, whether they involved attempts to negotiate, to mediate, or even to retaliate by gossip, were likely to be frustrated since channels for communication and shared value systems and acquaintance networks were unlikely to exist. This is reflected in the disproportionate presence of parties from outside the county on the personal injury docket.[16]

A more elusive but no less significant form of distance was suggested by interviews with the parties as well as by the court documents in several personal injury cases. In these cases, it became apparent that "social distance," which was less tangible but just as hard to bridge as geographic distance, separated the parties even when they were neighbors.

Social distance could take many forms in Sander County. In one personal injury case, the plaintiff, who lived in one of the outlying towns in Sander County, described himself as an outsider to the community although he had lived there almost all his life. He was a Democrat in a conservative Republican town; he was of German extraction in a community where persons of Norwegian descent were extremely clannish and exclusive; he was a part-time tavernkeeper in a locality where taverns were popular but their owners were not socially esteemed; the opposing party was a "higher up" in the organization for which they both worked, and there was a long history of "bad blood" between them.

In a second personal injury case, a Mexican immigrant and his family sued a tavernkeeper under the Illinois Dram Shop Act for injuries he had suffered as a bystander in a barroom scuffle. Latino immigration into the community had, as we have seen, increased greatly in recent years to the displeasure of many local residents. Cultural misunderstandings and prejudice ran high, and little sympathy could be expected for a Latino who was injured in the course of a barroom fight. Thus, the plaintiff's wife was quite worried about bringing the lawsuit. She feared that they would create more trouble for themselves and told me, "I was afraid that maybe they'd say our kind of people are just trying to

---

[16] The disproportionate number of cases involving geographically distant adversaries is especially striking when one considers the relative infrequency of interaction between persons living in separate counties and states as compared to persons living in the same county or town. In absolute terms, injurious interactions must have occurred far more frequently between neighbors than between distant strangers, yet injurious interactions between distant strangers ended up in the Sander County Court about as often as those involving local residents (compare Engel, 1978: 142–44).

get their hands on money any way we could ..." The decision to sue was made because they believed that people behind the bar had contributed to the injury by passing a weapon to the man who had struck the plaintiff (although, under the Dram Shop Act, the tavern could have been found liable without fault), and because they saw no other way to recover the income they had lost when the plaintiff's injury had kept him from working.

The tavernkeeper, who considered herself a member of the social under-class (although in a different sense from the Mexican immigrants), was bitter about the case and about the Dram Shop Act. When I asked her how the plaintiffs had known that she was liable under the Act, she answered, "I haven't any idea. How do they know about a lot of things is beyond me. They know how to come here without papers and get a job or go on welfare. They are not too dumb, I guess."

In this case, then, the two parties were separated from each other and from the community by a great chasm of social distance. One person was set apart from the general community by ethnicity and was well aware that his injuries were unlikely to be regarded with sympathy. The other party was also, by self-description, a "second class citizen." As a tavernkeeper, she told me, "you come up against many obstacles, prejudices, and hard times, you wouldn't believe." Both descriptions of social alienation were accurate. Yet the defendant had an established place in the traditional social order. She owned a small business in a town dominated by the ethos of individual enterprise. Her line of work was widely recognized and accepted, although not accorded great prestige, in a community where taverns were among the most important social centers. Her acquisition of Dram Shop insurance made her a "deep pocket" comparable to other local business enterprises that might provide substantial compensation in appropriate cases to injured persons. The plaintiffs in this case, far more than the defendant, were truly social "outsiders" in Sander County. For them, nonjudicial approaches appeared hopeless, and passively absorbing the injury was too costly. Only formal legal action provided a channel for communication between the two parties, and this ultimately led, despite the defendant's reluctance, to settlement.

Social distance also played a part in an action brought by a woman on behalf of her five-year-old daughter, who had suffered internal injuries when a large trash container fell on her. The little girl had been climbing on the trash container, which was located in back of an automobile showroom. The plaintiff and her husband were described by their adversaries as the kind of people who were constantly in financial trouble and always trying to live off somebody else's money. The plaintiff herself stated frankly that they were outsiders in the community, ignored or avoided even by their next-door neighbors. As she put it, "Everybody in this town seems to know everybody else's business ... but they don't know you."

Her socially marginal status in the community precluded any significant form of nonjudicial conflict resolution with the auto dealer or the disposal company, and the matter went to the Sander County Court, where the $150,000 lawsuit was eventually settled for $3,000. Since initiating the lawsuit, the plaintiff had become a born-again Christian and, from her new perspective on life, came to regret her decision to litigate. The little money they had obtained simply caused her to fight with her husband, who sometimes beat her. She came to believe that she should not have sued, although she did feel that her lawsuit had done some good. After it was concluded, she observed, signs were posted near all such trash containers warning that children should not play on them.

In my interviews with local residents, officials, community leaders, and legal professionals, I presented the fact situation from this last case (in a slightly different form, to protect the privacy and identity of the original participants) and asked them how similar cases were handled in the segments of the community with which they were familiar. From our discussion of this matter there emerged two distinct patterns of behavior which, the interviewees suggested, turned on the extent to which the aggrieved party was integrated into the community. If the parents of the injured child were long-time residents who were a part of the local society and shared its prevailing value system, the consensus was that they would typically take little or no action of any sort. Injuries, as we have seen, were common in a rural community, and the parents would tend to blame themselves for not watching the child more carefully or, as one interviewee put it, would "figure that the kid ought to be sharp enough to stay away" from the hazard. On the other hand, if the parents of the injured child were newcomers to the community, and especially if they were factory workers employed in the area's newly established industrial plants, it was suggested that their behavior would be quite different. One union steward assured me that the workers he knew typically viewed such situations in terms of a potential lawsuit and, at the least, would aggressively seek to have the auto dealer and the disposal company assume responsibility for the damages. Others described a kind of "fight-flight" reaction on the part of newcomers and industrial blue collar workers. One particularly perceptive minister said, "Those ... that feel put down perceive everything in the light of another putdown and I think they would perceive this as a putdown. See, nobody really cares about us, they're just pushing us around again. And so we'll push back." He also noted, however, that it was equally likely that aggrieved individuals in this situation would simply move out of the community – the "flight" response.

There was, then, some agreement that responses involving the aggressive assertion of rights, if they occurred at all, would typically be initiated by newcomers to the community or by people who otherwise lacked a recognized place in the status hierarchy of Sander County. Such persons, in the words of a local schoolteacher, would regard the use of the court as a "leveler" that could mitigate the effects of social distance between themselves and the other side. Persons who were better integrated into the community, on the other hand, could rely on their established place in the social order to communicate grievances, stigmatize what they viewed as deviant behavior, press claims informally, or, because they felt comfortable enough psychologically and financially, to simply absorb the injury without any overt response whatever.

Interestingly, this was precisely the picture drawn for me by the evangelical minister who had converted the mother of the five-year-old girl to born-again Christianity. Lifelong residents of the community, he told me, reacted to stressful situations with more stability and less emotion than newcomers to the community who were less rooted and whose lives were filled with pressures and problems and what he called, "groping, searching, grasping." For this minister, born-again Christianity offered socially marginal people a form of contentment and stability that was denied them by their lack of a recognized position in the local society. He argued that external problems such as personal injuries were secondary to primary questions of religious faith. He told me, "[I]f we first of all get first things straightened out and that is our relationship with God and is our help from God, all of these other things will fall into order." This was precisely the message that the plaintiff in this case – and many other socially marginal people in the community like her – had come to accept. On this basis, many social outsiders in Sander County could rationalize passivity in the face of personal injuries, passivity that was at least outwardly similar to the typical responses of Sander County's long-time residents.

The picture of the Sander County Court that emerges from this brief overview of personal injury cases differs substantially from that which might be suggested by conventional typologies of conflict resolution alternatives. In processual terms litigation, although rare, was not strikingly different from its nonjudicial alternatives. It was characterized by informal negotiation, bargaining, and settlement in all but the extremely infrequent cases that actually went to trial. Yet these processes occurred only as a result of the filing of a formal legal action. Because of the distance separating the parties, nonjudicial approaches, even with the participation of lawyers, sometimes failed to resolve the conflict. Resorting to the Sander County Court could vest socially marginal persons with additional weight and stature because it offered them access to the levers of judicial compulsion. The very act of filing a civil complaint, without much more, made them persons whom the other side must recognize, whose words the other side must hear, and whose claims the other side must consider. The civil trial court, by virtue of its legal authority over all persons within its jurisdiction, was able to bridge procedurally the gaps that separated people and social groups. In a pluralistic social setting, the court could provide, in the cases that reached it, a forum where communication between disparate people and groups could take place. In so doing, it substituted for conflict-handling mechanisms which served the well-integrated dominant group but which became ineffective for persons who were beyond the boundaries of the traditional community.

The communication that the court facilitated could, however, give rise to anger and frustration. Plaintiffs often viewed the process negatively, because even when they went to court they could not escape the rigid constraints imposed by a community unsympathetic to claims for damages in personal injury cases. Thus, the plaintiff whom I have described as a Democrat in a Republican town told me that the experience of filing and settling a personal injury claim was "disgusting ... a lot of wasted time." Low pretrial settlements were, not surprisingly, the rule.

Defendants viewed the process negatively because they were accustomed to a system of conflict resolution that screened out personal injury cases long before they reached the courthouse. Even though settlements might turn out to be low, defendants resented the fact that personal injuries had in the first place been viewed as an occasion to assert a claim against them, much less a formal lawsuit. Being forced to respond in court was particularly galling when the claimant turned out to be a person whom the core members of the community viewed with dislike or disdain.

In short, the Sander County Court was able to bridge gaps between parties to personal injury cases and to promote communication between those separated by social or geographic distance. It did so, however, by coercion, and its outcomes (particularly when both parties resided in the community) tended to exacerbate rather than ameliorate social conflict. In the court's very success as a mechanism for conflict resolution we may, therefore, find a partial explanation for the stigmatization of personal injury litigation in Sander County.

VIII. THE PRESERVATION AND DESTRUCTION
OF A COMMUNITY

In rural and archaic Japan ... people used to believe that calamity that attacked the community had its origin in an alien factor inside the community as well as outside it.

The malevolent factor accumulated in the community. It was related also to the sins committed wittingly or unwittingly by members of the community. In order to avoid the disastrous influence of the polluted element, it was necessary for the community to give the element form and to send it away beyond the limits of the village. However, the introduction of the alien element, which could turn into calamity at any time, was absolutely necessary for the growth of the crops. Thus the need for the alien factor had two facets which appear contradictory to each other on the surface: that is, the introduction of the negative element of expiation as well as the positive element of crop fertility

(Yamaguchi, 1977: 154).

The social and economic life of Sander County had undergone major changes in the years preceding this study, and the impact of those changes on the world view of local residents and on the normative structure of the community as a whole was profound. Small single family farms were gradually giving way to larger consolidated agricultural operations owned by distant and anonymous persons or corporations. The new and sizeable manufacturing plants, together with some of the older local industries, now figured importantly in the economic life of Sander County and were the primary reasons why the population had become more heterogeneous and mobile.

These changes had important implications for traditional concepts of individualism and for the traditional relationships and reciprocities that had characterized the rural community. Self-sufficiency was less possible than before. Control over local lives was increasingly exercised by organizations based in other cities or states (there were even rumors that local farmlands were being purchased by unnamed foreign interests). Images of individual autonomy and community solidarity were challenged by the realities of externally-based economic and political power. Traditional forms of exchange could not be preserved where individuals no longer knew their neighbors' names, much less their backgrounds and their values. Local people tended to resent and perhaps to fear these changes in the local economic structure, but for the most part they believed that they were essential for the survival of the community. Some of the most critical changes had been the product of decisions made only after extensive deliberations by Sander County's elite. The infusion of new blood into the community – persons of diverse racial, ethnic, and cultural backgrounds – was a direct result of these decisions. The new residents were, in the eyes of many old-timers, an "alien element" whose introduction was, as in rural Japan, grudgingly recognized as "absolutely necessary" to preserve the well-being of the community.

The gradual decay of the old social order and the emergence of a plurality of cultures and races in Sander County produced a confusion of norms and of

mechanisms for resolving conflict. New churches were established with congregations made up primarily of newcomers. Labor unions appeared on the
scene, to the dismay and disgust of many of the old-timers. New taverns and
other social centers catered to the newer arrivals. Governmental welfare and
job training programs focused heavily (but not exclusively) on the newcomers.
Newcomers frequently found themselves grouped in separate neighborhoods
or apartment complexes and, in the case of blacks, there were reported
attempts to exclude them from the community altogether. The newcomers
brought to Sander County a social and cultural heterogeneity that it had not
known before. Equally important, their very presence constituted a challenge
to the older structure of norms and values generated by face-to-face relationships within the community.

IX. PERCEPTIONS OF CONTRACT AND PERSONAL INJURY CLAIMS

The reaction of the local community to the assertion of different types of
legal claims was profoundly affected by this proliferation of social, cultural,
and normative systems. The contrast between reactions to claims based on
breaches of contract and those based on personal injuries is especially striking.
Contract actions in the Sander County Court were nearly ten times as numerous as personal injury actions.[17] They involved, for the most part, efforts to
collect payment for sales, services, and loans. One might expect that concerns
about litigiousness in the community would focus upon this category of
cases, which was known to be a frequent source of court filings. Yet I heard
no complaints about contract plaintiffs being "greedy" or "sue happy" or
"looking for the easy buck." Such criticisms were reserved exclusively for
injured persons who made the relatively rare decision to press their claims
in court.

In both tort and contract actions, claimants assert that a loss has been
caused by the conduct of another. In contractual breaches, the defendant's
alleged fault is usually a failure to conform to a standard agreed upon by
the parties.[18] In personal injury suits, the alleged fault is behavior that falls
below a general societal standard applicable even in the absence of any prior
agreement. Both are, of course, long-recognized types of actions. Both are

---

[17] Four percent of my case sample were personal injury cases and 37.5% were contract cases.
[18] On many occasions, of course, courts import external standards into contracts and impose them
on the parties regardless of their agreement or disagreement with such terms.

"legitimate" in any formal sense of the word. Why is it, then, that actions to recover one type of loss were viewed with approval in Sander County, while far less frequent actions to recover the other type of loss were seen as symptomatic of a socially destructive trend toward the overuse of courts by greedy individuals and troublemakers? The answer appears to lie in the nature of the parties, in the social meanings of the underlying transactions, and in the symbolism of individuals and injuries in the changing social order.

Most of the contract litigation in Sander County involved debts to businesses for goods and services. Typically, the contracts that underlie such debts are quite different from the classic model of carefully considered offers and acceptances and freely negotiated exchanges. Yet many townspeople and farmers in the community saw such obligations as extremely important (Engel, 1980). They were associated in the popular mind with binding but informal kinds of indebtedness and with the sanctity of the promise. Longtime Sander County residents viewed their society as one that had traditionally been based on interdependencies and reciprocal exchanges among fellow residents. Reliance upon promises, including promises to pay for goods and services, was essential to the maintenance of this kind of social system. One farmer expressed this core value succinctly: "Generally speaking, a farmer's word is good between farmers." Another farmer, who occasionally sold meat to neighbors and friends in his small town, told me:

> We've done this for 20 years, and I have never lost one dime. I have never had one person not pay me, and I've had several of them went bankrupt, and so on and so forth. I really don't pay any attention to bookkeeping or what. I mean, if someone owes me, they owe me. And you know, I've never sent anybody a bill or anything. I mean, sooner or later they all pay.

In these interpersonal exchanges involving people well known to one another there was, it appears, some flexibility and allowance for hard times and other contingencies. On the other hand, there was a mutual recognition that debts must ultimately be paid. When I asked a number of people in the community about a case in which an individual failed to pay in full for construction of a fence, the typical reaction among longtime residents was that such a breach would simply not occur. Of course, breaches or perceptions of breaches did occur in Sander County and the result could be, in the words of one farmer, "fireworks." I was told stories of violent efforts at self-help by some aggrieved creditors, and it was clear that such efforts were not necessarily condemned in the community (Engel, 1980: 439–40). A member of the county sheriff's department observed that small unpaid debts of this kind were often viewed as matters for the police:

We see that quite a bit. They want us to go out and get the money. He owes it, there's an agreement, he violated the law.... You see, they feel that they shouldn't have to hire an attorney for something that's an agreement. It's a law, it should be acted upon. Therefore, we should go out and arrest the man and either have him arrested or by our mere presence, by the sheriff's department, a uniformed police officer, somebody with authority going out there and say, hey, you know, you should know that automatically these people give the money and that would be it. So therefore they wouldn't have to go to an attorney. Boy, a lot of people feel that.

Other creditors, particularly local merchants, doctors, and the telephone company, brought their claims not to the police but to the Sander County Court. In some cases, contract plaintiffs (many of whom were long-time residents) appeared to litigate specifically to enforce deeply felt values concerning debt and obligation. As one small businessman explained:

I'm the type of a person that can get personally involved and a little hostile if somebody tries to put the screws to me.... I had it happen once for $5 and I had it happen once for $12. ... I explained to them carefully to please believe me that it wasn't the money, because it would cost me more to collect it than it'd be worth, but because of the principle of it that I would definitely go to whatever means necessary, moneywise or whatever, to get it collected. And which I did.

Even those creditors for whom litigation was commonplace, such as the head of the local collection agency and an official of the telephone company, shared the perception that contract breaches were morally offensive. This view appeared to apply to transactions that were routinized and impersonal as well as to the more traditional exchanges between individuals who knew each other well. As the head of the collection agency said, "When you get to sitting here and you look at the thousands of dollars that you're trying to effect collection on and you know that there's a great percentage of them you'll never get and no one will get, it's gotta bother you. It's gotta bother you." Certainly, business creditors felt none of the hesitancy of potential tort plaintiffs about asserting claims and resorting to litigation if necessary. Equally important, the community approved the enforcement of such obligations as strongly as it condemned efforts to enforce tort claims. Contract litigation, even when it involved "routine" debt collection, differed from tort litigation in that it was seen as enforcing a core value of the traditional culture of Sander County: that promises should be kept and people should be held responsible when they broke their word.

X. CONCLUSION

In Sander County, the philosophy of individualism worked itself out quite differently in the areas of tort and contract. If personal injuries evoked values emphasizing self-sufficiency, contractual breaches evoked values emphasizing rights and remedies. Duties generated by contractual agreement were seen as sacrosanct and vital to the maintenance of the social order. Duties generated by socially imposed obligations to guard against injuring other people were seen as intrusions upon existing relationships, as pretexts for forced exchanges, as inappropriate attempts to redistribute wealth, and as limitations upon individual freedom.

These contrasting views of contract and tort-based claims took on special significance as a result of the fundamental social changes that Sander County had experienced. The newcomers brought with them conceptions of injuries, rights, and obligations that were quite different from those that had long prevailed. The traditional norms had no doubt played an important role in maintaining the customary social order by reinforcing longstanding patterns of behavior consistent with a parochial world view dominated by devotion to agriculture and small business. But the newcomers had no reason to share this world view or the normative structure associated with it. Indeed, as we shall see, they had good reason to reject it.[19] Although they arrived on the scene, in a sense, to preserve the community and to save it from economic misfortune, the terms on which they were brought into Sander County – as migrant or industrial workers – had little to do with the customary forms of interaction and reciprocation that had given rise to the traditional normative order. The older norms concerning such matters as individual self-sufficiency, personal injuries, and contractual breaches had no special relevance or meaning given the interests of the newcomers. Although these norms impinged on the consciousness and behavior of the newcomers, they did so through the coercive

---

[19] Were personal injury lawsuits in the late 1970s, although relatively infrequent, more common than they had been before the recent influx of social "outsiders" in Sander County? Because of the unavailability of reliable historical data, it is impossible to say, nor is the answer central to the analysis presented here. It is true that recent social changes in Sander County had brought striking juxtapositions of insiders and outsiders, and some increase in the frequency of tort claims may have resulted; but in earlier periods there may have been other kinds of outsiders as well, and some of them may have brought personal injury actions. In this article, I am interested in the past primarily as it existed in the minds of Sander County's citizens at the time of my study. It is clear that current perceptions of Sander County's history and traditions, whether accurate or not, played a crucial role in constructing and justifying responses to the problems that now faced the community, and such perceptions were often invoked to support the assertion of "traditional values" in opposition to behavior that provoked long-time residents.

forces and social sanctions that backed them up and not because the newcomers had accepted and internalized local values and attitudes.

Indeed, it was clear that in the changing society of Sander County, the
older norms tended to operate to the distinct disadvantage of social outsiders
and for the benefit of the insiders. Contract actions, premised on the traditional value that a person's word should be kept, tended to involve collection
efforts by established persons or institutions[20] against newcomers and socially
marginal individuals. Such actions, as we have seen, were generally approved
by the majority of Sander County residents and occurred with great frequency.
Personal injury actions, on the other hand, were rooted in no such traditional
value and, although such claims were infrequent, they were usually instituted
by plaintiffs who were outsiders to the community against defendants who
occupied symbolically important positions in Sander County society. Thus, a
typical contract action involved a member of "the establishment" collecting a
debt, while the typical personal injury action was an assault by an outsider
upon the establishment at a point where a sufficient aggregation of capital
existed to pay for an injury. This distinction helps to explain the stigmatization
of personal injury litigation in Sander County as well as its infrequency and
its ineffectiveness.[21]

Yet personal injury litigation in Sander County was not entirely dysfunc-
tional for the traditional social order. The intrusion of "the stranger" into an
enclosed system of customary law can serve to crystallize the awareness of
norms that formerly existed in a preconscious or inarticulate state (See Fuller,
1969: 9-10 and Simmel, 1908/1971). Norms and values that once patterned
behavior unthinkingly or intuitively must now be articulated, explained,
and defended against the contrary values and expectations of the stranger to
the community.

---

[20] Frequent plaintiffs in collection cases were doctors, hospitals, merchants, collection agencies,
and the telephone company. Cases of this type constituted 76.5% of all contract actions. The
remaining 23.5% of contract cases involved actions based on construction contracts, promissory
notes, wholesale transactions, and other less frequent kinds of contractual transactions.

[21] Sander County tort and contract cases are not unique, of course, in these basic structural
differences. In other localities one might also expect to find that the majority of tort plaintiffs
are individuals asserting claims against "deep pocket" defendants, while the majority of contract
plaintiffs are business organizations attempting to collect debts from individuals. See, for
example, Galanter (1974) and Yngvesson and Hennessey (1975). It is possible that outside of
Sander County perceptions of the legitimacy and illegitimacy of contract and tort actions are
also influenced by these basic structural differences. In Sander County, however, this set of
distinctions between the parties to tort and contract actions combined with local reactions to
recent societal changes to produce a powerful symbolism of insiders and outsiders and of
injuries and individualism. The extent to which a similar symbolism may be found in other
localities is a subject for further investigation.

In Sander County, the entry of the stranger produced a new awareness (or perhaps a reconstruction) of the traditional normative order at the very moment when that order was subjected to its strongest and most devastating challenges. This process triggered a complex response by the community – a nostalgic yearning for the older world view now shattered beyond repair, a rearguard attempt to shore up the boundaries of the community against alien persons and ideas (compare Erikson, 1966), and a bitter acceptance of the fact that the "stranger" was in reality no longer outside the community but a necessary element brought in to preserve the community, and therefore a part of it.

Local responses to personal injury claims reflected these complexities. In part, local residents, by stigmatizing such claims, were merely defending the establishment from a relatively rare form of economic attack by social outsiders. In part, stigmatization branded the claimants as deviants from the community norms and therefore helped mark the social boundaries between old-timers and newcomers. Because the maintenance of such boundaries was increasingly difficult, however, and because the "alien element" had been deliberately imported into the community as a societal act of self-preservation, the stigmatization of such claims was also part of a broader and more subtle process of expiation (to borrow Yamaguchi's [1977] term), a process reminiscent of rituals and other procedures used in many societies to deal with problems of pollution associated with socially marginal persons in the community (Douglas, 1966; Turner, 1969; Perin, 1977: 110–15).

Local residents who denounced the assertion of personal injury claims and somewhat irrationally lamented the rise in "litigiousness" of personal injury plaintiffs were, in this sense, participating in a more broadly based ceremony of regret that the realities of contemporary American society could no longer be averted from their community if it were to survive. Their denunciations bore little relationship to the frequency with which personal injury lawsuits were actually filed, for the local ecology of conflict resolution still suppressed most such cases long before they got to court, and personal injury litigation remained rare and aberrational. Rather, the denunciation of personal injury litigation in Sander County was significant mainly as one aspect of a symbolic effort by members of the community to preserve a sense of meaning and coherence in the face of social changes that they found threatening and confusing. It was in this sense a solution – albeit a partial and unsatisfying one– to a problem basic to the human condition, the problem of living in a world that has lost the simplicity and innocence it is thought once to have had. The outcry against personal injury litigation was part of a broader effort by some residents of Sander County to exclude from their moral universe what they could not exclude from the physical boundaries of their community and to recall and reaffirm an untainted world that existed nowhere but in their imaginations.

REFERENCES

ABEL, Richard L. (1973) "A Comparative Theory of Dispute Institutions in Society," 8 *Law & Society Review* 217.

AUBERT, Vilhelm (1963) "Competition and Dissensus: Two Types of Conflict and of Conflict Resolution," 7 *Journal of Conflict Resolution* 26.

BLACK, Donald (1976) *The Behavior of Law*. New York: Academic Press.

BLACK, Donald and M.P. Baumgartner (1983) "Toward a Theory of the Third Party," in K. Boyum and L. Mather (eds.), *Empirical Theories about Courts*. New York: Longman.

DOUGLAS, Mary (1966) *Purity and Danger*. London: Routledge & Kegan Paul, Limited.

ENGEL, David M. (1978) *Code and Custom in a Thai Provincial Court*. Tucson: University of Arizona Press.

    (1980) "Legal Pluralism in an American Community: Perspectives on a Civil Trial Court," 1980 *American Bar Foundation Research Journal* 425.

ERIKSON, Kai T. (1966) *Wayward Puritans*. New York: John Wiley & Sons.

FELSTINER, William L.F. (1974) "Influences of Social Organization on Dispute Processing," 9 *Law & Society Review* 63.

FRIEDMAN, Lawrence M. and Robert V. Percival (1976) "A Tale of Two Courts: Litigation in Alameda and San Benito Counties," 10 *Law & Society Review* 267.

FULLER, Lon L. (1969) "Human Interaction and the Law," 14 *American Journal of Jurisprudence* 1.

GALANTER, Marc (1974) "Why the 'Haves' Come Out Ahead: Speculations on the Limits of Legal Change," 9 *Law & Society Review* 95.

    (1983) "Reading the Landscape of Disputes: What We Know and Don't Know (And Think We Know) about Our Allegedly Contentious and Litigious Society," 31 *UCLA Law Review* 4.

GEST, Ted, Lucia Solorzano, Joseph P. Shapiro and Michael Doan (1982) "See You in Court," 93 *U.S. News & World Report* 58 (December 20).

GREENE, Richard (1983) "Caught in the Better Mousetrap," 132 *Forbes* 66 (October 24).

GREENHOUSE, Carol J. (1982) "Nature Is to Culture as Praying Is to Suing: Legal Pluralism in an American Suburb," 20 *Journal of Legal Pluralism* 17.

McINTOSH, Wayne (1980-81) "150 Years of Litigation and Dispute Settlement: A Court Tale," 15 *Law & Society Review* 823.

NADER, Laura and Harry F. Todd, Jr. (1978) "Introduction: The Dispute Process— Law in Ten Societies," in L. Nader and H. Todd, Jr. (eds.), *The Disputing Process —Law in Ten Societies*. New York: Columbia University Press.

NATIONAL CENTER FOR STATE COURTS (1979) *State Court Caseload Statistics: Annual Report, 1975*.

    (1982) *State Court Caseload Statistics: Annual Report, 1977*.

PERHAM, John (1977) "The Dilemma in Product Liability," 109 *Dun's Review* 48 (January).

PERIN, Constance (1977) *Everything in Its Place*. Princeton: Princeton University Press.

ROSENBERG, Maurice (1977) "Contemporary Litigation in the United States," in H. Jones (éd.), *Legal Institutions Today: English and American Approaches Compared*. Chicago: American Bar Association.

ROSS, H. Laurence (1970) *Settled Out of Court*. Chicago: Aldine Publishing Co.

SEYMOUR, Whitney North, Jr. (1973) *Why Justice Fails*. New York: William Morrow & Co.

SIMMEL, Georg (1908/1971) "The Stranger," in D. Levine (éd.), *On Individuality and Social Forms: Selected Writings*. Chicago: University of Chicago Press.

STEELE, Eric H. (1975) "Fraud, Dispute and the Consumer: Responding to Consumer Complaints," 123 *University of Pennsylvania Law Review* 1107.

TAYLOR, Stuart, Jr. (1981) "On the Evidence, Americans Would Rather Sue Than Settle," *New York Times* (July 5) Section 4, 8.

TODD, Harry F., Jr. (1978) "Litigious Marginals: Character and Disputing in a Bavarian Village," in L. Nader and H. Todd (eds.), *The Disputing Process—Law in Ten Societies*. New York: Columbia University Press.

TONDEL, Lyman M., Jr. (1976) "The Work of the American Bar Association Commission on Medical Professional Liability," 43 *Insurance Counsel Journal* 545.

TURNER, Victor W. (1969) *The Ritual Process*. Chicago: Aldine Publishing Co.

YAMAGUCHI, Masao (1977) "Kingship, Theatricality, and Marginal Reality in Japan," in R. Jain (ed.), *Text and Context: The Social Anthropology of Tradition*. Philadelphia: Institute for the Study of Human Issues.

YNGVESSON, Barbara and Patricia Hennessey (1975) "Small Claims, Complex Disputes: A Review of the Small Claims Literature," 9 *Law & Society Review* 219.

3

Emulating Sherlock Holmes: The Dog That Didn't Bark, the Victim Who Didn't Sue, and Other Contradictions of the "Hyper-Litigious" Society

BARBARA YNGVESSON

This chapter moves backward from David Engel's most familiar research on missing plaintiffs in personal injury cases and the implications of this absence for our understanding of the role of law in everyday life, to take a retrospective look at key themes in his work over almost five decades. My focus is on his deep engagement with what he terms, following Emerson, "subject-lenses" with "a creative power," and his concern, building on the work of William James, with a "self" that is "an agent of continuity" in a world that is discontinuous and in constant flux.[1] Engagement with these themes has been central to Engel's work, beginning with his senior thesis at Harvard in 1967 and continuing through his interpretation of the injury narratives of Thai interlocutors in the first decade of the 2000s.[2] They are also key elements in his classic article, "The Oven Bird's Song."[3]

Engel's fascination with matters of subjectivity, time, and change has led to an extraordinarily productive engagement as a legal scholar with research in anthropology, psychology, and most recently neuroscience, and has drawn him to explanatory approaches that challenge conventional understandings of motivation and legal consciousness pervasive in the sociolegal literature on

---

[1] Ralph Waldo Emerson, *Selected Writings of Ralph Waldo Emerson*, edited, with a biographical introduction, by Brooks Atkinson (Modern Library, 1950); William James, *Principles of Psychology* (Henry Holt and Co., 1893).

[2] David M. Engel, "Theories of time and consciousness in the writing of Gertrude Stein and Ernest Hemingway," Presented to the Committee on Degrees in History and Literature in Partial Fulfillment of the Requirements for the Degree of Bachelor of Arts with Honors, Harvard College, Cambridge, Massachusetts, 1967; D. M. Engel, "Globalization and the decline of legal consciousness: torts, ghosts, and karma in Thailand," *Law & Social Inquiry*, 30 (2005), 469; D. M. Engel and J. S. Engel, *Tort, Custom, and Karma: Globalization and Legal Consciousness in Thailand* (Stanford University Press, 2010).

[3] D. M. Engel, "The Oven Bird's Song: insiders, outsiders, and personal injuries in an American community," *Law & Society Review*, 18 (1984), 551.

law, courts, and disputing. His detailed examination of injury narratives in Thailand and the United States instead provides an entry point for understanding victims' perceptions of self, of injury, and of loss, and the meanings they attribute to law, in the context of local and transnational changes affecting their lives. This approach signals Engel's close affiliation with the "interpretive turn" in American anthropology and the work of key figures, notably Clifford Geertz, whose emphasis on symbols and meanings, on the actor's point of view, and on local knowledge has been widely influential both within the discipline and in related fields.[4] As Geertz formulated the turn to interpretation in his classic essay "Thick Description: Toward an Interpretive Theory of Culture":

> This fact – that what we call our data are really our own constructions of other people's constructions of what they and their compatriots are up to – is obscured because most of what we need to comprehend a particular event, ritual, custom, idea, or whatever *is insinuated as background information before the thing itself is directly examined* (emphasis added).[5]

It also positions Engel – notably in his more recent work – in conversation with sociologist Pierre Bourdieu's theory of practice, as this has been deployed by a range of scholars who focus more on "habitus" and an unconscious "system of dispositions" to understand the force of law and culture than on decisions and strategic choice.[6]

This intellectual positioning provided important common ground for conversation and collaboration among legal scholars, historians, anthropologists, sociologists, and others who began to meet under the umbrella provided by the Law and Society Association as a forum for cross-disciplinary exchange in the 1970s and 1980s, and David Engel became a central figure in developing this exchange and extending its reach (particularly into East and Southeast Asia) from that period to the present. It is in this broad context of cross-disciplinary and transnational discussion and research that his approach to understanding the law through "non-events" – the dog that didn't bark, the

---

[4] C. Geertz, *The Interpretation of Cultures: Selected Essays* (Basic Books, 1973); C. Geertz, "From the native's point of view: on the nature of anthropological understanding" in J. L. Dolgin, D. S. Kemnitzer, and D. M. Schneider (eds.), *Symbolic Anthropology: A Reader in the Study of Symbols and Meanings* (Columbia University Press, 1977), pp. 480–92; Clifford Geertz, *Local Knowledge: Further Essays in Interpretive Anthropology* (Basic Books, 1983).

[5] C. Geertz, "Thick description: toward an interpretive theory of culture" in *The Interpretation of Cultures: Selected Essays by Clifford Geertz*, 3 (Basic Books, 1973), pp. 3–30.

[6] P. Bourdieu, *Outline of a Theory of Practice* (Cambridge University Press, 1977), pp. 72–87; P. Bourdieu, "The force of law," *Hastings Law Journal*, 38 (1987), 201. This issue will be discussed in more detail in the final section of this chapter.

phuyai [big person] who failed to appear, the victim who didn't sue – took shape, and that he came to an understanding of the self as "distributed" (following psychologist Jerome Bruner).[7] The "distributed" self, Engel argues, "is constituted by his or her relations with others and not just influenced by them from time to time."[8]

This perspective on subjectivity and identity, which has been honed over the course of many years of ethnographic observation and interviews, has contributed to Engel's critique of theories of agency modeled as "decision trees" or "disputing pyramids" and of action as a series of rational choices ("lumping," "blaming," "claiming," and so forth) that are intentional, active, and linear. It has also shaped his challenge to a familiar narrative of globalization in which liberal legalism is hegemonic and everyman is a hyper-litigious *homo juralis*.[9] Rather, by positioning the researcher as an erstwhile Sherlock Holmes seeking to unravel a sociolegal mystery – the experience of law's absence in a world that is increasingly legalized – Engel's fieldwork explores *how* the law engages local systems of meaning, the possibility that globalization may have "pushed legal consciousness in the direction of religiosity rather than rights," and the increasing tension between concepts of rights drawn from Western liberal legalism and experiences of (in)justice in everyday life.[10]

SUBJECT-LENSES WITH A CREATIVE POWER

Engel is perhaps best known for his research on law in Thailand, which has extended from the mid-1970s to the present and is punctuated by the publication of his first book, based on research in a Thai provincial court,[11] in 1978 and, just over thirty years later, the publication of a second book, co-authored with Jaruwan Engel, also based in northern Thailand.[12] Both focus on transformations of Thai legal practice in the context of processes of economic, political, legal, and cultural globalization. As in Engel's other scholarship – notably, dealing with disability rights in the United States – analytical focus is

---

7   Jerome Bruner, *Acts of Meaning* (Harvard University Press, 1990), p. 114.
8   D. M. Engel, *The Myth of the Litigious Society* (Chicago University Press, 2016), p. 79.
9   See J. L. Comaroff and J. Comaroff, *Ethnicity, Inc.* (University of Chicago Press, 2009), pp. 53–4, for an anthropological version of this narrative; and see B. Yngvesson, "Border politics" in James G. Carrier and Deborah B. Gewertz (eds.), *The Handbook of Sociocultural Anthropology* (Bloomsbury Academic, 2013), pp. 174–91 for a critique of the narrative.
10 Engel, "Globalization," 469.
11 David M. Engel, *Code and Custom in a Thai Provincial Court* (University of Arizona Press, 1978).
12 Engel and Engel, *Tort, custom and karma*.

on the lived experience of so-called ordinary people.[13] In his original study of a Thai provincial court, these are parties whose disputes are recorded in the court archives, but Engel's research included observations of judicial proceedings and interviews with litigants, village heads, attorneys, and judges as well. Likewise, in "The Oven Bird's Song"[14] and his subsequent "Law, Time, and Community"[15] he focused on plaintiffs and defendants in civil cases filed at a rural county court in Illinois, carrying out interviews with a selection of disputants, along with community "observers" from a wide range of walks of life. In his later research with Frank Munger on disability rights, the interlocutors were parents of children with disabilities contacted through the United Cerebral Palsy Association, as well as a range of adults with disabilities, with whom Engel and Munger conducted face-to-face interviews. In the Engels' most recent Thai research, their subjects are village or urban residents in northern Thailand who had been hospitalized for the treatment of injuries.

"Lived experience" is accessed in these projects either through details recorded in court files or through in-depth, semi-structured interviews in which people are encouraged to "tell stories about their lives, their experiences, their social relationships and interactions, and their sense of self."[16] While Engel emphasizes (referring to research in Thailand in the late twentieth century) that *"the subjectivity of the narrator – in this case, the interpretation offered by the injured person – is the object of the study,"*[17] he underscores the importance of injury narratives in illuminating a broad landscape in which subjectivity takes shape, revealing "with remarkable clarity how new information flows, new economic arrangements and activities, new patterns of internal migration, and new ideologies and religious belief systems create new human identities and new perceptions about the self and the community and about social practices and responsibilities."[18]

While the intersection of this broad cultural and political landscape with the "subject lenses" that are a hallmark of his work is most notable in his scholarship from the publication of "Oven Bird" in 1984 through his work in the first decade of the twenty-first century, it can be seen in incipient form in his first book, *Code and Custom in a Thai Provincial Court.*[19] It is there that he first begins to formulate a dynamic and relational theory of legal change

---

[13] D. M. Engel, "Origin myths: narratives of authority, resistance, disability, and law," *Law & Society Review*, 27 (1993), 785; D. M. Engel and F. W. Munger, *Rights of Inclusion: Law and Identity in the Life Stories of Americans with Disabilities* (University of Chicago Press, 2012).

[14] Engel, "The oven bird's song."

[15] D. M. Engel, "Law, time, and community," *Law & Society Review*, 21 (1987), 605–637.

[16] Engel, "Globalization," 477.   [17] Ibid, 478, emphasis added.   [18] Ibid, 472.

[19] Engel, *Code and Custom.*

in which "translation" displaces "modernization" and "subject lenses" displace the unique transformative power of liberal legal "forces" that originate in the global North and alter everything in their path, including the traditional understandings and values of "ordinary people." Engel's approach to legal change, by contrast, focuses on the space *between* two powerful systems of justice – "each founded upon a different set of concepts regarding injury and obligation, guilt and innocence, and social organization and behavior" – and the uneasy co-existence of both systems in this potential space, where they are "'translated,' as it were, from one language [one system] to another."[20]

In *Code and Custom*, Engel focuses on this process of translation not only as it takes place in the management of individual grievances in the Chiang Mai court, but also as it affects a much broader landscape in which the establishment of a centralized provincial judiciary and the drafting of modern law codes at the turn of the twentieth century were envisioned as a way of modernizing Thai society itself. Noting that "the transformation of Thai law has provided a powerful symbol of modernity"[21] and made possible the extension of the central government at a key period in the emergence of Thailand as a nation-state, Engel argues that the expectation that the modernization of law would fuel a radical transformation of the social order was never fully realized. Rather, the new Thai legal system was "strongly influenced – even subverted – by the persistence of customary patterns of justice in the Thai countryside,"[22] in an evolving relationship marked by "friction, by mutual accommodation, and by the interpenetration of rival theories of law and justice, a process taking place upon a stage that [was]... itself changing, shifting, and turning."[23] As he concludes:

> the process of translation from one system to another *results in the modification of both systems by extrinsic contacts*. The resulting changes should not necessarily be understood as an evolution of Thai law from one typical form to another or from one level of advancement to another – the stereotype of "modernization." Rather, it should be understood as a process of mutual adaptation in which the two distinctive systems of justice interlock and interact with one another over time. The significance lies not so much in the evolutionary changes that occur within either of the individual systems as it does in the evolution of the relationship itself.[24]

Engel's approach to social and legal change as accommodation and translation, rather than "advancement" or "modernization," is reflected most

---

[20] Ibid, 206; and see D. W. Winnicott, *Playing and Reality* (Tavistock Publications, 1971), pp. 100–10 for a discussion of "potential space" as "a third area of human living, one neither inside the individual nor outside in the world of shared reality" (p. 110).

[21] Engel, *Code and Custom*, p. 2.   [22] Ibid.   [23] Ibid, 207.   [24] Ibid, emphasis added.

clearly in his "thick descriptions" of a complex moral and legal landscape in which "new" legal codes are reshaped by "more traditional" systems of relationship and obligation.[25] The interactions and tensions within and between these entangled systems are both created by and reflected in the exchanges of everyday and "big" people with one another. Especially striking is Engel's exploration of how the tensions or discrepancies between the two systems *"create a form of potential energy that is released by the leap from one environment to the other."*[26] This release of energy, he suggests, "produces new distributions of power, new forms of relationship, and new perceptions of justice in the local community," a transformation that is possible "only because the two systems exist in such close proximity."[27]

Thirty years later, Engel's continued examination of the transformation of what (by the early 2000s) he was describing as the "legal consciousness" of everyday people in Thailand reveals not the eradication of more traditional, religiously inflected, approaches to justice in the face of an increasingly hegemonic liberal legalism, but rather the expansion of a de-localized religious "mediascape" in which Buddhist precepts of virtuous living through self-abnegation predominate.[28] In provincial Thailand in the early twenty-first century, the *absence* of law in everyday life, in the context of the seeming globalization of liberal legal forms and practices, is the paradox that needs explaining.[29] I return to Engel's exploration of this legal trajectory, in Thailand and elsewhere, later in this chapter. Here I simply underscore the productivity of an approach in which the analytical focus is on the evolution and transformation of *the relationship* of two entangled systems, as revealed through the "subject-lenses" of interlocutors who must negotiate the tensions and contradictions of a complex legal landscape that is at the same time both familiar and increasingly unresponsive to their needs.

THE REAL STORY OF THE "MODERNIZATION" OF THAI LAW: "WALK BEHIND THE *PHUYAI* AND THE DOGS WON'T BITE"

Engel's observation about the potential energy that is released by the "leap" from one environment to another as everyday people negotiate the landscape

---

[25] Ibid, 205.   [26] Ibid, 207, emphasis added.   [27] Ibid.

[28] Engel, "Theories of Time and Consciousness," 503, quoting Arjun Appadurai, *Modernity at Large: Cultural Dimensions of Globalization* (University of Minnesota Press, 1996), p. 35 ("Mediascapes ... tend to be image-centered, narrative-based accounts of strips of reality, and what they offer to those who experience and transform them is a series of elements ... out of which scripts can be formed of imagined lives, their own as well as those of others living in other places").

[29] See Engel and Engel, *Tort, custom, and karma*, p. 161.

of law also hints at the role of the ethnographer in the interpretation and translation of cultural meanings, echoing some of the most innovative work in the interpretive turn that was shaping anthropology at the time of his early fieldwork in Thailand. For example, anthropologist Roy Wagner, in his now classic *The Invention of Culture* (1981), suggested that the ethnographer confronting a "new [field] situation" must cope with a form of "culture shock" for which he must invent a solution. That is, "the fieldworker invents ... his own understanding" by constructing "analogies" that are

> extensions of his own notions and those of his culture, transformed by his experiences of the field situation. *He uses the latter as a kind of "lever," the way a pole vaulter uses his pole, to catapult his comprehension beyond the limitations imposed by earlier viewpoints* ... Gradually the subject, the objectified element that serves as a "control" for his invention, is invented through analogies incorporating progressively more comprehensive articulations, so that a set of impressions is re-created as a set of meanings.[30]

For Engel, a key such analogy in his account of "the real story of the 'modernization' of Thai law"[31] is the figure of the (missing) *phuyai*, a "big person" with sufficient status and authority to command respect (even that of dogs) in traditional Thai society. Drawing on a traditional Thai proverb – "Walk behind the *phuyai* and the dogs won't bite" – as an epigraph to Part Two ("Private Wrongs, Mediation, and the Traditional Legal Culture") of *Code and Custom*,[32] Engel argues that the "'missing *phuyai*,' like the dog in the Sherlock Holmes story conspicuous for its failure to bark, is the most important feature of [personal injury]... disputes in their pre-judicial stages."[33] As local systems of status and authority broke down and village remediation systems began to lose their efficacy in mid-twentieth century Thailand, the figure of the (missing) *phuyai* persisted as a powerful force for compromise in a legal system where mediation continued to be regarded as "the normal system for handling disputes"[34] and the litigation of private wrongs was experienced as "an aberrant pattern, a pathological development in the traditional setting."[35] In cases where a *phuyai* "fails to play his role as mediator ... the vacuum created by the missing *phuyai* is filled by the judge," even as the court of law replaces mediation in its traditional setting.[36]

Here, the role of the (missing) *phuyai* provides an unlikely but intriguing link to what ultimately became Engel's signature referencing of "the curious

---

[30] Roy Wagner, *The Invention of Culture* (University of Chicago Press [1975] 1981), p. 12, emphasis added.
[31] Engel, *Code and Custom*, 3.   [32] Ibid, 55.   [33] Ibid, 137.   [34] Ibid.
[35] Ibid, 138.   [36] Ibid, 137.

incident of the dog in the night-time" – from the popular Sherlock Holmes short story, *Silver Blaze* – in a number of publications.[37] In *Code and Custom*, the "missing *phuyai*" became a metaphor for absences and non-events (the dog that did not bite, the victim that failed to sue) and the conceptual lever for "catapulting"[38] Engel's grasp of the power of local forms and practices as they were incorporated into a centralized Thai legal system in the mid-twentieth century, "bending and adapting when necessary, yet retaining for the most part the basic values and patterns of behavior that have traditionally given meaning to life."[39]

These basic values included a concept of personality derived from Theravada Buddhism, in which character and temperament were constituted by the nature of each person's "heart." Thus people were described as "hot-" or "cool-hearted," "black-" or "good-hearted," "tender-" or "narrow-hearted," and so forth.[40] While injuries produced by wrongful acts did not typically "stimulate a consciousness of violated rights in any legal sense," Engel suggests that there is a different sense in which a set of rights is violated by such acts: "the right of individuals to maintain their coolness and psychic balance, the right to pursue a meritorious existence without being agitated or obstructed, the right to view oneself as a person respected by the community and worthy of that respect."[41] This different set of rights requires, Engel suggests, a different kind of judge, one that takes on the role of the missing *phuyai* in restoring psychic balance – a process that resembles more "a forceful hammering together of the heated disputants" than an effort to achieve any more abstract sense of justice, in a society where maintenance of a "cool heart" is a central value.[42]

As this discussion suggests, Engel's first major research project on the so-called modernization of Thai law, a topic that followed in the footsteps of other research by Western legal scholars of modernization in the 1960s and 1970s,[43] challenged the standard narrative of modernization with its assumption of development or progress toward liberal legal forms and practices, while documenting the resilience and independence of Thai understandings of justice. By focusing on the "subject-lenses" through which perceived wrongs were understood by his Thai interlocutors and drawing on familiar (Western) imageries to capture these perceptions, Engel provided a dynamic

---

[37] Arthur Conan Doyle, *The Adventure of Silver Blaze* (1892).
[38] Wagner, *The Invention of Culture*, 12.   [39] Engel, *Code and Custom*, p. 133.
[40] Ibid, 59–60.   [41] Ibid, 67–8.   [42] Ibid, 149.
[43] See, e.g., J. N. D. Anderson (ed.), *Changing Law in Developing Countries* (Allen and Unwin, 1963); Jerome Alan Cohen, "Chinese mediation on the eve of modernization, *California Law Review*, 54 (1966), 1201; Marc Galanter, "The Modernization of Law," in M. Weiner (ed.), *Modernization* (Basic Books, 1966), pp. 153–65.

and relational account of the ways that radically different systems of law "interlock and interact with one another over time," transforming each system through forms of "mutual adaptation" in the process.[44]

The productivity of this approach to the transformation of Thai law became apparent over the next several decades, culminating in Engel's co-authored book with Jaruan Engel which argues that by the time of their latest research in the late 1990s and early 2000s, conceptualizations of justice and injustice in Thailand had, if anything, moved further away from Western liberal legalism than was the case in the 1970s.[45] Indeed, as David Engel notes in "Globalization and the Decline of Legal Consciousness," while public discourse at the national level, and English-language media offering accounts of contemporary Thailand, may emphasize rights and the rule of law, "the language of rights is nowhere to be found in [provincial Thai] injury narratives."[46] Rather,

> although globalization may ... have transformed legal consciousness in Thailand, the accounts provided by injury victims suggest that the end result – somewhat unexpectedly – has been an atrophy of locality-based remediation systems, a further diminution of the role of law in everyday life, and a heightened sense that justice for the ordinary person is more likely to be achieved through self-abnegation than through the pursuit of rights.[47]

FROM LEGAL CULTURE TO LEGAL CONSCIOUSNESS: "FIND WHAT GAVE YOU THE EMOTION"

Just as Engel's attention to the "creative power" of "subject-lenses" influenced his challenge to processes of so-called modernization, contributing to a more nuanced understanding of legal change as relational and dynamic, so too did his engagement with the interpretive turn in anthropology complicate his understanding of subjectivity in light of what Raymond Williams describes as "structures of feeling"[48] or "practical consciousness."[49] This form of consciousness includes "affective elements of consciousness and relationship: not feeling against thought but thought as felt and feeling as thought: practical consciousness of a present kind, *in a living and interrelating continuity.*"[50] Williams argues that "a 'structure of feeling' is a cultural hypothesis, actually derived from attempts to understand such elements and their connections in a generation or period, and needing always to be returned, interactively, to such

---

[44] Engel, *Code and Custom*, p. 207.   [45] Engel and Engel, *Tort, custom and karma*, p. 2.
[46] Engel, "Globalization," 511.   [47] Ibid.
[48] R. Williams, *Marxism and Literature* (Oxford University Press, 1977), p. 128.   [49] Ibid, 130.
[50] Ibid, 132, emphasis added.

evidence," and notes that while the description is of "structures" of feeling, the reference is to "a social experience which is still *in process*, often indeed not yet recognized as social."[51]

The move to practical consciousness was a dimension of an analytic stance away from voluntarism (as rational or strategic choice) and toward an understanding of agency as embodied – an approach that is signaled ethnographically and most compellingly in the work of anthropologist Michelle Rosaldo. Rosaldo, like Engel, carried out fieldwork in Southeast Asia in the 1970s, where her research among the Ilongot of the Philippines provided a basis for highly innovative interventions into the complex dynamic of structure and agency that was a central problematic of social and cultural theory in the second half of the twentieth century.[52] Specifically, Rosaldo argued for the centrality of feeling and emotion in the analysis of agency, at a time when "psychological" approaches – understood at the time as an engagement with "internal" states – tended to be marginalized by anthropologists focused on cultural patterns or on social structure (kinship, economy, politics, law).

In a now classic volume on cultural theory that included papers presented at a workshop on the topic hosted at the University of Chicago in 1981, Rosaldo's contribution, published posthumously following her early death in the field in 1982, underscored "the limits of the ways in which the problem [of thought and feeling] has hitherto been posed" by cultural theorists.[53] In words that recall David Engel's discussion of the meanings of "heart" in Thai understandings of character and disposition, Rosaldo argued that

> the crucial point – and one much more profound than it initially appears – is recognition of the fact that feeling is forever given shape through thought and that thought is laden with emotional meaning ... I can then argue ... that what distinguishes thought and affect, differentiating a "cold" cognition from a "hot," is fundamentally a sense of the engagement of the actor's self. Emotions ... are *embodied* thoughts, thoughts seeped with the apprehension that "I am involved."[54]

---

[51] Ibid, 132–3, emphasis in original.
[52] See, e.g., Bourdieu, *Theory of Practice*; Williams, *Marxism and Literature*; Anthony Giddens, *Central Problems in Social Theory: Action, Structure, and Contradiction in Social Analysis* (University of California Press, 1979); Sherry B. Ortner, "Theory in anthropology since the sixties," *Critical Studies in Society and History*, 26 (1984), 126; Richard A. Schweder and Robert A. Levine (eds.), *Culture Theory: Essays on Mind, Self, and Emotion* (Cambridge University Press, 1984).
[53] Michelle Z. Rosaldo, "Toward an Anthropology of Self and Feeling" in R. A. Schweder and R. A. Levine (eds.), *Culture Theory: Essays on Mind, Self, and Emotion* (Cambridge University Press, 1984), p. 143.
[54] Ibid.

I note Rosaldo's important contribution to the understanding of emotion in cultural analysis in part because her research overlapped with Engel's and echoes his concern with the ways in which Western understandings of subjectivity and agency may bias our approach to other (less cognitive and more practical, in Raymond Williams' sense) forms of consciousness. Her work is also referenced by Jerome Bruner in his 1990 volume *Acts of Meaning*, a frequent reference point for Engel's work from the early 1990s forward.[55] Rosaldo's key move was her use of the phrase "embodied thoughts" to capture the sense of *how* cultural meanings are subjectively experienced: as thoughts *"seeped with the apprehension that 'I am involved.'"* Also important is that research on embodiment tended to focus not simply on *a* "system of meaning" but on multiple meanings (or systems of meaning) and the implications of such multiplicity for the affective power of cultural symbols in everyday life. Finally, by situating actors in what Raymond Williams terms "a living and interrelating continuity,"[56] the focus on embodiment places actors in the flow of time, directing attention to the layering of meanings over time, with meanings acquired in childhood or infancy forming "the intuitive basis for emotional responsiveness to symbols even after the latter have been understood at a reflective level."[57]

While Engel's interest in embodied thought is most fully theorized (and somewhat differently articulated) in his later work, and specifically in his forthcoming *The Myth of the Litigious Society*,[58] his understanding of subjectivity as emergent in the flow of consciousness through which individuals encounter the world has been a focal point of his writing since the time of his undergraduate thesis, "Theories of Time and Consciousness in the Writing of Gertrude Stein and Ernest Hemingway," which Engel generously made available to me in the summer of 2015. In the thesis, Engel quotes Hemingway's advice to a younger writer regarding the importance of emotion in his rendering of a character, and the ways that emotion could be rendered "by describing the small details associated with it."[59] Hemingway advised the

---

[55] B. Bruner, *Acts of meaning*, pp. 41–2. Rosaldo's contribution to debates about the place of emotion in cultural analysis predates by some thirty years the more recent resurgence of interest in the topic of affect and its relevance to issues of agency or of being "moved." See, e.g., Gregory J. Seigworth and Melissa Gregg, "An inventory of shimmers" in M. Gregg and G. Seigworth (eds.), *The Affect Theory Reader* (Duke University Press, 2010), pp. 2–25 for an overview.

[56] Williams, *Marxism and Literature*, p. 132.

[57] Robert A. Levine, "Properties of culture: an ethnographic view," in Schweder and Levine (eds.), *Culture Theory*, p. 85.

[58] Engel, *Myth of the Litigious Society*.   [59] Engel, *Theories of Time and Consciousness*, p. 56.

younger writer: "Find what gave you the emotion: what the action was that gave you the excitement. Then write it down ... making it clear so the reader will see it too and have the same feeling that you had."[60] As Engel explained this approach, underscoring a focus he would return to in the 1990s and 2000s, "Emotion is not dealt with as an entity in itself which the writer approaches directly. It is reduced to constituent sensations, and these sensations are described by the artist who believes that if the reader can share them then he will 'have the same feeling that you had.'" He notes that "the rationale [used by Hemingway] is similar to the Cubist concept of prelogical perception. Hemingway does not reason about what happens and seldom describes emotions analytically." Instead, he describes objects – "what gave you the emotion" – and was in this way "able to convey the inner life without indulging in any sentimentality. He could keep his coolness and poise even while showing how the protagonist lost his."[61]

Engel also notes that Hemingway abandoned traditional perspectives on chronological time in his writing, through character descriptions in which "[t]he history of the Self continually flows through the consciousness and exerts its pressure upon the mind and emotions of the character." In this way, "Hemingway balanced the Self, which is always significant," with an external world, which is discontinuous and static, and often unimportant in itself. As Engel argues: "The point of Hemingway's art, like that of Cezanne and of the Cubists, is to convey the essence of this Self by having the reader stand for a moment in the consciousness and look out as the Self does."[62]

In making this argument, Engel links Hemingway not only to the art of Picasso, Cézanne, and the Cubists, but also to the theories of William James, whose *Principles of Psychology* moved away from environmental determinism to focus instead on "the vital creative power of the human imagination."[63] Engel suggests that for Hemingway, if it can be truly shown how the character sees (how he imagines the world), then it can be truly understood how he feels. The weight of the past, which usually lies heavy upon Hemingway's characters, will thus be felt by anyone who reads his work with care."[64] This means, as Engel suggests, that to understand Hemingway's work – or that of the Cubists – one must pay careful attention, "in Gertrude Stein's words, both [to] 'the time of the composition and the time in the composition.'"[65]

---

[60] Ibid, quoting Charles A. Fenton, *The Apprenticeship of Ernest Hemingway: The Early Years* (Farrar, Straus, and Young, 1965), p. 155.

[61] Ibid, 56–8. [62] Ibid, 82. [63] Ibid, iii, citing James, *Principles of Psychology*.

[64] Ibid, 82.

[65] Ibid, iv, quoting Gertrude Stein, "Composition as Explanation 12," *Poetry Magazine* (1926), p. 12.

"THE ENIGMA OF BEING-IN-TIME"[66]

The fascination with "the weight of the past" shown by Engel in 1967, as he reviewed the work of Hemingway and Gertrude Stein, takes me both forward and backward in time: forward from the time of his undergraduate thesis to his subsequent research on injury, disability, and subjectivity; and backward, in the context of the gathering of sociolegal scholars who celebrated "The Oven Bird's Song" in October 2015, to core themes that were to become the focus of his writing. These themes include, first, an understanding of actors as embedded in dense relational networks which shape the ways they think and act in complex ways, rather than actors as autonomous individuals; second, a corresponding understanding of subjectivity – what anthropologist Sherry Ortner describes as "the ensemble of modes of perception, affect, thought, desire, and fear that animate acting subjects"[67] – as central to an understanding of agency; third, the privileging of nonconscious forms of motivation over conscious, strategic decision-making; and fourth, an approach to time and history that is nonlinear, in that, like Hemingway, he understands the "past" as constantly (if nonconsciously) involved in the present and affecting the impetus to act or not act in powerful ways.

In developing these themes, Engel turns in several publications to the work of Jerome Bruner, whose creative use of ethnographic research in the 1970s and 1980s led him to "locate ... Self not in the fastness of immediate private consciousness but in a cultural-historical situation as well."[68] Bruner suggests more specifically that the self might be understood as "distributed" throughout its relational networks and that in this sense this "wider circle of people ... might also be complicit in our narratives and our Self-constructions," producing a narrative of self that is "enmeshed in a net of others" rather than autonomous.[69] Bruner's focus on a self that is "told" is also a key theme in Engel's work, producing a self which varies "from time to time and from person to person ... in the degree to which it is unified, stable, and acceptable to informed observers as reliable and valid."[70] In this version of the creative

---

[66] Hayden White, *The Content of the Form: Narrative Discourse and Historical Representation* (Johns Hopkins University Press, 2009), p. 142.

[67] Sherry B. Ortner, *Anthropology and Social Theory: Culture, Power, and the Acting Subject* (Duke University Press, 2006), p. 107.

[68] Bruner, *Acts of Meaning*, p. 107.

[69] David M. Engel, "Perception and decision at the threshold of tort law: explaining the infrequency of claims," *DePaul Law Review*, 62 (2013), 293, 327, quoting Bruner, *Acts of Meaning*, 114.

[70] Bruner, *Acts of Meaning*, 113.

power of "subject-lenses," the human experience of time is a central consideration, as narrator and protagonist merge and separate from one another over the course of a narration. In Bruner's evocative framing of this complex dynamic, the story of a life

> is an account given by a narrator in the here and now about a protagonist bearing his name who existed in the there and then, the story terminating in the present when the protagonist fuses with the narrator ... The Self as narrator not only recounts but justifies. And the Self as protagonist is always, as it were, pointing to the future.[71]

Bruner's distinction between the Self as protagonist and the Self as narrator is reminiscent of Gertrude Stein's distinction between "the time of the composition and the time in the composition" that intrigued Engel at the time of his undergraduate thesis;[72] Engel turns again to Stein (in paraphrase) to underscore the significance of "'the time of the stories and the time in the stories'" in his analysis of the "origin myths" told by the parents of children with disabilities as they construct an emergent subjectivity for their children, in interviews elicited by Engel (the time *of* the story), that contradict the dire prognosis they received from medical experts – the "weight of the past," or the time *in* the story that is critical to the way it takes shape.[73]

In "The Oven Bird's Song," as in the Frost poem for which the article is named, the weight of the past is also a key concern – manifested as "a pervasive sense of social disintegration and loss,"[74] as expressed in the narratives of Sander County residents who lament the demise of community at a time (the time *of* the story) in which "a different crowd," with different understandings about the nature of personal responsibility, had seemingly taken over. This weight was also felt in comments by long-term county residents that indicated ambivalence about the roles of law and of going to court in this changing environment.[75] At the same time, Engel's analysis engaged with the instability of identity (between "insiders" and "outsiders") in his exploration of how the "'stranger' was in reality no longer outside the community" but central to its survival,[76] hinting at the powerful role of an imagined "other" in the construction of a no less imagined and unstable self.

Over the next decade, Engel came to conceptualize "community" (and implicitly "identity") as an ever-changing "fabric of differences"[77] in which

---

[71] Engel, "Perception and decision," 792, quoting Bruner, *Acts of Meaning*, 121.
[72] Engel, *Theories of Time and Consciousness*, quoting Stein, *Composition as Explanation*, 12.
[73] Engel, "Origin myths," 797.   [74] Engel, "The oven bird's song," 551.
[75] Ibid, 566–73; and see Engel, "Law, time, and community," 625ff.
[76] Engel, "The oven bird's song," 580–1.   [77] Engel, "Law, time, and community," 615.

"conceptions of time were a fundamental part of the largely subconscious process by which members of the community created meaning out of their experiences and attempted to give order to their world."[78] Likewise, talk about law was "a way of making claims about the legitimacy of a particular way of life."[79] Bourdieu's analysis of law as a form of symbolic power "which *creates* the social world, but only if we remember that it is this world which first creates the law"[80] is fundamental to this approach, in which struggles over court use position different factions as "virtuous" defenders of a way of life or disruptive outsiders intent on destroying it – a process in which "spatial references tacitly symbolize temporal ones," with shared geography standing in "for a deeper and more important set of claims to a shared relationship over time."[81]

EMULATING SHERLOCK HOLMES: FROM THE DOG THAT DID NOT BARK TO THE BRAIN THAT DID NOT THINK

In his most recent work, *The Myth of the Litigious Society* (2016), Engel returns to his thematic engagement over the course of his career with Sherlock Holmes and "the curious incident of the dog in the nighttime," positioning the researcher as an erstwhile detective systematically sifting through clues in order to reach a new understanding of plaintiffs in personal injury cases who fail to sue. In this book and his related 2013 article "Perception and Decision at the Threshold of Tort Law," Engel expands his critique of the decision-tree as a model of thought and action for victims of injury, while complicating his understanding of subjectivity as "being-in-time" through a broad engagement with literature in neuroscience on embodied cognition. Specifically, he turns to an alternative approach to perception and experience which he describes, following Daniel Kahneman and others, as "think[ing] with your body, not only with your brain."[82] Focusing on this version of an "embodied self" or "embodied mind"[83] positions humans "as quite literally the creatures of their environment, which leaves its traces in their minds and on their bodies."[84] Environment, in turn, is multifaceted and active, constituted culturally, historically, and biologically through the actions and interactions of human and

---

[78] Ibid at 636.
[79] Carol J. Greenhouse, Barbara Yngvesson, and David M. Engel, *Law and Community in Three American Towns* (Cornell University Press, 1994), p. 10.
[80] Bourdieu, "Force of law," 234.   [81] Greenhouse et al., "Law and community," 168.
[82] Engel, "Perception and Decision," p. 298, quoting Daniel Kahneman, *Thinking, Fast and Slow* (Farrar, Straus, and Giroux, 2011), p. 15.
[83] Engel, "Perception and decision," 304–5.   [84] Ibid, 306.

nonhuman others.[85] By locating decision and perception "at the threshold of tort law," Engel signals this complex interchange between humans who are subjects of an "environment" that is, in turn, an artifact of law and culture forged by humans.

Here, Engel builds on Bruner's notion of a self that is "distributed" in a network of others and may divide itself in the process of narration, to consider the ways a self "comes to mind" over time in a process of "gradual sedimentation and reworking of one's memory" that culminates in the emergence of an *"autobiographical self."*[86] The autobiographical self "operates both consciously and nonconsciously." In this sense, it "leads a double life," part of which "takes place offscreen," where memories or feelings laid down in the past may be triggered by events and experiences that occur in the future, subtly shaping and reshaping the ways in which response to an injury is perceived and acted (or not acted) upon.[87]

In developing this *"recursive* and interactional" analysis of "self" with "environment,"[88] Engel turns once again to Bourdieu, this time to his theorization of the *"dialectic of the internalization of externality and the externalization of internality,"*[89] through which a particular cultural formation is reproduced as a "system of dispositions ... [that] tends to perpetuate itself into the future by making itself present in practices structured according to its principles."[90] In the case of injury victims, the mystery of the victim who fails to sue is explained by (unconscious) dispositions produced in a legal and cultural environment that has itself been shaped by the history of the tort reform movement in the United States, as well as by a "moral ethos" that extols self-sufficiency and sanctions the monetization of loss, particularly in certain kinds of injuries, which are regarded as "individual," rather than social, problems.[91]

---

[85] Ibid, 314–27.

[86] Ibid, 303, quoting Antonio Damasio, *Self Comes to Mind: Constructing the Conscious Brain* (Pantheon Books, 2010), pp. 21–3, emphasis in original.

[87] Ibid, 210, quoting Damasio.   [88] Ibid, 306, emphasis in original.

[89] Bourdieu, *Theory of Practice*, 72, emphasis in original.

[90] Engel, "Perception and decision," 330, quoting Bourdieu, *Theory of Practice*, 82.

[91] Ibid, 330; *and see* Ortner, "Anthropology," 110–11, where she offers a critique of Bourdieu's *habitus* as insufficiently accessible to those whose lives are shaped by it: "In using the word 'consciousness' I do not mean to exclude various unconscious dynamics as seen, for example, in a Freudian unconscious or a Bourdieusian habitus. But I do mean that subjectivity is always more than those things, in two senses. At the individual level I will assume, with Giddens, that actors are always at least partially 'knowing subjects' ... They are, in short, conscious in the conventional psychological sense, something that needs to be emphasized as a complement to, though not a replacement of, Bourdieu's insistence on the inaccessibility to actors of the underlying logic of their practices. At the collective level I use the word 'consciousness' as it is

In this work, Engel expands conversations and collaborations in which he has been engaged for more than three decades with anthropologists interested in the nature of legal consciousness and the temporal character of law.[92] For example, his emphasis on humans as "quite literally the creatures of their environment" and the dialectic of internalization/externalization that produces embodied subjects recalls Carol Greenhouse's exploration of racial identity in her powerful 2008 essay "Life Stories, Law's Stories," which moves back and forth between the life stories of Supreme Court justice Clarence Thomas and Pecola in Toni Morrison's *The Bluest Eye*. Noting that "a life story is not one that can be limited to the skin-bound individual. It is not the individual who 'has' race, but the society as a whole,"[93] Greenhouse explores the effects of an absence of law on the vision of justice in Morrison's novel, suggesting that for its protagonists, justice "will not come from legal remedies yet cannot come without them."[94] Greenhouse also engages with the temporality of law in this essay, pointing to the "temporal doubling" in *Brown* v. *Board* as its "main literary feature" in that it "conjures two futures at once," a promising future for African American children who grow up to be productive citizens, a bleak one for those who are "damaged by the stigma of racial prejudice."[95]

Likewise, Engel's recent work on the dialectic between body and world, and on law's absence, is evocative of themes that Susan Coutin explores in her research on unauthorized migrants. For example, in her 2005 article "Being En Route," Coutin argues that although such migrants "cannot be" – in the sense that they officially "disappear" from jurisdictions that prohibit their

---

used by both Marx and Durkheim: as the collective sensibility of some set of socially interrelated actors. *consciousness in this sense is always ambiguously part of people's personal subjectivities and part of the public culture*" (emphasis added).

[92] See, e.g., Greenhouse et al., "Law and community"; Carol J. Greenhouse, *A Moment's Notice: Time Politics across Cultures* (Cornell University Press, 1996); Carol J. Greenhouse, "Life stories, law's stories: subjectivity and responsibility in the politicization of the discourse of 'identity'," *Political and Legal Anthropology Review* 31 (2008), 79–101; Justin Richland, *Arguing with Tradition: The Language of Law in Hopi Tribal Court* (University of Chicago Press, 2008) (on the ways that Hopi judges create "meaningful spaces" where the limited coherence of personal histories is acknowledged, momentarily destabilizing the truth-making practices of Anglo-American law); Susan Bibler Coutin, "Being en route," *American Anthropologist*, 107 (2005), 195; Susan Bibler Coutin, "Comment: the violence of being not quite there," *Law, Culture and the Humanities*, 7 (2011), 457; Susan Bibler Coutin, "Falling outside: excavating the history of Central American asylum seekers," *Law & Social Inquiry*, 36 (2011), 569 ; Sylvia Posocco, "Expedientes: fissured legality and affective states in the Transnational Adoption Archives In Guatemala, *Law, Culture and the Humanities*, 7 (2011), 434; Susan Bibler Coutin, *Exiled Home: Salvadoran Transnational Youth in the Aftermath of Violence* (Duke University Press, 2016).

[93] Greenhouse, "Life stories," 88.   [94] Ibid.   [95] Ibid, 82.

presence[96] – their bodies continue to occupy physical space, becoming "a sort of absent space or vacancy, surrounded by law."[97] In this way, migrants' embodiment of illegality transforms the landscape of law, even as the law, by deeming them illegal, positions them "outside of the territory that they occupy," in such a way that "local spaces become part of foreign territories and vice versa."[98] Coutin suggests that in this dialectic of body and law, the (migrant) body itself takes on "documentary qualities," with the potential to become "the principal document and archival form in which histories of violence and conflict sediment."[99] Coutin's analysis in these articles speaks to issues that are central to Engel's understanding of the injured body as constituted by a history of pain and violence in a world where "law itself *acts*" to perpetuate injustices.[100]

Like Greenhouse's exploration of the complexity of law's absence in a world where "justice does not come from legal remedies, yet is contingent on them," and Coutin's examination of how the undocumented reconfigure the legal landscape by embodying illegality even as they are situated outside the landscape of law, Engel's research on embodied cognition at the threshold of tort law provides a provocation to push beyond familiar assumptions about the hegemony of liberal legalism in order to complicate our understanding of the landscape of law. More specifically, his fascination over several decades with Sherlock Holmes and the dog that failed to bark focuses attention on the conundrums of law's absence, as discovered not simply in low rates of personal injury litigation, but also in stories that shed light on the place of human subjectivity in constituting what is considered to be the legal landscape. In this way, his research provides a compelling incentive for rethinking the significance of law's absence for our understanding of the power of law.

[96] Coutin, "En route," 199, quoting Mai M. Ngai, *Impossible Subjects: Illegal Aliens and the Making of Modern America* (Princeton University Press, 2004), p. 5.
[97] Ibid, 199.   [98] Ibid, 200.
[99] S. Coutin, "Comment: the violence of being not quite there," *Law, Culture, and the Humanities*, 7 (2011), p. 461.
[100] Coutin, "Falling outside," 592.

4

Karl's Law School, or The Oven Bird in Buffalo

ALFRED S. KONEFSKY

The idea for my reflection on "The Oven Bird's Song" originated in a conversation I had with David Engel almost thirty years after the publication of his article. When I was cleaning out my office files in anticipation of retirement, I discovered copies of David's first two drafts of the article, versions that had yet to incorporate – in title or text – the Robert Frost poem. I walked down the hall to David's office and presented these early drafts to him. He seemed very pleased to see, once again, the evidence of his preliminary work, and said "You remember this was my job talk when I interviewed here," to which I responded: "I know, we hired you anyway." And it was in the midst of our laughter at that moment that a conference and this volume of essays were born.

My task is to focus locally rather than globally and to try to situate David Engel and "The Oven Bird's Song"[1] within the intellectual life and context of the Buffalo Law School. In order to do that, we need to know a little about the institution that David joined in 1981, so that we might better understand both what brought David and "The Oven Bird" here and why the law school welcomed the addition of David and his intellectual project at that moment.

To take the full measure of my assignment, I think we have to go back a little further in time and ask how the Buffalo Law School became the Buffalo Law School of the 1970s and '80s, and in order to do that, I believe we have

University at Buffalo Distinguished Professor Emeritus, SUNY Buffalo Law School, The State University of New York. I am very grateful for the valuable comments on versions of this essay offered by Samantha Barbas, Anya Bernstein, Michael Boucai, David Engel, Patrick Long, Lynn Mather, Frank Munger, John Henry Schlegel, Robert Steinfeld, Matthew Steilen, Barry Sullivan, and Winnifred Sullivan. As usual, Dianne Avery contributed exceptional editorial and substantive suggestions. The standard disclaimer as to final responsibility applies.

[1] David M. Engel, "The oven bird's song: insiders, outsiders, and personal injuries in an American community," *Law & Society Review*, 18 (1984), 551.

to ask disarmingly simple questions: What do we want a law school to be, or what do we want out of a law school; and in a related sense, what do we want law to be, or what do we want out of law? David's journey and Buffalo's journey were very dependent on the answers to these questions, and in an attempt to answer them I think we have to recur to the early twentieth-century origins of an alternative vision of what legal education and legal scholarship might be, as distinct from the traditional Langdellian wisdom of the case method, the casebook, and its emphasis on rules, principles, and legal doctrine.[2] There is no legal doctrine in "The Oven Bird's Song," so why tolerate it in a law school at this time and in this place? The answer, I believe, can be traced to the influence of a singular figure in American legal education, writing at the outset of the Legal Realist movement: Karl Llewellyn.[3] In a sense, along with a handful of other law schools (Wisconsin included), Buffalo became Karl's law school – a law school in which "The Oven Bird's Song" seemed a natural outgrowth of what legal study should aspire to or become. We now take it for granted (it's almost a cliché) that one way or the other we are all legal realists (or "new" legal realists),[4] but how we got there can be found in part in Llewellyn's tearing away the mask of legal education about 100 years ago, and I want to sample briefly some of his observations and criticisms of law schools and explore why "The Oven Bird's Song" can be seen as a fulfillment of Llewellyn's promise of a new age of legal education.

Over the course of his life, Llewellyn had lots to say about legal education, and he was not always consistent. He sometimes changed his mind; for instance, at times he defended the case method and found it useful in a modified form while at others he was intensely critical of it, particularly when reflecting on it as the Great Depression in the 1930s stripped away its pretenses.[5] Yet, over time, for all his withering criticism (he complained of the "critical aloofness" of law schools and described them as "blind, inept, factory-ridden, wasteful, defective, and empty. If you prefer verbs: it blinds,

---

[2] For an analysis of Christopher Columbus Langdell's impact on legal education as the late-nineteenth-century Dean of the Harvard Law School, see Bruce A. Kimball, *The Inception of Modern Professional Education: C. C. Langdell, 1826–1906* (University of North Carolina Press, 2009), and Daniel R. Coquillette and Bruce A. Kimball, *On the Battlefield of Merit: Harvard Law School, The First Century* 304–83 (Harvard University Press, 2015).

[3] See generally William L. Twining, *Karl Llewellyn and the Realist Movement* (University of Oklahoma Press, 1985).

[4] See, for example, Stewart Macaulay, "The new versus the old legal realism: 'things ain't what they used to be,'" *Wisconsin Law Review*, 2005 (2005).

[5] Twining, *Karl Llewellyn*, 132–5, 232–9; Anders Walker, "Bramble Bush revisited: Llewellyn, the Great Depression and the first law school crisis, 1929–1939," *Journal of Legal Education*, 64 (2014), 161–2, 165–6, 171–2.

it stumbles, it conveyor-belts, it wastes, it mutilates, and it empties"),[6] he began to formulate a transformational vision of what legal education could be. He wanted to know what lawyers did because he wanted to prepare law students for the rigors of practice in an economically threatening time, and he thought law schools were failing miserably at their job. His idea was that theory could be practical, that is, understanding how things worked would be a very good thing for a law student to grasp in the real world, and simply focusing on legal rules and doctrines did students a disservice. And though he could be very practical, shrewd, hardheaded, and analytical, and was incredibly fluent in legal doctrine, Llewellyn, like many theorists of education, viewed education as primarily a moral enterprise. In *The Bramble Bush*, his series of lectures published in 1930 for entering law students (Lord knows what they made of it, let alone whether they truly were prepared to understand it), in a chapter called "Law and Civilization," he observed:

> By and large the *basic order* in our society, and for that matter in any society, *is not produced by law*. And one of the most misleading claims that has ever been put forward for law's contribution to civilization is the notion that it is law from which the basic order flows. The basic order grows, I repeat, not from law, but (at least every generation) *from the process of education*. With that process law may have much to do. But the much is not too much.[7]

Therefore, in Llewellyn's eyes, education was a moral imperative,[8] and his anger at the perceived failure of legal education was drawn from his belief that law schools were failing society and also failing law students in their preparation to serve society. "I think it is to law that we owe the conception of *justice*," he remarked.

> I am not wholly sure of this. There is a very remote chance that the matter runs the other way, that we owe law to the concept of justice. There is a greater chance that both are shoots of the same root. Still, I think law as a discipline may claim the concept. It should, if it can, for the concept marks a noble achievement.[9]

---

[6] K[arl] N. Llewellyn, "On what is wrong with so-called legal education," *Columbia Law Review*, 35 (1935), 651, 652–3.

[7] There are a number of editions of *The Bramble Bush*. I have chosen the most recent, which also has the virtue of having a perceptive introductory essay by Stewart Macaulay. Karl N. Llewellyn, *The Bramble Bush: On Our Law and Its Study* 116 (Quid Pro Books, 2012).

[8] In this regard, see Philip W. Jackson, *What Is Education?* (University of Chicago Press, 2012), pp. 20, 94.

[9] Llewellyn, *The Bramble Bush*, 124.

Having been charged with the responsibility for the concept of justice, law schools were in danger of abandoning their duty. What was to be done to prepare students to serve their society and assist law in attaining justice?

In a trenchant little essay entitled "On What Is Wrong with So-Called Legal Education," published in 1935 in the *Columbia Law Review*,[10] Llewellyn engaged in a wholesale assault on the form and substance of legal education, and offered proposals for remedying its evils.[11] Unlike *The Bramble Bush*, which sought to explain and defend the process of legal education, this 1935 article sought to demolish the apparatus that had been established since 1870. The moral edginess was still present: "Ideals without technique are a mess," he memorably observed, "[b]ut technique without ideals is a menace."[12] Social change, however, was taking place right under the very noses of law schools, and they had better adjust or perish. The nature of practice was shifting and the standard modes of education were going to be inadequate to face this brave new world. What was to be done? He had a number of suggestions. "The need is," he said, "in some fashion, for an integration of the human and the artistic with the legal. Not an addition merely; an integration."[13] How was that to be accomplished?

As Anders Walker has recently pointed out, Llewellyn, reacting to the impact of the Great Depression, "did not target interdisciplinary scholarship" as frivolous or useless, though he had once in the not too distant past been an avid defender of the case method. "While some reformers called for an increased attention to clinical work and practical skills, Llewellyn joined a cadre of pro-New Deal law teachers who advocated interdisciplinary, policy-centered coursework."[14] Ironically, in the face of economic crisis and diminishing job prospects, "Llewellyn did not," Walker observes, "view a more interdisciplinary focus to be less practical."[15] What was the point of introducing a wider lens into traditional legal study? It was to set legal rules and disputes into context. Llewellyn argued in his 1935 Columbia essay that "to set rules into their social context, into the context of how men do things, and of what difference the rule makes to those men – this is to give body to a rule for any student. It has graphic value, it has movement value, it has memory value."[16] According to Llewellyn, "[t]he fact is that legal rules mean,

---

[10] Llewellyn, "On what is wrong."

[11] Incidentally, though Llewellyn's essay originated as a speech at Harvard, the *Harvard Law Review* refused to publish it, causing him to comment archly that "their editor's canons of taste and policy did not jibe with mine." Ibid, 651*.

[12] Ibid, 662.   [13] Ibid, 663.   [14] Walker, "Bramble Bush revisited," 178.   [15] Ibid, 166.

[16] Llewellyn, "On what is wrong," 669.

of themselves, next to nothing."[17] When you introduce social context, instead, "[y]ou also make *critique* of the rule take on its human content. You make critique inevitable, because the human content, once introduced, will never be denied."[18] So, he asserted, it was time to "integrate the background of social and economic fact and policy, course by course, or fail of our job."[19] And he called for "wak[ing] faculty-members up to the job of *integrating* background – social or philosophical – into *every* course."[20] "The professor's job lies," he said, in preparing "the fact-background necessary to give to a policy-inquiry interest; to a rule, meaningfulness; to a counseling-question, body; to a critical evaluation, hands and feet."[21] In a talk at Duke Law School a year later, Llewellyn doubled down on his insights, commenting: "I think the most lamentable thing about American legal education is it has taken into account neither the society in which the job must be performed nor what we are educating for."[22] He suggested that "one of the things that goes to make lawyers is to make the law a cultural study. That is, curiously, today the most practical way to train for the trade,"[23] and he called for "the development of a realistic sense on the basis of fact."[24]

We have some sense of what Llewellyn meant by all of this in action, not simply in the classroom. An insight into his method and commitment to context is found not just in his prolific writing, but also in a recently discovered episode involving the NAACP. In 1933, after a post-Scottsboro lynching in Alabama, the NAACP submitted a brief to the Justice Department urging federal prosecution of the local sheriff, under an existing civil rights statute, for allowing or facilitating the lynching. When the brief was submitted and published, it included a foreword written by Llewellyn.[25] In searing language, he argued:

> The enclosed brief is a product of a situation. Behind the cold points of law is a crying need of fact. Pages (31) to (41) will burn like acid in any unsus-pecting reader's mind. Lynching is now being used, deliberately, to "teach" Negroes that *outside organizations must not be permitted to defend them in court*, though they be on trial for their lives. It is no longer a question of the individual defendants. Nor is it a question of the crime of which

---

[17] Ibid.   [18] Ibid.   [19] Ibid, 671.   [20] Ibid.   [21] Ibid, 678.
[22] Karl N. Llewellyn, "On the why of American legal education," *Duke Bar Association Journal*, 4 (1936), 19.
[23] Ibid, 24.   [24] Ibid.
[25] The account of this episode and its relationship to legal realism may be found in Alfred L. Brophy, "'Cold legal points into points of flame': Karl Llewellyn attacks lynching" (June 17, 2015), UNC Legal Studies Research Paper No. 2619895, available at SSRN: http://ssrn.com/abstract=2619895 or http://dx.doi.org/10.2139/ssrn.2619895.

the individual happens to be accused. It is, for the lynchers, a question of covering institutions as they are against implicit challenge *even in the courts of law*. "Keep this case from being another Scottsboro Case" – by driving the defendants' legal counsel out of town; and then by lynching the defendants. *With official connivance*.

It is against this background that the story of the Tuscaloosa lynching, on pp. (8)–(13), is to be read. It is this background that turns cold legal points into points of flame. The brief makes clear that the Federal Government has power to intervene. The brief makes clear that it is the duty of Federal officials to take action. When the baser elements of Southern communities turn, *not in sudden passion, but as a policy*, against the law, when even the decent elements of the same communities can "understand" such happenings (pp. (39)–(41)), the time has come for intervention of a stronger power. The statutes have provided for that intervention. *Will the Government act?*[26]

"[C]old legal points into points of flame"; "cold points of law" in "crying need of fact." Here on display are the elements and language of the legal realist agenda generally and, in particular, its link to Llewellyn's critique of legal education. Facts, situations (think situation sense and the Uniform Commercial Code[27]), background, communities, understanding – all in a piece of appellate advocacy.

What does all of this have to do with David Engel, "The Oven Bird," and the Buffalo Law School? David arrived in Buffalo in 1981 at a critical moment in the history of the school, and he arrived with his Sander County ethnography in tow from the American Bar Foundation, to be met and surrounded immediately by a sea of law and society and critical legal historian types. But the school's commitment to law and society and interdisciplinary work had two separate but related histories, one stemming from a period of time in the 1930s contemporaneous with Llewellyn's attempt to refashion legal education, and a more immediate one stemming from the decade of the 1970s.

As has been well chronicled, the Buffalo Law School in the late 1930s and '40s centered, at least initially, on the hiring of Frank Shea as Dean. Shea, a protégé of Felix Frankfurter, was brought in to get the law school accredited, and one of his many accomplishments (with Frankfurter's assistance) was to start a pipeline from the Harvard Law School to Buffalo (which often turned out to go back to Harvard) – a faculty pipeline fueled by the occasional former Holmes or Brandeis Supreme Court clerk, some of whom brought with them their interests in law combined with other disciplines, or went on to other

---

[26] Ibid, 16.   [27] Twining, *Karl Llewellyn*, 216–27, 313–21, 337–40, 369.

disciplines themselves.[28] If one thinks of Holmes, the skeptic and pragmatist ("The life of the law has not been logic: it has been experience"[29]), or Brandeis and his obsession with facts[30] (just substitute context for facts), one can see that the preconditions were set for viewing law in a more expansive way. Some of the scholarship done here at the time grappled with history, sociology, the development of the administrative state, tax policy, labor relations – not always the standard fare for legal academics then (though the Realists were beginning to make inroads into some forms of empirical social science[31]).

These traditions were revived in the early 1970s, when the law school had the temerity to hire as Dean Red Schwartz – a sociologist without a law degree – and brought to Buffalo some of the most significant figures in the early history of the formal Law and Society movement and its Association. Folks like Marc Galanter and Bob Gordon wrote early classics in the genre while at Buffalo,[32] but by 1977 a wholesale exodus had occurred, and Red, Marc, and Bob – on his way to critical legal studies and a rejection of functionalism[33] – and others had left. A new Dean, Tom Headrick, with a law degree in addition to a PhD, was in place on a new university campus, in a new law school building that was no longer located downtown as in the past. At the dedication of its cornerstone, the school's mission was tied directly to other university disciplines blessed as the wave and promise of the future by one of the leading practitioners of one of the leading local law firms, who observed:

[28] Daniel Horowitz, "David Riesman: from law to social criticism," *Buffalo Law Review*, 58 (2010), 1008–9; no author, "A gathering to remember Jacob D. Hyman, Dean and Professor," *Buffalo Law Review*, 57 (2009), 1129–30; Robert Schaus and James Arnone, *University at Buffalo Law School: 100 Years, 1887–1987: A History* (University at Buffalo Law Alumni Association, 1992), pp. 48–9.

[29] Oliver Wendell Holmes, Jr., *The Common Law* 1 (Little, Brown, and Company, 1881).

[30] Louis D. Brandeis, "The living law," *Illinois Law Review*, 10 (1916), 467 ("[N]o law, written or unwritten, can be understood without a full knowledge of the facts out of which it arises, and to which it is to be applied"). The ready translation of this insight about law into the iconic Brandeis Brief goes without saying. See Melvin Urofsky, *Louis D. Brandeis: A Life* (Pantheon Books, 2009), pp. 212–27, and Lawrence S. Zacharias, "Reframing the Constitution: Brandeis, "facts," and the nation's deliberative process," *The Journal Jurisprudence*, 20 (2013), 327.

[31] See John Henry Schlegel, *American Legal Realism and Empirical Social Science* (University of North Carolina Press, 1995).

[32] Marc Galanter, "Why the 'haves' come out ahead: speculations on the limits of legal change," *Law & Society Review*, 9 (1974), 95; Robert W. Gordon, "Introduction: J. Willard Hurst and the common law tradition in American legal historiography," *Law & Society Review*, 10 (1975), 9.

[33] Robert W. Gordon, "Critical legal histories," *Stanford Law Review*, 36 (1984), 57; John Henry Schlegel, "Notes toward an intimate, opinionated, and affectionate history of the Conference on Critical Legal Studies," *Stanford Law Review*, 36 (1984), 391.

Professional training alone, however, is not enough. The new law school must produce graduates who are educated and involved citizens in addition to being trained professionals. For this purpose the availability of relevant studies here on the campus must be put to use. Indeed, it is almost certain that one can no longer be considered a capable lawyer or public official unless he has been at least exposed to the greater problems of the world today, unless he has thought long and deeply about such present concerns as war and peace, environment, sociological, historical and political problems, the viability of democracy, culture and the arts, and the place of man in the universe.[34]

Armed with a 150-page single-spaced strategic plan,[35] along with a fifty-page mission statement,[36] Tom Headrick dedicated his tenure as Dean to the proposition that Buffalo should not be what was termed a "garden variety" law school, but instead should be a fully interdisciplinary "Buffalo model" that stood out for its distinctiveness, an island in a sea of convention. The problem now, however, was that some of the important contributors to that mission were gone, and the question was whether that new vision – or, for that matter, any vision – would long endure.

Intentionally or not, the place was crawling with people with historical interests of one type or another, though not all were full-time legal historians. Though that little corner of the world fit comfortably within the law and society canon, it was somewhat removed from the work of Galanter and others in the burgeoning law and society movement. And with law school appointments committees' penchant for replicating themselves, it was not exactly clear what direction the school would take. Of the thirteen people whom David thanks in the acknowledgments of "The Oven Bird's Song," six are from Buffalo, and five of those six had historical interests, or wrote on historical topics, or were full-time legal historians.[37] On the faculty at the time were about ten or a dozen people who at one point or another wrote on historical subjects, and a few more would soon join the faculty. This is the

---

[34] Manly Fleischmann, *Present at the Re-Creation* (Remarks . . . At the Cornerstone Ceremonies of the Law School of the State University of New York at Buffalo, May 11, 1971), 12–13 (copy on file with the author).

[35] "Long Range Plan of the Faculty of Law and Jurisprudence, State University of New York at Buffalo, June, 1975," Box 20, Folder 1, Law Special Collection 02, University at Buffalo Law School Records, 1898–2008, Charles B. Sears Law Library, The State University of New York at Buffalo.

[36] "'The Buffalo Model' and Mission Statement, 1976–1977," Box 9, Folder 2, ibid.

[37] Engel, "The oven bird's song," 552,**. The five are James B. Atleson, Guyora Binder, Fred Konefsky, John Henry Schlegel, and Robert J. Steinfeld. Only Virginia Leary did not write in the field.

environment that David joined, and in which substantial cross-fertilization took place, to the benefit of what might appear at first blush to be different approaches to sociolegal phenomena. So why was his article found so congenial here? Or is David's work so ecumenical that it speaks to a whole range of social science disciplines (in their various empirical configurations) that inform law and society (anthropology, sociology, political science, psychology, history, and maybe even law), and that each discipline gets to interpret "The Oven Bird" in its own image? Is it the case that one of its attractions and strengths is its accessibility to so many sides of the law and society coin?

John Henry Schlegel (who inhabits the SUNY Buffalo Law School building to this very day, in a kind of epigrammatic Llewellynesque outsized way) recently proclaimed that "[h]istorians, at least my kind of historians, like what Clifford Geertz called 'thick description,'" and that they

> have explanations or understandings or interpretations, rather than theories. They once had causes, but causation has fallen a bit out of style. For historians, things relate, cohere, suggest, lead to; they expose, clarify, elucidate, inform, reveal, illustrate. Buried by these words is a loss that our language tries to ignore. Historians really *know* a lot of things. One should never be allowed to forget this fact. But for us the difficulty comes, and so the serious work begins, when one leaves the archives or other sources and so it is time to say what those things mean. The question of meaning is the heart of historical practice.[38]

Likewise, David is on record, while reflecting on "The Oven Bird's Song," as having been somewhat influenced by Geertz and "thick description," and also writing "at a time when interpretive techniques had become more important for sociolegal researchers."[39] And, along the lines of Schlegel's observation, David thought "it seemed much more important to explore questions of meaning – not only what people did but how they explained and thought about what they did."[40] Though I agree with much of what Schlegel has to say, I would put it a little differently. I view my function as a historian as recreating the world as the actors have experienced it (almost by definition a contextual enterprise) – a kind of, if you will, ethnography of the dead

---

[38] John Henry Schlegel, "Philosophical inquiry and historical practice," *Virginia Law Review*, 101 (2015), 1198–9. The internal reference to Geertz is, of course, to the classic chapter "Thick description: toward an interpretive theory of culture," in Clifford Geertz, *The Interpretation of Cultures* 3 (Basic Books, 1973).

[39] "David Engel and 'The Oven Bird's Song,'" in Simon Halliday and Patrick Schmidt (eds.), *Conducting Law and Society Research: Reflections on Methods and Practices* (Cambridge University Press, 2009), pp. 83, 90.

[40] Ibid.

(without, of course, having to talk to them or interview them, and certainly not having to be on site with them). To the extent that it involves thick description, one can immediately understand why David's work on "The Oven Bird's Song" would appear so interesting, challenging, and captivating to a historian, and why a natural synergy would seem possible.

A lot has been said and will be said in this volume about what "The Oven Bird's Song" is about, and I do not want to intrude any more than is necessary into that part of the conversation. It is a story about law and litigiousness (or perceptions of litigiousness) in a small, rural community, and the apprehension and antipathy a portion of that community brought to both the specter and reality of personal injury claims, experiencing the claims as a betrayal of its core values. Most personal injury litigation (and there was precious little of it) was viewed as being brought on behalf of newcomers, outsiders who didn't understand the prevailing cultural attitudes in the place they had recently come to inhabit. By contrast, contract litigation was not frowned on by the same community and not seen as a threat to its cultural integrity. David sees these attitudes as stemming from the substantial social and economic changes that were underway in Sander County: Attitudes about law were shaped by social forces and differentially distributed within the community. Formal dispute-processing was acceptable in some circumstances but not in others, and that sorting followed from where one stood in the social and economic structure of the locality. Fears of upheaval and disintegration were displaced onto those who had recently joined the community. And the reigning elites exercised social control by disapproving of or stereotyping those who had been injured and who might contemplate seeking legal redress. The predominant culture emphasized that victims of injuries should generally just "lump it" and move on. Personal injury claims were deemed anti-communal; debt collection cases were not. The result was a series of social classifications that had an impact on whether legal rights were asserted, and some of the classifications were readily recognizable in certain corners of the worlds of sociology, anthropology, history, and political science: insiders and outsiders, inclusion and exclusion, core and periphery, and haves and have-nots (about which Llewellyn wrote in *The Bramble Bush*, by the way[41]).

I have always seen "The Oven Bird's Song" as a profound essay about cultural anxiety, which also just happens to be about attitudes about going to or invoking law. In the process of examining the cultural flux, we learn about a lot of things, including about law, and particularly its relationship to

---

[41] Llewellyn, *The Bramble Bush*, 153.

social context. All that formal and intricate and evolved tort doctrine is of absolutely no avail if the prevailing cultural practice and pressure counsels against using it. One might think that one would pursue legal rights and remedies when a sense of community fractures or breaks down, but that does not seem to have been the case in Sander County for those who experienced the sting of exclusion. Talk about legal realism. David mapped how ordinary people interpreted the social matrix in which they were embedded. On the one hand, they are endowed with a system of rights for redress of injury handed down from higher law authorities (courts or administrative bodies or legislatures) that seemed confident that they had identified and provided for the solution to social or policy problems. On the other, people may or may not know of the legal systemic approach to their situations, and even if they do, they may think, given the complex social environment in which they live, that it is meaningless (David's search for meaning again), because it does not represent a meaningful or realistic approach to what ails them. What is interesting is that the local social elites want the "ordinary people" who have been injured to ignore what the lawgivers have offered from the top down, and they have instead inserted their elite ideology on the ground to limit effectively or constrain the choices of those most in need.

In reading David, I often wonder what a good old-fashioned neo-Marxist would think of all of this. What would E. P. Thompson have looked for in interrogating class, and gender, ethnicity, and race?[42] Where do these attitudes come from and how are they formed? One of the troubling implications of David's portrait of Sander County is its import for what we might traditionally describe as the literature on the rule of law.[43] The threat to the rule of law in democracies is often conceived of as emanating from the abuse of formal, governmental or state power – flaunting traditional understandings, violating rules, engaging in inappropriate exercises of discretion. But David's work may reveal the soft underbelly of the rule of law in a democracy, that is, the extent to which ordinary people are meant to feel or experience in their communities

---

[42] E. P. Thompson, *The Making of the English Working Class* (Vintage Books, 1963).

[43] For a good introduction to the complexity of debates about the rule of law in twentieth-century American legal history, see chapter 8, "Legal realism, the bureaucratic state, and the rule of law" in Morton J. Horwitz, *The Transformation of American Law, 1870–1960: The Crisis of Legal Orthodoxy* (Oxford University Press, 1992), pp. 213–46, as well as Sanford Levinson and Jack M. Balkin, "Morton Horwitz wrestles with the rule of law" in Daniel W. Hamilton and Alfred L. Brophy (eds.), *Transformations in American Legal History: Law, Ideology, and Methods, Essays in Honor of Morton J. Horwitz* (Harvard University Press, 2010), p. 483 (particularly the authors' analysis of Horwitz's review essay, "The rule of law: an unqualified human good?" *Yale Law Journal*, 86 (1977), 561).

that the rules or laws are not really available to them, that there is danger in vindicating their rights because the social context in which they live disapproves of legally constituted regimes of protection and social responsibility, legal protections ostensibly provided by the democratic state. (It is a little reminiscent of the role of private actors in the Reconstruction South, in collaboration, of course, with state actors and courts.[44]) The handful of lawyers we encounter in Sander County seem somewhat uncomfortable in their role in the system of dispute processing, even those who approve of deterring people from claiming or suing.[45] "We have met the enemy and he is us."[46] We cannot begin to grasp that possibility of the subtle subversion of the rule of law unless we start to unpack the deep insights into the relationship between legal culture and social culture that David has provided.

I want to end where I began, by returning to Karl Llewellyn's vision of a law school (which includes legal scholarship) and tying it to David's work in "The Oven Bird's Song" and elsewhere, and to the revival of law and society here at Buffalo after the departure of some of its standard-bearers. It seems quite clear that "The Oven Bird's Song" is a pretty close embodiment of the model set out in Llewellyn's call for reformation of legal education. From the idea that "[b]y and large the *basic order* in our society . . . *is not produced by law*"[47] (a pretty fair conclusion to draw from Sander County, though "basic order" ironically may have something to do with the reaction to law), to the assertion that the academic discipline of law must remain a steward of the concept of justice, to the insistence that law belongs in the humanities as well as aspiring to be humane, to the argument that the best and most useful method for legal education in making a continuing social contribution to the larger culture and the greater good is to provide an understanding of background, facts, and context (with its multiplicity of definitions and meaning), to the use of interdisciplinary approaches – all these measures seem to be hallmarks of "The Oven Bird's Song." It is humane in its treatment of the "ordinary people" who live in its pages; it raises questions about the justness

---

[44] See generally Eric Foner, *Reconstruction: America's Unfinished Revolution, 1863–1877* (Harper & Row, 1988); Pamela Brandwein, *Rethinking the Judicial Settlement of Reconstruction* (Cambridge University Press, 2011); George Rutherglen, *Civil Rights in the Shadow of Slavery: The Constitution, Common Law, and the Civil Rights Act of 1866* (Oxford University Press, 2013); Laura F. Edwards, *A Legal History of the Civil War and Reconstruction: A Nation of Rights* (Cambridge University Press, 2015); G. Edward White, *Law in American History: From Reconstruction through the 1920s, vol. 2* (Oxford University Press, 2016), 6–49, 424–94.

[45] Engel, "The oven bird's song," 564–6.

[46] Walt Kelly, *Pogo: We Have Met the Enemy and He Is Us* (Simon and Schuster, 1972).

[47] Llewellyn, *The Bramble Bush*, 116.

of a system – social or legal or economic – that turns its back on the people who are injured as that system continues to function; it movingly catalogs the fate or plight of those considered to be outside the mainsprings of power and influence; it brings up questions about the efficacy of law itself (what is a lawyer supposed to do when faced with the knowledge of how the community operates?); and, though it is careful not to judge and treats all its ethnographic encounters with tact and delicacy (it is David, after all), it is also a moral argument challenging the effectiveness of law in society – and ultimately, in Llewellyn's sense, it teaches or educates. It is quite an accomplishment, which was shared with pride in the institution at which it was finally written. And ultimately, it asked in a law and society sense not just whether law matters, but rather of what matter law is made. Llewellyn would have approved.

PART II

The Oven Bird's Insights into the Legal System and Legal Process

5

Challenging Legal Consciousness

Practice, Institutions, and Varieties of Resistance

ANNA-MARIA MARSHALL

Even though the term never appears in the article, "The Oven Bird's Song" is one of the foundational articles in studies of legal consciousness. Engel did not define the concept in "The Oven Bird's Song," even though we could reasonably say that the entire article is about what we have come to recognize as legal consciousness. In the article, Engel analyzes how individual members of a community think about law and legal institutions. The article is also about the things that people did – and didn't do – to put those beliefs into practice. Engel demonstrated that the community's value system (to which many individuals subscribed) shaped the way they thought about conflict and even about what an injury was. And in turn, this "mangle" of action and belief created a unique legal environment – what we now refer to as legality: "the meanings, sources of authority and cultural practices that are commonly recognized as legal, regardless of who employs them, or for what purposes."[1]

Even as he laid a foundation for studies of legal consciousness, Engel also anticipated some of the significant debates in that tradition. By analyzing the legal significance of what ordinary people think and do, Engel demonstrated that law is a thread that runs through everyday life. In this chapter, I describe three debates in legal consciousness research and show how reading Engel's study of Sander County offers a fresh perspective on those debates and poses challenges for those of us working in the field. First, I consider the significance of silence as the practice of legal consciousness, particularly when that silence is wielded by the powerful. Second, context is important. People develop legal consciousness through the institutions they navigate. Thus, legal consciousness is related to the different identities that people develop in different settings. Finally, while law is hegemonic, constructing systems for

---

[1] Susan S. Silbey, "After legal consciousness," *Annual Review of Law and Social Science*, 1(1) (2005), 323–68.

the powerful in ways that preserve their privilege, people nevertheless draw on legal concepts when trying to resist authority. Thus, I ask whether and what varieties of resistance are made possible through legal consciousness.

I have been thinking through these challenges as I embark on a new project that draws on a legal consciousness perspective in analyzing farmers' conservation practices. Specifically, I seek to understand what role law and policy might play in shaping farmers' decision-making. I illustrate the enduring significance of "The Oven Bird's Song" with examples of questions from this project.

LAW AS SOCIAL AND PRACTICE: ACCOUNTING FOR SILENCE

The many definitions of legal consciousness have emphasized social and cultural practice – what people say about law and the ways they behave when they invoke their rights. These social and cultural practices are the foundation of law's hegemonic power to structure our relationships. As I explain below, in "The Oven Bird's Song," Engel demonstrated the importance of including silence as a form of social practice worth studying.

Sally Engle Merry defined legal consciousness as "the ways people understand and use the law ... the way people conceive of the natural and normal way of doing things, their habitual patterns of talk and action and their common sense understandings of the world."[2] Similarly, Michael McCann defined rights consciousness as "the ongoing, dynamic process of constructing one's understanding of, and relationship to, the social world through the use of legal conventions and discourses."[3] These definitions not only stress the meaning that people give to their experiences and their relationships, but also include the active construction of those meanings – what people do in addition to what they think.[4]

The emphasis on social and cultural practice is important in light of the well-established gaps between what we think and what we do.[5] We are buffeted along by actors and institutions outside of our control – our families, our friends, our neighbors, our colleagues, our employment manuals, our religious leaders. Through our interactions in all these settings with all these

---

[2] Sally Engle Merry, *Getting Justice and Getting Even: Legal Consciousness among Working-Class Americans* (University of Chicago Press, 1990).

[3] Michael W. McCann, *Rights at Work: Pay Equity Reform and the Politics of Legal Mobilization* (University of Chicago Press, 1994).

[4] Anna-Maria Marshall, "Idle rights: employees' rights consciousness and the construction of sexual harassment policies," *Law & Society Review*, 39(1) (2005), 83–124.

[5] Silbey, "After legal consciousness."

different people and structures, we send out cues about the law's significance and meaning in structuring our ongoing relationships or in resolving conflict. In those settings, law has competition from other normative systems, such as religion, which may shape our views of justice,[6] for example, or work, which shapes our expectations about how to balance family obligations.[7] It is through interactions and relationships with others that law and other values are enacted and implemented. For example, in my own research, I found that women facing unwanted sexual attention in the workplace routinely used legal categories to make sense of their experiences. Without legal training, they developed their understandings by talking to employees, reading their employment manuals, attending training workshops, and watching how supervisors reacted to other similar cases. Through these social and cultural practices, the women in my study understood their rights, applied them to their situations, and made decisions about what to do in response. In other words, legal consciousness is not simply in our heads – it can't be if it has enduring power to structure social relations. That structural power works when legal consciousness emerges through our words and our deeds. So both words and deeds should be scrutinized in our studies of legal consciousness.[8]

This emphasis on social and cultural practice was foreshadowed in "The Oven Bird's Song," where Sander County residents enacted their thoughts about the legal system in their social practices, often with dramatic consequences for their neighbors. For example, residents sought out alternatives to litigation when they faced conflict with others. Mostly, they engaged in self-help by simply seeking sympathy and advice from their friends, neighbors, and physicians.[9] On occasion, they might have directly requested compensation for their injuries from the responsible party. Engel describes one such story:

> A doctor told me that one of his patients was seriously burned during a trip out of state when an airline stewardess spilled hot coffee on her legs, causing permanent discoloration of her skin. This woman refused to contact a lawyer

---

[6] Carol J Greenhouse, *Praying for Justice: Faith, Order, and Community in an American Town* (Wakefield Press, 1989).

[7] Catherine R. Albiston, "Bargaining in the shadow of social institutions: competing discourses and social change in workplace mobilization of civil rights," *Law & Society Review*, 39(1) (2005), 11–50.

[8] Ibid; Carol A. Heimer, "Competing institutions: law, medicine, and family in neonatal intensive care," *Law & Society Review*, 33(1) (1999), 17; Erik W. Larson, "Institutionalizing legal consciousness: regulation and the embedding of market participants in the securities industry in Ghana and Fiji," *Law & Society Review*, 38(4) (2004), 737–68.

[9] David M. Engel, "The oven bird's song: insiders, outsiders, and personal injuries in an American community," *Law & Society Review*, 18(4) (1984), 551–82, at 561.

and instead settled directly with the airline for medical expenses and the cost of the one-week vacation she had missed. Regarding the possibility of taking formal legal action to seek a more substantial award, she said simply, "We don't do that."[10]

Public officials also reported hearing complaints from public-spirited people who were not interested in compensation but rather in protecting others from the hazards that caused their injuries. Thus, Sander County residents modeled their rejection of the legal system by finding other ways to redress their injuries.[11]

Moreover, Sander County residents' hostility to tort claims was reflected in the social and cultural practices of both insiders and outsiders. Engel described the "outsiders" in Sander County as newcomers to what was predominantly a farming community, including the tavern keeper, union members, and immigrants who worked in the new factory. These "outsiders" understood the community they lived in and their place in it, yet, in spite of this realistic perspective, they actively engaged the legal system: They hired lawyers, they made insurance claims, and they filed complaints in court – social and cultural practices that openly invoked legal institutions. These "outsiders" knew what the "insiders" thought of them, not because they could read minds but because "insiders" engaged in social and cultural practices that conveyed their disdain for those who used the legal system. Through gossip and ostracism, long-time residents were able to exert social pressure. The discomfort felt by outsiders illustrates why it is important to study both thought and deed in analyzing legal consciousness. Everyone in Sander County knew that formal claiming was unpopular, but what they chose to do and how the community responded are what gave rise to the community's culture. These outward social interactions were the foundation of the widespread belief in Sander County that litigation was a poor way of resolving conflict.

"The Oven Bird's Song" also challenges us to be attentive to silence as a form of social and cultural practice that constitutes legal consciousness and legality. "Insiders" in Sander County established their community's particular forms of legality by, in some senses, failing to act. Because they did not invoke the law or pursue legal action when they had a right to do so, they undermined the formal authority of law. In this context, their legal claims for compensation for their injuries were "idle rights"[12] – those occasions where law should matter, but has lost the competition to other sets of values and sources of meaning. And if members of a community routinely reject the law, then law's role in constituting a community's hegemonic order is minimized.

---

[10] Engel at 561.   [11] Engel at 562.   [12] Marshall, "Idle rights."

Law's competition with other systems of meaning is a recurring theme in the research on legal consciousness. For example, studies of the workplace suggest that employee rights vie with management prerogatives in the implementation of grievance procedures.[13] Both supervisors and their employees internalize a logic that emphasizes efficiency and ongoing relationships, often at the expense of formal legal requirements. Employees soon learn that complaints can be fruitless, leading to more trouble with little tangible benefit. Their silence in the face of discriminatory behavior creates a legality of the workplace where discrimination is accepted practice.[14]

Recent studies have also suggested that in some Islamic communities, law and religion are rival sources of authority in establishing social order in areas of family law and women's rights.[15] These struggles do not simply take place among policy-makers. Rather, women encountering family problems in their everyday lives may draw on different sources of authority – legal, religious, and others – to understand those problems and seek solutions. Thus, where we might expect law to level the playing field, the powerful can – through their silence – render law invisible and impotent.

The search for silence raises important methodological issues. How do we listen for law's silences, and what inferences can we draw from frames that have no meaning in a particular community? Recent studies have drawn on survey methods to identify general patterns of legal consciousness among different groups of people.[16] Yet the effort to identify other systems of meaning beyond law – systems that compete with law or that coincide with it – requires qualitative methods, especially narrative analysis.[17] We have to listen to people describe in their own words how they think about their problems and what options they have to resolve them. By listening to them, without prejudging

---

[13] Lauren B. Edelman, "Legal ambiguity and symbolic structures: organizational mediation of civil rights law," *American Journal of Sociology*, 97(6) (1992), 1531–76; Lauren B. Edelman, Christopher Uggen, and Howard S. Erlanger, "The endogeneity of legal regulation: grievance procedures as rational myth," *American Journal of Sociology*, 105(2) (1999), 406–54; Marshall, "Idle rights."

[14] Marshall, "Idle rights."

[15] Tamir Moustafa, "Islamic law, women's rights, and popular legal consciousness in Malaysia," *Law & Social Inquiry*, 38(1) (2013), 168–88; Friso Kulk and Betty De Hart, "Mixed couples and Islamic family law in Egypt: legal consciousness in transnational social space," in *Law in the Everyday Lives of Transnational Families*, vol. 3(6) (Onati Socio-Legal Series, Onati International Institute for the Sociology of Law, 2013), https://papers.ssrn.com/sol3/papers.cfm?abstract_id=2365888##.

[16] Moustafa, "Islamic law"; Mary Nell Trautner, Erin Hatton, and Kelly E. Smith, "What workers want depends: legal knowledge and the desire for workplace change among day laborers," *Law & Policy*, 35(4) (2013), 319–40.

[17] Patricia Ewick and Susan Silbey, "Narrating social structure: stories of resistance to legal authority," *American Journal of Sociology*, 108(6) (2003), 1328–72.

the matter, we can identify the ways in which law weaves in and out of
their lives and, if they are silent about law, what other normative order is
more important.

Institutions and Social Networks

In "The Oven Bird's Song," Engel attributed the residents' different perspectives on the legal system to their different social networks. The "insiders" were
members of a close-knit farming community, where everyone knew each
other and strangers were scarce. The introduction of a manufacturing plant
(and the immigrants and unionized workers that came with the plant) represented an external shock to the community, loosening previously close ties.
According to Engel, the insiders and outsiders traveled through different social
networks, rarely overlapping. And the repeated interactions occurring in those
networks re-enforced residents' views about the nature of injury, conflict
resolution, and the value of the legal system.

Engel's emphasis on Sander County's social networks anticipated the
research on institutional influences on legal consciousness. Resisting the urge
to atomize the individual, many studies of legal consciousness situate individuals in specific institutional settings, such as workplaces, schools, families, and
religious practice. We know that these institutions organize people's lives by
setting expectations and defining what is possible through patterned interactions that occur on a daily basis. We also know that structural forces shape
these institutions. So, for example, our understanding of gender is created in
the context of our families. We develop our gender identity by responding to
our parents' and our siblings' demands that we behave in ways expected of
little girls and boys. In turn, the gender roles our families impose on us come
from their own interactions with the rest of the social world. When we study
legal consciousness in these institutional contexts, we can incorporate the
"social" into our analysis. We can examine the way that individual encounters
with law are connected to broader social forces even in relatively intimate and
private settings.

For example, the law has extensively penetrated the American workplace.[18]
Edelman and her colleagues have extensively documented the ways in which

[18] Edelman, Uggen, and Erlanger, "The endogeneity of legal regulation"; Edelman, "Legal
      ambiguity and symbolic structures"; Lauren B. Edelman, "Legal environments and
      organizational governance: the expansion of due process in the American workplace,"
      American Journal of Sociology, 95(6) (1990), 1401–40; Frank Dobbin and Erin L. Kelly, "How to
      stop harassment: professional construction of legal compliance in organizations," *American
      Journal of Sociology*, 112(4) (2007), 1203–43.

employers have adopted legal rules to serve their own interests. By developing institutions – such as grievance procedures – employers stage repeated interactions where supervisors receive, investigate, and adjudicate employee complaints. In these interactions, employees get information from their supervisors about their legal rights – information that may be colored by the employer's own interests. Thus, employees' civil rights to equal treatment free of discrimination in the workplace may, in practice, do more to protect management imperatives such as efficiency and workforce discipline. As employees make complaints (or watch their colleagues complain), they can observe the grievance procedure in action and evaluate the results. Thus, employees' legal consciousness is shaped in these grievance procedures. In this way, the workplace can shape what employees think about and expect from the law.

We might then wonder what the institutions in Sander County social networks looked like and think about how "insider" and "outsider" institutions differed in their approach to conflict. For example, some of the "outsiders" were factory workers, including union members. Union members' working lives are governed by contracts, with well-defined grievance procedures for handling conflict. To them, grievances may have been a daily occurrence, and the process might have seemed like a well-ordered way of handling a dispute, especially among parties with unequal power. Thus, routine interactions with the institutions of a unionized workplace could have shaped their legal consciousness in ways that made the legal system feel more familiar, less aberrant.

On the other hand, the "insiders" were mostly farmers whose working lives were not structured by hierarchical organizations. Rather, as Engel noted, the farmers were largely independent and self-sufficient, although they were members of wide-ranging networks of industry representatives; financial brokers; not to mention neighbors. They had few employees and little in the way of formal structure. Rather, as in many industries that count on repeated interaction, the farmers relied on cooperative relationships, and institutions in those work settings probably encouraged accommodation rather than conflict.[19]

In Sander County, the problem was that these social networks did not overlap. Farmers did not mix with factory workers; they did not participate in organizations that might have brought them together. Had they gone to school together – or played on the same sports teams, or joined the Garden Club – they may have had the social interactions that allowed them to share

[19] Stewart Macaulay, "Non-contractual relations in business: a preliminary study," *American Sociological Review*, 28(1) (1963), 55–67, doi:10.2307/2090458.

or even challenge each other's values as they engaged in or resolved conflict. If they had shared institutional spaces, we might have seen the Sander County attitudes about the legal system re-enforced or perhaps undermined.

This raises a question for our existing studies of legal consciousness. People are rarely confined to a single institution, although most of our existing studies are limited to a single institutional space. Most people navigate many social networks, institutions, and settings: They go to work; they care for their spouses, children, and parents; they house-sit for their neighbors; they practice a religion; they go to the doctor; they play in a sports league. Law's authority in organizing these different spheres of life varies, and thus, people will have different – sometimes competing – views of it. How people reconcile these differences remains an open question in research on legal consciousness.

VARIETIES OF RESISTANCE: LAW AND SOCIAL CHANGE

The relationship between law and social change is very much an unsettled question in law and society literature. On the one hand, social movements often draw on legal concepts and strategies in their campaigns for social change. The language of rights has been empowering to many marginalized people, and legal battles have been one tactic that have led to social transformations in the United States,[20] including school desegregation,[21] reproductive rights,[22] and marriage among same-sex partners.[23] Of course, critics point to the fragile nature of those "rights." Children in the United States mostly attend segregated schools; many women live in states where it is impossible to get an abortion; and while they may now have the right to marry, members of the LGBT community continue to face discrimination in many other crucial spheres of life.[24] Critics also argue that legal tactics narrow the possibility of radical challenges to the status quo because the range of legal remedies is too constrained to dismantle oppressive social conditions.

Existing theories of legal consciousness and legality are pessimistic about the possibilities of law for social change.[25] In many studies, law is hegemonic,

[20] McCann, *Rights at Work*.
[21] Thomas M Hilbink, "Defining cause lawyering: NAACP v. Button and the struggle over professional ideology," *Studies in Law Politics and Society*, 26 (2002), 77–108.
[22] Helena Silverstein, *Girls on the Stand: How Courts Fail Pregnant Minors* (NYU Press, 2007).
[23] Scott L. Cummings and Douglas NeJaime, "Lawyering for marriage equality," *UCLA Law Review*, 57 (2010), 1235.
[24] Gerald N. Rosenberg, *The Hollow Hope: Can Courts Bring about Social Change?* (University of Chicago Press, 2008).
[25] Patricia Ewick and Susan S. Silbey, *The Common Place of Law: Stories from Everyday Life (Chicago Series in Law and Society)* (University of Chicago Press, 1998).

constructing systems for the powerful in ways that preserve their privilege, and our social relations are constituted in a very real sense by legal threads. People can try to struggle against the power of law; they may even use law to challenge existing conditions that they find unfair. Merely invoking the law, however, recreates the law's power and authority, rather than dismantling those structures in any meaningful way.[26] This view has plenty of support in "The Oven Bird's Song," where people who were injured could have complained by filing a lawsuit or an insurance claim, but it rarely did any good. Not only were they unlikely to be compensated, but their complaints simply re-enforced their status as outsiders.

But can legal consciousness be a mechanism for social change? What are its possibilities for resistance to power and authority? Ewick and Silbey, for example, articulated a theory of resistance in their theoretical elaboration of legal consciousness. Describing this orientation as being "against the law," they described legality as "a net in which [people] are trapped and within which they struggle for freedom."[27] In this aspect of legal consciousness, respondents felt powerless in the face of law's authority to define them as criminals, for example, or to deny them compensation for their injuries. In light of the poor treatment they received at the hands of the legal system, they rejected it and sought out alternatives. In this theory, then, resistance is a means of escaping law's authority rather than invoking it to demand change.

"The Oven Bird's Song" does not fit comfortably in this theory of resistance. Indeed, the residents of Sander County "resisted" the law's authority to define and address injuries and conflict, but it was hardly the product of powerlessness. It was the dominant social groups – the insiders – who so forcefully rejected the law. Thus, the residents of Sander County offer a compelling reminder that the dominant groups do not always or exclusively rely on law to preserve their power. Other values and systems of meaning can dominate our institutions, and not always with fair and equitable results. In Sander County, the insiders explicitly rejected tort law as a way of constructing their experiences with injury. The taken-for-granted rules of Sander County society were *not* inscribed in legal rules. The legal consciousness there, especially among the outsiders, did not construct a hegemonic social order; rather, it identified the gaps where resistance was possible.

Thus, in "The Oven Bird's Song," legal consciousness contains the possibility of resistance to forms of oppression that are taken for granted. Legal rules can define conduct as being harmful, violating well-established community norms. Moreover, legal rules allocate blame, identifying the parties

[26] Ibid.   [27] Ibid, 184.

responsible for causing injuries. And the adversarial structure of legal claims consists of direct confrontation in a public setting. Law levels the playing field between insiders and outsiders, although not by much. Still, in communities where marginalized people have little access to social, political, or economic power, filing a legal claim might be one of the few available means of challenging existing social relations.

FARMING, CONSERVATION, AND LEGAL CONSCIOUSNESS

I am traveling through many places just like Sander County as part of my current research project about farmers' legal consciousness in Illinois. I am exploring a different but still curious dimension of farmers' skepticism to legal institutions: Rather than inquiring about their hostility to personal injury claims, I am studying their opposition to environmental regulation requiring conservation practices. This is a pressing issue for environmental policy-making. Scientists agree that the Dead Zone in the Gulf of Mexico is being caused by decisions made by individual farmers upstream and the agricultural practices they use on their land.[28] The farmers I am studying very purposefully try to keep their conservation practices outside of the legal arena.

Like the "insiders" in Sander County, farmers rarely say that they oppose regulatory conservation. Rather, their unwillingness to participate in conservation programs is a form of silence signaling their opposition to state interference. The conservation measures that they are most likely to adopt are those that save them money, like applying less fertilizer fewer times a year, for example. Other strategies, such as planting cover crops or building wetland filters, are less popular. While it is true that they require a financial investment, there are programs that subsidize the costs associated with adopting the strategies. By declining to participate – by remaining silent – they make it clear to their social networks that the state has no role in dictating the way that they manage their land.

For those farmers who are willing to adopt conservation measures voluntarily, we know that they find support from actors and institutions in their social

---

[28] Stefanie Hufnagl-Eichiner, Steven A. Wolf, and Laurie E. Drinkwater, "Assessing social–ecological coupling: agriculture and hypoxia in the Gulf of Mexico," *Global Environmental Change*, Special Issue 21(2) (2011), 530–9; Nancy E. Rabalais, R. Eugene Turner, and Donald Scavia, "Beyond science into policy: Gulf of Mexico hypoxia and the Mississippi river nutrient policy development for the Mississippi river watershed reflects the accumulated scientific evidence that the increase in nitrogen loading is the primary factor in the worsening of hypoxia in the northern Gulf of Mexico," *BioScience*, 52(2) (2002), 129–42.

networks.[29] Farmers' environmentalist attitudes and identities are re-enforced through repeated interactions with neighbors and organizations, such as soil and water conservation districts and drainage districts, which promote the benefits of conservation and provide information and training on specific land management practices. In Illinois, the network of support for conservation is growing through the Nutrient Loss Reduction Strategy. The NLRS brought together stakeholders from across the agricultural community in Illinois – retailers, agronomists, commodity groups, the Farm Bureau, and the research community – to promote voluntary conservation measures among individual farmers.[30] Thus, when farmers seek advice from a fertilizer sales representative or a crop advisor, they are much more likely to hear about conservation practices. Still, progress is slow, and the acres using conservation represent a relatively small fraction of the total farming acreage in Illinois.

Thus resistance to the state and command-and-control environmental regulation remains strong in current-day Sander County. In fact, command-and-control regulation seems to be out of the question, unthinkable. Thus, farmers retain their hegemonic power as "stewards of the environment," without state interference. Just as Sander County farmers created their own culture of dispute resolution, my research suggests that they create their own regulatory culture, free of the state, for better or worse.

[29] Timothy Conley and Christopher Udry, "Social learning through networks: the adoption of new agricultural technologies in Ghana," *American Journal of Agricultural Economics*, 83(3) (2001), 668–73; Annemie Maertens and Christopher B. Barrett, "Measuring social networks' effects on agricultural technology adoption," *American Journal of Agricultural Economics*, 95(2) (2013), 353–9.

[30] Illinois Department of Agriculture, Illinois Nutrient Loss Reduction Strategy, 2015, www.epa .illinois.gov/Assets/iepa/water-quality/watershed-management/nlrs/nlrs-final-revised-083115.pdf.

6

Client Selection

How Lawyers Reflect and Influence Community Values

LYNN MATHER

In "The Oven Bird's Song," David Engel investigates the relationship between law and social change in a rural Midwestern community through an ethnographic study of civil litigation, especially personal injury cases. The evocative title of his article refers to Robert Frost's poem "The Oven Bird," in which the bird/singer responds to perceived disintegration and decay from change in the seasons. The poem is similar, Engel writes, to popular perceptions of personal injury claims in Sander County – perceptions that were strongly influenced by "social changes as local residents experienced them and by the sense that traditional relationships and exchanges in the community were gradually disintegrating."[1] In Chapters 5 and 7 of this book, Marshall and Hans each explore ways in which institutionalized legal practices mediate between people's perceptions of the law and their engagement with law. In this chapter, I focus on lawyers, because lawyers also constitute a crucial set of institutional actors connecting culture, community, and law.

When representing community residents, lawyers articulate their ideas and values while simultaneously translating abstract legal concepts, rights, and procedures for those who need – or want – to use them. Lawyers thus play a significant intermediary role in society. How do they perform this role? The most visible way lies in lawyers' advocacy at trial, through public performances of attorneys arguing before judges and juries on behalf of their clients. But over time, fewer and fewer legal cases in the United States have been resolved by adversary trial. Bench and jury trials constituted only 1.1 percent of all civil case dispositions in federal courts in 2015,[2] and only 4 percent of all civil

---

[1] David M. Engel, "The oven bird's song: insiders, outsiders, and personal injuries in an American community," *Law & Society Review*, 18 (1984), 551, 556–7.

[2] www.uscourts.gov/sites/default/files/c04mar15_0.pdf.

cases in state courts in 2013.[3] Since most cases are settled by negotiation without trial, a second way to observe lawyers' intermediary role lies in the process of case settlement. For example, what is the "going rate" for a guilty plea in different kinds of crimes or for settling cases in civil law? Such settlements anticipate likely outcomes at trial and are thus bargained "in the shadow of the law."[4] Plaintiffs' lawyers in Sander County, knowing that local judges and juries were hostile to personal injury suits, generally counseled their clients against trials and advised them to accept informal negotiated settlements instead.

Yet even before attorneys engage in negotiations or argue a case at trial, they must agree to represent someone. A lawyer's decision to represent a client or to reject someone's claim constitutes a third way in which lawyers mediate between communities and the law. Claimants or defendants in civil cases proactively seek out legal counsel, but individual lawyers are under no obligation to represent any particular client. The most common reason suggested for rejecting clients is economic: Either clients lack sufficient funds to pay for an hourly fee lawyer or else their cases are unlikely to generate sufficient reward for a contingency fee lawyer. Unlike criminal cases in which indigent clients are legally entitled to a defense lawyer, clients in civil cases in the United States have no such constitutional right. I discuss client selection in this chapter because, although rarely visible, lawyers' discretionary actions in choosing clients are crucial for determining access to the civil legal system. Moreover, such decisions illustrate well how attorneys reinforce community values when they embrace certain cases and reject others. We also see occasions where lawyers seek to challenge and perhaps change those values by representing the claims of "outsiders" – those socially or culturally marginal members of the community.

Engel's study of community and law shows that residents of Sander Country disapproved of formal legal action to recover for personal injuries. Instead, they believed in individual responsibility and self-sufficiency, seeing accidents as just part of life and not wanting to "cash in" on their misfortune by blaming others. Those who did file injury claims were seen as "troublemakers" and often were newcomers to the community – migrants, Latinos, union workers, and so forth. Lawyers reinforced community perceptions by discouraging

---

[3] Paula Hannaford-Agor, Scott Graves, and Shelley Spacek Miller, "The Landscape of Civil Litigation in State Courts 2015" National Center for State Courts, 20, www.ncsc.org/~/media/Files/PDF/Research/CivilJusticeReport-2015.ashx.

[4] Robert H. Mnookin and Lewis Kornhauser, "Bargaining in the shadow of the law: the case of divorce," *Yale Law Journal*, 88 (1979), 950.

potential plaintiffs and accepting as clients only those with "real, nonfrivolous grievances."[5] Unlike the stereotypical plaintiff attorney who zealously pursues tort litigation, attorneys in Sander County actively discouraged it. The question is: Why? Engel's article suggests three reasons for the lawyers' behavior in client selection: lawyers' economic incentives, social networks, and – most significant in his analysis – shared cultural values. In what follows I will focus on these three, plus a fourth: formal law. Each explanation provides insight into how and why lawyers reflect community values when they agree to represent certain clients. Yet each answer also suggests why some lawyers might challenge or seek to change those traditional community values. For example, lawyers who perceive themselves to be outside of a homogeneous community might select clients who share their outsider status or whose cases could provide an impetus for legal or social change.

The empirical literature on the legal profession – including client selection – has grown enormously since 1984, when Engel's article was published. Interestingly, Engel's provocative analysis anticipates findings that emerged after his pathbreaking study, such as the importance of cultural over economic incentives for lawyers and the lack of any formal law constraining lawyers in client selection. I draw on this recent research to explore how lawyers select clients not only in personal injury cases but in other civil matters as well. I confine my discussion to areas of law with individual (rather than organizational) clients, given the well-known differences in the legal profession between these two hemispheres.[6]

Individuals with claims of personal injury or employment discrimination rarely have funds to pay attorneys an hourly fee and thus depend on lawyers in contingency fee practices. Lawyers in such practices are quite selective, rejecting the majority of clients who contact them.[7] Rates of rejection vary widely, however, depending on a lawyer's specialization, experience, location, case volume, and average case value.[8] Lawyers paid by hourly fees also

---

[5]   Engel, "The oven bird's song," 564.
[6]   John Heinz and Edward Laumann, *Chicago Lawyers: The Social Structure of the Bar* (Russell Sage Foundation and American Bar Foundation, 1982).
[7]   Herbert M. Kritzer, *Risks, Reputations, and Rewards: Contingency Fee Legal Practice in the United States* (Stanford University Press, 2004), p. 71.
[8]   For comparison of research findings in this area, see Table 2 in Mary Nell Trautner, "How social hierarchies within the personal injury bar affect case screening decisions," *New York School Law Review*, 51(2006–7), 215. Recent research on case selection by employment discrimination lawyers reports their accepting only "a very small percentage" (10 percent or less) of potential clients: see Amy Myrick, Robert L. Nelson, and Laura Beth Nielsen, "Race and representation: racial disparities in representation for employment civil rights plaintiffs," *New York University Journal of Legislation and Public Policy*, 15 (2012), 705–58, 742.

scrutinize individuals seeking their help in order to be assured of payment and to avoid ethical problems such as conflict of interest or malpractice complaints. Divorce lawyers in one study overwhelmingly said that they screened potential clients before agreeing to representation.[9] And considerable bar commentary warns lawyers to choose their clients carefully since, by avoiding difficult clients, attorneys may prevent problems later on in a case. This all suggests, as Trautner notes, that the *process* of client selection may be as important for understanding as the *rate* of client acceptance: "How do lawyers *think* about screening?"[10] The answers below explore the four different perspectives on this question – economic, sociological, cultural, and legal – and in the end they reinforce Engel's insistence on the powerful role of culture for explaining lawyers' behavior.

ECONOMIC INCENTIVES

Although lawyers perform a public service, they also must earn a living. When representing individuals in family matters, torts, real estate, or other civil matters, new attorneys quickly learn that hard work and sympathy for clients only go so far. They don't pay the rent, the phone bill, or a secretary. The most common explanation of how lawyers think about screening centers on economic incentives. For contingency fee lawyers (who earn nothing unless the client wins), what is the likelihood of their "winning" the case? Cases most likely to be accepted should have legal merit and high damages. Kritzer's survey of contingency fee lawyers, for example, found that "lack of liability and inadequate damages (together or singly) are the dominant reasons for declining cases, accounting for about 80 percent."[11] Other researchers, such as Trautner, have found tort lawyers' perceptions of potential damages to be even more important than liability in the decision to accept or reject a case.[12]

Stratification in the plaintiffs' bar produces varying rates of client acceptance due to differences in the lawyers' practices. While many lawyers handle auto accidents or slip-and-fall cases, a smaller group specializes in cases involving more severe injuries or greater complexity (such as medical malpractice). Daniels and Martin distinguish between "bread and butter" plaintiff lawyers and "heavy hitters" according to the average value of their typical cases, and

[9]   Lynn Mather, Craig A. McEwen, and Richard J. Maiman, *Divorce Lawyers at Work: Varieties of Professionalism in Practice* (Oxford University Press, 2001), p. 93.
[10] Trautner, "Social hierarchies," 240.   [11] Kritzer, *Risks, Reputations, and Rewards*, p. 84.
[12] Mary Nell Trautner, "Tort reform and access to justice: how legal environments shape lawyers' case selection," *Qualitative Sociology*, 34 (2011), 523–38, 530; see also Myrick et al., "Race and representation," 747.

find the latter to be more selective in choosing clients.[13] High-end lawyers scrutinize potential cases for reassurance that the damages recovered will justify the time they invest. Kritzer, on the other hand, finds that high-volume attorneys reject proportionately more clients than low-volume attorneys do, perhaps because of the different referral patterns.[14] Lawyers handling a large number of cases often rely on mass advertising or client referral for their contacts, while those with fewer cases depend on attorney referrals, which means that some lawyer screening has already occurred. Each of these various personal injury practices rests on its own pattern of risks and rewards.[15]

Hourly fee lawyers also balance risk and reward in client selection. The risks for these attorneys involve investing more time than the client will be able to pay for, not getting paid at the end of a case, taking on too many cases and consequently neglecting some, or being pushed by a client to engage in ethical misconduct. Research on the divorce bar in New England conducted by myself and two co-authors reveals how some lawyers charge low fees and attract a large number of lower-income clients, others charge more per hour and require a modest retainer up front, and high-end divorce attorneys demand a large retainer and charge high fees.[16] We found that the average number of hours lawyers invested in a case, the nature of advocacy, and the length of the divorce process were associated with these different business models of divorce practice. That is, "having clients with few financial assets prompts attorneys to limit sharply what they do in the average case, while having clients with deeper pockets encourages expansion of billable hours and increased use of the formal legal process."[17]

Economic incentives in client selection are also shown in Michelson's study of Chinese lawyers at work. He finds that lawyers' financial insecurity and the conditions of solo legal practice in Beijing lead to their frequent rejection of cases with low fee potential.[18] As noted earlier, the legal merit of a case matters in client selection because it could produce a good financial outcome for both the lawyer and the client. But as Michelson notes, "the boundaries of 'legal merit' are flexible and malleable," reflecting and

---

[13] Stephen Daniels and Joanne Martin, "It was the best of times, it was the worst of times: the precarious nature of plaintiff's practice in Texas," *Texas Law Review*, 80 (2002), 1781–828, 1789; see also Trautner, "Social hierarchies," and Sara Parikh, "How the spider catches the fly: referral networks in the plaintiffs' personal injury bar," *New York Law School Law Review*, 51 (2006–7), 243–83.

[14] Kritzer, *Risks, Reputations, and Rewards*, pp. 71–2.   [15] See ibid for this phrase.

[16] Mather et al., *Divorce Lawyers at Work*.   [17] Ibid, p. 142.

[18] Ethan Michelson, "The practice of law as an obstacle to justice: Chinese lawyers at work," *Law & Society Review*, 40 (2006), 1–38.

reproducing cultural stereotypes.[19] Chinese lawyers' aversion to clients with labor disputes (compared to clients with housing or commercial conflicts) underscores Michelson's point. Client characteristics such as attractiveness, credibility, or "likeability"[20] also influence lawyers in client selection, in part because of how such characteristics might influence a judge or jury. As Engel explains in "The Oven Bird's Song," personal injury lawyers evaluate potential clients and negotiate case settlements using their "shared knowledge of the likely juror reaction if the case actually went to trial."[21] Trautner's research comparing client selection in states with tort reform and those without reform strongly supports this argument, showing how "lawyers frame cases in ways they expect to appeal to what they believe the jury will find compelling in the context of their own localized legal cultures."[22] Hence, even when attorneys are thinking about their own self-interest – if and how they will be paid – they are reflecting community values in their predictions about case outcomes.

Attorneys (especially those in solo practice) have considerable autonomy in setting fees, so they can adjust them downward for sympathetic individuals or upward to deter to difficult ones. The category of the "difficult" client emerges frequently in studies of client selection. When divorce lawyers in New England were asked to describe which clients they rejected, about half said those who are "difficult," variously defined as "vengeful, unrealistic, stubborn, or demanding"; "those who won't listen to you"; and "clients I'm not comfortable with."[23] Lawyers in Beijing said they rejected clients "who are unreasonably demanding," "who try to direct my work," or "who won't stop pestering me."[24] Personal injury lawyers interviewed by Kritzer said they sometimes hesitated to represent "high-maintenance" clients or those who engaged in lawyer shopping.[25] And employment discrimination lawyers considered the plaintiff's demeanor when deciding on representation; one lawyer interviewed "said he had a 'sixth sense' for 'difficult' clients, meaning that they would become 'accusatory' or 'whin[y]' in the course of the lawyer-client relationship."[26] Since lawyers hesitate to turn away business – even that of difficult or "whiny" clients – they sometimes charge a higher hourly fee or increase the size of their retainer to compensate for the difficulty anticipated in representation. As one divorce lawyer said, "I don't mind a pain if they are going to

[19] Ibid, 5.   [20] Trautner, "Tort reform."   [21] Engel, "The oven bird's song," 564–5.
[22] Mary Nell Trautner, "Personal responsibility v. corporate liability: how personal injury lawyers screen cases in an era of tort reform," *Sociology of Crime, Law and Deviance*, 12 (2009), 203–30, at 227.
[23] Mather et al., *Divorce Lawyers at Work*, pp. 93–4.   [24] Michelson, "The practice of law," 20.
[25] Kritzer, *Risks, Reputations, and Rewards*, p. 86.
[26] Myrick et al., "Race and representation," 744.

pay me!"[27] Similarly, Michelson reports that some Chinese lawyers would tolerate the "risk and the annoyances associated with 'difficult' clients if the fee potential of the case [was] sufficiently attractive."[28]

A small number of divorce lawyers in New England took this rational calculation even further to carve out a market niche for themselves – one that appealed directly to vengeful or unreasonable clients and offered to act as a hired gun for them. Unlike most divorce lawyers, who invoked the norms of reasonableness of their legal communities, these attorneys rejected cooperation and instead embraced a more aggressive "Rambo"-style representation. They knew they could attract clients this way, especially those stubborn or angry clients who were unwilling to listen to attorneys' pleas to be patient and realistic about their divorce.[29]

By pursuing their economic self-interest when selecting clients, lawyers thus reflected community values by predicting jurors' responses to those clients, or by aiding clients in resolving their conflicts in cooperative or adversarial ways depending on the interests of the individuals – and the lawyers.

SOCIAL NETWORKS AND RELATIONSHIPS

The fact that lawyers practice within social networks offers a second explanation for how they select their clients. Lawyers' ongoing interactions and close relationships in a community profoundly shape the way in which they do their work. In "The Oven Bird's Song," Engel explains the local bar's disinterest in filing personal injury claims as due in part to the social network of professional practice: "Sander County lawyers were seen as closely linked to the kinds of individuals and businesses against whom tort actions were typically brought."[30] That is, since lawyers are embedded in a social hierarchy, they are reluctant to accept clients wanting to sue those whom the lawyers generally represent. Indeed, Engel's data from a sample of civil cases confirms this point: Only 12.5 percent of the plaintiffs in tort cases were represented by attorneys from Sander County, in contrast to 72.5 percent of the non-tort plaintiffs who had legal counsel from the county.[31] Thus, local lawyers did not hesitate to represent plaintiffs in other areas of law – it was only the tort cases that they avoided. Consequently, Sander County residents who sought legal help for personal injury claims were often represented by one particular lawyer

---

[27] Mather et al., *Divorce Lawyers at Work*, p. 95.   [28] Michelson, "The practice of law," 21.
[29] Mather et al., *Divorce Lawyers at Work*, pp. 85–6.   [30] Engel, "The oven bird's song," 565.
[31] Ibid.

who lived just over the county line, a lawyer who readily admitted to Engel: "I'm not part of the establishment."[32]

This lawyer's comment underscores two different aspects of a lawyer's social network. Not only do ongoing relationships constrain lawyers in their work; so also does the hierarchy of the legal community. Van Hoy's research on Indiana lawyers, Parikh's on the Chicago bar, and Daniels and Martin's on the Texas bar reveal a great deal about the role of hierarchy among personal injury lawyers.[33] Each finds substantial stratification shaped by geographic reach, type and volume of cases, and specialization. Parikh notes that this hierarchy is "less obvious to outsiders," although well known within the bar.[34] Ranging from attorneys with a small number of high-value, complex cases to those handling many routine auto accidents, the bar depends heavily on cooperation for referrals. High-end practitioners refer low-value cases down the hierarchy and low-end practitioners return the favor (since the latter lack the resources to handle a specialized case and also could not shoulder that degree of risk). Additional referral partners come from small firms representing individuals on matters outside of personal injury. Parikh finds that the ties among referral partners are long-lasting, involve frequent contact, and are personal (rather than firm-based). These embedded ties among personal injury lawyers, Parikh suggests, not only shape the clientele that each represents, but also reproduce the stratification and hierarchy of the profession as a whole.[35]

Throughout the United States, 63 percent of private practitioners work either as solo practitioners or in small firms of one to five lawyers.[36] That does not mean, however, that these individuals are working entirely on their own, unconstrained in selecting clients or deciding how to represent them. Networks of attorneys, stemming in part from market considerations but also from ongoing social and professional interactions, create informal norms, mutual dependencies, and common standards. These "communities of practice," as my co-authors and I call them, include groups of lawyers practicing in a particular locality and those within a specific legal field such as personal injury or divorce.[37] Our research on divorce lawyers in Maine and

---

[32] Ibid, 566.

[33] Jerry Van Hoy, "Markets and contingency: how client markets influence the work of plaintiffs' personal injury lawyers," *International Journal of the Legal Profession*, 6 (1999), 345–66; Parikh, "How the spider catches the fly"; Daniels and Martin, "Best of times."

[34] Parikh, "How the spider catches the fly," 247.   [35] Ibid, 267.

[36] www.americanbar.org/content/dam/aba/administrative/market_research/lawyer-demographics-tables-2016.authcheckdam.pdf.

[37] Mather et al., *Divorce Lawyers at Work*, p. 6.

New Hampshire, for example, describes a hierarchy among divorce practitioners quite similar to the personal injury bar: High-end attorneys often face each other in two-lawyer divorce cases involving considerable assets, while divorce attorneys with working-class clients rarely face a lawyer on the other side and seek to finalize divorces as quickly and efficiently as possible. We also found among most of the divorce lawyers whom we interviewed a generally shared commitment to being reasonable, sharing information when asked, seeking to settle cases amicably, and avoiding unnecessary litigation. As noted in the previous section, however, a few lawyers in each locality rejected this norm of the reasonable lawyer and sought to carve out a market niche of their own, in some ways acting similarly to the lawyer in Sander County who said he wasn't part of the establishment.

Research on legal practice in small towns and rural areas shows how pervasive and influential these social networks can be. In small, tightly knit communities with ongoing social relationships, lawyers advocate for clients within the confines of those networks. Landon's study of lawyers in rural Missouri shows how lawyers redefined advocacy to avoid excessive zeal, cooperating with other attorneys and tamping down any client expectations of adversarial conflict in order to preserve the social fabric.[38] Recent research by Li on case screening in rural China points to a similar phenomenon – i.e., "relational embeddedness," referring to "concrete and durable relationships among law practitioners, clients, adversaries, and the communities these individuals inhabit."[39] Li's fieldwork in Chinese law offices finds that economic incentives explain some of their decisions on client selection, but she argues that economics was not the overriding determinant. Indeed, this 2016 study provides considerable evidence showing that "when faced with social obligations derived from kinship, friendship, and community membership, legal workers often put monetary interests on the back burner."[40] Some of the crucial non-monetary incentives that influenced client selection include the exchange of favors, the need to uphold moral obligations and show respect, and a desire to avoid social fallout.

Although research on relational embeddedness typically emphasizes its positive benefits for communities, Li draws on her research to point out its negative aspects, namely legal workers' tendency to support the more

---

[38] Donald D. Landon, *Country Lawyers: The Impact of Context on Professional Practice* (Praeger, 1990).

[39] Ke Li, "Relational embeddedness and socially motivated case screening in the practice of law in rural China," *Law & Society Review*, 50 (2016), 920–52, 921.

[40] Ibid, 935.

powerful party in disputes and thereby reinforce existing social inequalities. By agreeing to represent some clients and reject others, and to give priority to certain types of cases, law practitioners in rural China – like the lawyers in Sander County who would not represent personal injury clients – reinforce dominant community values.

SHARED CULTURAL AND PERSONAL VALUES

In his discussion of lawyers and local values, Engel emphasizes that many of the lawyers he interviewed "were born and raised in the area" and thus "shared the local tendency to censure those who aggressively asserted personal injury claims."[41] Just like the insurance adjusters who downgraded injury claims and the jurors and judges who disapproved of tort cases, lawyers in Sander County grew up in the community and shared its ideas and beliefs. That is to say, even the few attorneys who agreed to represent plaintiffs in injury cases had internalized the community's hostile view of these claims.

In the traditional bar account of lawyers' choices about client representation or advocacy, lawyers' personal values have no bearing on their professional conduct. Instead, the norms of the profession and professional socialization have ostensibly "bleached out" attorneys' personal attributes based on race, gender, religion, or social background.[42] But the indeterminacy of law and the wide discretion enjoyed by attorneys provide considerable space for lawyers' own personal identities and values to affect their professional decisions. Implicit biases regarding race, religion, or gender also influence lawyers' judgment. Further, the fact that others (judges, opposing lawyers, clients, witnesses, etc.) consciously or unconsciously treat lawyers according to their gender or race may lead – or even in some way oblige – women and minority attorneys to reflect their own personal identities in their professional work.[43]

When seeking an attorney, potential litigants often look for someone with certain personal attributes in addition to the requisite professional qualities. Representation by an attorney of the same gender, race, or ethnicity can promote trust, and some clients believe it may improve the lawyer-client

[41] Engel, "The oven bird's song," 565.
[42] Levinson coined the term "bleached out professionalism" to describe the belief that lawyers' personal characteristics have no bearing on their professional values or conduct. He then critiques that view for Jewish lawyers in various situations. See Sanford Levinson, "Identifying the Jewish lawyer: reflections on the construction of professional identity," *Cardozo Law Review*, 14 (1993), 1577–1612, 1578.
[43] See, e.g., David B. Wilkins, "Identities and roles: race, recognition, and professional responsibility," *Maryland Law Review*, 57 (1998), 1502; and Mather et al., 2001.

relationship. Thus, regardless of how gender or race-blind the attorney is, or aspires to be, client perceptions and expectations may affect their relationship. At the same time, implicit or explicit biases can influence lawyers' responses to those seeking their services. A large study of employment discrimination claims in federal court found that African-Americans are almost twice as likely as whites to lack legal representation. Part of this may be due to Black plaintiffs' lack of trust in the legal profession (given that nearly all specialist lawyers are white), but part might also be explained by lawyers' implicit biases – their perceptions of Black clients as being more difficult, less credible, or harder to work with.[44]

Women divorce lawyers report that potential clients often contact them because of their gender. Some wives say they feel more comfortable talking to a woman lawyer, while others believe that a woman will better understand their problems and fight harder for them. And some women divorce lawyers admit they prefer to represent wives. Checking the docket records of over 6,000 divorce cases in New England, my colleagues and I found that female attorneys disproportionately represent wives in divorce cases.[45] Some women divorce lawyers we interviewed described their enjoyment of divorce work due to the intimacy and close emotional bond they could forge with a largely female clientele. Women attorneys are also more likely than men to specialize in divorce, and one specialist, for example, extolled the perfect match between her personal values and divorce law: "It was just a very good fit because I love people, and I've always been very interested in human relations, so it's a just a natural."[46]

Research on immigration lawyers reveals the importance of national and ethnic background for this area of practice. Levin's survey of immigration lawyers in New York City found that one-third were immigrants themselves, while the same proportion were born in the US and had at least one parent who was foreign-born.[47] Although these attorneys had many different reasons for initially entering the immigration field, they continued to represent immigrants because this area of practice "resonated with their own history or because of a desire to help others" – especially others like themselves.[48]

Historically, religious identity directly affected lawyers' selection of clients and areas of practice, as Jews and Catholics were barred from elite law firms for much of the twentieth century. Consequently, these attorneys gravitated

---

[44] Myrick et al., "Race and representation," 720.
[45] Mather et al., *Divorce Lawyers at Work*, pp. 56 and 208 (fn 16).   [46] Ibid, 157.
[47] Leslie C. Levin, "Guardians at the gate: the backgrounds, career paths, and professional development of private US immigration lawyers," *Law & Social Inquiry*, 34 (2009), 399.
[48] Ibid, 411.

to personal plight fields of law, representing individuals in criminal cases, personal injuries, or family matters, and contributing to the social stratification of the legal profession still noted today.[49] Lawyers' religious beliefs may affect the selection of individual clients through the particular values of their practice, as, for instance, when Jewish lawyers work for social justice or serve the poor as part of their religious faith,[50] or when Catholic lawyers integrate moral analysis with their legal counseling.[51] But religious values can exert an even stronger influence on attorneys through legal obligation – for example, to canon or Jewish law. During the 1950s, for instance, Catholic lawyers were forbidden by Church doctrine from representing clients in a divorce action without prior approval from their local bishop and any lawyer ignoring this command would be committing "a seriously sinful act."[52] Similarly, some rabbis have ruled that Jewish lawyers should not represent clients as plaintiffs unless they have first sought to resolve their conflicts in a rabbinical court.[53] Levinson notes, however, that the question of the Catholic or Jewish lawyer "is not precisely analogous to questions involving other attributes like gender, race, or ethnicity," since the latter may suggest "distinctive way of looking at the world" whereas the former may in fact involve a matter of competing legal obligation.[54]

Increased diversity in the contemporary legal profession and changing expectations of the lawyer-client relationship pose challenges for a distinct professional identity. For instance, Mah argues that new Latino and Asian-American immigrant communities have social norms and worldviews that are poorly served by the bar, not because of too few Latino and Asian lawyers but because of professional norms such as client autonomy and lawyer neutrality, which clash with the norms of these immigrant communities.[55] Similarly, a detailed analysis of American Indian tribal litigation by Carpenter and Wald underscores the obstacles confronting tribal attorneys when representing their tribes because of professional bar rules that are not well suited for group lawyering.[56] These scholars see great advantage in allowing lawyers to have "thick" professional identities – closely identifying with their clients – but

---

[49] John P. Heinz et al., *Urban Lawyers: The New Social Structure of the Bar* (University of Chicago Press, 2005).

[50] Russell G. Pearce, "The Jewish lawyer's question," *Texas Tech Law Review*, 27 (1996), 1259.

[51] Thomas L. Shaffer, *On Being a Christian and a Lawyer* (Brigham University Press, 1981).

[52] Albert L. Schlitzer, "Catholic lawyer and divorce cases," *Notre Dame Law Review*, 29 (1953), 37, 44.

[53] Levinson, "Identifying the Jewish lawyer," 1603.   [54] Ibid, 1611.

[55] Liwan Mah, "The legal profession faces new faces: how lawyers' professional norms should change to serve a changing American population," *California Law Review*, 93 (2005), 1721.

[56] Kristen A. Carpenter and Eli Wald, "Lawyering for groups: the case of American Indian tribal attorneys," *Fordham Law Review*, 81 (2013), 3085.

others, such as Spaulding, view such intense identification as "self-interested perversion" of the professional norm of service.[57]

These last points have special resonance in light of Engel's exploration of law and social change in Sander County. When social outsiders in that community – newcomers or those with a different ethnic or religious background – were injured in accidents, they struggled to find help from the local lawyers. But lawyers located outside of the county were willing to represent the injured claimants and to fight in court on their behalf. Being outsiders themselves, these attorneys were less likely to share the cultural values of Sander County.

FORMAL LAW

Interestingly, as Konefsky notes in his chapter about "The Oven Bird's Song," formal law plays little or no role in explaining civil litigation in Sander County. Cultural, social, and economic influences loom much larger in Engel's analysis, both for understanding who uses the court to recover for injuries and for showing how lawyers decide which injury plaintiffs to accept or reject. Indeed, the broader question of how lawyers think about client selection in civil cases is also surprisingly unconstrained by law. Historically, lawyers in the US have enjoyed nearly complete professional autonomy to decide upon client representation. By contrast, barristers in the UK have traditionally followed a "cab-rank" rule in which they are expected to take clients in the order in which they arrive at barristers' chambers. Empirical research, however, shows that this English rule is "widely thought to be honored mostly in the breach."[58]

Professional rules of conduct in the US focus on those whom lawyers *cannot* represent, but the rules impose no conditions on client acceptance. Specifically, ABA Model Rule 1.16 prohibits lawyers from accepting a client if the representation would result in a violation of professional conduct rules, such as a lawyer's conflict of interest. Even if a court appoints an attorney to represent a client, the attorney can refuse the appointment if the client or the cause is "repugnant" to the lawyer.[59] Moreover, once the client is accepted,

---

[57] Spaulding distinguishes between what he calls "thick" and "thin" professional identity and argues forcefully against the former, i.e., close identification of lawyers with their clients. See Norman W. Spaulding, "Reinterpreting professional identity," *University of Colorado Law Review*, 74 (2003), 1, 6.

[58] W. Bradley Wendel, "Institutional and individual justification in legal ethics: the problem of client selection," *Hofstra Law Review*, 34 (2006), 987, 994.

[59] ABA Model Rule 6.2 (c).

a lawyer can still withdraw if he/she "considers [the client's objectives] repugnant or with which the lawyer has a fundamental disagreement."[60] In short, other than avoiding conflicts of interest or clients who want to commit fraud, attorneys are generally free to reject clients for any reason whatsoever.

Nevertheless, the question of whether lawyers may refuse to represent individuals based on race, ethnicity, religion, gender, or any other protected category – just as other private businesses are legally constrained – has been a controversial subject of debate for decades. The ABA and state bars have wrestled with how best to promote anti-discrimination within the legal profession – whether by the more general state anti-discrimination statutes or by ethical conduct rules specific to the legal profession. Although nearly all states have public accommodations statutes prohibiting discrimination, there is only one case on record applying such law to lawyers – a 2003 Massachusetts court decision against a feminist lawyer who refused to represent a man in a divorce action.[61] Other states have professional conduct rules that prohibit discrimination in the practice of law or within the profession, but these do not apply to client selection. In August 2016, this debate came to a head with a vote by the American Bar Association to add a new paragraph (g) to 8.4 in the Model Rules of Professional Conduct to explicitly prohibit lawyers from knowingly engaging in harassment or discrimination in the practice of law. However, following this statement of prohibition, 8.4(g) adds a qualification: "This paragraph does not limit the ability of a lawyer to accept, decline or withdraw from a representation in accordance with Rule 1.16."[62] In other words, even with this controversial new rule change, it appears that attorneys continue to enjoy professional autonomy to accept or reject clients as they see fit.

Commenting on this ethical gap in the rules, Professor Allen described the dilemma raised by a student in her Professional Responsibility class: "Wait a minute, are you telling me that after I graduate I could hang out a shingle that says, 'Lawyers for White People'?" Professor Allen acknowledged that numerous websites already advertise gender-based legal services in family law – such as DAWN ("Divorce Attorneys for Women") or Family Law Attorneys for Men.[63] Allen argues in her comments to the ABA that the harm of the current ABA rule and the non-enforcement of most state anti-discrimination laws for client selection by lawyers greatly undermine the legitimacy of the legal

---

[60] ABA Model Rule 1.16 (b) (4).
[61] *Nathanson v. Mass. Commission against Discrimination*, 16 Mass L. Rptr 761 (Mass. Sup. Ct. 2003).
[62] ABA Model Rule 8.4 (g).
[63] Jessie Allen, Comments to ABA Committee on Ethics and Professional Responsibility, March 17, 2016, Re: Proposed Amendment to ABA Model Rule of Professional Conduct 8.4.

system. It is certainly ironic that one's access to legal rights and legal institutions depends on lawyers as gatekeepers choosing to grant such access, and
yet the lawyers' own conduct in this process is largely unconstrained by law.

CONCLUSION

Lawyers express and reinforce dominant community values through their
screening of potential clients. Engel's article alerted scholars to the importance of this stage of the legal process, and, even more, to the nuance and
complexity involved in the process of client selection. Although economic
incentives for lawyers are the easiest to observe in screening decisions, when
examined more closely by Engel and then by later researchers those incentives
often turned out to rest on cultural assumptions – assumptions that are
reinforced by social networks. Thus, the emphasis in "The Oven Bird's Song"
on the cultural values of residents and lawyers in Sander County to explain
client acceptance was prescient. Moreover, Engel's lack of attention to formal
law exerting constraints on lawyers remains accurate today, since lawyers are
still largely unregulated in their selection of clients.

Let me conclude by suggesting that these same factors that link the process
of client selection to community values also point to how and why lawyers
may occasionally help to bring about change. That is, by representing marginal voices in society, initiating new kinds of lawsuits, or making new legal
arguments, lawyers select clients and present their cases in ways that may
influence community values. The process of litigation requires, as Engel
writes, that "norms and values that once patterned behavior unthinkingly
or unconsciously must now be articulated, explained, and defended."[64] For
example, when a criminal lawyer defended her female client for killing her
husband after years of his physical abuse, the lawyer introduced *the wife*, not
the husband, as the victim, and thereby extended the concept of self-defense
to include victims of domestic violence. In so doing, the lawyer asked the
community to re-think its norms about violence within families, gender
relations, and protections of criminal law. When a lawyer agreed to represent
a gay client seeking a marriage certificate, he was challenging taken-for-
granted assumptions about the legal definition of marriage and forcing them
to be "articulated, explained, and defended."[65] As gay marriage cases made
their way through the appellate courts, the traditional defense of marriage as a
heterosexual institution broke down against constitutional claims of equal

[64] Engel, "The oven bird's song," 579.   [65] Ibid.

protection. Numerous other cases abound in which minority views within a local community (whether liberal or conservative voices) have found expression through litigation and ended up challenging community values and ultimately changing the law.

Why do lawyers agree to represent clients against such overwhelming odds? For the same reasons that lawyers select clients based upon dominant community values. These lawyers may share the cultural ideas of their clients, perhaps seeing themselves as cause lawyers who use law to confront dominant norms. Or, the lawyers may have also experienced the marginal social status of their clients, whether due to gender, sexual orientation, race, ethnicity, or something else within the social hierarchy of the legal profession. Or, the lawyers may be willing to take a risk with certain clients because they see possible economic benefits from representing them. For instance, my research a few decades ago revealed a small number of women divorce lawyers in New England who represented their clients – wives – in ways that challenged the status quo of small-town family law practice, which tended to favor husbands. These women lawyers embraced aggressive legal advocacy because of a commitment to feminist principles (cultural values), their own marginalization by the largely male divorce bar (social network), and recognition of a market niche (economic incentive).[66] Other examples abound in which lawyers marginalized within their own communities, such as lawyers from racial or ethnic minority backgrounds, represent their peers to reflect and confront wrongful treatment or to assert legal rights. While in some cases these practitioners were part of organized political networks seeking legal change, others were simply individual lawyers who felt sidelined in their own communities because of their identities or values and sought to represent clients in order to remedy the situation.

The study of lawyers as they decide whom to represent in litigation may seem at first blush to be an insignificant topic, but "The Oven Bird's Song" showed its importance for understanding the role lawyers play in mediating community values and law. Considerable scholarship since Engel's article has built on and extended his insights. The process of client selection shows how lawyers typically reflect, but on occasion may influence, community values.

---

[66] Mather et al., *Divorce Lawyers at Work*, p. 127.

7

Do Jurors Hear the Oven Bird's Song?

VALERIE P. HANS

Three decades ago, David Engel set out to interview members of rural "Sander County" about their views of civil litigation, asking them about their attitudes toward fellow community members who brought lawsuits over personal injuries. The results of these fascinating interviews were published in "The Oven Bird's Song: Insiders, Outsiders, and Personal Injuries in an American Community."[1] The article immediately captured attention. One might imagine that, hearing of severe injuries suffered by their fellow citizens, community members would feel and express sympathy and understanding. Instead, Engel was surprised to find strong currents of hostility toward injured people who sued others. These observers saw personal injury plaintiffs as violating the deeply cherished value of personal responsibility, by attempting to place blame elsewhere for injuries that were thought likely to be their own fault. Special scorn was heaped upon those who sued business owners and other community leaders, especially if the plaintiff was a newcomer or an outsider. Community members told David Engel that for the most part, "life's little accidents" did not warrant lawsuits. Instead, it was best to lump it: to pick up and go on with one's life rather than try to shift the burden of responsibility onto others. Not surprisingly, Engel found that lawsuits were infrequently brought in Sander County, and those that were brought were not wildly successful.

A sharp contrast can be drawn between these Sander County residents, insistent on plaintiffs' personal responsibility and reluctant to award them money damages, and popular images of the contemporary American civil jury. Accounts of civil juries often depict them as modern-day Robin Hoods,

---

[1] David M. Engel, "The oven bird's song: insiders, outsiders, and personal injuries in an American community," *Law & Society Review*, 18 (1984), 551–82.

who cheerfully plunge into the deep pockets of defendants to award substantial sums to undeserving plaintiffs.

The portrayal of the American jury as a Robin Hood figure has a long history. As far back as the 1950s, insurance companies asserted that jurors were "[r]unled by emotion rather than facts, they arrive at unfounded and excessive awards."[2] One 1950s ad shows a court officer outside a jury room door with the accompanying statement: "Your Insurance Premium is Being Determined Now."[3] The ad complains about "excessive jury awards, rendered by jurors who feel they can afford to be generous with the 'rich' insurance company's money";[4] widely distributed at the time, it asserts that "as jurors tend more and more to give excessive awards in cases that do go to court, such valuations are establishing the 'going' rate for the day-to-day out-of-court claims all of which means increased insurance premium cost to the public."[5]

The same refrain was sounded in advertising during the 1980s.[6] The insurance company Johnson and Higgins placed an ad in the *Wall Street Journal* that featured a jury box filled with menacing-looking jurors. The ad, entitled "Insurance Is Getting Killed in Self-Defense," reports that "In 1974, the average product liability jury award was $345,000. Last year it was $1.07 million ... Worse yet, as juries hand out larger and larger awards, judges keep expanding the definition of liability ... And the public pays the bill in the end."[7]

The trope of the Robin Hood jury persists today. Recently, a Tennessee jury awarded $55 million to sports caster Erin Andrews in her lawsuit against a Nashville hotel company after she was unknowingly videotaped by a stalker who learned of her room location through a hotel employee.[8] One commentator complained that the verdict against the hotel company was not likely to have been based on its actual negligence: "The main consideration

[2] *People* v. *American Automobile Insurance Company*, 132 Cal. App. 2d 317 (1955).
[3] American Associated Insurance Companies, "Your insurance premium is being determined now," *Life*, January 26, 1953, p. 91; *People* v. *American Automobile Insurance Company*.
[4] American Associated Insurance Companies, "Your insurance premium"; *People* v. *American Automobile Insurance Company*.
[5] American Associated Insurance Companies, "Your insurance premium"; *People* v. *American Automobile Insurance Company*.
[6] Stephen Daniels, "The question of jury competence and the politics of civil justice reform: symbols, rhetoric, and agenda building," *Law and Contemporary Problems*, 52 (1989), 269.
[7] Johnson & Higgins, "Insurance is getting killed in self-defense," *Wall Street Journal*, November 19, 1985, p. 3.
[8] Associated Press, "Erin Andrews awarded $55M in lawsuit over nude video posted online," *Hollywood Reporter*, March 7, 2016, www.hollywoodreporter.com/news/erin-andrews-awarded-55m-lawsuit-873313.

seems to be, not what objective blame the hotel companies held, but how deep their pockets were."[9]

A substantial body of research on the views, attitudes, and decisions of civil jurors allows us to examine whether contemporary jurors are more akin to rural Sander County residents or Robin Hood and his band. The modern field of empirical jury research began in the 1950s and has continued to expand.[10] The initial focus of much research was on juries in criminal cases. However, the civil justice system and civil juries came under concerted attack in the 1980s, leading many scholars to examine the tort system and civil jury decisions.[11] Multiple public opinion polls tapped Americans' views about civil litigation.[12] Interviews with civil jurors and analysis of civil trial verdicts and awards provided both qualitative and quantitative evidence about the perspectives and decisions of civil jurors.[13] Thus, we now are in a position to answer the question: Do jurors hear the oven bird's song?

This chapter presents what we know about civil jurors' approach to personal injury plaintiffs, drawing on diverse types of research. As striking and surprising as Engel's results were at the time, the research on jury decision-making in personal injury lawsuits shows remarkable convergence with his discovery of anti-plaintiff hostility. A tendency to blame plaintiffs for their own injuries is not, it appears, limited to rural communities. Instead, research from surveys, juror interviews, jury experiments, and case outcomes across the

---

[9] Walter Hudson, "Hotel must pay Erin Andrews millions after stalker filmed her nude, but why?" PJ Media.com, March 8, 2016, https://pjmedia.com/lifestyle/2016/03/08/hotel-must-pay-erin-andrews-millions-after-stalker-filmed-her-nude-but-why/.

[10] Dennis Devine, *Jury Decision Making: The State of the Science* (New York University Press, 2012); Shari Seidman Diamond and Mary R. Rose, "Real juries," *Annual Review of Law and Social Science*, 1 (2005), 255; Valerie P. Hans and Neil Vidmar, "The American Jury at twenty-five years," *Law & Social Inquiry*, 16 (1991), 323–51; Valerie P. Hans and Neil Vidmar, "Jurors and juries" in Austin Sarat (ed.), *Blackwell Companion to Law and Society* (Blackwell Publishers, 2004), pp. 195–211; Neil Vidmar and Valerie P. Hans, *American Juries: The Verdict* (Prometheus Books, 2007).

[11] Stephen Daniels and Joanne Martin, *Tort Reform, Plaintiffs' Lawyers, and Access to Justice* (University Press of Kansas, 2015); David M. Engel and Michael McCann (eds.), *Fault Lines: Tort Law and Cultural Practice* (Stanford University Press, 2009); Marc Galanter, "Real world torts: an antidote to anecdote," *Maryland Law Review*, 55 (1996), 1093; Marc Galanter, "An oil strike in hell: contemporary legends about the civil justice system," *Arizona Law Review*, 40 (1998), 717.

[12] See, e.g., H. Taylor, M. R. Kagay, and S. Leichenko, "Public attitudes toward the civil justice system and tort law reform," Survey conducted for Aetna Life and Casualty by Louis Harris and Associates (1987).

[13] Valerie P. Hans, *Business on Trial: The Civil Jury and Corporate Responsibility* (Yale University Press, 2000).

country reveals that civil jurors frequently derogate personal injury plaintiffs, express doubts about their credibility, minimize their injuries, and discount their awards.

COMMUNITY VIEWS OF PERSONAL INJURY PLAINTIFFS

> ATRA's goal is not just to pass laws. We work to change the way people think about personal responsibility and civil litigation. ATRA programs shine a media spotlight on lawsuit abuse and the pernicious political influence of the personal injury bar. ATRA redefines the victim, showing how lawsuit abuse affects all of us by cutting off access to health care, costing consumers through the "lawsuit tax," and threatening the availability of products like vaccines.[14]

Around the time that David Engel published the results of his ethnography and interviews with Sander County residents, the movement to impose limits on recovery through the tort system gained significant ground.[15] Tort reform groups affiliated with businesses and the insurance industry worked at both the state and the federal levels to reform the civil litigation system. A critically important part of their strategy was to develop broad public support for the idea that the civil litigation system was out of control and needed to be reined in.[16] Expanding on the advertising approach dating back to the 1950s, tort reform groups embarked on a multi-faceted and sustained effort "to change the way people think about personal responsibility and civil litigation."[17] Their ad campaigns developed the theme of profligate juries who cost the public serious money.

Another approach taken by tort reform groups was to publicize "horror stories" about runaway litigation. These stories typically portrayed greedy plaintiffs who sued at the slightest provocation, short-sighted judges who allowed meritless claims to proceed, and overly generous juries who cared more about emptying the defendant's deep pockets than about ascertaining the defendant's negligence.

Included in the horror stories that circulated in the popular media in 1986 were cases in which thieves, sloppy workmen, and other overreaching plaintiffs sued, often successfully, when their own bad behavior caused

---

[14] American Tort Reform Association website, www.atra.org/about.
[15] Daniels and Martin, *Tort Reform*.
[16] Stephen Daniels, "The question of jury competence and the politics of civil justice reform: symbols, rhetoric, and agenda building," *Law and Contemporary Problems*, 52 (1989), 269.
[17] www.atra.org/about.

injury.[18] Consider the story of a workman who set up a ladder in a pile of manure. The ladder slipped in the manure while the workman was aloft; he fell and was injured. The story continues with the news that the workman successfully sued the ladder manufacturer for failing to warn him about the danger of setting up a ladder in manure or other slippery substances.[19] Another horror story features a man in a telephone booth who was injured when a drunk driver crashed into the booth. The appellate court found the company that designed the booth liable.[20] In both these instances, someone is clearly to blame – the careless worker, the drunk driver. But, as the stories emphasize, despite the clear wrongdoing of others, the blameless manufacturing company or designer is found liable and must foot the bill.

As Daniels explains, however, these anecdotes are wrong or incomplete, leaving out critical details that make the cases and outcomes more understandable. In the ladder and manure lawsuit, "the manure had nothing to do with the verdict. The jury found that the ladder broke with less than a 450-pound load on it. The ladder's safety rating indicated that it could support 1000 pounds."[21] Similarly, the phone booth story is full of inaccuracies and fails to tell the whole story. It had been the site of a previous accident, and when the plaintiff in the booth saw the car coming toward it he tried unsuccessfully to flee the booth but the door would not open. The driver was not drunk. After the plaintiff was severely injured in the accident, which crushed one of his legs and cut off the other leg, he brought suit. The appeals court ruling permitted the case to go to trial, rather than ruling on liability.[22]

Stella Liebeck's successful lawsuit against McDonald's for the burns she received from hot coffee at McDonald's was immediately cast as yet another illustration of out-of-control juries and absurd results in the civil litigation system.[23] As Haltom and McCann describe in compelling detail, after the elderly Albuquerque, New Mexico woman received such severe burns from spilled coffee that she required skin-graft surgery, she asked McDonald's to cover her hospital bills. The company refused, and in the subsequent lawsuit, Liebeck prevailed. Initially, the jurors thought the trial was a waste of their time.[24] But after hearing evidence about the severity of Liebeck's

---

[18] Daniels, "The question of jury competence"; Daniels and Martin, *Tort Reform*; William Haltom and Michael McCann, *Distorting the Law: Politics, Media, and the Litigation Crisis* (University of Chicago Press, 2004); Michael J. Saks, "Do we really know anything about the tort litigation system – and why not?" *University of Pennsylvania Law Review*, 140 (1992), 1147.

[19] Daniels, "The question of jury competence," 294.   [20] Ibid.   [21] Ibid.   [22] Ibid.

[23] Haltom and McCann, *Distorting the Law*.

[24] Andrea Gerlin, "How a jury decided that a coffee spill is worth $2.9 million," *Wall Street Journal*, 1 September 1994, A1.

burns, the seeming indifference of McDonald's to customer injuries, and the company's unwillingness to modify procedures even though it had become aware that its hot coffee was causing injuries, the jury found for Liebeck and awarded her both compensatory and punitive damages.

The McDonald's hot-coffee case, the ladder lawsuit, and the phone booth story all paint a dramatic (if inaccurate) picture of a civil justice system run amok. As Marc Galanter observed: "Unfortunately, much of the debate on the civil justice system relies on anecdotes and atrocity stories and unverified assertion rather than analysis of reliable data."[25]

But did the collected ads and horror stories change jurors' minds? Was the decades-long campaign by business and insurance groups successful in modifying Americans' views about civil litigation? As a scientific matter, whether the ads and horror stories contributed to more negative views is challenging to determine definitively. Perhaps the closest we can come is an experiment conducted some time ago by the memory psychologist Elizabeth Loftus.[26] In her experiment, a number of mock jurors saw an insurance company ad raising the potentially negative impact of high damage awards, which asked the question: "You *really* think it's the insurance company that's paying for all those large jury awards?" Others did not see the ad. Those who were exposed to the advertising gave lower damage awards for pain and suffering to a plaintiff in a mock lawsuit. This simple laboratory demonstration shows that insurance advertising certainly has the potential to influence jury awards.

There are other reasons to expect that media coverage of civil litigation has influenced Americans' perceptions of civil lawsuits. News reports tend to highlight plaintiff wins and large damage awards, giving the average person an atypical view of what goes on in civil litigation.[27] Bailis and MacCoun calculated the median jury awards in state civil trial courts and in the stories reported by popular national magazines.[28] The median awards in the courts ranged from a low of $51,000 to a high of $318,000. The median award in the cases covered in the magazines? $1,750,000! When people are asked about their views of civil litigation, these unusually large, high-visibility cases will

---

[25] Galanter, "Real world torts," 1098.

[26] Elizabeth F. Loftus, "Insurance advertising and jury awards," *American Bar Association Journal*, 65 (1979, January), 68–70.

[27] Daniel S. Bailis and Robert J. MacCoun, "Estimating liability risks with the media as your guide: a content analysis of media coverage of tort litigation," *Law and Human Behavior*, 20 (1996), 419; Jennifer K. Robbennolt and Christina Studebaker, "News media reporting on civil litigation and its influence on civil justice decision making," *Law and Human Behavior*, 27 (2003), 5.

[28] Bailis and MacCoun, "Estimating liability risks."

come more readily to mind. In turn, through the availability heuristic – a psychological phenomenon in which people estimate the frequency of events by the ease with which they can recall them – these readily available examples will lead people to assume they occur frequently.[29]

That said, it seems likely that if the ads worked, it was because they resonated with many citizens' strong ethic of individual responsibility, similar to Sander County residents who saw lawsuits as violating that ethic. The ads and horror stories spoke to citizens – and jurors – who were already primed with concern about plaintiffs' abrogation of personal responsibility. Then, too, a tendency to blame victims is very consistent with the "fundamental attribution error," the psychological predisposition to focus on individual rather than situational factors.[30]

SURVEY EVIDENCE: PUBLIC OPINION ABOUT CIVIL LITIGATION

Whatever the relative causal roles of the ATRA strategy and underlying norms of individual responsibility, surveys conducted over the past several decades show that public opinion lines up rather neatly with ATRA claims. Surveys find again and again that Americans hold negative views of the civil justice system.[31] They are convinced that a large proportion of the lawsuits are illegitimate. For example, approximately 80–90 percent of respondents in different polls agree with the statement that "There are far too many frivolous lawsuits today."[32] They see that more people are bringing lawsuits than they should, that there is an explosion of (unworthy) litigation, and that the size of awards has increased faster than litigation.[33] As did Engel's Sander County residents, other Americans also tend to doubt the credibility of plaintiffs who sue others. Fully 77 percent of the respondents in one poll said that people who sue are just trying to blame others for their problems. In another poll, two-thirds thought that juries were awarding too much money.[34]

Public opinion poll results are in line with the ads' emphasis on adverse effects of excessive jury verdicts on the economy. In one survey, at least

---

[29] Hans, *Business on Trial*, p. 74.

[30] Jennifer K. Robbennolt and Valerie P. Hans, *The Psychology of Tort Law* (New York University Press, 2016).

[31] Valerie P. Hans, "Faking it? Citizen perceptions of whiplash injuries" in Brian H. Bornstein, Richard L. Wiener, Robert F. Schopp, and Steven L. Willborn (eds.), *Civil Juries and Civil Justice: Psychological and Legal Perspectives* (Springer, 2008), pp. 141–142.

[32] Hans, *Business on Trial*, pp. 59–60.   [33] Taylor, Kagay, and Leichenko, "Public attitudes."

[34] Hans, *Business on Trial*.

70 percent of respondents said that frivolous lawsuits have led to higher insurance premiums, higher taxes, and lost jobs.[35] In sum, the majority of citizens surveyed in national and regional polls over the past few decades voice remarkably similar concerns as the residents of rural Sander County.

ATTITUDES AND VIEWS OF JURORS

In my own jury research, I have found abundant evidence of disapproval of civil litigation and anti-plaintiff sentiment. In one of my research projects, I interviewed jurors who decided civil cases involving a business or corporation as one of the parties. Similar to the findings of public opinion polls, four out of every five of the jurors I interviewed agreed that frivolous lawsuits are too numerous, channeling Engel's Sander County residents. And the "we all pay" theme of insurance and business advertising was voiced by a juror in these words: "Basically, I feel that people are too quick to sue nowadays. They're looking for the big pockets."[36] In jurors' eyes, businesses will suffer as a result:

> Well, the way I look at it is a big corporation is made up of a bunch of people, and if you take this money from this corporation it's bound to suffer somewhere. Someone invariably is gonna lose their job and that's the way I look at it from my perspective as a working person. In the court system nowadays, it is a completely opposite scene with some of the judgments that go on. It's stupid, there's no reason for some of the judgments that I've seen today.[37]

Jurors often voiced serious doubts about plaintiffs in the lawsuits decided by those jurors. In several cases in which plaintiffs who had worked with the harmful substance asbestos brought suit against asbestos manufacturers and distributors, jurors derogated the plaintiffs as money-hungry: "I think [the plaintiffs] were out to get money, all they could get" and "I just thought as though they felt they were going to come into a big sum of money and just live the rest of their life on easy street ... They figured they were going to take the companies for a large amount, and they really played a good part."[38] Some plaintiffs were seen as taking illegitimate advantage of the opportunity: "this was his chance to make some money," a juror said of one; another was accused of trying to "cash in on this knee injury."[39] Like Sander County residents who believed that people assumed the risk of their actions, jurors

[35] Citizens Against Lawsuit Abuse, "Lawsuit abuse in California," survey performed for Pacific Research Institute by Charlton Research Company (1993).
[36] Hans, *Business on Trial*, p. 61.   [37] Ibid, p. 65.   [38] Ibid, p. 29.   [39] Ibid, pp. 29–30.

thought that a plaintiff who was severely injured playing sports had assumed the risk: "If you decide that you're going to play any sport, I feel as though any consequence coming from playing that sport and getting hurt, that's the way it is"; "That's a risk you always take."[40]

In related research, I conducted a mock jury study that varied whether an individual or corporate defendant was being sued, in which mock jurors deliberated to reach a group verdict on liability and a possible award. The plaintiff was a woman who, depending on the condition, was walking around either a store or a private home during a furniture sale. She tripped over a rip in the carpet and fell hard to the floor, hitting her head and causing injury.

Some striking themes emerged during the videotaped mock jury deliberations. The mock jurors focused relentlessly on what the injured person could have done to avoid her own injury: "She could have prevented this if she would have been looking"; "She was plain careless; that was not very bright"; "what a fall; she must have been a klutz!"; "she's just as much at fault." They also expressed doubts about her credibility, sometimes colorfully: "She previously had headaches, she's either a hypochondriac and looking for trouble or she's a born litigator and maybe she was glad and maybe she even fell on purpose."[41] Jurors often expressed doubts about plaintiff claims as a general matter: "In this day and age everybody wants to sue"; "There are a lot of people who file lawsuits and are not that injured"; "Things happen to people and it's never their fault, it's always someone else's fault."[42] Multiple jurors emphasized the causal link between lawsuits and negative economic impact: "These awards, we all end up paying"; "You have to understand that every time the store pays one of these claims, you're paying for it because the prices go up"; "That's why we're paying the premiums we are"; "In this country we're just suing ourselves out of business."[43]

I found similar resonances in another line of research in which I studied reactions to whiplash cases through a national survey, focus groups, and mock juries. Frivolous lawsuits are widespread, focus group members say: "Yeah, if you are in a car accident and you sprain your thumb and now you can't flip the remote and you want ten grand because you can't flip the remote for two months, give me a break"; "I think we're a sue-happy society. And I think so many people are out for what they can get from the insurance company, from whoever."[44]

Whiplash cases are the prototypical fraudulent injury, in the eyes of the public: "A lot of people complain of it when they have an accident and

---

[40] Ibid, p. 30.   [41] Ibid, pp. 44–5.   [42] Ibid, p. 51.   [43] Ibid, p. 66.
[44] Hans, "Faking it," 141.

a lot of lawsuits are won because you can't see it. I just figure when they go with whiplash, a lot of times they don't have whiplash, but the first thing they think of is, 'Oh, my neck . . . Like how much can I get for this one?";[45] "I tend to think that they're wearing [a neck brace] and as soon as the check comes in, they take it off";[46] "[Injuries] are permanent until the payment comes and then it is gone."[47] And the likely fraud is connected to economic impact: "People try to milk it just because they've got a little neck injury . . . that kind of lawsuit's filed probably every day and that's why our court systems and our premiums are so high."[48]

IMPACT OF JURORS' ATTITUDES AND VIEWS ON CASE SELECTION

Not surprisingly, jurors' anti-plaintiff tendencies are very much on the minds of trial lawyers as they screen and select cases.[49] Trial lawyers interviewed by Mary Nell Trautner told her that the business and insurance advertising campaigns have reshaped the landscape of personal injury jury practice and have to be taken into account in case screening:

> The insurance companies and all the medical organizations . . . had an overwhelming amount of, just staggering amount of advertising, constant commercials about this poor doctor, as he walks down the stairs, locks the door to his office and there's all these poor impoverished kids crying because they have no doctor. "And pretty soon, there'll be no more doctors in this state. And then where will you go?" They ran so many of those that, I think it was just beating the public's head. And so now, they're so ingrained now that everyone thinks all your doctors are going out of business and we've got to save them and we can't punish them.[50]

---

[45] Valerie P. Hans and Nicole Vadino, "Whipped by whiplash? The challenges of jury communication in connective tissue injury lawsuits," *Tennessee Law Review*, 67 (2000), 569, 573–5.

[46] Hans and Vadino, "Whipped by whiplash," 575–6; see also Valerie P. Hans and Nicole Vadino, "After the crash: citizens' perceptions of connective-tissue injury lawsuits," Cornell Legal Studies Research Paper No. 07-016 (2008), available at: http://papers.ssrn.com/sol3/papers.cfm?abstract_id=1012392.

[47] Hans, "Faking it," 143.   [48] Hans and Vadino, "Whipped by whiplash," 573.

[49] Daniels and Martin, *Tort Reform*; Mary Nell Trautner, "Screening, sorting, and selecting in complex personal injury cases: How lawyers mediate access to the civil justice system," unpublished Ph.D. thesis, University of Arizona (2006); Mary Nell Trautner, "Tort reform and access to justice: how legal environments shape lawyers' case selection," *Qualitative Sociology*, 34 (2011), 523.

[50] Trautner, "Tort reform and access to justice," 532–3.

Another lawyer asserted that

> because insurance companies have spent so much money trying to change
> the reality, that people perceive that all lawsuits are frivolous. I think they
> perceive that. And so we have to prove up front that this case is valid, and we
> waste a lot of time talking about frivolous lawsuits and things like that ... And
> juries tend to be sympathetic to the defendant, I think, more so than the
> injured party, whereas 20 years ago that was different.[51]

Another lawyer agreed that the "propaganda wave" had definitely influenced
jurors: "early on, there was a very sympathetic response if you represented a
victim in a medical malpractice case. And then came this huge propaganda
wave ... They had billboards everywhere, they had TV campaign ads, and
it really was a powerful and very effective tool."[52] As a result, trial lawyers
reported to Trautner that they had to shift the way they presented their
plaintiffs' cases:

> When I first started practicing law I think the jurors' perceptions were
> different ... The way plaintiffs' [lawyers] approached their cases ... was
> almost always "Why should the plaintiff win?" The first part of our case
> always ... dwelt on the plaintiff, and focused on what happened to the
> plaintiff, what the plaintiff lost, what the plaintiff's entitled to – and we all
> believed that that's what drove jurors and their decisions. And then we'd talk
> about what the defendant did – the defendant caused this. The reverse has
> happened now ... Jurors first want to know what the defendant did wrong ...
> As plaintiff's lawyers we used to think that [presenting the victim's side of the
> story] was great for us because it told jurors what great people our plaintiffs
> were, but I think what's happened is that jurors have changed the way they
> look at things ... They've changed and they want to know what did the
> defendant do wrong – how did the defendant violate the rules.[53]

As a result, trial attorneys reported that they were much more judicious about
the cases and plaintiffs they chose to represent.

IMPACT OF JURORS' ATTITUDES AND VIEWS
ON JURORS' CASE JUDGMENTS

Jury research offers concrete documentation of these trial lawyers' suspicions.
Negative views about frivolous lawsuits and general doubts about plaintiff
credibility and the legitimacy of injuries have an impact on juries. In my
Business on Trial research, I analyzed the relationship between my study

---

[51] Ibid, 533.   [52] Trautner, "Screening, sorting and selecting," 109.   [53] Ibid, 106–7.

participants' views about civil litigation and their verdicts and awards. For civil jurors who had decided actual cases, I found that the collective anti-litigation views of the civil jurors I interviewed were significantly related to their verdicts and awards. The more strongly a jury perceived a litigation explosion and believed there were many unjustified lawsuits, the lower the jury award was in the case.[54] I found the same pattern in mock jury and scenario experiments. The more individual mock jurors believed that there were far too many frivolous lawsuits today, the less they favored the plaintiff and the lower the damage awards.[55] In short, attitudes toward civil litigation mold evidence interpretation and decision-making in civil lawsuits.

Other researchers have documented the impact of general anti-plaintiff sentiment among jurors. One mock jury study employed a product liability case with ambiguous evidence about the defendant's liability.[56] One of the strongest predictors of whether mock jurors found the defendant liable was the response to the question: "When plaintiffs sue in a lawsuit and receive money damages, would you say that in general they receive too much or too little?" Those who saw awards as excessive were less likely to find the defendant liable. As in my research, general views about civil litigation led to more anti-plaintiff decisions.

In ambiguous situations, these anti-plaintiff sentiments may lead jurors to over-attribute fault to plaintiffs. In two experimental studies that varied the degree of plaintiff fault, study participants weighed plaintiff responsibility more heavily, in one case even attributing some fault to plaintiffs who were described as blameless.[57]

What is more, Neal Feigenson, Jaihyun Park, and Peter Salovey found that plaintiffs who were partly at fault were doubly penalized financially in the damage awards they received.[58] These researchers presented scenarios to their study participants in which the plaintiff's fault and the plaintiff's injury severity were both experimentally varied. In some variations, the plaintiff was not at fault, whereas in others the plaintiff was partly at fault for the injury.

---

[54] Hans, *Business on Trial*, 75.   [55] Ibid, 76.

[56] Shari S. Diamond, Michael J. Saks, and Stephan Landsman, "Juror judgments and liability and damages: sources of variability and ways to increase consistency," *DePaul Law Review*, 49 (1998), 301.

[57] Neal Feigenson, Jaihyun Park, and Peter Salovey, "Effect of blameworthiness and outcome-severity on attributions of responsibility and damage awards in comparative negligence cases," *Law and Human Behavior*, 21 (1997), 597; Ewart A. C. Thomas and Mary Parpal, "Liability as a function of plaintiff and defendant fault," *Journal of Personality and Social Psychology*, 53 (1987), 843.

[58] Feigenson, Park, and Salovey, "Effect of blameworthiness."

The participants first assessed the percentage of fault that was attributable to both the plaintiff and the defendant. They then decided on damage awards – both an overall damage award that represented the full cost of the plaintiff's injury, and an adjusted damage award that decreased the award to take into account the plaintiff's proportionate fault. In actual trials, the adjustment would typically be made by the judge rather than the jury. Feigenson and his colleagues found, as they anticipated, that the percentage fault increased in line with the plaintiff's fault for the injury. However, they also discovered that the initial total damage award that represented the full cost of the injury to the plaintiff – *before* the damage award was discounted by the percentage of plaintiff fault – was significantly lower for plaintiffs who were described as partially at fault. So the awards to the plaintiff were discounted twice: first in the initial total award judgment, and second when the percentage of fault was applied to the initial total award.

Douglas Zickafoose and Brian Bornstein also discovered double discounting in a medical malpractice mock juror experiment they conducted.[59] Plaintiff fault was varied, as in the study by Feigenson and colleagues, and the mock jurors were asked to give an overall damage award, one that would be reduced later to take into account the percentage of plaintiff fault. However, when the plaintiff was described as partly responsible, the overall damage award before reduction was $38,273, compared to an average award of $54,103 for a completely blameless plaintiff.

Finally, researchers analyzing actual jury decisions in auto accident cases found awards showed evidence of double discounting.[60] Initial damage awards, before judicial reductions for plaintiff fault, were lower in cases with plaintiffs who bore some share of the responsibility for their injuries; indeed, the reductions were proportionate to plaintiff fault.

Plaintiff fault is part of the full situational context of the injury that jurors take into account as they assess how to price the injury. That is not surprising, as fact finders in tort cases often take a holistic view to determining the worth of an injury.[61] Focusing on the plaintiff as opposed to the situation is also consistent with the psychological tendency for observers to attribute responsibility to individual rather than situational factors. But the way in which damage awards are calculated by the courts in contributory

[59] Douglas J. Zickafoose and Brian H. Bornstein, "Double discounting: the effects of comparative negligence on mock juror decision making," *Law and Human Behavior*, 23 (1999), 577–96.
[60] James K. Hammitt, Stephen J. Carroll, and Daniel A. Relles, "Tort standards and jury decisions," *Journal of Legal Studies*, 14 (1985), 756.
[61] Robbennolt and Hans, *Psychology of Tort Law*, pp. 156–7.

and comparative negligence jurisdictions gives rise to double discounting, systematically disadvantaging plaintiffs.

The research summarized here, including David Engel's path-breaking article, public opinion surveys, interviews with trial lawyers, juror interviews, and experiments, all points to the substantial challenges that many plaintiffs confront. Plaintiffs who are injured face an uphill battle in establishing the credibility of their claims. They encounter difficulties as they attempt to convince lawyers to take their cases, insurance companies to offer compensation, and legal fact-finders to find in their favor and award appropriate damages. This raises an important question for both theory and practice: What might be done to counter the lure of the oven bird's song?

To explore strategies that might be employed to shift anti-plaintiff attitudes, I conducted a mock jury experiment of a civil trial over injuries arising from an automobile accident.[62] The car driven by the defendant, who was distracted by her children, rear-ended the plaintiff's car, injuring the plaintiff. The defendant's case did not vary between conditions. The defendant admitted liability, but nonetheless disputed the existence and severity of the plaintiff's injury through a defense expert, vigorous cross-examination of the plaintiff, and attorney arguments.

The experiment varied how the plaintiff's case and his injury were presented. In the control condition, the plaintiff's neck injury was described as whiplash, and the plaintiff and other witnesses, including an expert medical witness, gave traditional testimony documenting the nature and impact of the injury. The experimental condition incorporated a number of suggested trial tactics to shore up the credibility of the plaintiff and to convince fact-finders of the legitimacy of the plaintiff's injury. For example, instead of whiplash, the term "neck injury" was employed to refer to the plaintiff's injury. Additionally, the experimental condition included multiple efforts to improve the perceived credibility of the plaintiff. To address concerns about sue-happy plaintiffs, in the experimental video the plaintiff and other witnesses provided justification for bringing a lawsuit, describing it as a last resort. Anticipating low plaintiff credibility and minimization of the plaintiff's injury, the experimental version supplemented the traditional medical expert evidence about the

---

[62] Hans, "Faking it."

injury with lay witnesses who also confirmed the impact of the injury on the daily life of the plaintiff and his family.

The combined efforts worked. Mock jurors in the experimental condition were significantly more likely to see the plaintiff's case as stronger than the defense case than were mock jurors in the control condition, who saw the defendant's case as relatively stronger. The plaintiff and his attorney also got a boost in perceived credibility in the experimental condition. Most participants in the control condition did not see the whiplash as very serious at all. With the addition of neck injury terminology and pro-plaintiff arguments, participants in the experimental condition evaluated the plaintiff's neck injury as more serious.[63] Although multiple factors were varied in this experiment, meaning it is difficult to pinpoint which ones were most effective, the experiment suggests that carefully addressing plaintiff credibility and injury legitimacy can shift jurors' perceptions in a way that counteracts anti-plaintiff tendencies.

CONCLUSION

It has been decades since David Engel conducted his remarkable community interviews in Sander County. The interviews revealed what for many readers was a surprising hostility to tort plaintiffs who invoke the civil justice system to redress their wrongs. Political and legal debates have altered some features of the landscape of our civil justice system. However, much social science research, including research on jury decision-making, reinforces the deep insights into culture that David Engel discovered years ago. Jurors, too, hear the oven bird's song. Recognizing the allure of plaintiff-blaming, however, is a first step to counteracting it. Like David Engel's "The Oven Bird's Song," research that documents and illuminates a community's predispositions and concerns offers a path forward.

---

[63] Ibid.

8

Having a Right but Using It Too:
"The Oven Bird's Song" about Contracts

STEWART MACAULAY

The modern law and society movement began somewhere in the 1950s, and much of the early work tended to focus on the gap between the law in the books and the law in action. We often found that courts and legislatures had created lots of new rights for individuals, but the world had not changed drastically as a result. People often did not assert their rights. David Engel's "The Oven Bird's Song" pointed to American cultural assumptions about vindicating rights by going to court. People who became plaintiffs will not always be applauded by their friends and relatives. Engel's study was a real achievement; it made salient that law is only one of many systems of norms and sanctions.

The decision to assert legal rights is a mixture of the kinds of cultural assumptions that Engel stressed plus the risks of incurring all kinds of costs. Litigation is expensive, but defendants also can retaliate against plaintiffs and their family members. Moreover, one who would assert a claim may run the risk of not being believed and supported by a relevant community. More recent studies extend "The Oven Bird's Song." For example, Phoebe Morgan looked at the litigation choices of women who had been sexually harassed. Morgan found that "The decision to sue rested upon assessments of their abilities to do so while also being good mothers, wives, and daughters. If the filing of the suit threatened the well-being of family members or to strain family ties, then potential plaintiffs were reluctant to embrace such a choice."[1]

K. T. Albiston looked at decisions to assert rights under the family medical leave laws. She found that one who takes time from work to care for a member

---

[1] Phoebe A. Morgan, "Risking relationships: understanding the litigation choices of sexually harassed women," *Law & Society Review*, 33 (1999), 67, 75.

of the family may fear he or she will be viewed as not taking the job seriously. The 'good employee' puts the job first.[2]

"The Oven Bird's Song" reports that in the county that Engel studied, potential tort plaintiffs were reluctant to assert claims. Contract claims, however, were different. Engel tells us:

> In ... interpersonal exchanges involving people well known to one another there was, it appears, some flexibility and allowance for hard times and other contingencies ... On the other hand, there was a mutual recognition that debts must ultimately be paid ... Contract litigation ... was seen as enforcing a core value of the traditional culture of Sander County: that promises should be kept and people should be held responsible when they broke their word.[3]

Undoubtedly, the cultural norm that one must perform one's promises is a strong one in American society. However, I want to offer a long footnote to Engel's study that qualifies the "a deal is a deal" norm. As so often is true, there are inconsistent norms in our culture. I recognize that my point might be reduced to little more than "context matters," but a contracts teacher cannot forget this normative conflict.

Professor David Campbell is, among other things, one of the leading writers about relational contracts. I summarized his conclusions about counter-norms to those that seem to insist on performance at all costs.[4] I reported that Campbell tells us:

> There may be an implicit norm in at least some long-term continuing relationships calling for buyers to help sellers who run into trouble trying to perform. Campbell points out that errors in forecasting the future cannot be eliminated. Some contracts inevitably will impose on a party unanticipated costs that are beyond its ability to absorb. Buyers always take the risk of their suppliers going into bankruptcy or another kind of creditors' proceeding. They also take some small risk of their supplier being excused by the doctrines of mistake or frustration. The law of contract remedies limits damages for breach, and, as a result, it allows the threat of breach to induce adjustments. The law of remedies serves to keep contract as a

---

[2] Catherine R. Albiston, "Bargaining in the shadow of social institutions: competing discourses and social change in workplace mobilization of civil rights," *Law & Society Review*, 39 (2005), 11, 30–40.

[3] David M. Engel, "The oven bird's song: insiders, outsiders, and personal injuries in an American community," *Law & Society Review*, 18 (1984), 551, 576–7.

[4] Stewart Macaulay, "Renegotiations and settlements: Dr. Pangloss's notes on the margin of David Campbell's papers," *Cardozo Law Review*, 29 (2007), 261.

useful institution, and not one that imposes such great risks so that only fools would make contracts.[5]

In my comment, I accepted most of Campbell's argument. However, I added other factors in contract law as delivered that push parties to renegotiate and to settle potential contracts causes of action. There is always the risk of losing a lawsuit. Often it is hard for a party considering litigation for breach of contract to judge the likelihood of winning a judgment. Much of the contract law that deals with performance is very qualitative. Ideas such as giving remedies only for a "material breach," offering in some situations an opportunity for a defaulting supplier to "cure" its defective performance, and providing for excuses upon the happening of a contingency the non-occurrence of which was a basic assumption of the contract, create relative certainty only in extreme situations. More typically, these kinds of qualitative standards provide both sides with at least somewhat plausible arguments. Moreover, if the plaintiff can jump the barrier of motions for summary judgment that often delay the process, the plaintiff will assert arguments before a jury which may or may not apply the law as written.

The law in action adds disincentives to assert rights in court. Litigation is slow and costly. Furthermore, litigation is public, and the buyer, the seller, or both may not want others to know their secrets. Finally, it is hard to sue a contract partner and keep the relationship alive.

I argued that in many situations, contract law as delivered served to push suppliers to work hard to perform, but also to push buyers to accept something less than promised performance in order to reach the least bad solution available. Messy and uncertain law and procedures might serve real purposes in at least some situations.

This pressure on buyers to accept something less than what the seller promised may be matched by a contract term or a social norm that allows buyers to cancel some or all of what they ordered. Cancellation-for-convenience clauses are very common in contract documents put forward by buyers. Moreover, in at least some industries, sellers accept that buyers have such a right as a matter of ill-defined custom.[6]

---

[5] Ibid, 264.

[6] A lawyer with many large industrial clients said: Often business people do not feel they have "a contract" – rather they have "an order."

> They speak of "canceling the order" rather than "breaching our contract." When I began practice I referred to order cancellations as breaches of contract, but my clients objected since they do not think of cancellation as wrong. Most clients, in heavy industry at least, believe that there is a right to cancel as part of the buyer-seller relationship.

Almost always, social norms and customs are uncertain and offset by other practices. There may be a right to cancel orders for convenience, but buyers cannot go too far. The story of US Airways' order of 737 and 757 jet planes from Boeing offers an example.[7] In the early 1980s, US Airways (US Air) ordered many of these planes from Boeing, but the written contract documents did not include a cancellation-for-convenience clause. From the late 1980s to the mid-1990s, US Air was in great financial difficulty and faced the threat of bankruptcy. Several times during this period Boeing agreed to postpone delivery and payment dates for the aircraft. The final deal was that the planes were to be built and delivered between 1998 and 2003.

In November of 1996, a new management team at US Air selected Airbus, Boeing's major competitor, as the supplier of a large number of Airbus A320 planes to replace a substantial part of US Air's fleet. US Air told Boeing to tear up the original contracts for the 737 and 757 planes. When US Air failed to make a scheduled payment, Boeing sued for $450 million. US Air argued that Boeing's failure to accept cancellation of the order violated a long pattern in the aircraft industry. Moreover, it pointed to Boeing's many concessions over the years since the orders had been placed as indicating a waiver of the obligation to buy. The parties finally settled the case: US Air paid Boeing an undisclosed sum of money, but as part of the settlement, US Air acknowledged that it was bound to a contract with Boeing. Of course, this settlement could have affected US Air's future willingness to once again buy planes from Boeing. However, US Air is now a part of American Airlines, and I doubt whether the current management of American would be influenced by this past history.

Boeing figures in a more recent example of practices in the aircraft industry related to performing contracts. Since the 1980s, many large organizations have sought to create elaborate relationships with those firms that supply goods and services to them. Sellers must seek supplier status. This involves opening the seller firm to the buyer's officials so that the buyer's people can evaluate potential suppliers. To a great extent, the process involves tearing down the

There is a widespread attitude that one can back out of any deal within some very vague limits. Lawyers are often surprised by this attitude.

See Stewart Macaulay, "Non-contractual relations in business: a preliminary study," *American Sociological Review*, 28 (1963), 55.

7   See Stewart Macaulay, "Relational contracts floating on a sea of custom? thoughts about the ideas of Ian Macneil and Lisa Bernstein," *Northwestern University Law Review*, 94 (2000), 775, 792–3. "It was one thing to roll over delivery and payments dates in the face of US Air's grave financial problems. It was something else to tear up the contract entirely so that US Air could turn to a competitor to supply its needs for the foreseeable future": at 793.

formal boundaries of the buyer and its suppliers. Ideally, the engineers of all concerned work together to produce quality products more cheaply and to innovate in many ways. These steps attempt to create mutually beneficial long-term continuing relations which have their own norms and sanctions beyond those established by contract law. Under the master supply agreements, ideally the parties avoid breaches of contract, lawyers, and litigation. Instead, they just fix the problems.

Boeing fashioned a daring plan that could not be carried out.[8] It designed the "787 Dreamliner." Instead of aluminum, the plane was to be built from carbon fiber. In addition, it had highly efficient engines. The 787 was supposed to be 20 percent cheaper to fly and a third less costly to maintain. Boeing created an elaborate outsourcing process for building the plane. Suppliers from around the world would build the various parts of the plane, such as the wings, the tail, the main cabin, and suchlike, and then ship them to Boeing's plant in Washington. Boeing would assemble everything to produce completed 787 aircraft. The original goal was to put everything together in only three days.

The plan collapsed – it was a disaster. Many of the suppliers were not able to work with carbon fiber technology. The various components often failed to fit into the parts made by other suppliers. Some parts arrived at Boeing's factory only partially completed. Ultimately, Boeing was three years late in delivering the first 787 to the Japanese airline ANA. This delay cost Boeing a great deal of money.[9]

How did Boeing cope with all of these defaults by its suppliers? The law of contract and litigation before the public courts had little to do with Boeing's response. Essentially, whatever the law might have said, Boeing pushed its suppliers into becoming part of the Boeing organization. Boeing sent out teams of engineers to take over production of the various components.[10] One newspaper said that Boeing was "parachuting in dozens or

---

[8]   See, e.g., J. Lynn Lunsford, "Jet blues: Boeing scrambles to repair problems with new plane – layers of outsourcing slow 787 production; hostage to suppliers," *Wall Street Journal*, Dec. 7, 2007, A1; J. Lynn Lunsford, "Boeing delays Dreamliner delivery again – six more months needed despite making progress on jet 'start-up issues,'" *Wall Street Journal*, April 10, 2008, B3; David Kesmodel, "Boeing examines supply chain for weak links – as it prepares to boost output, jet maker intensifies reviews of vendors to make sure they can keep up," *Wall Street Journal*, Dec. 30, 2011, B3.

[9]   James Fontanella-Kahn and Andrew Parker, "India says Boeing to pay $500m for delays to 787," *Financial Times*, Mar. 15, 2012, 14; David Kesmodel and Anirban Chowdhury, "India clashes with Boeing – compensation for delayed delivery of new Dreamliner aircraft sparks discord, *Wall Street Journal*, Mar. 15, 2012, B2.

[10]   Lunsford, "Jet blues."

hundreds of its own employees to attack problems at plants in Italy, Japan and South Carolina."[11] Boeing bought two of the large supplier's plants and turned their facilities into Boeing factories. Finally, parts started flowing to Washington, and Boeing was able to start deliveries of these planes to airlines that had ordered them.

What about Boeing's legal rights? As far as I know, it did not seek to recover its lost anticipated profits from any of the suppliers. Another right which the law gives an aggrieved buyer is the power to walk away and not deal with the defaulting party in the future. Mike Blair had been the Boeing executive in charge of the 787 program, but he was reassigned because of all of the problems involved in carrying out the original plan. Blair gave a speech about what had happened in developing the 787. He suggested that some suppliers had stumbled so badly that "some of these guys we won't use again"[12] on future programs.

Many Boeing officials, and many suppliers, did not like this speech. Boeing had agreements with most suppliers that extended, potentially, over the thirty-year-plus projected life of the 787 program. After the Boeing engineers had parachuted in and straightened out matters, it would have made sense for them to continue to work together in the future.[13]

We can view Boeing's power under these contracts to impose its engineers on its suppliers as a kind of self-help specific performance. If Boeing had a typical breach of contract cause of action against a supplier, courts would award it the damages that it could prove with reasonable certainty limited by ideas of the supplier's assumption of the risks of such losses. Of course, such a right always would be subject to defenses that would arise if the award pushed the supplier into bankruptcy. In a few instances, courts might award Boeing a decree of specific performance, ordering the defaulting supplier to perform the contract. However, courts seldom will make such an award if it would require the court to supervise a complex performance over time. Moreover, in some of the Boeing 787 contracts the problem was that the supplier was not able to perform because it did not know how to do what it had promised. The master supply agreements between Boeing and its suppliers allowed Boeing to send in its engineers and take over production of the needed part of the new airplane. Boeing could push the supplier into performing rather than going to court seeking a judgment.

---

[11] Ibid.   [12] Ibid.

[13] But see David Kesmodel, Boeing examines supply chain for weak links – as it prepares to boost output, jet maker intensifies reviews of vendors to make sure they can keep up," *Wall Street Journal*, December 30, 2011, B3.

We can view this arrangement as consistent with the norms Engel reported in his "Oven Bird's Song." Courts and litigation are avoided, and a form of cooperation creates the conditions necessary to get the contract performed. In this way, the "a deal is a deal" norm is carried out. At the same time, however, Boeing aided its supplier to help it carry out the bargain.

What is the cultural norm involved here? In a sense, the deal had to be carried out and performed. However, no one could paste pages back into the calendar: At the end of the process, Boeing got the various pieces of each 787 that were needed, but it could not make timely delivery of completed planes to the airlines that had bought them. Of course, Boeing offered its defaulting suppliers far more help than most creditors give their debtors who are in trouble. It did not get the performance originally promised, but perhaps it should have known that a new, complex technology was very likely to pose major problems.[14]

As I said at the outset of this chapter, I have taken us far away from Sander County where the oven bird flew. But in the context of major corporations, we have found elements of the norm calling for deals to be performed and the qualifying norm that demands that one party to a relational contract help its partner cope with difficulties in doing what was promised.

At the very least, "The Oven Bird's Song" alerts us to norms affecting when we can use legal rights. When the citizens of Sander County could not make the payments on a car that they had purchased, the creditor that had financed the deal was likely to repossess the vehicle and perhaps seek a default judgment. But in other contexts, suits for breach of contract may be seen as inappropriate or as warranted only as a last resort after great efforts to find acceptable ways to share losses. Engel reports that there was "some flexibility and allowance for hard times and other contingencies."[15] However, he emphasizes "deeply felt values" that insist that "debts must ultimately be paid."

Lawrence Friedman tells us: "No legal intervention takes place in a vacuum. It lands in a crowded, pre-existing social space; and the reaction is tempered and determined by what that space is like."[16] Long ago, I was a law student at Stanford, when the Supreme Court of the United States decided *Brown v. Board of Education*. My classmates and I, and even some members of the faculty, talked as if the problems of race in this country were over.

---

[14] Compare Josh Whitford, *The New Old Economy: Networks, Institutions, and the Organizational Transformation of American Manufacturing* (Oxford University Press, 2005).

[15] Engel, "The oven bird's song," 576.

[16] Lawrence M. Friedman, *Impact: How Law Affects Behavior* (Harvard University Press, 2016), p. 56.

Undoubtedly, *Brown* has affected life in this country. Nonetheless, the crowded, pre-existing social space had its influence too. Having read "The Oven Bird's Song," we could not and should not forget that rights do not enforce themselves. People must act, and action likely has real costs. For example, a legal victory often damages or destroys long-term continuing relations. The winner cannot count on future cooperation from the loser. Those who do not like a legal victory often are able to evade much of its impact. Still, law matters. But it is part of a complex process that can only be described as messy.

PART III

Insiders, Outsiders, Class Conflict, and Difference

9

Indigenous Litigiousness

The Oven Bird's Song and the Miner's Canary

EVE DARIAN-SMITH

The oven bird's song, as captured in Robert Frost's evocative poem, speaks to the marking of time and the inevitable changes wrought by the passing of the seasons. The bird's clear sweet song reminds us that youth and adulthood is followed by old age and death, and that the world cannot remain the same. David Engel refers to the song in the title of his essay to evoke the ways in which the people of Sander County voiced opposition to personal injury litigation.[1] Their collective concerns are interpreted – as is the oven bird's song – as a lament; a lament to the lessening in their minds of a traditional way of living and being.

In this chapter I turn to another bird: the "miner's canary," which refers to canaries being used by coal miners in Britain as an early warning system and an essential element in keeping miners safe from harm. The bird was taken in a cage with the men down to the bottom of the shaft. When the delicate bird showed signs of distress it meant that fresh air had turned sour and the miners needed to quickly get out of the deep underground tunnels, or succumb to carbon monoxide poisoning.[2] I like to think of the oven bird and the miner's canary singing to each other across time and space in ways that both resonate and contradict. Their commonality lies in the sense that both evoke the marking of time, transition, and change, as well as impending threat.[3]

---

[1] David M. Engel, "David Engel and the oven bird's song" in Simon Halliday and Patrick Schmidt (eds.), *Conducting Law and Society Research: Reflections on Methods and Practices* (Cambridge University Press, 2009), pp. 83–93.

[2] In Britain, canaries were used extensively throughout the nineteenth and twentieth centuries. They were finally phased out in 1986 and replaced with new monitoring technologies for carbon monoxide, which is odorless, colorless, and hard for humans to detect.
http://news.bbc.co.uk/onthisday/hi/dates/stories/december/30/newsid_2547000/2547587.stm.

[3] Why birds are used as vehicles of social commentary is an interesting question. Perhaps it is because birds, particularly small birds, often go unnoticed and are part of the unseen

From spring to winter, from fresh to poisonous air, the birds symbolize shifting conditions, nostalgia, melancholy, and ultimately a deep sense of loss.

In David Engel's chapter, personal injury litigation becomes the legal front through which Sander County locals voiced their dismay at the increasing encroachment by industry and "foreigners" into their established set of social, political, and economic relations.[4] Opposition to personal injury lawsuits became the official mechanism through which to sort the "insiders" who belonged and shared the town's cultural values (including notions of injury) from "outsiders" who didn't understand how the system worked. As Engel compellingly argued, opposition to personal injury lawsuits operated to galvanize thinly veiled articulations of social anxiety and racialized fear that informed the local blaming of outsiders for the inevitable altering of the rural small-town community.

In this chapter I explore both similarities and differences between the ways in which "outsiders" brought personal injury lawsuits in Sander County and lawsuits in Santa Barbara County (in the latter case a Native American tribe). However, whereas Engel was interested in the category of litigation (personal injury, contract) and the differences this made to people's understanding of the legal system's appropriateness to address grievances, I am interested in the very fact that Native Americans – in this case the Santa Ynez Band of Chumash Indians – are bringing lawsuits at all. So it is not the type of legal action that is of central importance in my narrative, but rather that more and more Indians are using the formal legal system to resolve a variety of historical and contemporary disputes and grievances.

In the following, I discuss Indian gaming, which informs the background to the lawsuits being brought by the Santa Ynez Band of Chumash Indians, and describe more fully the reference to the miner's canary. I then explore the similarities and differences between the "outsider" politics of Sander County and the "outsider" politics of Santa Barbara County as each is refracted through people's use of formal and informal legal processes. The similarities and differences of these two case studies – separated by approximately forty years – provide a way to think about comparable forms of legal consciousness

---

landscape. At the same time, their capacity to watch us go about our business is immense, precisely because we generally ignore them. They sit on the tree branch outside our living room, watching, chirping, waiting, and ultimately moving on with little notice from most of us. Their taken-for-granted presence and assumed innocence is exactly what Alfred Hitchcock played to in his film *The Birds* (1963), which released frenzied swooping, murdering flocks onto the heads of schoolchildren.

4 David M. Engel, "The oven bird's song: insiders, outsiders, and personal injuries in an American community," *Law & Society Review*, 18(4) (1984), 551–82.

as well as emerging legal subjectivities in contexts of rapid change and the diminishing of a romanticized American past that never existed.

INDIAN GAMING

Native Americans accessing the formal legal system is a relatively new phenomenon, brought about almost entirely by the introduction of the Indian Gaming Regulatory Act (IGRA) in 1988. At the time the act was passed, a few tribes had casinos on their reservations. The Seminole Tribe of Florida was the first to open a high-stakes bingo parlor in 1981, and other tribes quickly followed suit. While the Seminole casino operation was enormously successful,[5] most Indian operations were far less so because of reservations' isolation from urban communities and a sustainable clientele. Moreover, each state had specific laws relating to Indian gaming within its state borders.[6] These state laws were aggressively defended against the Bureau of Indian Affairs (BIA), which, as a federal agency, has historically governed all matters pertaining to Native Americans. Many states challenged the federal oversight of Indian gaming because they wanted to either block Indians establishing high-stakes gaming (which competed with state lotteries and horse-racing) or illegally demand revenue-sharing from tribes when their casinos were successful.[7]

IGRA was introduced in response to the confusion about federal and state jurisdictional control over reservation casinos. IGRA's goals were to regulate Indian gaming operations and to provide tribes some federal protection from state governments. IGRA was also introduced to try and encourage economic growth and financial independence for Indian communities on reservations, many of whom were living in abject poverty. As stated in the case *Rincon Band v. Schwarzenegger* (2010), "Congress enacted IGRA to provide a legal framework within which tribes could engage in gaming – an enterprise that holds out the hope of providing tribes with the economic prosperity that has so

---

[5] Jessica Cattelino, *High Stakes: Florida Seminole Gaming and Sovereignty* (Duke University Press, 2008).

[6] Kathryn R. L. Rand and Steven Andrew Light, *Indian Gaming Law and Policy*, 2nd ed (Carolina Academic Press, 2014).

[7] The Cabazon Band of Mission Indians sued the state of California, claiming it had no right to shut down its gambling operations and seize cash and goods held by the tribe. In 1986, in *California v. Cabazon Band*, the Supreme Court held that Indian reservations are governed exclusively by Congress and the federal government and upheld the principle of tribal sovereignty against state encroachments on native lands. See Ralph A. Rossum, *The Supreme Court and Tribal Gaming: California v Cabazon Band of Mission Indians* (University Press of Kansas, 2011).

long eluded their grasp – while settling boundaries to restrain the aggression by powerful states."[8] To facilitate federal oversight of Indian gaming, the National Indian Gaming Commission (NIGC) was also established by Congress in 1988. Over the years it has become a powerful presence in Washington DC, providing a national platform to represent and lobby for a wide diversity of issues and concerns raised by tribes with gaming operations across the entire United States.[9]

There are 566 federally recognized tribes in the United States, of which 486 tribes are involved in some form of gaming on their reservations. However, not all of these involve high-stakes gaming and many of these casino operations are not financially successful. The 2008 economic recession has taken a toll, and in certain areas the proliferation of casinos has saturated the market. That being said, in 2013 gross gaming revenues reached $28.5 billion. Much of this revenue has been diversified into a range of businesses, resorts, health clinics, educational facilities, housing, infrastructure, and the building of cultural centers and museums. Many tribes "realize that the success of gaming is not an end in itself. Rather, it is a bridge to help regain what was once ours long ago – true self-respect, self-determination and economic self-sufficiency."[10] NIGC's Former Associate Commissioner Daniel notes that "Indian gaming is an American success story for addressing the social and economic needs of Indian country."[11]

One success story has been unfolding over the past two decades in Santa Barbara County with respect to the Santa Ynez Band of Chumash Indians. While other bands of Chumash exist in Southern California, together numbering around 5,000 people, only the Santa Ynez band received federal recognition in 1901 and were granted a small reservation landholding close to the Santa Ynez Mission for their population of less than 200 members. At that time, the Chumash had experienced centuries of colonial oppression by the Spanish, Mexican, and then Californian governments, and their populations had been decimated in the process.[12] The social and economic marginalization of the tribe continued throughout the twentieth century,

8   *Rincon Band* v. *Schwarzenegger* (2010) at pp. 5887–8, http://cdn.ca9.uscourts.gov/datastore/opinions/2010/04/20/08-55809.pdf.
9   Indian gaming has a very rich history and a large body of literature has developed around the issue which is beyond the scope of this chapter. See Eve Darian-Smith, *New Capitalists: Law, Politics and Identity Surrounding Casino Gaming on Native American Land* (Wadsworth, 2004); Cattelino, *High Stakes*; Paul H. Gelles, *Chumash Renaissance: Indian Casinos, Education, and Cultural Politics in Rural California*. CreateSpace Independent Publishing Platform, 2013).
10 www.santaynezchumash.org/gaming_history.html.
11 www.nigc.gov/images/uploads/Fact%20Sheet%20August%202015.pdf.
12 See Gelles, *Chumash Resistance*; Darian-Smith, *New Capitalists*.

and it was not until the 1960s that the reservation had running water; electricity came many years later.

Faced with extreme economic disadvantage, in 1994 the Santa Ynez Band of Chumash Indians opened up a modest bingo parlor. Encouraged by other tribes entering the casino business, the Chumash began planning for a more fancy and lucrative full-scale casino and resort. In 2003 the tribe opened up a 190,000-square-foot gaming facility; a year later a 106-room luxury hotel. The tribe's current plan is to place into federal trust lands it purchased in 2010 adjacent to its reservation. The primary purpose for the purchase was to build homes for tribal members, since only 17 percent of the tribal members can currently be accommodated on their reservation lands. According to the tribe's website, the effort to provide new housing is regarded as a creating "a meaningful opportunity for tribal members and their families to be part of a tribal community revitalization effort that rebuilds tribal culture, customs and traditions."[13]

Casino operations on reservations represent the most important challenge to the enduring legal discrimination against Indian peoples by both federal and state governments. In a sense, the future of Indian legal sovereignty, which determines the extent to which a tribe is allowed to control what goes on within its bounded territory, is being shaped by the gaming industry. And nowhere is this more evident than in the state of California, where more Native Americans live than in any other state in the country.[14] In a very real sense, what unfolds in California points to the future of Native Americans and their legal sovereignty across the whole of the United States. This future is not clear – many Native Americans are anxious that the good times won't last, given a general decline in the economy coupled with a glut of gambling venues. These contemporary economic worries are compounded by native people's memories of centuries of racism and discrimination. "Owing to the historic distrust between Native Americans and the people who displaced them, there's a sense they must be alert to the prospect that their 'rights' to open casinos could be snatched back or curtailed."[15]

California (and more generally the American West) also performs a highly symbolic role in the popular US imagination. Philip Burnham, a scholar and

---

[13] www.chumashfacts.com/. Also see Gelles, *Chumash Resistance*.

[14] California's relatively large native population is the direct result of the prevailing ideology of manifest destiny in the nineteenth century, which justified the deliberate dismantling of tribes and their members driven westward across the American continent throughout the nineteenth century. See Dee Brown, *Bury My Heart at Wounded Knee: An Indian History of the American West* (with foreword by Hampton Sides) (Picador, 2007); Theda Perdue and Michael Green, *The Cherokee Nation and the Trail of Tears*, reprinted edition (Penguin, 2008).

[15] Steve Friess , "Indian tribes look beyond casinos for income," *New York Times*, October 23, 2015.

journalist who has lived and taught for several years on the Rosebud Sioux Reservation in South Dakota, sums up the significance of the West in thinking about the future of Native Americans:

> Since the creation of the reservations in the mid-nineteenth century, the West is where the vast majority of Indian trust land resides. Land is seminal to our understanding of Indian history, and in recognition of the claims that remain to be settled in US courts, of the future of Indian Country as well ... The native has literally "returned."[16]

This sense of native peoples "returning" to take a rightful place in the cultural, political, and economic institutions of their historical oppressors is a theme picked up by James Clifford in the opening passage of his 2013 book *Returns: Becoming Indigenous in the Twenty-First Century*. Clifford writes: "Indigenous people have emerged from history's blind spot. No longer pathetic victims or noble messengers from lost worlds, they are visible actors in local, national, and global arenas."[17]

Building on this theme, the overarching question in this chapter is: How is mainstream American society responding to the use of formal law by "outsiders" to redress wrongs and fight enduring discrimination? Specifically, how is the sense of Native Americans returning to take a place at the table of national politics heightening non-Indian cultural and social anxieties and forging new forms of contestation? In the context of Santa Barbara County, I am interested in thinking about the backlash against the Santa Ynez Band of Chumash Indians, who are often derogatively labeled "rich Indians" and who have been engaged in years of lawsuits and litigation with local activist groups. What does this backlash, as articulated by an upsurge in litigiousness involving native peoples, suggest more generally about the future of American society and its fraught postcolonial relations with its Indian populations?

THE MINER'S CANARY

The phrase "miner's canary" is relatively common in referring to a person or thing serving as an early warning of a coming crisis.[18] In the United States it is

---

[16] Philip Burnham, "The return of the native: the politics of identity in American Indian fiction of the West" in Michael Kowalewski (ed.), *Reading the West: New Essays on the Literature of the American West* (Cambridge University Press, 1996), pp. 199–212, see pp. 202–3.

[17] James Clifford, *Returns: Becoming Indigenous in the Twenty-First Century* (Harvard University Press, 2013), p. 13.

[18] See, e.g., Lani Guinier and Gerald Torres, *The Miner's Canary* (Harvard University Press, 2002).

most famously linked to Felix S. Cohen, who used the phrase in 1949 with reference to American Indians.[19] In a passage that reads with as much relevance today as it did more than sixty years ago, Cohen wrote:

> It is a pity that so many Americans today think of the Indian as a romantic or comic figure in American history without contemporary significance. In fact, the Indian plays much the same role in our society that the Jews played in Germany. Like the miner's canary, the Indian marks the shift from fresh air to poison gas in our political atmosphere; and our treatment of Indians, even more than our treatment of other minorities, reflects the rise and fall of our democratic faith.[20]

Felix Cohen is a fascinating and inspirational figure on many fronts, and is widely known for his early foray into what we would recognize today as sociolegal scholarship. Before joining the Department of the Interior under Franklin Roosevelt's New Deal, Cohen was considered a leading force in the Legal Realism movement.[21] He railed against a science of law that did not ground analysis in criticism or context, writing in a much cited article in the *Columbia Law Review* that even "the most intelligent judges in America can deal with a concrete practical problem of procedural law and corporate responsibility without any appreciation of the economic, social, and ethical issues which it involves."[22] Building upon his belief that law must be

---

[19] There are apparently nearly 50,000 references on the internet to Cohen's use of the term "miner's canary". For a fascinating discussion of this phrase, see "Getting a bead on Felix Cohen's miner's canary," *Indian Country Today Media Network.com*, June 9, 2006, https://indiancountrymedianetwork.com/news/getting-a-bead-on-felix-cohens-miners-canary/.

[20] Cohen concluded with the following: "If we fight for civil liberties for our side, we show that we believe not in civil liberties but in our side. But when those of us who never were Indians and never expect to be Indians fight for the cause of Indian self-government, we are fighting for something that is not limited by the accidents of race and creed and birth; we are fighting for what Las Casas and Vitorio and Pope Paul III called the integrity or salvation of our own souls." Felix S. Cohen, "Indian self-government," *The American Indian*, 5(2) (1949); see reprint in *The Legal Conscience: Selected Papers of Felix S. Cohen*, ed. Lucy Kramer Cohen S. (Yale University Press, 1960), pp. 305–14.

[21] On legal realism see Thom Brooks, "David Ingersoll, behavioralism and the modern revival of legal realism" *Beijing Law Review*, 6(3) (2015), 190–2, and for discussions of the New Legal Realism movement see Howard Erlanger et al., "Is it time for a new legal realism?" *Wisconsin Law Review*, 2005(2) (2005), 335–63; Stewart Macaulay, "The new versus the old legal realism: 'things ain't what they used to be'," *Wisconsin Law Review*, 2005(2) (2005), 365–403; and Mark Suchman and Elizabeth Mertz, "Toward a new legal empiricism: empirical legal studies and new legal realism," *Annual Review of Law and Social Science*, 6(1) (2010), 555–79.

[22] Felix Cohen, "Transcendental nonsense and the functional approach," *Columbia Law Review*, 35(6) (1935), 809–49 at 812.

understood in its wider social contexts, Cohen turned to the issue of Native Americans and is widely considered to have established Indian law in his path-breaking 1941 work *The Handbook of Federal Indian Law*. Throughout his later career he was a vocal champion of Indian land rights and sovereignty in the face of the Bureau of Indian Affairs' efforts to undermine tribal self-government. Despite his great efforts, the BIA eventually pushed into law the Indian Termination Act (1953), which resulted in the widespread disbandment and dispossession of many Indian tribes across the country.

Cohen's insistence that prevailing attitudes toward Native Americans are emblematic of more general attitudes about cultural and racial difference in American society is as pertinent now as it was back in the 1940s and 1950s.[23] The treatment of Native Americans in law and governmental policy over many decades can be used to historically chart the ebbs and flows of racism, intolerance, and capitalist greed that have periodically washed across the political and cultural landscape of American society. Of course, racism, intolerance, and greed have always been intertwined forces sustaining the United States' belief in manifest destiny and its own inherent exceptionalism. But I am interested in the conditions of its periodic upswing – how and why people change their attitudes over time from less tolerant to more tolerant, and back again.

Despite the development of tribal gaming that has enriched a number of tribes, Native Americans remain the most socioeconomically marginalized of all ethnic groups in the United States. Historically, they have been disproportionately vulnerable to the shifting tempo of mainstream racism and xenophobia. As a collective people, they have been subject to swings back and forth in social attitudes toward them as reflected in federal governmental policies: The Indian Removal Act (1830) systematically forced native populations off their lands in the hope of breaking up their way of life and eradicating the

---

[23] Interestingly, some native communities have embraced the idea of being thought of as a miner's canary. In January 2016, a coalition of activist organizations including the Indigenous World Alliance marched on Washington DC to promote the "Clean Up the Mines!" campaign, which focuses attention on the exposure of communities to nuclear radiation resulting from an estimated 15,000 abandoned uranium mines across the United States. "Native American nations of North America are the miners' canaries for the United States trying to awaken the people of the world to the dangers of radioactive pollution," said Charmaine White Face from the South Dakota-based organization Defenders of the Black Hills: see Klee Benally, "We are the miner's canary: indigenous organizations call for clean up of "homegrown" radioactive pollution crisis," www.cleanupthemines.org/press-release-we-are-the-miners-canary-indigenous-organizations-call-for-clean-up-of-homegrown-radioactive-pollution-crisis/.

"Indian problem"; the General Allotment (Severalty) Act (1874) sought Indian assimilation by splitting up reservations into individual allotments in order to undermine tribal communities and take their lands; the Indian Reorganization Act (1934) sought to restore to Indians the management of their lands and culture; the Indian Termination Act (1953) again sought to aggressively assimilate natives into the white population; the Indian Civil Rights Act (1968) recognized that the polices of Indian termination were a failure; the Self-Determination and Education Act (1975) granted tribes the right to contract with the BIA directly and manage their own health and education services; and the Indian Gaming Regulatory Act (1988), as discussed earlier, was designed to protect tribes from predatory state governments and encourage tribal economic development.

Across the centuries of federal Indian policies, one can read different sets of mainstream attitudes toward native peoples. However, common to what seem at times contradictory attitudes is that native peoples are consistently treated by the dominant white society as social and cultural "outsiders." This treatment ranges from Anglo/Americans originally seeing them as a threat to be exterminated during the Indian Wars, to being seen as a hopeless waste of federal funds, to being seen as obstacles to land grabs and exploitation of natural resources, to being seen as culturally resilient and deserving of government support, to being seen in the 1980s as non-threatening but ultimately useless, wretched, and pitiful. Against this turbulent backdrop, how are Native Americans viewed today, and what does that say about our current dominant society? Are they still considered outsiders by mainstream America, and if so what are the current conditions of their alienation? To what degree do Native Americans function as the miner's canary and point to more generalizable attitudes with respect to a spectrum of cultural, ethnic, and religious minorities?

Taking one step back and putting the US national framework within a global context, to what degree are attitudes toward Native Americans as the nation's internal "outsiders" informed by the increasing hysteria raised by trans-border threats of external "outsiders"? To ask this differently: In what ways may domestic indigenous politics relate to immigration politics and escalating fears of "illegals" and brown-skinned others who will forever change idealized notions of a traditional, white, and culturally monolithic American society?[24] These are the questions that capture my imagination as we move forward into the middle decades of the twenty-first century.

---

[24] Jamie Longazel, *Undocumented Fears: Immigration and the Politics of Divide and Conquer in Hazelton, Pennsylvania* (Temple University Press, 2016).

SIMILARITIES AND DIFFERENCES – OUTSIDERS IN SANDER
AND SANTA BARBARA COUNTIES

The first similarity between Sander County as described by David Engel in "The Oven Bird's Song" and Santa Barbara County is a sense of a changing demographic within the established rural community. Sander County's widespread opposition to personal injury claims was in part related to the new industries that moved into the region in the 1970s and altered the small farming practices of the region. The new industries were accompanied by union members, southerners, blacks, and Latinos, bringing "to Sander County a social and cultural heterogeneity that it had not known before."[25] These new faces were considered "alien elements" by the long-term residents.

In contrast to the arrival into Sander County of new ethnic and racial groups, in Santa Barbara County Native Americans did not arrive from somewhere else. Hence they are not "outsiders" in a literal sense but rather social and cultural outsiders, and have recently been able to revitalize their local presence. The Chumash Indians have a very long history with the region, and once numbered in the tens of thousands before being wiped out by disease and encroachments on their lands by Spanish Catholic missionaries and military.[26] The Santa Ynez Band of Chumash Indians was federally recognized in 1901 and granted a small reservation in Santa Barbara County, some forty miles inland from the coastal city of Santa Barbara. As narrated on the Santa Ynez Band of Chumash Indians website:

> For many years, few tribal members lived on the Reservation. It was difficult to live a modern existence on the Reservation without running water or electricity. We began a housing program in 1979 and more tribal members moved on to the Reservation – both lower and upper Reservation ... Thanks to the revenue generated from the tribe's Chumash Casino Resort, our tribal members are on the path to economic self-sufficiency. Some continue to live on the Reservation and others live in homes in surrounding towns. Today there are 249 residents on the Santa Ynez Reservation and 97 homes.

---

[25] Engel, "The oven bird's song," 574, n. 4.

[26] In 1769 a Spanish land expedition, led by Gaspar de Portola, left Baja California and reached the Santa Barbara Channel. In short order, five Spanish missions were established in Chumash territory. The Chumash population was eventually decimated, due largely to the introduction of European diseases. By 1831, the number of mission-registered Chumash numbered only 2,788, down from pre-Spanish population estimates of 22,000. http://santaynezchumash.org/history.html.

The second similarity between Sander County and Santa Barbara County is the phrases used by the local rural community to describe "outsiders." In Sander County, according to David Engel, long-term residents referred to the newcomers, and specifically those that brought personal injury claims, as "very greedy," "deviant," "troublemakers," "looking for the easy buck." The overwhelming feeling was that litigants were people eager to "cash in" without doing the long hours of hard work that everyone else was obliged to undertake to make ends meet. In other words, the outsiders were considered to be not morally worthy of receiving financial compensation.

In Santa Barbara County, the accusations flung by non-Indian residents at the Chumash Indians are surprisingly similar to those heard decades earlier in Sander County. The Chumash are described at various times as "lawless," "unsophisticated," "shifty," "greedy," and as trying to take advantage of a system that supposedly grants them "special rights."[27] There is a general consensus that native peoples are in a profound sense not worthy of making lots of money because they don't work for it, and that if they do become wealthy they will somehow cease to be authentic Indians. As noted in an interview with Gail Marshall, 3rd District Santa Barbara County Supervisor:

> [T]hey have, you know, taken up a really beautiful legacy of basketry and tommel building, and really interesting lifestyles and sort of erased it with one fell swoop. I'm not sure how it's going to affect their generations to come, but I have a feeling it's going to be very negative. Because when you get $300,000 a year for sitting on the couch watching a Lakers game, not working, you model that lifestyle to the next generations. I'm not sure what it's going to be like. They'll have money but I wonder what else.[28]

The third similarity between Sander County and Santa Barbara County is the recognition that the local community no longer has control over the terms of engagement with "outsiders." In Sander County this was expressed by the older members of the town as nostalgia for a past era in which neighbors all knew each other face-to-face. As the township grew in size, locals commented on the growing geographic and social distance between people who were no longer familiar, no longer eating at each other's tables, no longer minding each other's kids, no longer growing up together knowing each other's business and functioning as a tightly knit community. As a result, "the gradual

---

[27] Jon Goldberg-Hiller and Neal Milner, "Rights as excess: the politics of special rights," *Law & Social Inquiry*, 28(4) (2006), 1075–118; Jeffrey R. Dudas, "In the name of equal rights: "special" rights and the politics of resentment in post-civil rights America," *Law & Society Review*, 39(4) (2008), 723–57.

[28] Taped interview; see Darian-Smith, *New Capitalists*, p. 92.

decay of the old social order and the emergence of a plurality of cultures and races in Sander County produced a confusion of norms and of mechanisms for resolving conflict."[29]

In Santa Barbara County, the old rules of the game have also changed. Much to the dismay of local residents in the valley, the Chumash are accessing formal legal processes to bring their demands to the table. Many of the white locals interpret this as the Chumash thumbing their nose at them and not paying attention to established behavioral norms. The long-term residents are being forced to engage with the tribe and come to terms with the fact that they can no longer "manage" local Indian communities as they have in the past. Moreover, they are being forced to deal with native peoples holding legal rights "that are quite different from those that had long prevailed."[30] This has caused a media outpouring of nostalgic rhetoric about a pristine natural landscape that will be tainted by Indian housing and development. Just as in Sander County, in Santa Barbara County there is "a confusion of norms and of mechanisms for resolving conflict."[31]

Yet among Chumash tribal members there is no nostalgia for a romanticized past, nor much confusion over how best to proceed. And this is where my story builds out from David Engel's tale about Sander County, in that I have been following the emerging legal consciousness of the Chumash "outsider" over a period of some decades. At first in the early 2000s, when the tribe was developing its casino plans, it sought the cooperation and involvement of Santa Barbara County as part of what it called government-to-government relations. Unfortunately, the County refused to acknowledge the Chumash as a sovereign tribe and failed to treat the attempted negotiations with any respect. In 2013 the Board of Supervisors voted by a 3–2 margin "against entering into government-to-government negotiations with the tribe, sending a clear message to the Chumash that the tribe's status as a sovereign government is meaningless to the county."[32] As a result, communications have almost entirely broken down and the tribe's efforts to discuss their plans to build homes on purchased lands adjacent to their reservation have stalled and been rejected.

In recent years, the situation has escalated way beyond a refusal to communicate. The County has taken aggressive action – again via the legal system – to challenge the tribe's historical claim to reservation land that was allocated by the federal government back in 1901. A lawsuit was brought against the tribe, claiming that it did not own reservation land, but this was

---

[29] Engel, "The oven bird's song," 574, n 4.   [30] Ibid, 578, n 4.   [31] Ibid, 574, n 4.
[32] Editorial, "Talking through problems," *The Lompoc Record* (June 25, 2015).

subsequently thrown out by a US District Court judge on the basis that it had no jurisdiction over a tribal sovereign entity. Vincent Armenta, tribal chairman of the Santa Ynez Band of Chumash Indians, stated: "Unfortunately, we know this will not be the last time these angry anti-tribal individuals will sue the tribe. They simply refuse to live in an evidence-based world, where facts can't be ignored. Instead, they prefer to make up their own set of facts and ignore the rich historical evidence that proves our tribe's existence and documents our reservation."[33] In public statements and across social media, the county and other citizen groups have called the Chumash people "untrustworthy" and "disingenuous."

Some of the county supervisors have even publicly questioned the existence of tribal governments. But as chairman Armenta responded:

> For Supervisor Adam to suggest that the "whole reservation system" should be revisited is laughable. Does he think that the Santa Barbara County Board of Supervisors has the authority to revoke the passage of the Indian Removal Act of 1830? ... Even more preposterous is Supervisor Adam's assumption that Native American tribes liked having their land taken away from them and liked being relegated to a small plot of land. Perhaps if the Board of Supervisors could wave a magic wand and "revisit the whole reservation system", the Chumash people could reclaim the 200-mile stretch of California coastline from Malibu to Paso Robles rather than being relegated to 99 acres in a creek bed.[34]

For the past twelve years the Chumash have engaged in an effort to be legally recognized and exert their legal rights to build on purchased lands, while Santa Barbara County has simply refused to hear their case or brought actions against them for attempting to exert their sovereign rights and status. As noted in an editorial in a local newspaper:

> The valley squabble has expanded into county government, with the majority of the supervisors generally taking side with those that oppose the tribe's plans, now and in the future. Attempts to mitigate the hostilities with actual face-to-face negotiations – or even civil conversation – have failed, miserably. One reason is that both sides are being stubborn about reconciliation. The county apparently feels obligated to stress its own self-importance when it comes to land – use concepts and rules, while tribal officials apparently feel compelled to fall back on the sovereignty angle, refusing to cede any authority to the other sovereign entity. It's a classic standoff, one that shows no sign

---

[33] Vincent Armenta, "Relying on history facts to validate tribe," *The Lompoc Record* (July 16, 2015).
[34] Vincent Armenta, "You can't rewrite history," *The Santa Barbara Independent* (February 6, 2015).

of breaking any time soon – and one that is doing very little in the way of good for the general population of the Santa Ynez Valley ... We also believe the fact that the Chumash have morphed from among the poorest citizens of the Valley to some of the wealthiest, and in a relatively short period of time, simply rubs some neighbors the wrong way.[35]

Finally, in frustration, in June 2015 the Chumash bypassed both Santa Barbara County and state agencies and made a federal appeal to have their right to build houses on adjacent land granted. The House Subcommittee on Indian, Insular and Alaskan Native Affairs heard the case in a public hearing on June 16, 2015. After hearing from both the county and the tribe, Representative Don Young, chairman of the subcommittee, forcefully condemned the actions of Santa Barbara County and charged it to engage in intergovernmental relations with the Chumash. "It's a pretty damning case, so you had better go back and tell your friends that we will [pass this bill] if they don't cooperate," Young told county executive Mona Miyasato.[36] While the federal agency firmly reinforced the sovereignty authority of the tribe, the decision was immediately appealed by the county.

Where this legal battle in Santa Barbara County will end up is not yet clear. It seems that relations between the white wealthy "insiders" and native "outsiders" will probably get worse before they get better. Chumash tribal members relate that they are afraid of going into local shops because they are harassed and bullied. Hate speech and attacks in local media continue. However, what does appear very clear is that the Chumash are now setting the terms of engagement through legal channels and evoking what Jean and John Comaroff have called "lawfare."[37] Across the United States, more and more tribes who own successful casinos and increasingly diversified commercial interests are asserting greater political and economic clout and engaging in various forms of legal action. In short, by forcefully claiming their legal rights, some tribes are pushing back against long-held stereotypes carried over from a former colonial era that presented them as being legally and politically irrelevant. Contributing to campaign election funds, negotiating tribal land deals, creating new sustainable environmental practices, and providing better health and educational services for their own communities – all of these activities are steadily improving the chances that more and more Native Americans will be able to take a seat at the center of mainstream American society.

---

[35] Editorial, "Talking to break impasse," *The Lompoc Record* (July 10, 2015).

[36] Editorial, "Lawmakers slam county for poor dealings with the Chumash Tribe," *The Lompoc Record* (June 18, 2015).

[37] John L. Comaroff and Jean Comaroff, *Ethnicity, Inc.* (Chicago University Press, 2009).

Notably, tribes are engaged in lawfare in increasingly creative ways. They have created subnational and transnational legal forums that include leveraging UN treaties, participating in pan-indigenous networks, and creating solidarity across national borders, ethnic differences, and socioeconomic classes. For instance, the Cowboy Indian Alliance, which is a coalition of tribal members, ranchers and landowners, came together in April 2014 to march in Washington DC to protest the laying down of the Keystone XL Pipeline. This unlikely alliance reflects a generation of young Indian activists who use new social media to form "networks that are connecting both indigenous and nonindigenous people in truly unprecedented ways."[38] These coalitions are acutely aware that they may have to use law as a means to resist against government agencies and commercial enterprises taking lands and resources. As John and Jean Comaroff have noted, "the rise of neoliberalism ... has intensified greatly the reliance on legal ways and means."[39] As a result, we are witnessing "a planetary culture of legality" and "law has become *the* prime space of contestation."[40] Across the United States, tribes such as the Chumash are demonstrating a newfound capacity to use the formal legal system to negotiate that space to their own advantage.[41]

CONCLUDING COMMENTS

Among non-Indian Americans, be these long-term residents of Santa Barbara County or elsewhere, a national anxiety is emerging about Native Americans "returning" to the national polity as fully matured and involved citizens.[42] In a sense the "outsiders" are becoming the "insiders," and the cultural, social, political, and economic divides between them are not so obvious or differentiated as they were only three decades ago. Mainstream American anxiety about who belongs to what ethnic group often takes the form of a deep lament for a simpler time, when white Americans did not have to think much about native populations and, if they did, the relationship was constructed as one of supposed harmony. This lament conveniently silences or ignores centuries of violence and oppression, as well as genocidal and assimilationist policies that often involved the deliberate dissolution of Indian tribal communities and the removal of Indian children from their families.

[38] Kristin Moe, "Cowboys and Indians Stand Together against Keystone XL," http://voices .nationalgeographic.com/2014/05/14/cowboys-and-indians-stand-together-against-keystone-xl/.
[39] Comaroff and Comaroff, *Ethnicity, Inc.*, 53–54, n 37.   [40] Ibid, 54; 80, n 37.
[41] Eve Darian-Smith, "Environmental law and Native American law," *Annual Review of Law and Social Science*, 6 (2010), 359–86.
[42] Clifford, *Returns*, n 17.

Accompanying this nostalgic romanticism, there is also an emergent sense of anger among residents of Santa Barbara County and elsewhere toward Native Americans, whom many people feel must be stopped at whatever cost from demanding their sovereign rights and legal presence. Often painted as "greedy," "illegal," and "dispassionate," Native Americans are experiencing a national backlash against them by mainstream white society, which remains keen to keep them at arm's length. But whereas in the colonial era native peoples were relegated to barren reservation lands out of sight and mind, today implementing processes of marginalization is not so straightforward. Racism and racial discrimination are taking more insidious forms, often under cover of the law, as experienced by the protesters against the Dakota Access Pipeline, who have been subject to tear gas, water cannon, and arrest by law enforcement officers. It should never be forgotten that across the mounting legal conflicts and cultural wars between indigenous and non-indigenous communities, Native Americans' continuing vulnerability to racial discrimination is very real and experienced on a daily basis by rich and poor Indians alike.

In building upon David Engel's enormously important work of more than thirty years ago, and returning to the title of this chapter, I like to think of the oven bird and the miner's canary singing to each across time and space in ways that resonate. They both evoke the marking of time, transition, and change, as well as impending threat. From spring to winter, from fresh to poisonous air, the birds symbolize shifting conditions, nostalgia, melancholy, and ultimately a deep sense of loss. In a profound sense, both birds are singing about what Felix Cohen explored back in 1949 when he wrote about "the rise and fall of our democratic faith."

10

Listening for the Songs of Others

*Insiders, Outsiders, and the Legal Marginalization
of the Working Underclass in America*

MICHAEL MCCANN

David Engel's evocative, masterfully constructed essay is one of the most intriguing texts in the entire sociolegal canon. I have taught it every year – sometimes in two to three classes, both at the undergraduate and graduate level, perhaps thirty-five times in all – since the mid-1990s, when it first appeared as a chapter in Engel, Greenhouse, and Yngvesson's book *Law and Community in Three American Towns*.[1] Moreover, I and co-author William Haltom spent the better part of a decade researching, writing, and following up an empirically ambitious book committed to demonstrating that the communal romance Engel identifies in a small suburban context in fact consumed the entire nation for several decades and was closely tied to the power dynamics of the hegemonic neoliberal, corporate-governed order that most of us now take for granted.[2]

I thus enthusiastically accepted the invitation to write about how my teaching of the essay has evolved over several decades. In the process, I have come to reflect more deeply on why Engel's ethnographic account speaks to me so powerfully, and also how my reading of the essay differs a bit from, or goes beyond, that of most scholars, and also differs from Professor Engel's own articulated interpretive focus.[3] Engel's focus in the essay is on the romance

---

[1] David Engel, Carole Greenhouse, and Barbara Yngvesson, *Law and Community in Three American Towns* (University of Chicago Press, 1994). I had read the initial essay in 1984 in *Law & Society Review*, as I was becoming more familiar with sociolegal scholarship. However, during the first decade of my academic career, I mostly taught classes on constitutional law, American political development, and American political thought. My initial classes in sociolegal studies were on law and social change, and I did not begin teaching core classes that focused on sociolegal texts until the mid-1990s.

[2] William Haltom and Michael McCann, *Distorting the Law: Politics, Media, and the Litigation Crisis* (University of Chicago Press, 2004).

[3] Professor Engel and I have had a number of awkward, head-scratching conversations about our different readings of his essay, reflecting in part the fact that he is a rigorous anthropologist and I am a scholar of politics and power.

that developed among community insiders about their imagined happier past grounded in citizen self-reliance and cooperation, which subsequently came under assault by outsiders whose alleged selfish, irresponsible rights-claiming behavior was eroding communal bonds. The essay's title refers to the inter-subjective world of the insiders, to their fantastic accounts of their shared history,[4] and to their "perception of disintegration and decay" that allegedly was caused by the invasion of alien outsiders.[5] "The Oven Bird's Song" is a fitting, memorable image for this story about a community imagining itself in decline, and its stifling implications for those labeled as outsiders.

A curious feature of the essay, however, is that we learn very little about those outsiders, who they are, how they view the insiders, how they are affected by community power structures, and how they imagine their own quests for a good life. There are a few snatches of anecdotal disputes involving outsiders, but their experiences and aspirations, what we might call their subaltern subjectivities, do not receive nearly the same investigation as the communal consciousness of insiders. Almost everything we know about the outsiders is filtered through the particularistic, privileged lens of the insiders' obsessions. To recognize this is not to offer a critique of Engel; in coming pages I will defend the author's focus in terms of sophisticated ethnographic commitments. But this desire to recognize the outsiders, or "others," on their own terms sets up my own project – that of linking the subject position of outsiders to the long history of racialized and gendered low-wage workers and their relatively rightless status in American society. In short, my teaching aims to listen for the outsiders' songs, as we might imagine them through hearing other similarly marginalized, stigmatized Others in the American underclass throughout history, along with and likely in contrast to the loud, familiar, ideologically infused moralistic tunes of insiders. We cannot hear the out-siders' music directly in the story, but learning about the history of the outsider underclass can sensitize us to what to listen for, and for what we might hear.

The following engagement with Engel's essay unfolds in five parts. First, I outline the overall logic of my longstanding undergraduate course, "Law in Society," and elaborate the themes and texts that we cover prior to engaging Engel's essay, and which play a key role in the developing sociolegal logic of inquiry that I teach. The focus is on Stuart Scheingold's macro-level account about the tensions between the "myth of rights" and the "politics of rights,"[6]

---

4   Engel himself refers to the insiders' conception of community as "nostalgia" for what never existed.

5   David M. Engel, "The oven bird's song: insiders, outsiders, and personal injuries in an American community," *Law & Society Review*, 18(4) (1984), 551.

6   Stuart A. Scheingold, *The Politics of Rights: Lawyers, Public Policy, and Political Change*, 2nd ed. (University of Michigan Press, 2004).

which I illustrate in lectures through histories of struggles by African American, Asian-American, Mexican, and women workers – all confined to relatively rightsless status as low- or no-wage underclass laborers – to win various types of citizenship rights throughout US history. Second, I outline how I teach the "conventional" reading of "The Oven Bird's Song," about the dynamics of insider community. My focus is on the questions that I ask of students; this section is rather brief, because other chapters in this volume cover the essay so well. Third, I develop the core insight that we actually know little about the so-called outsiders, and I try to enlarge their significance and speculate about their circumstances, challenges, and experiences by linking them to similarly situated others discussed earlier (and later) in my course. I also draw on earlier course readings by sociolegal scholars to explore why (due to limited access, knowledge, status, money, time, etc.) the "have nots" often do not or cannot make good on the promises of even those rights that they are formally granted, and also on the question of whether and when subaltern populations embrace and act on "rights consciousness." My aim is to amplify Engel's powerful story of exclusion by embedding the outsiders, including especially low-wage immigrant workers, in a long history of legal disenfranchisement. Fourth, I briefly summarize the topic that I teach following "The Oven Bird's Song": my research on the cultural obsession with hyperlexis and imagined communal decline that occupied the entire American nation from the 1980s until at least 2001. My aim is to put Engel's carefully documented ethnography of a small community into a bigger framework, again to amplify his findings and insights. In all of these sections, my aim is to develop a more direct, frank, critical understanding about how "The Oven Bird's Song" provides a window into the different dimensions of unequal social power and how they clash with the pretenses to "equality under the law" at the heart of Scheingold's "myth of rights" that arguably has sustained the fantasies of white, property-owning (mostly male) Americans. My brief conclusion summarizes my assessment of the centrality of "The Oven Bird's Song" to my teaching agenda now and into the future.

INTERROGATING THE MYTH OF RIGHTS: LIBERAL COMMUNITY AND ITS HISTORICAL UNDERCLASS

LSJ/PolS 363: An Overview

The class in which I have taught OBS most often is my undergraduate 300-level (sophomore/junior) "Law in Society." It was originally the gateway course for our Law, Societies, and Justice program, for which I served as founding director for a dozen years; the course is cross-listed also with Political

Science, which accounts for around half the students. The class usually enrolls 100–200 students during the regular academic year. I teach it as a mix of lectures, using questions to generate answers and to propel the class in an active, somewhat instructor-decentered way. Students are required to engage texts of many sorts: academic books and essays, mainstream news stories, fictional parables and poems, social media communications, speeches, lots of YouTube clips, and the like. I very self-consciously present and call attention to the many sources of knowledge that inform us about law and socialize us as legal subjects; I underline the multiple ways in which we comprehend law and the challenges of making legal judgments as we navigate different types of knowledge and epistemological terrain.

The overall aim of my class is to explore how legal conventions, knowledge, and practices constitute all dimensions of social life in various ways and degrees. This goal is especially important for political science students, given the disciplinary bias to focus on politics in and among nation-states, and to identify "the law" mostly with federal appellate courts. Moreover, while the empirical focus is on the United States, I draw on cross-national and trans-national legal institutions and practices to offer comparative analytical perspective. The course is divided into two parts. The first half emphasizes law as traditions of knowledge and discursive meaning-making activity, what Robert Cover calls "law's words,"[7] constituting an imagined symbolic community of loosely shared understandings among citizens in everyday social interaction. The second half emphasizes that law's words are backed up by the routinized violence exercised by state officials and indirectly by authorized non-state actors, especially members of dominant groups, in civil society.

Law as Inclusionary Myth and Resource
for Political Contestation

The course begins, as do many such courses, with a long, free-ranging discussion of the classic, highly evocative parable by Franz Kafka, "Before the Law."[8] I ask students open-ended questions about law – Where is it? What is it? Who makes it and who is affected by it? How does law work? What prevents the man from the country from gaining access to law, or does he in fact do so? Does law not deliver on its promises? If not, why? And so on. By exploring

---

[7] Robert Cover, "Violence and the word," *Yale Law Journal*, 95 (1986), 1601.

[8] Franz Kafka, "Before the law," from *The Trial*, 1925, www.kafka-online.info/before-the-law .html. Also used in class is the opening scene from Orson Welles' classic 1962 cinematic version of the book.

paradoxes at the start, I introduce the persistently questioning, critical character of the course activity, the elusiveness of clear or one-dimensional answers to our questions, and a variety of complex themes that will be explored in the course. Kafka's parable also enables me to introduce briefly Ewick and Silbey's classic conceptions of "with" and "against" as well as "before" the law that structure legal consciousness and practice.[9] I often illustrate these concepts with recent events in the media, such as President Obama's memorable speech about Trayvon Martin, the black teenager who was killed in Florida by a whitish Hispanic man who claimed to be informally policing the neighborhood.[10]

The first two weeks of the class are dedicated to an intense engagement with Stuart Scheingold's *The Politics of Rights*,[11] which students read in four segments, from start to finish. My aim is to derive from Scheingold three perspectives on American law – the mainstream romance with law that "beguiles" the haves, the "myth of rights"; a less developed and implicit but important "radical critical" perspective, which anticipated the critical legal studies movement that was percolating in law schools and developed soon after the book was published; and the "politics of rights," which borrowed from both perspectives but advanced a more complex, politically nuanced, and power-sensitive view of how law, in both official and unofficial guises, works "in practice." After fortifying Scheingold's argument about the substantive elements of the myth of rights, how it is generated, and how it matters, I examine empirical reasons to think that "rights talk" has lost some of its resonance in the decades since he wrote the book. We end by examining Scheingold's pessimistic chapters about how legal education and professional responsibilities divert lawyers from the type of activity that he identifies with the politics of rights.

My primary pedagogical gambit is to illustrate how each of the three theoretical angles offers a story about the mid-twentieth century civil rights movement. In my version, the mythical story that prevails in politicians' rhetoric, middle-school civics classes, fictional fables such as "To Kill a Mockingbird," and even still among many law professors is largely ahistorical, apolitical, and moralistic. While there are strands of truth in such stories, the "critical" account I develop next exposes their myopia. I begin by enumerating

---

[9] Patricia Ewick and Susan S. Silbey, *The Common Place of Law: Stories from Everyday Life* (University of Chicago Press, 1998).

[10] Barack Obama, "Speech on Trayvon Martin," www.cbsnews.com/8301-250_162-57594598/transcript-obamas-remarks-on-race-trayvon-martin/.

[11] See n 4 above.

the long history of protections for slavery written into the US Constitution and tracing the role of courts at all levels in perpetuating the subjugation of African workers, first as slaves, then as third-class citizen laborers for nearly another century, and continuing for most to this day. I then extend this legacy of marginalization for the working underclass to experiences of three waves of Asian immigrants, of Mexican immigrants, and of women long confined to unpaid domestic labor or low-wage factory labor. From this perspective, one third to one half of "American" inhabitants have been excluded from the promise of rights enjoyed by property-owning white men until the post-World War II era. Even when formal rights have been expanded to more persons by statutes and court decisions, moreover, the experiences of many people have continued to be little more empowering than was the case for the man from the country in Kafka's tale which opened the course.

Then I turn to the "politics of rights" angle. I retrace the previous historical steps, beginning with the many abolitionist opponents of slavery and exclusion who embraced rights, often along with Christian principles, through Jim Crow and the mid-century civil rights movement. I underline the intersection of race and class issues, discussing points of solidarity and conflict between labor unions and African Americans. Sometimes I add a brief story about the long legacy of Filipino and Mexican migrant workers, as well as generations of women whose invaluable work is mostly unpaid. This survey covers a huge amount of ground all too superficially, but together these brief accounts underline the systematic subordination of a persistent laboring underclass and their struggles for rights status throughout our history. My aim in all this is to illustrate the relevance of Scheingold's analysis, for my historical narratives both expose the fantasy of the myth of rights and illustrate how the politics of rights makes sense of legal mobilization struggles demanding that the myth of legal equality become a reality. These histories underline how law is a blend of fantastic delusion, aspirational struggle, and sensuous, material relationships in many spheres of social life. They also underline how law is best understood to structure, or "constitute," institutional terrains of contested claims as well as instrumental resources deployed in those contests. Finally, I aim to exemplify Scheingold's mostly pessimistic and critical-realist analytical position while refusing to abandon an aspirational egalitarian, inclusionary commitment to legal, if not social, justice.

Individual Disputing and the Constraints on Legal Mobilization

The second quarter of the class shifts from historical, nation-wide macro-struggles over rights to focusing on contemporary micro-contexts of individual experiences with legal marginalization as well as aspirational struggles for making rights real. We continue the "legal mobilization" framework with Frances Kahn Zemans' classic essay on that topic.[12] I underline Zemans' methodologically individualistic framework, especially her argument that rights-claiming is a form of democratic citizenship often overlooked by political scientists. This individual-level model, like Scheingold's, emphasizes that rights-claiming need not lead to litigation or involve lawyers; it is routine activity "in" society, in social life. Rights are "all over" in social relations and practices, as Austin Sarat famously wrote.[13] But I also emphasize the several sections in which Zemans points out that the *capacities* to claim rights effectively are highly unequal among differently situated people. My lectures connect this claim to the Kafka story, to the skeptical Scheingold perspectives, and to the focus on the unequal rights status of variously marked (especially racialized and gendered laborers) groups, as well as to the constraints of many people's capacities to mobilize law.

The discussion of Zemans opens the way for the next five class periods. Students read the classic essay by Miller and Sarat on "Grievances, Claims & Disputes,"[14] which introduces them to the core concepts of the disputing pyramid and empirical facts showing that legal disputes are common but litigation is uncommon in American society. We build on the earlier discussions to ask why people may not escalate and formalize disputes when they have genuine grievances, and why they may not even make claims, instead "lumping it" when they experience harm. Students are invited to raise issues about constraints, resuming a discussion that goes back to the first day, and we eventually get to a list that includes: scarce money and time; limited legal knowledge; poor access to lawyers; low status or lack of respect; racial, gender, and/or religious bias; and fear of reprisal. We add to the list recognition that the legal rules are "fixed" in favor of dominant groups and "repeat players," taking up Galanter's famous essay on "Why the Haves Come Out Ahead."[15] The aim is to summarize what we have learned about what is "real" and hollow regarding the hopes for justice and empowerment in a society organized in large part around rights.

---

[12] Frances Kahn Zemans, "Legal mobilization: the neglected role of the law in the political system," *American Political Science Review*, 77(3) (1983), 690–703.

[13] Austin Sarat, "'. . . The law is all over': power, resistance and the legal consciousness of the welfare poor," *Yale Journal of Law & the Humanities*, 2(2), http://digitalcommons.law.yale.edu/yjlh/vol2/iss2/6.

[14] Richard Miller and Austin Sarat, "Grievances, claims & disputes: assessing the adversary culture," *Law & Society Review*, 15 (1980–1), 525–66.

[15] Marc Galanter, "Why the 'haves' come out ahead: speculations on the limits of legal change," *Law and & Society Review*, 9(1) (1974), 95–160.

One final interpersonal constraint is examined in detail by engagement with Sally Merry's article "Rights Talk and the Experience of Law."[16] Merry's brilliant but accessible study shows clearly the interpersonal and experiential factors that figure into individual women's decisions about calling the police and prosecuting abusers. In particular, Merry underlines three types of factors that she observed among abused women in Hilo, Hawaii. One is culturally defined norms and roles that shape women's subject positions, or their "subjectivities." Many women found it hard to act as "rights bearers" because of conflicts with other social roles – as "good" wives, daughters, mothers, Christians, etc. – that prescribe inaction against abusive men, and hence, literally, "lumping it." Second, Merry emphasizes the roles of familiar others – parents, siblings, friends, religious counselors, women's shelters – as well as official legal actors – police, court clerks, lawyers, judges, jurors – in reinforcing different subjectivities, either as reticent victim or active rights claimant. The actions and assessments of people in the surrounding local context matter a great deal. Finally, abused women are greatly influenced by their overall experiences with official law, either directly or indirectly through accounts by others; the more empowering the initial experiences, the more likely women will be to pursue rights claims, and vice versa. Extensive discussion of these three factors in the Merry essay is profoundly helpful to my pedagogical engagement with Engel's *OBS*.

THE DOMINANT COMMUNITY'S SONG:
RESPONSIBLE INSIDERS VS UNDISCIPLINED OUTSIDERS

The readings and discussions outlined above very self-consciously prepare students to understand Engel's essay of communal fantasy by dominant social groups of insiders at a relatively sophisticated level. I start the class on "The Oven Bird's Song" by showing contrasting cartoons about both empowered and feeble rights-bearing citizens, followed by another pairing of images that capture Engel's changing faces of Sander County: a large group of happy, smiling, white youth in a sunny pastoral setting of a field with farmhouse in the background; and pictures of sterile new row houses bunched together, the parking lot in a tacky strip mall, and a crowded Walmart stuffed with mostly people of color as both consumers and workers. I then ask the class about the meaning of a legal "tort," and we discuss briefly the range of harms that routinely emerge in personal injury disputes.

---

[16] Sally Engle Merry, "Rights talk and the experience of law: implementing women's human rights to protection from violence," *Human Rights Quarterly*, 25 (2003), 243–81.

For the first half or more of the class, we interrogate the dynamics of Engel's communal song of woe by insiders in Sander County. I mostly ask simple questions, and students invariably compete to provide smart answers that incisively dissect the dynamics of relational practices in the local community around personal injury. My first question is usually: "If you were a resident in Sander County, what would you do if you experienced a personal injury caused by another person? Say, a neighbor's tree falls on your house; or a neighbor runs over your child's bike; or a fellow worker drops a heavy tool box on your foot, breaking several toes; or your employer's old tractor breaks down and throws you in a ditch, breaking your arm; or you are hurt while a bystander to a barroom fight?" Students usually begin by noting that, in Sander County, they probably would be reluctant to claim a rights violation or call a lawyer, as it would mark them as an undesirable community member. They might call their insurance company, but otherwise they would absorb the costs of injury and lump it. Then other questions follow:

- *Would this sort of response be true for everyone in Sander County?* This leads to discussions about the allegedly different behaviors of insiders and outsiders as portrayed through the dominant cultural narrative.
- *What distinguishes insiders and outsiders?* I encourage recognition that non-cooperative, adversarial, or legalistic behavior is only one of many markers, just one of many bricks that build walls separating groups of people. We make a list of other likely or possible markers: length of time living in Sander County, including family ties over generations; membership in local civic organizations, clubs, and churches; geographic location and type of residence (owned/rented); type of job and level of income; racial and ethnic status; modes of dress, speech, outward appearance; connections to "support groups" in the community; etc.[17] Students are usually very insightful about these markers and how they matter; invariably, some offer that they suspect that race and class play a bigger role than Engel's account suggests. We also discuss what happens when an insider, say a nephew of a former mayor, files a lawsuit for a personal injury claim, say a broken fence and mangled leg when a neighbor's teenage son misses the turn into the driveway. Would the insider become

---

[17] All of these markers are found in anecdotal stories in "The Oven Bird's Song," but I and the students spend more time fleshing them out and grappling with the differences than Engel does in his ethnographic narrative. In this sense, and more throughout my teaching and this chapter, I quite frankly take liberties in interpreting and analyzing the essay in ways that fit my pedagogical purposes.

an outsider? What if the person who allegedly "caused" the accidental injury was viewed as an outsider? Is suing that person acceptable?

- *How does the hostility to rights-claiming and litigation both reflect and reinforce community values?* We proceed into discussion of cooperation and self-reliance as performance modes strongly endorsed over rights claiming as selfish greed. This always takes us to Engel's profound distinction between two sorts of "individualism," which I supplement with a digression into Tocqueville's theorization of the topic.

- *Who enforces community values?* Students usually volunteer a multitude of answers, and eventually we get to "everybody" among the insiders – neighbors and friends, clergy and church members, employers, local media, and legal officials, including lawyers, insurance agents, court clerks, police, judges, jurors. One key point is that, in "The Oven Bird's Song," filing a personal injury lawsuit usually requires seeking counsel from outside Sander County, such claims are highly unlikely to be successful, and the costs of stigma and ostracism are high even for those few who do win in court. This builds on earlier discussions about socialization processes and the institutionalized mechanisms of enforcing socially constructed norms, values, and disciplinary practices. The discussion invariably returns us to Merry's article, where expressed attitudes by familiar others (family, friends, clergy) and legal officials figure prominently into encouraging or, as in Sander County, strongly discouraging rights-claiming. Due to our earlier discussions about the context-specific constraints on rights-claiming, most students have little trouble understanding these dynamics.

- *What is the role of official law in this setting? Should not the official legal system recognize, respect, and enforce citizens' rights to have their day in court and win compensation for injuries they suffer at the hands of others?* This leads to discussion of courts as sites of legal construction and community-building, a theme more fully developed in the co-written 1994 book in which "The Oven Bird's Song" appeared. I point out a key paradox of "The Oven Bird's Song": official legal practices informally deter claiming of the very rights that official law documents place "on the books" as entitlements equally available to all citizens. But courts still do offer a potential, highly constrained forum for rights-claiming and contestation. One might say that courts, like law generally, are sites for both enforcing and contesting hegemonic relations, echoing again the complex argument of Scheingold that runs through the course.

- *Engel makes the concept of "community" central to his argument; he uses the term nearly 100 times in the article. What does Engel mean by the term "community," and why does he end his analysis by portraying it as "nostalgic" longing for "an untainted world that existed nowhere but in their imaginations," i.e., a fantasy? Is this a fair assessment of this local public culture?* This question takes us back to the enduring theme of how narratives can be myths or fantasies and still be very "real" in shaping meaning construction and social practice. The Japanese parable about the need for unwelcome aliens, implying that a "we" always needs a "not us" or "other" to sustain cohesion, very effectively expands on how community is constructed and sustained. At this point I often ask whether any students grew up in a small rural community, and whether Engel's narrative is familiar. That question always draws a number of testimonies, usually affirming the resonance of the fantasy of an anxious, exclusionary white community in "The Oven Bird's Song." Students from more urban areas often chime in that they have relatives who live in such rural communities, or they are familiar with them through television, movies, novels, and the like. But everyone has an experiential understanding of how "communities," however constructed, whether geographic or functional or voluntary, both include and exclude as routine practices basic to survival.

- *How do Sander County residents view legal disputes over contracts? Why is it acceptable to formalize and litigate contracts, but not personal injuries?* This returns the discussions to matters of individual responsibility and how contracts enforce responsibility for fulfilling commitments of trust, whereas personal injury lawsuits undermine trust and reflect abdication of individual responsibility. To be honest, students often have trouble with this seeming inconsistency, so I often offer a few examples and illustrative cartoons. I then follow up with a broader question about who benefits from contract litigation and personal injury litigation. Whereas the latter often provide leverage to the less powerful and wealthy against the more wealthy, and especially against business interests, the primary claimants in contract cases are usually business interests, landlords, banks, and other haves aiming to enforce financial obligations on the have-nots. I counsel against overstating these tendencies, but they do make sense to students in general.

LISTENING FOR THE OUTSIDER'S SONG:
IMAGINING THE LEGAL CONSCIOUSNESS OF "OTHERS"

Most of Engel's account is about and from inside the worldviews shared (and enforced?) by insiders of Sander County. The narrative provides lots of revealing anecdotes about the behavior of insiders – a minister, a social worker, a middle-aged farmer, an elderly farmer, an elderly woman from a farming family – who follow or avoid at some cost community norms, and lots of quotes and interview evidence about salient meanings of the community norms that identify and stigmatize adversarial legalism as a corrosive force.[18] Engel thus masterfully offers what we expect of ethnography – a mapping of the symbolic imaginations that structure meaning-making and the social practices of his subject population. Ethnographies explore cultural lives from the point of view of the defined social groupings or communities.[19] In this regard, "The Oven Bird's Song" fits very well the aims of my class, because endeavoring to understand the culturally constructed imaginary of, and regarding, law that has developed in American society (and to some degree increasingly around the world) is one of my primary aims in the course. One virtue of beginning my class with Scheingold is that he explicitly invokes and identifies the ethnographic project of studying systematic meaning construction. Scheingold invokes the famed anthropologist Clifford Geertz as a specific source of his thinking about "the myth of rights" as well as his overall approach to cultural ideology.[20] And Engel's skillful construction provides readers with a deep sense of "being there" in Sander County.

However, Engel's relatively "pure" ethnography at the same time eschews two related projects that political scientists find equally important. First is the expansion of the ethnographic project to the distinct legal and social imaginations of the stigmatized outsiders. Engel himself identifies a deep if volatile fissure within Sander County, but his study is almost entirely focused on the insiders and how they construct differences. Hence, almost all we know about identified outsiders is filtered through the stigmatizing lens of insiders. Engel gives us few direct entries into the thoughts, experiences, aspirations, and strategic gambits of those who are viewed as outsiders in Sander County. We do encounter a couple of anecdotes, including the story of the farmworker who was injured in the field, who went to court and then lost in a jury trial. But the account is mostly about events and behavior; we are provided little access to the subjective experience and worldview of this person. Engel does speculate about why newcomers and outsiders *might* be more inclined to take rights claims to court, because "channels for communication and shared value

---

[18] I take the liberty of using the term "adversarial legalism" to summarize what Engel found to be the alien, corrosive element. See Robert Kagan, *Adversarial Legalism: The American Way of Law* (Harvard University Press, 2009).

[19] See *American Ethnography Quasimonthly*, "What is ethnography?" www.american ethnography.com/ethnography.php.

[20] Scheingold, *Politics of Rights*, pp. 14–15, 17.

systems and acquaintance networks were unlikely to exist" for many new-comers and marginalized groups.[21] Litigation is more likely where people are separated by social distance, Engel notes, drawing on an old insight about legal behavior.

But what do people identified as outsiders think about relationships in Sander County? What "songs" do they sing among themselves? Do they see the world through the same normative lens as do insiders? Almost everything we read in the class before "The Oven Bird's Song" provides evidence that marginalized, stigmatized groups – which seems a fitting characterization of the outsiders – see the world differently. For example, Scheingold devotes a chapter to evidence suggesting that African Americans and other racial minorities do not buy into the myth of rights as much as do majority white Americans. My lectures add many bits of both statistical and qualitative evidence supporting that people in marginal sub-communities – from black slaves, sharecroppers, and unemployed or underemployed workers; to low-wage Asian farmworkers and pink-collar female workers; to dissidents and activists – often develop different and somewhat resistant worldviews, or what Merry calls "subjectivities."[22] Indeed, Merry's account, which we read imme-diately before "The Oven Bird's Song," underscores how the experiences, understandings, and strategic choices of abused working-class, often low-income women are quite different from the perspectives of others, especially white legal officials, many men of different classes, and middle-class residents.

Hence, we wonder: Do those marked as outsiders understand the terms and implications of the enforced communal norms? Do they agree that commu-nity norms of non-adversarial behavior and rights avoidance make for a good, desirable, or just community? Do they actually litigate more than insiders? If not, is it because of fear of stigma and reprisal, or... what? Engel presents descriptive statistics to suggest that litigation has not increased as new low-wage workers of color and women have invaded the community, but then speculates that litigation might still be attractive when they experience per-sonal injury, so there is a question that a study of outsiders more directly might help to answer. And if the numbers of newcomers and outsiders increases in the community, could they represent a bloc of citizens who might press for change, through voting for political leaders and initiatives, through informal political action or even protests, or through appeals to opinion and the media? Do they put up with the community pressures quietly, agreeably, or do they resist and aim to subvert in various ways? And, more fundamentally, how do

[21] Engel, *Oven bird's song*, 567.   [22] Merry, *Rights Talk*.

other markers – skin color, ethnicity, religion, gender, education, income, job status, organizational affiliation, mode of dress and talk, etc. – interact with the stigma of litigiousness to marginalize various people as outsiders? Indeed, it is important to inquire whether litigiousness is itself not a coded signaling of other, more invidious types of marking others, especially racialization.

This question points to another of feature of "The Oven Bird's Song": the lack of detailed demographic data, which leaves much vague about characteristics shared by insiders and outsiders. Specific incidental references in "The Oven Bird's Song" suggest that the world of insiders is mostly white and propertied or employed, although many may not be not wealthy; I could find no explicit mention of "white/s" in the essay, though, which is extremely surprising, in many ways. The demographics of the outsiders are even more vague, although Engel is highly suggestive. His early section on "social changes" explains that small farms were undergoing change and loss, while "manufacturing plants brought in blue collar employees" and one plant employed "seasonal migrant workers, many of whom were Latinos." But a "variety" of outsiders had come to stay. Perhaps the most revealing statement follows a long quote about "a certain element that you've never had before," which one must suspect in part is code for race, ethnicity, class, and other differences. "Others were more blunt about the 'certain element' that had entered Sander County: union members, southerners and southwesterners, blacks and Latinos," as well as "Commies" and "strangers."[23] But explicit references to "Latino" and "Black" are few. While demographic detail is absent, virtually all of these terms are well-known coded signals for constructing racialized low-wage workers of color, immigrants, ethnic minorities, and the like. I take this limited information, along with anecdotes in "The Oven Bird's Song" and knowledge about changing population dynamics around the United States during and since the 1980s, to connect the outsiders to the history of racialized and gendered low-wage, often migrant, worker populations. I am not sure that the connection is fully warranted, but what we learn from the limited data in "The Oven Bird's Song" supports my approach, at least for me and students in my classes. I have no reservations about acknowledging that I am concerned less about fidelity to (unknown) demographic realities in Sander County than about understanding how community norms work to construct and sustain hierarchical power, which in most of the United States is inextricably tied to race, class, gender, ethnicity, religion, immigrant status, and the like. My project, like Engel's, is mostly attuned

---

[23] Engel, *Oven Bird's Song*, 555.

to the social construction of identities, which is only loosely tethered, and in complex ways, to demographic categories.[24]

The questions above are those that my students often ask and to which they offer speculative answers. In fact, many students want to raise these issues from the very start, and I must ask them to hold off until we can address the account that Engel offers. These questions, which I encourage and students engage routinely, do not by any means signal a failure of Engel's ethnography. His project is to map the symbolic meaning-making practices of Sander County, which are largely "governed" by the norms of the insiders. But raising questions about the experiences and worldviews of the outsiders can amplify the relevance and expand the significance of his story. For one thing, students quickly see the connections between outsiders in Sander County and racialized and gendered laboring classes, including especially recent immigrants of color, throughout American history. Sander County in many ways is unique, as Engel encourages us to consider, but the story of invading workers of color who are denied full access to rights, status, and community power is very old and important. It is worth repeating that many students in my classes have taken social science classes addressing these issues and themselves are already engaged social justice activists. Moreover, raising these questions is hugely important for many students in the class who identify in various degrees with those marginal identities – as people of color, as recent immigrants, as people connected through other religious traditions, as offspring of families stuck in low-wage work and near-poverty. Indeed, many students from such contexts who were reticent earlier in the course are commonly empowered by reading their experiences into Engel's narrative, filling the blank space of insider consciousness, thus infusing the text with great meaning and power. Such students routinely recall personal examples of stigmatizing episodes and powerlessness before communal pressure and an inaccessible legal system. Sometimes these stories are about relatives in jail, families fearing deportation, exploitation (wage theft) and discrimination at work, job loss, and the like. Class discussions often encourage students to speak of their own experiences in their own words, introducing perspectives that are largely silenced by (mostly white, propertied) insiders in Sander County as well as actual

---

[24] Demographics and social construction of differences are different, of course, but interrelated. The strength of Engel's essay is his focus on constructions of differences between insiders and outsiders by dominant groups, grounded in part on imputed but questionable characteristics and nostalgia for a lost, purer past. My effort is to question whether these social constructions are linked closely to the racialized, gendered, ethnic, and class constructions of low-wage workers through which dominant, white, propertied Americans have sustained their privileges throughout American history.

communities in our proximate region. And sometimes, this produces a bit of friction in the class that mirrors the differences one might imagine in Sander County, where outsiders were actually allowed to speak up, which no doubt did happen. I welcome spirited but respectful exchanges, and the discussion of "The Oven Bird's Song" usually produces robust discussion, although less so than later classes directly on legal violence. In sum, both by historical materials covered in the course and by lived experiences, students are primed to extract (or impose?) great relevance from "The Oven Bird's Song."

This leads me to a second related departure from Engel's ethnographic method of studying Sander County. I encourage the development of independent critical social theory frameworks to explain how these norms and practices developed in Sander County as well as how they mattered for sustaining or, at least potentially, disrupting established hierarchies of power. From the start, with Scheingold, the class aims to incorporate and deploy a variety of realist, structuralist, and post-structuralist tools to critically analyze social relations and practices in terms of differential *power*.[25] But the word "power" is almost entirely absent from Engel's insider account, as are other terms central to contemporary critical analysis – inequality or unequal, inclusion and exclusion, hierarchy, domination, resistance, disciplinary power, and the like.[26] I tend to focus most on the first two sets of terms, but I often end up talking about hierarchy. My previous summary of class discussion regarding different norms about contracts, where we shift from "meanings" of terms among insiders to the material and political interests that benefit from and dominant groups that enforce such meanings, is an important type of move that drives critical analysis. Again, it would be interesting and, most likely, revealing to probe what low-wage immigrants and minority outsiders think about how contract enforcement serves "responsibility," trust, and communal bonds. Moreover, a focus on the "intersectionality" of race, class, gender, ethnicity, sexuality, and the like emphasizes the institutional challenges of outsiders, including especially their limited capacities – in money and time, legal knowledge, access to lawyers, respect, fear of reprisal, etc. – that long

---

[25] One big difference between my undergraduate course and most graduate courses is in the knowledge and sophistication that students bring regarding critical social theory. Most of my classes are focused on skill-building and critical analysis. See Michael McCann, "Dr. Strangelove: or how I learned to stop worrying and love methodology" in Austin Sarat (ed.), *Studies in Law, Politics, and Society* (JAI/Elsevier Press, 2007), pp. 19–60.

[26] A quick word count of "The Oven Bird's Song" reveals that the word "community" appears more than 100 times and "norms" are mentioned a dozen times, but the word "power" is used only twice and never in the ways I suggest, while other terms related to differential power – inequality, unequal, in/justice – show up never or rarely.

have figured into the marginalization of the low-wage, largely immigrant laboring populations. Again, bringing earlier discussions of material capacities from previous class sessions adds new dimensions of understanding and relevance to "The Oven Bird's Song." Finally, the robust literature in and beyond sociolegal studies on the themes of domination and resistance, and especially on the legal consciousness and practices of subaltern resistance, strongly invite exploration of subaltern outsider groups' world views.

I underscore that our aim in addressing what is excluded or muted by Engel's ethnography is *not* to identify intellectual shortcomings, but rather to illustrate how Engel's well-crafted insider narrative provides space for us to deploy our own critical analytical and historical tools to make sense of Sander County. Ironically, Engel's anthropological discipline as a scholar proves to be golden for my pedagogy as a teacher. This is even more true when I teach "The Oven Bird's Song" at the graduate level. I often begin my graduate course on "Rights (as Practices)" with Marx's brilliant treatise "On the Jewish Question,"[27] and students cannot resist putting that essay into conversation with "The Oven Bird's Song" later in the class. Cheryl Harris's "Whiteness as Property"[28] also proves to be a highly charged intellectual analysis to bring to the world of Sander County. Much as in my undergraduate courses, once students read Engel's "The Oven Bird's Song" it continues to be an intellectual reference point that connects with almost everything else.

FROM LOCAL TO NATIONAL: EXPLAINING THE DEVELOPMENT AND IMPACT OF THE HYPERLEXIS FANTASY

I complete my review by recognizing how engagement with "The Oven Bird's Song" continues to inform the remainder of the class. The discussion of Engel's essay feeds immediately into the next class session (the last class of the first half), where I lecture on how the same anxiety about, and condemnation of, legal rights-claiming and litigation over personal injury proliferated on a national scale throughout the United States from the late 1970s (when Engel was conducting research) until the tragedy of September 11, 2001, altered the public agenda. I draw directly on the research for the 2004 book that William Haltom and I wrote, titled *Distorting the Law: Media, Politics, and the Litigation Crisis.* The text for the class that day is a chapter from the book

---

[27] Karl Marx, "On the Jewish question," 1844, www.marxists.org/archive/marx/works/1844/jewish-question/.
[28] Cheryl Harris, "Whiteness as property," *Harvard Law Review*, 106 (1993), 1707.

on the infamous McDonald's coffee case, titled "Java Jive."[29] The widely reported popular media version of the lawsuit fits very well the types of "rumored" behavior that Engel identified as condemned in Sander County: An elderly working-class woman, Stella Liebeck, poured hot coffee on herself and then sued for huge bucks to line her pockets amply, wrongly victimizing the virtuous, family-favorite corporate giant. I ask: How would the story of Stella Liebeck have played in Sander County? Students immediately, often incisively, see the connections. "She would be stigmatized as an outsider," someone often volunteers. Some astute students might add: "Maybe, but it depends on whether she was well connected locally – but obviously that would not matter for national news stories." Not surprisingly, this single story and the quick overview of national data about news from our book multiplies hugely the reach of Engel's humble ethnographic account of a small Mid-western community. My lecture presents other culturally resonant "tort tales" of this sort, documents news coverage that mimics in form and substance the stigmatizing anecdotes, and links these narratives to state and national congressional legislative campaigns to reduce civil litigation in the decades immediately following Engel's study of Sander County. Paralleling Engel, I also offer abundant social science research to show that the fears of excessive litigation lacked empirical verification in actual disputing practices. In sum, Sander County is, or was, all over; it is us!

But our study, and my lecture, adds other dimensions that Engel's ethno-graphic account resists. Specifically, our study demonstrates at length how the national fear of hyperlexis grew out of the convergence of three interrelated developments: first, a massive *instrumental* campaign by big business, with insurance companies, the tobacco industry, the Business Roundtable, and the Chamber of Commerce in the lead, to saturate mass media with anecdotes, vignettes, news stories, editorials, and paid advertisements decrying the epi-demic of frivolous litigation by undeserving individuals, mostly against good, deserving producer organizations; second, the *institutional* complicity of the news media in extending huge attention to tort cases, tort reform politics, and the cartoonish images of citizen behavior that matched the campaign by big business, who lobbied reports with their storylines at great length; third, the savvy appeal of business campaigns and deference of media producers to the obsession with lost individual responsibility that matched the *ideological* position of neoconservatives and neoliberals in the "culture wars." In short, we offer a complex but clear three-dimensional "causal story" about how the

---

[29] Haltom and McCann, *Distorting the Law*. The specific text that students read, referenced here, is chapter 5, but my lecture presents the argument and evidence of the larger book.

fable developed and attained status as "common sense" truth in modern corporate capitalist society.

Moreover, the lecture incorporates two intellectual moves made in the book to build on what I discussed in the previous section of this chapter. First, I draw on our book to outline a variety of ways in which the cultural narrative of excessive litigation shaped both micro and macro politics in ways that bolstered corporate power and conservative ideology, themes I posited earlier through questions in discussion of "The Oven Bird's Song." For example, lawsuits against corporations declined over the quarter of a century we studied, as jurors and judges increasingly ruled against plaintiffs and plaintiffs' attorneys found the prospects for winning at trial increasingly dim. This in turn reduced corporate liability and insulated consequential corporate decisions concerning consumer and worker safety from accountability. Large tobacco companies were among the prime movers of the hyperlexis smear campaign, and they were among the primary beneficiaries, at least until the mid-1990s, when one judge and a number of whistleblowers exposed industry perfidy. Other public agendas were skewed as well. For example, our book questions why the story of 79-year-old Stella Liebeck was interpreted as an example of excessive frivolous litigation rather than bolstering support for the national health-care bill proposed by President Bill Clinton in the same year and other measures increasing social security benefits on which many low-income, working-class people depend to cover health needs. In fact, the charge that health care legislation was "a lawyers' bill" was leveled to stigmatize many forms of egalitarian legislation, dooming the fate of health-care, safety regulation, and other bills. At the same time, the animus against personal injury litigation dovetailed with and, arguably, multiplied the large backlash against civil litigation generally, and against civil rights litigation in particular. Meanwhile, politicians (e.g. George W. Bush) rose and fell based on their positions regarding the litigation "crisis." My lecture introduces the class to a variety of dimensions of unequal political and social power that help explain both *causes* and *effects* of the fantasy common-sense narrative, much as I had aimed to do in pushing beyond the analysis of Engel in "The Oven Bird's Song." My gambit works because, again, it builds on earlier course materials and discussions as well as other classes and experiences that students bring into my class.

Second, our interrogation of the McDonald's coffee case and other parallel real-life (as opposed to the many fictional tort tales) stories enables us to hear the "other songs" of those stigmatized by the litigation deterrence narrative, and who suffered as a result. Telling the "real" story of Stella Liebeck as she experienced it, fortified by accounts from family members and her doctor, provides the basis for a powerful counternarrative to the prevailing hyperlexis story. I use the first third of the now familiar advocacy documentary "Hot Coffee" to provide voice to those twice victimized by the anti-litigation crisis, first by physical harms wrought by corporate negligence and second by the psychological pain of public ridicule.[30] To this I add public and interview testimony from others also twice victimized as well as from everyday plaintiffs' attorneys (including Liebeck's attorney, who quit his practice under the strain of the public ridicule), local judges, and jurors who supported rights advocates. Like many of the voices from civil rights and women's rights struggles which I present in the early weeks of the class, these people are much more likely to identify the power imbalances that both sustain and benefit from the cultural narrative stoking anxieties about excessive litigation. Indeed, where corporate executives and paid advocates of tort reform speak the moralistic insider language of declining individual responsibility, stigmatized outsiders speak of corporate hierarchy, hypocrisy, greed, power politics, and a legal system rigged in favor of corporations (think "repeat players"). They speak to the constraints endured by ordinary people facing injuries – scarce resources of time and money, inadequate legal knowledge, limited access to lawyers, fear of reprisal – that we discussed in the previous weeks of the course. And this sometimes prompts us to momentary revisiting of the question: What and how might the outsiders – most of whom presumably are low-wage, minority, and female recent immigrants – think about community power dynamics and promises of rights entitlement in Sander County?

The class on the politics of the national litigation crisis concludes the first half of my course. I know from systematic student evaluations and later anecdotal exchanges that what students later remember most is the pairing of Engel's narrative of Sander County with the McDonald's coffee case to show how or why the promises of rights mobilization are routinely thwarted in American society.

The second half of the course shifts ground quite abruptly toward interrogating law's violence. We begin by discussing Robert Cover's "Violence and the Word"[31] and putting it into conversation with the amazing documentary

---

[30] *Hot Coffee*, www.hotcoffeethemovie.com/. I always acknowledge ambivalence about this film, because it glorifies our civil legal system and plaintiffs' attorneys. By the time they view the film, though, most students are attuned to the limitations and biases of the civil law system as a resource for ordinary people and the cultural propensities to lionize as well as castigate lawyers. I do feel compelled to recognize that I and our book figured into that very effective documentary, but that does not make me reluctant to distance myself from some dimensions of its primary storylines.

[31] See n 5 above.

The Thin Blue Line. We take up issues of excessive police violence, both in the street and in the station house; the politics of punishment and mass incarceration; the parallels of domestic state violence and global state violence, as manifest in reliance on torture, rendition, military imprisonment, and drones; and, finally, judicially authorized state killing (the death penalty). The graphic accounts of white, propertied insiders and racialized outsiders discussed in the first half of the class and captured deftly by "The Oven Bird's Song" take on new dimensions in these discussions of legal violence. In fact, in my opening lecture, I invite students to shift from thinking about the hierarchies enforced by personal injury and contract law practices in Sander County to those practices of police regarding insiders and outsiders. What might we expect, I ask? This enables students to assemble their expectations, impressions, and ideas as we begin our analytical descent into the intricacies of state violence.[32] Engel's powerful account of the anxious, quick-to-stigmatize community of (mostly white) Sander County insiders is never far from any moment in the remainder of the course.

CONCLUSION

My aim in this chapter has been to show how I teach Engel's haunting ethnography of Sander County. That article plays a critical, powerful role in my course, and I have tried to show how the essay builds on and adds to my pedagogical project. My focus on the larger context of the course flirts with critiquing "The Oven Bird's Song" for its limitations, but my aim has been to show that the intellectual trajectory of the course primes students not only to understand the intersubjective world of Sander County insiders, but also to see beyond their anxious nostalgia to the dimensions of likely (but uncertain) class, racial, ethnic, and gender (among other) inequalities that are expressed in stigmas against excessive rights-claiming and litigation over personal injury. Indeed, students raise these topics even before I am ready to address them in my orchestrated engagement with Engel; I am the one who must rein in the rush to fill in meaning beyond Engel's literal text. The students draw on earlier course readings and discussions as well as their own experiences to raise

---

[32] This reference to analysis as "descent," as relentless digging down to ever greater depths, is intentionally evocative. I sometimes use the opening scenes from David Lynch's evocative film *Blue Velvet*, where a camera panning a happy community of smiling white people and white picket fences witnesses a man stricken by heart attack, and the camera begins to dig down into the grass, which is dark, dirty, mysterious, infested with ugly insects. Sometimes I use this cinematic device on the first day of class, but usually I deploy it as we begin discussion of "The Oven Bird's Song."

questions about the exclusionary biases of the myth of rights and the civil legal system that appear to be at work in "The Oven Bird's Song," even if they are not the primary focus of Engel's ethnography. And students yearn to hear the songs that the outsiders sang (or might have sung) about the community that their presence was viewed as changing. "The Oven Bird's Song" enhances the course greatly, but my aim and experience is that the class also enlarges the significance of Engel's essay. It is relevant, I think, to conclude by noting that I have routinely substituted specific course readings in the class over nearly twenty years, both to keep my thinking fresh and to integrate great new materials I encounter. But Engel's "The Oven Bird's Song" is the only essay that I have never seriously considered replacing. I hope that I have made clear why that is the case. For that, and much else, I and my students owe a great debt to Professor Engel.

11

Racing the Oven Bird

Criminalization, Rightlessness, and the Politics of Immigration

JAMIE LONGAZEL

When Barack Obama issued the Deferred Action for Parents of Americans (DAPA) policy in November 2014, an executive order promising deportation relief to undocumented parents of US-citizen children, his political opponents pounced. A cadre of Republican presidential hopefuls, elected officials, and conservative pundits called the order a "lawless"[1] and "wholly unconstitutional"[2] abuse of power comparable to that of "[Vladimir] Putin,"[3] "a Latin American Dictator,"[4] and "the tyranny of King George."[5] Ben Carson suggested DAPA was part of the President's "nefarious agenda to bring

---

[1] The comments in this paragraph all come from a summary of Republican commentary on the DAPA program offered by Michael B. Keegan, president of People for the American Way. However, subsequent notes list the original source.

   Michael B. Keegan, "Edit memo: responses from republican presidential candidates, former and current elected officials and their far right base to President Obama's executive actions on immigration," *People for the American Way*, May 18, 2015, www.pfaw.org/press-releases/2015/05/edit-memo-responses-republican-presidential-candidates-former-and-current-ele; AV Press Releases, "Think immigration reform has a chance in the next Congress? Listen to Ted Cruz and Jeff Sessions to understand why it doesn't," *America's Voice*, September 9, 2014, http://americasvoice.org/blog/think-immigration-reform-chance-next-congress-listen-ted-cruz-jeff-sessions-understand-doesnt/.

[2] America's Voice, "UPDATED: Meet the 2016 GOP candidates for President – and their positions on immigration," *America's Voice*, February 9, 2016, http://americasvoice.org/research/meet-2016-gop-candidates-president-positions-immigration/.

[3] Al Weaver, "Ben Carson: Obama 'very much like Putin' with executive amnesty," *The Daily Caller*, November 21, 2014, http://dailycaller.com/2014/11/21/ben-carson-obama-very-much-like-putin-with-executive-amnesty-video/.

[4] David Weigel and Michael C. Bender, "Jeb Bush, confronted by DREAMer, compares Obama orders to decrees of 'Latin American dictator,'" *Bloomberg*, March 7, 2015, www.bloomberg.com/politics/articles/2015-03-07/jeb-bush-confronted-by-dreamer-compares-obama-orders-to-decrees-of-latin-american-dictator-.

[5] America's Voice, *UPDATED*.

government dependent voters to the U.S."[6] Alabama representative Mo Brooks saw DAPA as part of a plot to "dilute the vote of American citizens by bringing in millions of foreigners who are going to be dependent on welfare and handouts and hence will be dependent on the Democratic Party for their livelihoods."[7] By "encouraging the invasion"[8] and "opening the flood gates to the Third World,"[9] others said the President had "[insulted] the American people,"[10] potentially inciting "violence," "anarchy,"[11] and "an abrupt decent into an abyss that we have never seen in the history of this country."[12]

Blocking the action was not enough; Obama's adversaries wanted to see him punished. Representative Walter Jones said that he and his Republican colleagues had a "constitutional duty"[13] to impeach the President. Rep. Steven King echoed this stance, noting, "The 'I-word' (Impeachment) is on the table because our republic is on the table."[14] Others went even further, claiming Obama's "reckless conduct"[15] was "a treasonous act against the American people"[16] that warranted his arrest. "This is the only way you deal with a

[6]   Keegan, *Edit Memo*.

[7]   Miranda Blue, "Mo Brooks: immigration action will lead to 'insolvency and bankruptcy of our government,'" *Right Wing Watch*, November 24, 2014, www.rightwingwatch.org/post/mo-brooks-immigration-action-will-lead-to-insolvency-and-bankruptcy-of-our-government/.

[8]   Miranda Blue, "Ken Cuccinelli: 'We're being invaded . . . one person at a time,'" *Right Wing Watch*, March 6, 2015, www.rightwingwatch.org/post/ken-cuccinelli-were-being-invadedone-person-at-a-time/.

[9]   Media Matters Staff, "Limbaugh: Obama's immigration action intended to 'Open the flood gates to the third world,'" *Media Matters*, November 21, 2014, http://mediamatters.org/video/2014/11/21/limbaugh-obamas-immigration-action-intended-to/201666.

[10]   America's Voice, *UPDATED*.

[11]   Susan Page, "GOP senator warns of violence after immigration order," *USA Today*, November 20, 2014, www.usatoday.com/story/news/politics/2014/11/19/usa-today-capital-download-with-tom-coburn/19263969/.

[12]   Miranda Blue, "Steve King: immigration action would send country 'descending abruptly into an abyss,'" *Right Wing Watch*, November 14, 2014, www.rightwingwatch.org/post/steve-king-immigration-action-would-send-country-descending-abruptly-into-an-abyss/.

[13]   Brian Tashman, "GOP rep.: Republicans have 'constitutional duty' to impeach Obama," *Right Wing Watch*, February 11, 2015, www.rightwingwatch.org/post/gop-rep-republicans-have-constitutional-duty-to-impeach-obama/.

[14]   Miranda Blue, "Steve King threatens government shutdown, impeachment over immigration executive action," *Right Wing Watch*, October 22, 2014, www.rightwingwatch.org/post/steve-king-threatens-government-shutdown-impeachment-over-immigration-executive-action/.

[15]   Brian Tashman, "Rep. Mo Brooks: Obama should face jail time for immigration actions," *Right Wing Watch*, February 3, 2015, www.rightwingwatch.org/post/rep-mo-brooks-obama-should-face-jail-time-for-immigration-actions/.

[16]   Brian Tashman, "Michael Savage: GOP-led Congress should arrest Obama," *Right Wing Watch*, October 23, 2014, www.rightwingwatch.org/post/michael-savage-gop-led-congress-should-arrest-obama/.

hooligan," conservative talk radio host Rick Wiles said; "you tell him we're coming with handcuffs, we're going to lock you up."[17]

* * *

In a testament to its generalizability, David Engel's classic article, "The Oven Bird's Song," provides a lens for seeing the reaction to DAPA as something more than partisan bickering.[18] His study of Sander County, Illinois is perhaps best known for laying bare a glaring discrepancy between legalistic rhetoric and reality. The actual frequency of personal injury lawsuits filed in Sander County, he noted, "bore little relationship" to the level of concern residents expressed about them.[19] A similar discrepancy is evident here: President Obama did not do anything out of the ordinary – let alone *criminal* – by issuing DAPA. The truth is, Obama issued fewer executive orders than his predecessors, and he was not the first modern president to offer deportation relief with the goal of keeping families together.[20]

Engel also described how legal mobilizations and evocations of rights tend to be selectively accepted. When Sander County "outsiders" used the law, they were lambasted, accused of acting in their own self-interest, going against the community's norms, and threatening its stability. When "insiders" turned to the law, in contrast, they regarded their own efforts as virtuous, egalitarian attempts to preserve cherished norms and protect "community harmony." Selective acceptance of law is evident in the DAPA example, too. Opponents constructed the action as a "lawless," "anarchistic" initiative executed by

---

[17] Brian Tashman, "Conservative activists dream of military arresting Obama," *Right Wing Watch*, November 21, 2014, www.rightwingwatch.org/post/conservative-activists-dream-of-military-arresting-obama/.

[18] David Engel, "The oven bird's song: insiders, outsiders, and personal injuries in an American community," *Law & Society Review*, 18(4) (1984), 551–82.

[19] Ibid., 580.

[20] Obama issued fewer executive actions per year than any president since Harry S. Truman. See, e.g., The American Presidency Project, "Executive Orders: Washington – Obama," www.presidency.ucsb.edu/data/orders.php. During his eight years in office, he issued 276 executive actions, or thirty-five per year. In comparison, George W. Bush issued thirty-six per year, Bill Clinton forty-six per year, and George H. W. Bush forty-two per year. Franklin Roosevelt issued the most executive actions of any president, at 3,721 – more per year (307) than President Obama issued over his entire presidency.

What is more, Obama was not the first recent president to use his executive authority to halt deportations for family members of undocumented immigrants. Ronald Reagan and George H. W. Bush supported a similar policy in the wake of the 1986 Immigration Reform and Control Act. See, e.g., American Immigration Council, "Reagan-Bush family fairness: a chronological history," December 9, 2014, www.immigrationpolicy.org/just-facts/reagan-bush-family-fairness-chronological-history.

a "self-interested" president (e.g. "bringing Democratic voters") who, by allegedly overstepping his bounds (e.g. behaving like a "King"), posed an unprecedented threat to the nation (e.g. "descending abruptly into an abyss that we have never seen in the history of this country"). Yet the subsequent call to mobilize law *in opposition to* DAPA (e.g. "impeachment," "arrest," "coming with handcuffs") is presented as legitimate and, indeed, necessary (e.g. "a constitutional duty") to preserve the republic.

What I consider the most impressive aspect of Engel's classic article was how he placed these small-town reactions in a much bigger context. He interpreted Sander County residents' complaints about "outsider" litigiousness as one of the ways in which they grappled with the deep uncertainty they felt during a shift to an industrial economy. The construction of "insiders" and "outsiders" there, as he eloquently put it, was part of a "more broadly based *ceremony of regret* that the realities of contemporary American society could no longer be averted from their community if it were to survive."[21] For the case at hand, Engel's example prompts us to keep in mind that DAPA came on the heels of an economic crisis, amid nearly unprecedented economic inequality, and at a time when the wages of American workers had stagnated despite increases in productivity. Moans about Americans being "backed into a corner" by an "immigrant invasion" and a "reckless president" were understandably attractive to many in an historical moment characterized by economic and social insecurity.[22]

I suggest in this chapter that we can make a similar argument regarding critical race theory's (CRT) applicability to such cases.[23] From a CRT perspective, opponents' claims about immigrants being violent, government-dependent, and capable of "watering down" the vote of American citizens, beyond being untrue,[24] coincide with contemporary iterations of a racist narrative with deep roots in the United States.[25] Racialized distinctions between rhetoric and reality have likewise been pervasive in the resistance

---

[21] Engel, *Oven Bird's Song*, p. 580 (emphasis added).

[22] Jock Young, *The Vertigo of Late Modernity* (Sage, 2007). Compare also Kitty Calavita, "The new politics of immigration: 'balanced budget conservatism' and the symbolism of Proposition 187," *Social Problems*, 43(3) (1996), 284–305; Ian Haney López, *Dog Whistle Politics: How Coded Racial Appeals Have Reinvented Racism and Wrecked the Middle Class* (Oxford University Press, 2014).

[23] Richard Delgado and Jean Stefancic, *Critical Race Theory: An Introduction*, 2nd edn. (New York University Press, 2012).

[24] See, e.g., Avia Chomsky, *"They Take Our Jobs!" and Twenty Other Myths about Immigration* (Beacon Press, 2007).

[25] Joe R. Feagin, *Racist America: Roots, Current Realities, & Future Reparations* (Routledge, 2000).

Obama confronted as the first Black president (e.g. opponents continuing to bring up the disproven theory that he is not a US citizen). Because he acted on his own to grant undocumented people even the slightest legal protection (i.e. protection from deportation), his opponents saw DAPA as an affront. On the other hand, the President's opponents embraced legalistic efforts to subvert an "immigrant invasion" and to strip Obama of his power and, indeed, his freedom.[26] Context is also relevant in that DAPA came amid a heightened sense of racial threat felt by the white majority. In addition to economic uncertainty, the United States has been experiencing increasing racial/ethnic diversity and continued movements for immigrant rights and racial justice that intertwined with Obama's ascendance to the presidency.

While there are clear conceptual similarities between these two approaches, dialogue across them has been minimal. For instance, "The Oven Bird's Song" and Cheryl Harris's seminal CRT article "Whiteness as Property"[27] have simultaneously been in print for more than twenty years. At the time of this writing, however, scholars have cited both in the same work only twice.[28] In an effort to bridge this gap, this chapter acknowledges the far-reaching and seemingly timeless implications of David Engel's classic piece while at the same time arguing that increased attention to recent developments in CRT make possible an even deeper sociolegal analysis of the politics of belonging.

My specific focus is on racialized criminalization in the politics of immigration. The chapter begins with a review of relevant CRT scholarship that illustrates how race and criminalization are used to construct not only belonging but also, more profoundly, *personhood* – which, in turn, determines who is considered eligible for resources, rights, and legal recognition. Following Engel, I also place the contemporary backlash against Latina/o immigrants in its broader political economic context, exploring specifically how race and class intersect in these debates. From there, I revisit my previous work on the politics surrounding Hazleton, Pennsylvania's 2006 passage of the

---

[26] Leo Chavez, *The Latino Threat: Constructing Immigrants, Citizens, and the Nation* (Stanford University Press, 2008); Jamie Longazel, "Moral panic as racial degradation ceremony: racial stratification and the local-level backlash against Latina/o immigrants," *Punishment & Society*, 15(1) (2013), 96–119.

[27] Cheryl I. Harris, "Whiteness as property," *Harvard Law Review*, 106(8) (1993), 1707–91.

[28] A recent dissertation and a recent annual review article were, at the time of this writing, the only scholarly publications that cited both articles. See: Erin Kerrison, "The crux of context: an examination of how collateral consequences legislation impacts the desistance process," unpublished Ph.D. thesis (University of Delaware, 2014); Carroll Seron, Susan Bibler Coutin, and Pauline White Meeusen, "Is there a canon of law and society?" *Annual Review of Law and Social Science*, 9 (2013), 287–306.

Illegal Immigration Relief Act (IIRA).[29] Placing some of the data from that study more squarely in this theoretical context is revealing, particularly in light of Hazleton's striking resemblance to Sander County.

RACE, CRIMINALIZATION, AND PERSONHOOD

In "Whiteness as Property," Cheryl Harris argues that whiteness has value accrued by the historic devaluation of people of color.[30] Recognizing that whiteness is a "relational concept, unintelligible without reference to non-whiteness,"[31] her point is that it is through the denial of some people's humanity that others come to understand their own. Race, therefore, is centrally about granting and denying *personhood*. As Harris describes it, the chief purpose of whiteness as a socially constructed category in US history has been the protection it offers from devaluation. During slavery, she writes,

> Whiteness became *a shield from slavery*, a highly volatile and unstable form of property. In the form adopted in the United States, slavery made human beings market-alienable and in doing so, subjected human life and person-hood – that which is most valuable – to the ultimate devaluation. Because whites could not be enslaved or held as slaves, the racial line between white and Black was extremely critical; it became a *line of protection and demar-cation* from the potential threat of commodification, and it determined the allocation of the benefits and burdens of this form of property. White identity and whiteness were sources of privilege and protection; their absence meant being the subject of property.[32]

Immigration scholars have been noting how criminalization characterizes contemporary immigration politics. This is most evident, for example, in the

---

[29] Jamie Longazel, *Undocumented Fears: Immigration and the Politics of Divide and Conquer in Hazleton, Pennsylvania* (Temple University Press, 2016). See also Benjamin Fleury-Steiner and Jamie Longazel, "Neoliberalism, community development, and anti-immigration backlash in Hazleton, Pennsylvania" in M. W. Varsanyi (ed.), *Taking Local Control: Immigration Policy Activism in U.S. Cities and States* (Stanford University Press, 2010), pp. 157–72; Jamie Longazel and Benjamin Fleury-Steiner, "Exploiting borders: the political economy of local backlash against undocumented immigrants," *Chicana/o-Latina/o Law Review*, 30 (2011), 43–64; Longazel, "Moral panic as racial degradation ceremony"; Jamie Longazel, "Rhetorical barriers to mobilizing for immigrant rights: white innocence and Latina/o abstraction," *Law & Social Inquiry*, 39(3) (2014), 580–600.

[30] Harris, *Whiteness as Property*.

[31] Howard Winant, "Behind blue eyes: whiteness and contemporary U.S. racial politics" in Michelle Fine, Lois Weis, Linda C. Powell, and L. Mun Wong (eds.), *Off White: Readings on Race, Power, and Society* (Routledge, 1997), p. 48.

[32] Harris, *Whiteness as Property*, pp. 1720–21, emphasis added.

militarization of the border,[33] the doctrinal convergence of immigration and criminal law,[34] and political rhetoric that assumes those who cross the US-Mexico border are inherently crime-prone.[35] However, Lisa Marie Cacho suggests, following Harris, that although scholars often use "criminalization" interchangeably with "stereotyping" (e.g. "to be *misrecognized* as someone who committed a crime"[36]), we can more accurately understand it as a contemporary "demarcation line."

Many marginalized people of color, Cacho goes on to elaborate – including, especially, those without documentation – suffer a veritable social death.[37] They are "prevented from being law-abiding";[38] their lives and the spaces they occupy are what "make an unsanctioned action legible as illicit and recognizable as a crime."[39] In contrast, white criminality is "inconceivable to imagine." Whiteness, in effect, is *"decriminalized."*[40] Therefore, for critical race scholars like Harris and Cacho, racialized criminalization runs much deeper than misrecognition. It is not behavior, but rather *being*, that it targets.[41]

The consequences of this cannot be overstated. Cacho notes how the denial of personhood renders criminalized populations "ineligible for sympathy and compassion"[42] – that is, "undeserving" of resources, rights, and legal

---

[33] Joesph Nevins, *Operation Gatekeeper: The Rise of the Illegal Alien and the Making of the U.S.–Mexico Boundary* (Routledge, 2002).

[34] Juliet Stumpf, "The crimmigration crisis: immigrants, crime, and sovereign power," *American University Law Review*, 56 (2006), 367–419.

[35] Carolina Moreno, "9 outrageous things Donald Trump has said about Latinos," *Huffington Post*, November 9, 2016, www.huffingtonpost.com/entry/9-outrageous-things-donald-trump-has-said-about-latinos_us_55e483a1e4b0c818f618904b.

[36] Lisa Maria Cacho, *Social Death: Racialized Rightlessness and the Criminalization of the Unprotected* (New York University Press, 2012), p. 4; emphasis added.

[37] Compare Orlando Patterson, *Slavery and Social Death: A Comparative Study* (Harvard University Press, 1985).

[38] Ibid, 4.   [39] Ibid, 38.

[40] Ibid, 38 (emphasis added).

This is not to say that someone who identifies as white cannot be *convicted* of a crime. Mass incarceration has also disaffected poor whites, especially in recent years. Cacho's point is that when white law-violating occurs, it becomes difficult to comprehend, particularly within a scheme designed to punish the racial "outsider." In her words:

[T]he interpretation and application of criminal law is never race-neutral, no matter how race-erased individual laws appear to be. Recognizable as rights-bearing subjects and able to access pervasive discourses of white innocence, injury, and entitlement, [white offenders are] read and represented as explicitly not criminal and even unable to become criminal in a way that effectively render[s] their intent and their culpability irrelevant. They would be rendered innocent even if guilty. Ibid, 38.

[41] Ibid, 6.   [42] Ibid, 37.

recognition, not necessarily from a formal legal perspective, but certainly in the opinion of many "insiders" on the ground. Hence how debates over resources (e.g. government services) usually hinge not on the deprivations that criminalized populations endure but rather on the so-called "excessive" amount of resources the majority complains they require. When the taken-for-granted assumption is that a group deserves nothing, *anything* seems undue.

In debates over immigration, the myriad harms that immigrants experience – e.g. structural violence, disproportionate criminal victimization, exploitation, and discrimination – often take a back seat to complaints about their perceived "overreach." And again, this construction of ineligibility feeds a parallel construction of eligibility: labeling "them" as undeserving reinforces the idea that these resources are "ours."

The same goes for rights. There exists a similar "settled expectation," that whites will be "overrepresented on a neutral playing field."[43] The white majority does not measure rights claims brought by the criminalized by "the scope of the injury to the subjugated, but . . . the extent" to which such settled expectations are perceived to have been infringed.[44]

Another way of saying this is that the white majority determines whether criminalized populations of color are "deserving" of resources or rights. In those cases when the majority does award resources/rights to otherwise "ineligible" or "rightless" populations, they present them as "gifts"[45] – or, in Cacho's words, as honorable sacrifices made "as if legal recognition was a contract between unequals that formalizes the dominant populations' willingness to share their power and privileges."[46] But such gifts are conditional. They come with the assumption that whites can rescind what they have granted if they perceive the recipient is either pursuing more than they are "permitted" or challenging the prevailing politics of personhood.[47]

And when the "socially dead" *demand* resources or rights, particularly when they use a race-cognizant language that runs counter to colorblind racial ideology's façade of neutrality,[48] their "uninvited" assertions are met with

---

[43] Ibid, 25.   [44] Harris, *Whiteness as Property*, 1768.

[45] Cacho, *Social Death*; Derrick Bell, *Faces at the Bottom of the Well: The Persistence of Racism* (Basic, 1992); Miranda Cady Hallett, "Temporary protection, enduring contradiction: the contested and contradictory meanings of temporary immigration status," *Law & Social Inquiry*, 39(3) (2014), 621–42.

[46] Cacho, *Social Death*, p. 8.

[47] Dana Cloud, "Hegemony or concordance? The rhetoric of tokenism in 'Oprah' Winfrey's rags-to-riches biography," *Critical Studies in Mass Communication*, 13(2) (1996), 115–37.

[48] Eduardo Bonilla-Silva, *Racism without Racists: Color-Blind Racism and the Persistence of Racial Inequality in America* (Rowman and Littlefield, 2006).

scorn. Not unlike the "outsiders" targeted in Sander County, "insiders" accuse criminalized rights-seekers of self-interestedly demanding "special," rather than equal, rights and/or of inappropriately "playing the race card." As Derek Bell put it, although people of color may now be able to get into court, they are nevertheless "denied ... standing when they discuss their negative experiences with racism" and "are eyed suspiciously" because it is assumed they "cannot be objective on racial issues."[49] Expectations of white overrepresentation thus make it possible for social and legal actors to flip the discursive script, ironically creating a widespread perception that racism is "a zero-sum game that [whites] are now losing" in a climate where institutionalized white supremacy remains robust.[50]

Any attempt to challenge the settled expectation of white overrepresentation, in fact, usually leads the majority to reinforce the subordinate status of marginalized claimants. Building on the work of Engel and others,[51] Jonathan Goldberg-Hiller and Neal Milner describe how marginalized groups regularly have their rights claims turned against them.[52] The so-called "inappropriate" demands of outsiders, they write, become "evidence" that they are "morally dangerous, irrational, profligate people whose very rights claims become indicators of [their] general unseemliness."[53] Adding race to the equation extends that observation. Criminalized populations often face punishment – rhetorical or literal – for "overstepping" their oppressor-defined bounds. They are accused of being "racist," not egalitarian (and therefore a threat to "community harmony"/ "national stability"), and, I would add, are often *re-criminalized* and thus stripped of any "gifts" they have been conditionally granted (e.g. recall the rhetorical criminalization of President Obama after he offered legal protection to a "rightless" group of people).

The inclination of many would be to stop the analysis at this point – to chalk this up as another instance of detestable racism, much like many observers might have attributed the bogus claims about litigation coming out of Sander County to the "backward" nature of those small-town residents. But it is here that both Engel and Harris impressively take their arguments one step further, theorizing about how material concerns intersect with the

---

[49] Bell, *Faces at the Bottom of the Well*, p. 111, 113.

[50] Micahel Norton and Samuel Sommers, "Whites see racism as a zero-sum game that they are now losing," *Perspectives on Psychological Science*, 6(3) (2011), 215–18.

[51] Engel, *Oven Bird's Song*; Carol Greenhouse, Barbara Yngvesson, and David Engel, *Law and Community in Three American Towns* (Cornell University Press, 1994).

[52] Jonathan Goldberg-Hiller and Neal Milner, "Rights as excess: understanding the politics of special rights," *Law & Social Inquiry*, 28(4) (2003), 1075–118.

[53] Ibid, 1079.

construction of "insiders" and "outsiders." Harris notes how the "value" of whiteness represents a form of "compensation" for economic misfortune, akin to what W. E. B. Du Bois described as a "psychological wage."[54] Du Bois famously pointed out how, despite having shared economic interests, poor and working-class whites during Reconstruction opted to identify themselves as "not slaves" and "not blacks" in exchange for the "public deference and titles of courtesy"[55] that came with an embrace of their white identity. Whiteness in this way, Harris explains, "retains its value as a *'consolation prize'*: it does not mean that all whites will win, but simply that they will not lose, if losing is defined as being on the bottom of the social and economic hierarchy."[56]

CRIMINALIZATION AND RIGHTLESSNESS IN HAZLETON, PENNSYLVANIA

Hazleton is located in the Anthracite Coal Region of Pennsylvania – a place that, for historians, represents the "face of decline."[57] Once a coal boomtown, Hazleton's mining industry dissipated in the first half of the twentieth century. The city's shift to a manufacturing economy in the 1950s provided some stability in the ensuing decades. However, demanufacturing prompted the local economy to falter again beginning in the 1980s. By the late 1990s, even enhanced efforts to attract industry were mostly futile.[58] More than 40,000 people worked in the manufacturing sector in Hazleton's Luzerne County in the late 1970s; twenty years later, the total was less than half of that.

It was at this point that local developers turned to a massive tax incentive for help luring industry to the area. The tactic was a success in that it brought jobs; unfortunately, though, most of them were with low-wage firms: distribution centers, warehouses, and a meatpacking plant. These economic changes in turn prompted demographic changes. Latina/o migrants began arriving in large numbers in subsequent years, many seeking work in these industries. Hazleton's population was 95 percent white at the time of the 2000 census and approximately 36 percent Latina/o by 2006, the year Hazleton passed the Illegal Immigration Relief Act (IIRA).

---

54 W. E. B. Du Bois, *Black Reconstruction in America* (Meridian, 1935); see also David Roediger, *The Wages of Whiteness: Race and the Making of the American Working Class* (Verso, 1991).
55 Du Bois, *Black Reconstruction*, p. 700.   56 Ibid, 1758–9.
57 Thomas Dublin and Walter Licht, *The Face of Decline: The Pennsylvania Anthracite Region in the Twentieth Century* (Cornell, 2005).
58 See Longazel, *Undocumented Fears*.

The IIRA sought to punish landlords and businesses who rented to or hired undocumented immigrants and to make English the official language of the city. Its passage was prompted by a moral panic over the murder of a white resident allegedly committed by two undocumented Latino men (notably, those charges were later dropped for lack of evidence). The message circulating locally was that this crime was an example of the threat undocumented immigrants posed to the city. In time, the reaction to this single incident expanded into a broader set of claims that *all* undocumented immigrants were crime-prone and burdensome, wreaking havoc in Hazleton.[59]

In line with an emerging "scholarly consensus"[60] that immigration does not increase crime, local assumptions of immigrant criminality, it turns out, were uncorroborated. To provide but one example of the distinction between rhetoric and reality in this case,[61] undocumented immigrants accounted for just 0.25 percent of all arrestees in the city in the years leading up to the IIRA's passage.

This was not just oversight. Officials never even bothered to examine local crime statistics,[62] despite remaining insistent that undocumented immigrant criminality was a serious problem warranting legislative action. "I don't need to know how many homeruns Barry Bonds has to know that [if] I throw him a bad pitch, he can knock it out of the park," Hazleton Mayor Lou Barletta, who spearheaded the ordinance, declared while defending the local measure; "I knew we had a problem here. I didn't need numbers ... My people in my City did not need numbers."[63]

Comments like this imply that criminality is an inherent tendency of undocumented immigrants – in Cacho's words, they are "presumed guilty even if proven innocent." This is especially evident in remarks which Hazleton Police Chief Robert Ferdinand made while on the stand in the subsequent trial over the IIRA's constitutionality (*Lozano et al. v. City of Hazleton*). Defending his argument that there is a link between undocumented immigration and crime in Hazleton, he said:

> I think that we're seeing a penchant of these guys for carrying weapons and using weapons, not only firearms, but baseball bats and sticks and swords and knives, that we haven't seen in previous years. I mean, that, to me, is a plain fact, because I keep myself abreast of what goes on with the police

---

[59] See Longazel, "Moral panic as racial degradation ceremony"; Longazel, *Undocumented Fears*.
[60] Matthew Lee and Ramiro Martinez Jr. "Immigration reduces crime: an emerging scholarly consensus," *Sociology of Crime, Law and Deviance*, 13 (2009), 3–16.
[61] For more, see Longazel, *Undocumented Fears*.   [62] Ibid.
[63] *Lozano v. Hazleton*, trial testimony.

department, the reports from the police officers themselves. I get a picture of what is occurring through their eyes, and that is plainly the truth that we're having an increase in violent crimes of that nature, utilizing weapons and gang activity and large fights.

For instance, when I was young in high school, the way to resolve a difference would be two guys squaring off after school and punching it out. Now we're talking about these guys don't have the honor or the courage to fight one on one. They are talking about utilizing weapons against each other and having a whole crew of their buddies jump in there, too.

This is completely different from what we have seen years ago. This is a way of resolving disputes of this nature to resort to violence. This is truly something that we have not seen before. I don't care what the numbers say. I'm telling you that the reality is that this is the trend now, this type of activity, this kind of violent crime.[64]

Like Barletta's baseball analogy, Ferdinand maintains that his taken-for-granted "truth" about immigrant criminality trumps any consideration of empirical data. Again, it is not that he gets the numbers wrong; it is that he does not "care what the numbers say." Also significant is how his description of "this type of activity" in which "these guys" are engaging enables a parallel construction of whiteness. Recounting his youth as a resident in a more homogeneously white Hazleton, Ferdinand fails to label as "criminal" that which we would expect an officer of the law to identify as an assault: "two guys squaring off ... and punching it out." This illustrates the unintelligibility of white law-breaking.[65] Ferdinand actually goes so far as to bring up the violence of these hypothetical, presumably white youth as an example of behavior that is more "virtuous" (e.g. youth exhibiting "honor" and "courage") than that exhibited by today's "criminals." For those operating with the conception that "we" *cannot* be criminals and "they" *must* be, the arrival of criminalized populations in Hazleton is proof enough that crime is on the rise, even if offending is not.

By implication, those on one side of the line of demarcation are undeserving, those on the other entitled. Commentary in favor of the IIRA was littered with declarations that "unmotivated" immigrants were burdening the city (again, without any supporting evidence). "Some people have taken advantage of America's openness and tolerance," Mayor Barletta told Hazleton City Council; "Some come to this country and refuse to learn English, creating

---

[64] Ibid.   [65] Cacho, *Social Death*, p. 38.

a language barrier for city employees."[66] There are even traces of this in the subtext of Ferdinand's testimony: Unlike "us" – we who "courageously" and "honorably" fight one-on-one – "they" seek an "unfair advantage," even in skirmishes, by "utilizing weapons" and "having a whole crew of their buddies jump in."

Regardless of the accusation, the underlying message is that "shortcutting" immigrants are burdening "hardworking" and "law-abiding" Americans. Importantly, this narrative contains a material component in that it has the "capacity to explain"[67] the economic marginality of poor and working-class whites. Hazleton *is* declining; its resources *are* limited. But rather than pointing to the political economic factors responsible for this decline (e.g. demanufacturing, corporate tax breaks, etc.) – factors which were scarcely discussed publicly in Hazleton – officials introduced and local residents embraced a version of events that blames immigrants for the city's social ills.[68] Following Harris, one interpretation of this is that such scapegoating provides local white residents with assurance that, despite their economic plight, they will remain a step above Latina/o newcomers on the social and economic ladder.[69]

Criminalizing Resistance

After Hazleton City Council introduced the IIRA, a small group of longtime Latina/o community leaders led efforts to oppose it. The members of this group were upfront about their distaste for the ordinance. It called it discriminatory, challenged accusations that immigrants committed crime and drained resources, and urged officials and city residents to appreciate immigrants' humanity.[70] The group's protests, however, met harsh counterresistance. Many accused these activists of demanding not equal but "special" rights and of bringing race into an otherwise "raceless" debate. A comment from Hazleton City Councilwoman Evelyn Graham aimed at one of these leaders captures this quite well:

---

[66] Lou Barletta, "An open letter from Mayor Lou Barletta." See http://lawprofessors.typepad.com/immigration/2006/07/amother_local_g.html.

[67] Katherine Beckett, *Making Crime Pay: Law and Order in Contemporary American Politics* (Oxford University Press, 1997), 87.

[68] Longazel, *Undocumented Fears.*   [69] Ibid.

[70] For a more detailed description of this activism, see Longazel, *Rhetorical Barriers*; Longazel, *Undocumented Fears.*

I have tried twice to explain to you the serious problems we face, and you have dismissed these problems by insisting they are just the result of a different culture. You seem to believe that we must accept them. When I and the mayor tried to give you and [other community leaders] examples of troubles in the community which we believe are caused by illegal aliens, your response was to discount "illegal" as just a word that changes with time. You belittle any implications of criminality. You show no desire to help solve the problems and will not even discuss them. I must confess, I am dismayed by this attitude. I was hoping that you would help build the bridge we need. Based on your statements in front of City Council [calling for acculturation rather than assimilation] ... I could accuse you and [another community leader] of racism. You, not the mayor or council, are the ones who are inciting segregation instead of encouraging integration. I believe it is you who are practicing divisiveness. Look into your hearts and you may find that you are advocating separatism ... I believe that most of Hazleton's immigrants came here to become a part of the community and build a better life, a new life. I believe they seek unity rather than diversity. And I believe that you, the mayor, City Council, and community leaders owe it to them and future legal immigrants to get behind them and encourage their adaptation to a new life and a loyalty to America, their new home. We welcome them. And you do them a disservice when you deliberately misrepresent our actions for your own purposes.[71]

Elsewhere, I have used these data to show how members of the majority in effect abstracted away the concerns of the Latina/o community while maintaining the innocence of the white majority.[72] The theoretical perspective I am advancing here extends that analysis. There is evidence that Latina/os in Hazleton experienced hardships, including increased discrimination,[73] yet notice how in this statement the Councilwoman does not mention those harms as a concern. The real affront, Graham seems to imply, is the Latina/o leaders' tenacity in bringing forth race-cognizant resistance, therefore challenging several of the community majority's taken-for-granted assumptions and "settled expectations." Specifically, the Latina/o leaders drew criticism for questioning that immigrant criminality is a given. Graham also chided them

---

[71] Hazleton City Council, meeting transcript, July 13, 2006.

[72] Longazel, *Rhetorical Barriers*; Longazel, *Undocumented Fears*; Thomas Ross, "The rhetorical tapestry of race: white innocence and black abstraction," *William and Mary Law Review*, 32(1) (1990), 1–36.

[73] See Réne Flores, "Living in the eye of the storm: how did Hazleton's restrictive immigration ordinance affect local interethnic relations?" *American Behavioral Scientist*, 58(13) (2014), 43–63; Longazel, *Undocumented Fears*, pp. 40–2.

for evoking race at all, and especially for drawing attention to discrimination, both of which challenge the majority's insistence that the playing field is in fact neutral, even if white overrepresentation is the reality in practice.

Having "overstepped" these bounds, the Latina/o community leaders found their claims turned upside down. Comments such as Graham's discursively transform the racially oppressed into oppressors, and vice versa. Notice, especially, how this narrative re-applies familiar tropes after those whom white leaders "trusted" (e.g. "I was hoping that you would help build the bridge we need") apparently violated the terms of their "award" by insisting on Latina/o personhood. Having "disappointed" officials, the Latina/o community leaders now face accusations of being stubborn ("I have tried twice to explain to you"), manipulative ("you deliberately misrepresent our actions"), and self-serving ("for your own purposes"). To go against the status quo is to exhibit "no desire to help" and an "unwillingness to discuss" the city's problems. And because they brought up race, Graham accuses them of "inciting segregation" and "practicing divisiveness," actions which run counter to the egalitarian approach that supporters of the IIRA swear they have embraced ("we welcome them").

Take, as another example, comments a former Hazleton resident made in front of Hazleton City Council in response to the Latina/o leaders challenging the IIRA:

> I really feel after reading the newspapers that the Hazleton Area Latino Taskforce (whose membership is comprised of the Latina/o community leaders mentioned above) is the cause of a lot of these problems. They are telling the Latino community that we are against all of them, not just the illegals. It is almost like blackmail. They are blackmailing our community with litigation threats. I'm hearing them all night. We're threatened about our economy going down, litigation. It has to come to an end. We survived for many years before this mass immigration came into Hazleton. We're going to survive again. Blackmail is a crime, just like being illegal is a crime ... You're threatening Hazleton, threatening everybody else and I think it is wrong.[74]

Especially noteworthy here is how this resident makes an effort to criminalize the Latina/o leaders. He accuses them of a "crime" (blackmail) that I think not coincidentally involves manipulation and the taking of money. Seemingly as a way to put these activists "back in their place," he also aligns their behavior with that of already degraded undocumented immigrants

---

[74] Hazleton City Council, meeting transcript, July 13, 2006.

("Blackmail is a crime, just like being illegal is a crime") as he portrays a "dual threat" from which Hazleton must defend itself.[75]

Lozano v. Hazleton: *Re-Asserting Rightlessness*

Despite not gaining any traction locally, this group of Latina/o leaders persisted. They contacted the American Civil Liberties Union (ACLU) and other prominent litigating organizations who ultimately filed a lawsuit against the City of Hazleton for passing the IIRA. In formal legal terms, the suit was a success. US District Court Judge James Munley declared the IIRA unconstitutional, prohibiting it from ever being enforced. Higher courts upheld his ruling after several years' worth of appeals.[76] Yet his initial decision sparked what was perhaps the most vitriolic backlash of the entire local conflict.[77]

Harris points out that in recent decades courts have "refused to extend continued legal protection to white privilege"[78] as they had in the past, but that there remains a hesitancy to "guarantee that white privilege would be dismantled."[79] As a result, she says, it is often "the level of white resistance [that dictates] the parameters of the remedy."[80] And, indeed, when a legal ruling favors "rightless" "outsiders," "insiders" tend to mobilize with stiffer opposition, refusing to accept any challenges to their settled expectations.[81]

Responding to Munley's ruling, officials in Hazleton spoke out against those so-called "powerful special interest groups and lobbyists"[82] who in their minds stood in the way of an "innocent small town" doing what it thought was

---

[75] Longazel, *Rhetorical Barriers*; Longazel, *Undocumented Fears*.

[76] Following the initial ruling, the case was appealed to the US Court of Appeals for the Third Circuit. That court upheld Munley's decision. After a subsequent appeal, the Supreme Court remaindered the case in light of its recent decisions on a pair of Arizona laws. The Third Circuit Court again reaffirmed the IIRA's unconstitutionality and the Supreme Court refused to hear an appeal of that decision. See Kent Jackson, "Supreme Court refusal ends city's illegal immigration case," *Standard-Speaker*, March 14, 2014, http://standardspeaker.com/news/supreme-court-refusal-ends-city-s-illegal-immigration-case-1.1644404.

[77] Longazel and Fleury-Steiner, *Exploiting Borders*; Longazel, *Rhetorical Barriers*; Longazel, *Undocumented Fears*.

[78] Harris, "Whiteness as property," 1751.

[79] Ibid, 1751.
     For additional analysis of this opinion, see Doris Marie Provine, "Justice as told by judges: the case of litigation over local anti-immigrant legislation," *Studies in Social Justice*, 3(2) (2009), 231–45; Longazel and Fleury-Steiner, "Exploiting borders."

[80] Harris, "Whiteness as property," 1756.

[81] Compare Jeffery Dudas, *The Cultivation of Resentment: Treaty Rights and the New Right* (Stanford University Press, 2008).

[82] L. A. Tarone, "Barletta team vows appeal," *Standard-Speaker*, July 27, 2007.

necessary to protect itself. They called Munley's ruling "judicial activism"[83] ("It is clear we were not only battling [the plaintiffs in the case], but a hostile court as well"[84]) and depicted the ACLU as a bully ("The ACLU and their twenty-five lawyers thought that this little city would roll over and back down, but we're not going to back down"[85]).

In short time, a group of ordinary residents mobilized to form a grassroots group that held rallies in the streets of Hazleton and across the state that summer "in support of Mayor Barletta and the IIRA."[86] Many who got involved became active for the first time, provoked by the perception that the momentum "unfairly" generated by pro-immigrant activists posed a threat to their rights and to their way of life. The following recollection is similar to what I heard from many:

> I saw [Mayor Barletta] on TV speaking the same language I am … Then I see where the ACLU is taking him to court. Then this is playing out in the courts. Then I hear that during his trial [that] the ACLU and … La Raza and a couple other militant organizations are going to be staging a protest outside of the courthouse in Scranton on Public Square … So I pull over and I go out and here is all the pro-illegal immigration activists – not immigration activists, [but] *illegal* immigration activists … I said, "Something has to be done here. There has to be a counter-demonstration, a counter show of support for *legal* immigration and against *illegal*." So I went ahead and made a couple of phone calls … I called talk radio and said, "Look, tomorrow I am going to have a rally in support of Mayor Lou Barletta and the IIRA."[87]

Those who mobilized in favor of the IIRA identified as strong supporters of the "rule of law," and were most appreciative of legalistic efforts brought forth by the community majority (e.g. passing the IIRA). When it came to the rights claims and legal filings of pro-immigrant groups, however, they were quick to dismiss them, and, as we see here, were apt to mobilize in opposition. It is probably safe to say that the more momentum immigrant rights groups gained, the more forceful the resistance they faced became.[88]

A passage from an interview I conducted with a pro-IIRA activist captures this quite well. During our discussion, the interviewee referenced the 2008 murder of Luis Rameriz, which occurred in neighboring Shenandoah, Pennsylvania. Rameriz, an undocumented Mexican immigrant, was beaten to

---

[83] Ibid. [84] Ibid.
[85] Lou Barletta, "Rally in support of Mayor Lou Barletta," Hazleton, PA, June 3, 2007. Transcript of speech is on file with the author.
[86] Author's interview with a pro-IIRA activist, May 2009. [87] Ibid.
[88] See Longazel, *Undocumented Fears*, pp. 45–65.

death by four white teenagers from Shenandoah who, while carrying out the attack, called him a "fucking spic" and shouted, among other things, that "this is Shenandoah" and Rameriz should "go back to Mexico."[89] Initially a jury exonerated the teens of serious charges. However, the Mexican American Legal Defense and Education Fund (MALDEF) urged the federal government to reopen the case in light of revelations that local law enforcement had corroborated with the family of one of the accused.[90] That prosecution resulted in federal hate crime convictions for two of the attackers. The pro-IIRA activist saw the efforts of MALDEF and the federal government as unacceptable:

> It was just unbelievable; they wanted to lynch these kids – MALDEF and all of them. First of all, MALDEF has no right in our legal system. This is our country, not the Spanish country. You know what I mean? What right does MALDEF have to put their nose in our legal system?

It seems obvious from this statement that this activist considers neither Ramirez nor the overtly pro-Mexican-American organization working on his behalf as having rights or being legitimately able to access legal recourse ("MALDEF has no right in *our* legal system"). That MALDEF even tried to use the law at all to protect a murder victim is something he considers "criminal" – ironically, on par with a lynching. His words epitomize how *being* trumps *behavior* when it comes to criminalization. An attempt to seek justice on behalf of a marginalized person of color beaten to death by a group of white teens draws comparisons to a similar crime to the one they arguably committed.[91] Meanwhile, the actual criminal behavior of Ramirez's killers goes unrecognized (e.g. many dismissed the murder as a "fight gone wrong").

CONCLUSION

"The Oven Bird's Song" ends with the following passage:

> [T]he denunciation of personal injury litigation in Sander County was significant mainly as one aspect of a symbolic effort by members of the community to preserve a sense of meaning and coherence in the face of

---

[89] For an analysis of this case, see Kevin Johnson and Joanna E. Cuevas Ingram, "Anatomy of a modern-day lynching: the relationship between hate crimes against Latina/os and the debate over immigration reform," *North Carolina Law Review*, 91 (2013), 1613–56.

[90] See, e.g., CNN, "Men convicted of hate crime sentenced to 9 years in prison," February 27, 2011, www.cnn.com/2011/CRIME/02/23/pennsylvania.hate.crime/.

[91] Johnson and Ingram, *Anatomy of a Modern-day Lynching*.

social changes that they found threatening and confusing. It was in this sense a solution – albeit a partial and unsatisfying one – to a problem basic to the human condition, the problem of living in a world that has lost the simplicity and innocence it is thought to have had. The outcry against personal injury litigation was part of a broader effort by some residents of Sander County to exclude from their moral universe what they could not exclude from the physical boundaries of their community and to recall and reaffirm an untainted world that existed nowhere but in their imaginations.[92]

Engel describes the ontological pain experienced by Sander County residents. Their sense of loss was deep, akin to what Jock Young described as *vertigo* – "a sense of insecurity of insubstantiality, and of uncertainty, a whiff of chaos and a fear of falling."[93] This particular insight is what I have always admired most about this classic article. To begin with varying reactions to contract and personal injury litigation and end up vividly capturing how local residents puzzle over their individual and collective senses of self is a truly magnificent intellectual accomplishment that showcases the importance of decentering law and capturing how it intersects with society in complex ways.

To argue that we ought to incorporate race into such analyses might therefore strike some as an unnecessary suggestion. Would doing so not take away from the depths of this interpretation? Why ask whether residents in places like Sander County are "racist" when we can explore problems "basic to the human condition"? Such concerns may be understandable if we limit our understanding of race to bias or individual-level malice. What I have tried to emphasize here, however, is that critical race theorists have articulated more nuanced, expanded understandings of race that can enrich Engel's classic interpretation without sacrificing any of its insights.

As we carve out a research agenda in this tradition moving forward, it is therefore paramount that we appreciate the layers of critical race theorizing and avoid, as Laura Gómez put it in her 2011 Presidential Address to the Law and Society Association, "looking for race in all the wrong places."[94] Too often, we treat race as static rather than dynamic. Race is more than a variable.[95] And it exists even when we cannot see it,[96] including deep down alongside that soulful mourning Engel describes. As we have seen here, many

---

[92] Engel, *Oven Bird's Song*, pp. 580–1.   [93] Young, *Vertigo*, p. 12.

[94] Laura Gómez, "Looking for race in all the wrong places," *Law & Society Review*, 46(2) (2012), 221–45.

[95] Tukufu Zuberi, *Thicker than Blood: How Racial Statistics Lie* (University of Minnesota Press, 2001).

[96] Osagie Obasogie, *Blinded by Sight: Seeing Race Through the Eyes of the Blind* (Stanford University Press, 2014).

cling to whiteness with strong emotion to retain a sense of worth, especially when prospects seem grim. My point is that, rather than wondering whether this is a case of racialized backlash *or* an expression of elemental fear, we ought to recognize the two as inextricably linked. As jon a. powell writes, the former was "born of" the latter:

> The problematic and isolated white self forms the backbone of resistance to a truly robust, inclusive America ... This self is all too easily controlled by fears – in part because it was born of fear – whether declining property values, the "predatory" black man, the other's "culture of poverty," or any of a range of similar racialized images. Beyond these distortions, however, lies a more fundamental fear: self-annihilation. For in the context of this society's unwillingness to come to terms with its racial organization, to ask people to give up whiteness is to ask them to give up their sense of self.[97]

He goes on to say that in order to overcome this, it is important that we "provide space – institutional space, political space, social space, and conceptual space – for the emergence of new relationships and a new way of being that exists beyond isolation and separation." Given the relative inattention to critical race scholarship, we should probably add "scholarly space" to his list, as well. Since it emerged as a critique of mainstream legal thought, critical race theorists remain on the margins of law and society scholarship, regarded as "outsider scholars"[98] despite having produced a theoretically rich body of work and maintaining the strong commitment to social justice that inspired this intellectual movement in the first place.[99] In this regard, we might also say that "The Oven Bird's Song" offers a lesson for scholarly communities: As we pursue a richer understanding of how law interacts with society, and especially as we study the politics of belonging, it becomes incumbent upon us, as well, to break down our boundaries.

---

[97] jon a. powell, *Racing to Justice: Transforming Our Conceptions of Self and Other to Build an Inclusive Society* (Indiana University Press, 2012), pp. xvii–xviii.
[98] Delgado and Stefancic, *Critical Race Theory*, p. 150.   [99] Ibid, p. 150.

12

Irresponsible Matter

Sublunar Dreams of Injury and Identity

ANNE BLOOM

I can't imagine anything
  that I would less like to be
  than a disincarnate Spirit...

the sublunar world is such fun,
  where Man is male or female
  and gives Proper Names to all things.

I can, however, conceive
  that the organs Nature gave Me...

dream of another existence
  than that they have known so far

yes, it well could be that my Flesh

is praying for "Him" to die,
  so setting Her free to become
  irresponsible Matter.

        W. H. Auden, *No, Plato, No* (1973)[1]

Like David Engel's "The Oven Bird's Song," the title of this chapter borrows from a poem. Engel's title referred to Robert Frost's poem "The Oven Bird," which, like Engel's essay, describes a response to the perception of a rapidly changing landscape.[2] In a note beneath the text, Engel explains that, in the poem, the oven bird "sings loudly" in an apparent protest against the changing

---

[1] W. H. Auden, "No, Plato, no" in *W.H. Auden: Collected Poems*, 2007 Modern Library Edition, ed. Edward Mendelson (The Modern Library, 2007), p. 891.
[2] David Engel, "The oven bird's song: insiders, outsiders, and personal injuries in an American community," *Law & Society Review*, 18(4), 551–82.

environment: "The question that he frames in all but words/Is what to make of a diminished thing."[3] Engel's research subjects, whose stories are told in the essay, experienced a similar struggle as they faced the seeming disintegration of their community that accompanied globalization. By referencing Frost's poem, Engel beautifully conveys both the sadness of his subjects and his compassion for their experience.

The title of my chapter borrows from a line in W. H. Auden's "No, Plato, No," which also describes a response to a rapidly changing environment. Auden wrote the poem a few months before he died; the poem is a response to his dying body. Similar to the oven bird, Auden sings a song of resistance: he "can't imagine anything that [he] would less like to be than a disincarnate Spirit." But while it is clear that Auden does not want to say goodbye to his body, "No, Plato, No" strikes a more hopeful note than "The Oven Bird," and so does this chapter. Unlike the oven bird of Frost's poem – and the subjects of Engel's essay – Auden does not ask himself what to make of his body's diminished state. Instead, he dreams of a different bodily existence, one in which his body would be free to become what he called "irresponsible matter."

Following Engel, I borrow from Auden's poem in this chapter to signify both the message and the mood of the chapter's subject: how changing perceptions of bodily identity may be shaping the future of tort law. Like Auden, today's gender and disability activists seek freedom from bodily categorization, or from what Auden called "giv[ing] Proper Names to all things." There are also signs of increasing resistance to organizing the body as "responsible matter," not only among activists but in the culture writ large. These growing demands for bodily freedom echo the dreams of Auden in "No, Plato, No" in both substance and spirit and, as in Auden's poem, the tone of the resistance is more playful than sad. This chapter is about how these new understandings of the body may shape the future of tort law.

As in "The Oven Bird's Song," this is also a story about community "insiders" and "outsiders." But, again, the tenor of the story strikes a very different note. Here, the "outsiders" are not only "outsiders" in the community (as they were in Engel's essay) but also outsiders to law. In many instances, their outsider identities effectively preclude them from making a claim at all. Despite this, as compared to the "outsiders" in Engel's study, it is not uncommon for bodily identity "outsiders" to relish their "outsider" status. They do not seek to become "insiders," through law or any other means, even as the

---

[3]   Ibid, 551.

communities around them have become more accepting of bodily differences. Instead, today's gender and disability activists seem to be seeking to legitimize "outsider" status, not by becoming "insiders," but through bodily performances that call into question the assumptions upon which "insider"/ "outsider" distinctions are made.

The thesis of this chapter is that tort law is currently not well equipped to deal with these developments. Its preoccupation with what I call the "categorical productivity" of bodies – through which "insiders" and insiders to the law are clearly defined – is losing its cultural relevance. More fundamentally, the growing disconnect between tort law's approach to the body and contemporary understandings of bodily identity raises questions about tort law's capacity to deliver on its promise of meaningful justice, especially for the growing number of those who either refuse or are unable to comply with the assumptions about bodies on which tort law currently relies.

My argument proceeds in three steps. The first section considers tort law's reliance on categorical assumptions about bodily productivity as a historical feature of tort law. It considers the different ways in which the body has been categorized in tort law and how these categories have been linked with conclusions about productivity to determine the viability of claims. Drawing on Engel, this section also describes how this emphasis on "categorical productivity" has helped to construct certain categories of individuals as "outsiders," both in and outside of courts.

The second section explores the current cultural challenges – both theoretical and practical – to tort law's demand for categorical productivity. It describes the emerging resistance to identification along categorical lines and the devaluation of productivity as a desirable bodily aim. Instead, many people seem to be seeking a more playful existence for their bodies, where there is less concern with conforming to bodily expectations and the demand for productivity. This section also suggests that these changing attitudes may be representative of a new form of individualism, grounded in a desire for self-expression, that was not identified by Engel in "The Oven Bird's Song."

The third section assesses the implications of these developments for the future of tort law. It argues that emerging, more complex conceptions of bodily identity will require tort law to move away from its current reliance on category-driven assessments of injuries. What replaces it is less clear. One possibility is a return to a more individualized approach to injuries that places more emphasis on suffering and pleasure than on productivity. Another possibility, perhaps related to the first, is the development of new legal rules that protect and foster what appears to be a growing interest in bodily self-expression.

Tort Law's Reliance on Categorical Assumptions About Productivity

For many years now, tort law has been preoccupied with the categorization and productivity of bodies, so much so that, in most instances, the possession of what we might call a "categorically productive" body is a condition precedent to recovery. As evidence of this, the two most dominant approaches to tort law – corrective justice theory and law and economics – both assume that the body *should* be restored to productivity after injury or compensated for any loss in productivity that cannot be restored. While in recent years there has been some progress toward recognizing non-bodily harm as a basis for claims, the productivity of the body remains the focal point of analysis in most tort cases.[4] Perhaps as a result, it is not usually possible to make a viable claim unless some injury to the productivity of the body is alleged. Notably, this emphasis on the productivity of the body marks a departure from early tort law, where injuries were primarily understood in terms of damage to honor and reputation.[5] Foucault blamed the increasing emphasis on the body on the rise of capitalism, which demanded increasingly productive bodies to maintain and increase profits.[6] But we know that as early as the thirteenth century, English courts began to place more emphasis on the physical aspects of the injury and its impact on productivity.[7] This important shift in the concept of injury, during what Marx would have called the pre-capitalist era, survives to this day.

As the law developed, jurisdictions utilized different criteria in their assessments of bodies. For example, some jurisdictions treated all fingers the same, while others focused on injuries to particular fingers.[8] Similarly, some jurisdictions considered the loss of smell or speech to be injurious while others did not.[9] That differential treatment exposes the cultural biases at play in assessing bodies for purposes of injury law which continue to this day.[10]

There are generally two steps in contemporary analyses of the body's productivity in tort cases. The first step is the categorization of the body. During this phase, bodies are categorized according to race, gender, age,

---

[4] Martha Chamallas and Jennifer B. Wriggins, *The Measure of Injury: Race, Gender, and Tort Law* (New York University Press, 2010), p. 90.

[5] Anne Bloom, "Plastic injuries," *Hofstra Law Review*, 42(3) (2014), 759–98, 788–91.

[6] Michel Foucault, *The History of Sexuality, Volume I: An Introduction* (trans. Robert Hurley) (Random House, 1990).

[7] Lisi Oliver, *The Body Legal in Barbarian Law* (University of Toronto Press, 2011).

[8] Ibid.   [9] Ibid.

[10] Sarah S. Lochlann Jain, *Injury: The Politics of Product Design and Safety Law in the United States* (Princeton University Press, 2006).

disability, etc. The second step is the linking of the categorizations with expected levels of productivity, based on assumptions about the categories. For example, aging bodies and the bodies of women are generally assumed to be less productive. Similarly, certain categorizations are linked with a pre-existing failure of productivity, such that the body is deemed incapable of experiencing a legally cognizable injury. A body that is categorized as "disabled" before injury, for example, might find it difficult to obtain compensation for any losses associated with new injuries. A body that is re-categorized as "disabled" *after* an injury, in contrast, typically has a very strong claim. This is because the plaintiff's injuries will be deemed to have led to a failure of bodily productivity, which tort law has historically considered a compensable loss.

We can see the two steps of the analysis operating in a 1909 case involving the alleged false imprisonment of an African-American man.[11] After first categorizing the plaintiff's body according to race, the court then linked the categorization to assumptions about expected levels of productivity associated with the plaintiff's designated racial category. These assumptions led the court to conclude that it was appropriate to award a smaller amount of damages to the plaintiff because the amount of injury experienced by an African-American man for false imprisonment was not as great as that of a white man in the same position.[12] There were two categorical assumptions at play in the court's analysis. The first had to do with the assumed relatively lower baseline of economic productivity of the plaintiff's body before injury. The second involved an assumption about the plaintiff's capacity to experience injury. In both instances, the assumptions flowed directly from the court's initial categorization of the plaintiff's body, according to race.

A very similar practice is followed in contemporary tort cases, where categorical conclusions about the productivity of would-be plaintiffs enter into the legal analyses of tort claims under the guise of actuarial analyses, which rely on prior economic performance data as a marker of current and future productivity. It remains fairly common, for example, for courts and parties to use race-based and gender-based methods of damage computation in tort litigation.[13] These practices effectively make it more difficult for individuals categorized as women or non-white to state a financially viable claim. The same is true for older plaintiffs, whose productive years are largely assumed to be behind them.

---

[11] The case is described in Chamallas and Wriggins, *The Measure of Injury*, 52–3.
[12] Ibid, 53–4.   [13] Ibid, 155–82.

In recent years, the movement toward capping non-economic damages has placed even greater emphasis on productivity. As a result, those with bodies associated with relatively less productivity before injury can find it especially difficult to succeed with their claims. Generally, young white men will find it much easier to retain a lawyer and pursue successful injury claims than old white men; whites will find it easier than non-whites; and men will usually find it easier than women. In each instance, the categorization of the body predicts the result, rather than the degree of pain and suffering that the injured individuals experienced.

While legal analyses in contemporary tort cases generally focus on the economic productivity of bodies, some conclusions are reached on the basis of the presumed failure of bodies to be productive in other aspects of cultural life. For example, in jurisdictions where hedonic damages are recognized, courts typically permit a jury to award hedonic damages on the basis of a disability diagnosis alone.[14] In a similar way, courts also presume injury in so-called wrongful birth cases where the child is categorized as "disabled" at birth.[15] The operational presumption in both instances is that a life with a disability is inherently less pleasurable than a life without one, even when there is no evidence offered to support this conclusion.

A similar type of categorical discrimination is at play in the treatment of plaintiffs whose pre-injury bodies do not fit clearly into a binary (male/female) sex categorization. Intersex infants and other children who undergo sex-assignment surgery, for example, find it difficult to state a claim for the often very serious injuries that result.[16] The categorical assumption is that a body that cannot be clearly classified as male or female cannot be injured by actions that attempt to make the body conform, even when those actions lead to the loss of sexual function.

Because bodies classified as disabled and intersex are clearly able to lead economically productive lives, the failure of productivity in these examples relates to the presumed failure of the bodies to be productive in other aspects of life, such as experiencing pleasure or having physical attributes that the law associates with binary sex identification. By making this presumption, tort law assumes that to be classified as "intersex" or "disabled" is inherently undesirable, without any consideration of how the individuals involved might

---

[14] Samuel R. Bagenstos and Margo Schlanger, "Hedonic damages, hedonic adaptation, and disability," *Vanderbilt Law Review*, 60 (2007), 745–97, 771–72.

[15] Wendy F. Hensel, "The disabling impact of wrongful birth and wrongful life actions," *Harvard Civil Rights and Civil Liberties Review*, 40 (2005), 141–95.

[16] Anne Bloom, "To be real: sexual identity politics in tort litigation," *North Carolina Law Review*, 88(2) (2010), 357–426, 404–8.

experience the attributes that prompted the classifications of their bodies in these ways. Thus, here the demand for categorical productivity presents not as a demand for bodies to demonstrate economic productivity but, rather, as a requirement that bodies accept the presumptions of the categories; e.g. individuals designated as "disabled" will experience less pleasure and individuals classified as "intersex" should attempt to qualify for binary gender classification instead.

These examples illustrate the role of bodily categorization in the analysis of tort claims. In each of the examples cited above, courts reached conclusions about whether plaintiffs could recover based on categorizations of the plaintiffs' bodies. In some instances, such as those involving the claims of women, people of color, and older plaintiffs, the categorizations are linked with a failure of economic productivity. In other cases, the categorization of the body will prompt courts to presume injury without further evidence. While the recovery outcomes differ, the analysis is roughly the same. In each instance, an assessment of the body's productivity follows its categorization. These analytical practices reflect the liberal legal presumption – so prevalent in tort law – that bodies are meant to be categorically productive; that is, productive as men or women, as able-bodied or disabled, and as raced or aged, in both the economic and cultural realms. Moreover, bodies that are not categorically productive – bodies that cannot be categorized and linked with assumptions about productivity – cannot state a claim. Put differently, the presentation of a categorically productive body is a condition precedent to recovery in tort law.

Each of these examples also illustrates how legal practices help to construct certain categories of individuals as "outsiders" to tort law, in ways that are similar to those observed by Engel in "The Oven Bird's Song." In the bodily identity context, claimants are constructed as "outsiders" both in terms of the limited viability of the claims of those who are deemed categorically unproductive *before* their claim of injury and in terms of the rapidity with which tort law assumes that other types of bodies can no longer be productive *after* injury (e.g. people with disabling injuries). In each case, the bodies are "outsiders" to tort law in the sense that they are no longer (or never were) linked with productivity.

The "outsiders" in "The Oven Bird's Song" faced a similar fate. In most instances, the individuals were considered "outsiders" even before they attempted to pursue legal claims. Going to court did not help them to escape this assessment, despite the promise of a fair hearing. Although it is not a focus of Engel's study, the "outsider" designation stemmed, in some instances, from perceived bodily differences. Engel notes, for example, that some community members alluded to race and ethnicity when describing their own "outsider" status or the status of others.[17] For these community members, as with many others who attempt to pursue tort claims, the "outsider" classification is literally written on the body.

As Engel recognized, tort litigation operates in ways that reproduce and help to construct social hierarchies. Of course, legal narratives reproduce and construct hierarchies in other areas of the law as well. But it is in tort law that the body itself is most closely scrutinized and that bodies act – more so than any other field of law – as material repositories of culture.[18] Because of this, it is in tort law that the growing cultural demand for freedom from bodily categorization is likely to be experienced most acutely.

CHALLENGES TO THE DEMAND FOR
CATEGORICAL PRODUCTIVITY

2016 opened with the deaths of two wildly popular, gender-fluid cultural icons: David Bowie and Prince. Among their many fans, Bowie and Prince came to signify a desire to be free of the expectations of gender and other bodily categories. Like Auden, both Bowie and Prince in their early days associated freedom with the death of "Him" and the emergence of Her. Bowie and Prince both wore eyeliner, high heels, and catsuits; Prince was partial to ruffles as well. As their popularity grew, however, both increasingly expressed a desire not to be categorized at all. Bowie was famously noncommittal about his sexuality. Prince sang, "I'm not a woman/I'm not a man/I am something that you'll never understand."[19] Later, when Prince got into a feud with his record label, he changed his name to an unpronounceable symbol that fused the sex signs for male and female. When asked what he was doing, Prince declared that he was trying to tune into to a new, undefined "freequency."

Although Bowie and Prince were not especially political, many gender activists consider them heroes. *The New York Times* eulogized Bowie as the "patron saint of defiant outcasts" and credited him with bringing queer culture into the mainstream.[20] Prince was described as "an artist who defied genre."[21] But Bowie and Prince were not just admired by gender activists. Public grieving over their deaths was widespread. Spontaneous tributes to both artists

---

[17] Engel, *Oven Bird's Song*, 555.   [18] Jain, *Injury*, 152.
[19] Prince and the Revolution, "I Would Die 4 U," *Purple Rain* (USA: Warner/Chappel Music Inc., 1984).
[20] Katie Rogers, "Was he gay, bisexual or Bowie? Yes," *The New York Times*, January 13, 2016.
[21] Jon Pareles, "Prince, an artist who defied genre, is dead at 57," *The New York Times*, April 21, 2016.

erupted all over the world, especially for Prince. Even the White House was lit purple for a night in his memory.

In an article entitled "Listen to My Body Tonight: How Prince's Transgressive Spirit Broke Boundaries," NPR's Ann Powers tried to explain why so many people were finding Prince's death so difficult. According to Powers, it was partly Prince's defiance of categories: "Prince gave us a new way into our bodies that was brainy, full of feeling and committedly defiant of categories."[22] But it was also that Prince provided a vision of how things might be different, of how people might "truly overcome the divisions that both define and continually limit our lives" and become more fully themselves. Prince's music, Powers wrote, taught us "something vital" about the "multiple realities that pulsed beneath our own skins."[23] Others wrote similar things about Bowie's cultural significance.[24]

These sentiments are remarkable because of how well they correspond with more academic perspectives on the current cultural emphasis on the classification and categorization of bodies. Susan Bordo, for example, has expressed concern about the obsession with medical categorization of body "pathologies" and the demand for homogeneity of women's bodies through plastic surgery, dieting, and physical training.[25] Foucault described this type of control as "biopower," which he believed was a response to the need for well-regulated bodies to maintain the capitalist system of production.[26] Since the aim of biopower is to make people more productive, medical baselines increasingly focus on idealized conceptions of how bodies *should* perform, rather than the performance characteristics of average bodies.[27] Over time, Foucault argued, we have become expert in diagnosing and treating the pathologies ourselves.

Foucault's description of the operations of biopower resonated with many cultural and political figures, especially in the United States, where it seemed that what Foucault described had special relevance for contemporary cultural

---

[22] Ann Powers. "Listen to my body tonight: how Prince's transgressive spirit broke boundaries," *the record: Music News from NPR*, April 22, 2016, www.npr.org/sections/therecord/2016/04/22/475210984/listen-to-my-body-tonight-how-princes-transgressive-spirit-broke-boundaries.

[23] Ibid.   [24] See, e.g., Rogers, *Was He Gay, Bisexual or Bowie? Yes.*

[25] Susan Bordo, *Unbearable Weight: Feminism, Western Culture, and the Body* (University of California Press, 2003).

[26] Michel Foucault, *The History of Sexuality, Volume I: An Introduction.* Translated by R. Hurley, reissue edition (Vintage Books, 1990 [1976]).

[27] Nikolas Rose, *The Politics of Life Itself: Biomedicine, Power, and Subjectivity in the Twenty-First Century* (Princeton University Press, 2007); Robin Mackenzie, "Somatechnics of medico-legal taxonomies: elective amputation and transableism," *Medical Law Review*, 16 (2008), 390–412 (describing the regulation of bodies in several contexts).

and political experience.[28] Drawing upon Foucault, several American scholars decried the demand for bodily normalization, especially in the contexts of gender and disability.[29] Bordo, for example, described the myriad ways in which women's bodies were controlled through bodily classifications and how women learned to control themselves in response. Around the same time as this scholarly outpouring, Bowie and Prince became icons of cultural resistance to these same forces.

The politics of this cultural resistance, on the surface at least, have little to do with Foucault and his broader claims about the relationship of biopower to capitalism. Social critic Camille Paglia, for example – a defender of capitalism and no fan of Foucault – has named David Bowie as one of her most important influences.[30] But there is a common theme of resistance to the increasing regulation, classification, and categorization of bodies – practices Foucault had described as critical to the operation of biopower. There are also some similarities in the tenor of the resistance. Foucault believed that resistance would take the form of an insistence on bodily pleasures. This is a clear theme in Paglia's work, but also one that runs through the cultural performances of musical icons such as Bowie and Prince (especially). It can also be seen in the new emphasis on pleasure, rather than productivity, among legal scholars writing about the body.[31]

There are also echoes of Gilles Deleuze, with whom Foucault shared a close intellectual relationship. The similarities with the sentiments expressed by Auden in "No, Plato, No" are also remarkable. Deleuze's scholarship called for experimentation with bodily identity. Of particular note, Deleuze asked us to try to imagine bodies without organs.[32] For Deleuze, a body without organs was a way of imagining the body as something other than an organized whole with the aim of productivity. Like Auden, Deleuze was concerned with freeing up the body to experience pleasures that cannot be captured by categorical demands such as male/female, crazy/sane, or, we might add, able-bodied/disabled. Experimentation with bodily identity, Deleuze speculated, might allow for individuals to get outside the categories and experience a more authentic "becoming."

[28] Francois Cusset, *French Theory: How Foucault, Derrida, Deleuze, & Co. Transformed the Intellectual Life of the United States* (trans. J. Fort) (University of Minnesota Press, 2008).
[29] Bordo, *Unbearable Weight*; Mackenzie, "Somatechnics of medico-legal taxonomies."
[30] Camille Paglia, *Sexual Personae* (Yale University Press, 1990).
[31] See, e.g., Elizabeth Emens, "Intimate discrimination: the state's role in the accidents of sex and love," *Harvard Law Review*, 122 (2009), 1307–402.
[32] Gilles Deleuze, *The Logic of Sense* (trans. M. Lester and C. Stivale) (Columbia University Press, 1990 [1969]).

Judith Butler tackled a similar theme in *Bodies that Matter* (2003). Butler began with the observation that social survival requires individuals to enact the expectations of their designated categories, not only through social performance but also by corporeally enacting the physical demands of their categorization.[33] Surgeries on the bodies of intersex infants are an excellent example of this. Butler noted that the gap between the normative expectations of the categories (binary sex identity) and the performance (an intersex body) exposes the limitations of the categories but also creates opportunities for resistance. The behavior of parents who refuse to consent to surgery on their intersex infants, for example, might be read as resisting the practice of binary sex categorization.

Butler suggested that those who engage in cross-dressing practices, like Bowie and Prince, also engage in resistance that, perhaps unintentionally, disrupts categories. And it is worth noting that Prince's alter ego – Camille – is widely believed to have been inspired by a nineteenth-century French intersex person, sometimes known as Camille, whose private journals were published by Foucault. Whether the nineteenth-century Camille was truly the inspiration for some of Prince's gender category-defying performances is almost beside the point. What is remarkable is that many of his fans understand Prince's performances as a form of resistance, in ways that are reminiscent of Foucault, Deleuze, and Butler.

Importantly, Bowie and Prince did not simply refuse to perform within the accepted categories; they also seemed to resist the concept of categorization itself. Something similar can be seen in the work of the French performance artist, ORLAN. In a project she calls "The Reincarnation of Saint-Orlan," ORLAN is undergoing plastic surgeries to make parts of her body look more like elements of bodies that are portrayed in famous works of art. Because ORLAN is drawing from different periods of time, and because her body is undergoing constant change, she is disrupting the notion of a stable categorical identity associated with the body. But it is also a project of affirmative identity-formation, as she selects different bodily elements based on what she feels they may presently represent, while simultaneously leaving herself open to further changes in what she refers to as her "nomadic" bodily identity.

Resistance to categories, and to categorical productivity, can also be seen increasingly in the choices and actions of many people who do not identify as gender activists or artists. The emerging practice of individuals with disabilities seeking to use in vitro fertilization processes to affirmatively select children

[33] Judith Butler, *Bodies that Matter: On The Discursive Limits of Sex* (Routledge, 1993).

with the genetic traits associated with disabilities, for example, has been interpreted as a form of resistance to the category of "disability" and its negative connotations.[34] Similarly, for individuals categorized as women, "letting yourself go" by not dying grey hair, or refusing to diet when society says you look too fat, might be read as resistance to the categorical demands of gender.

A subtler form of resistance emerging in everyday office practice involves placing one's preferred pronouns and form of address at the end of an email. While many prefer conventional binary gender pronouns, e.g. she/he/her/ him, there is a growing movement toward requesting the use of non-binary pronouns, such as "ze" and "hir." Some people request the use of non-binary pronouns because they do not identify within the binary gender regime. Others request non-binary pronouns to show solidarity for others or simply because they would prefer not to be categorized according to a binary gender system, even if they do generally identify as male or female.

Sometimes the resistance takes a playful turn. As dying one's hair has become increasingly *de rigueur* for women of a certain age, young women have begun dying their hair gray as a fashion statement. Many young celebrities, including Pink, Lady Gaga, Rihanna, and Jennifer Lawrence, have joined the trend and gone gray in recent times, and the practice has also started to become popular with young men. Perhaps unintentionally, the practice disrupts the categorical linkage between gray hair and aging. The widespread practice of tattooing among young, college-educated women is having a similar effect. While they were previously associated almost exclusively with the bodies of lower-working-class men, tattoos are no longer a reliable marker for this category, typically linked with lower productivity.

With these practices, we can also see the ways in which bodily identity is increasingly centered on creative presentation and alternative identity construction, rather than productivity (economic, social, or otherwise). For some, practices such as tattooing, hair-color changes, and piercings are a vehicle for personal reconstruction from the outside in, rather than the inside out. Through bodily identity, they are expressing the complexity of their identity experience, which is neither stable nor categorically confined. It is also worth noting that interviews with women dying their hair gray and obtaining tattoos reveal that these practices are, in part, an expression of a desire to become what David Engel's community members might have viewed as "outsiders." In other words, individuals are engaging in these practices *because they do not*

---

[34] Brigham A. Fordham, "Disability and designer babies: rethinking the debate over genetic interventions in favor of disability," *Valparaiso University Law Review*, 45 (2011), 1473–528.

wish to fit in. Following Auden, we might also read these practices as a desire to be *less responsible* matter, both in terms of categorical productivity (conforming with the expectations of the categories) and with respect to economic productivity. For whatever reason, there appears to be simply less concern about complying with the demands for productivity.

These changing attitudes may be representative of a new form of individualism that will make its mark on law as well. Engel identified two distinct strains of individualism at play in "The Oven Bird's Song." One version emphasized the vindication of rights; a second emphasized self-sufficiency and personal responsibility.[35] Engel found that the second brand of individualism was more prominent in the community he studied, particularly in discussions of personal injury cases. But the bodily identity practices described above suggest a third type of individualism in which an emphasis on creative self-expression may trump concerns about rights assertion or self-sufficiency. What remains to be seen is how these new values will shape the future for tort law, both in terms of how injuries are understood and the legal remedies that may available to address them.

IMPLICATIONS FOR TORT LAW

Currently, the two most dominant approaches to tort law – corrective justice and law and economics – focus heavily on the productivity of bodies. Both approaches look to changes in the productivity of the body to determine injury. Both approaches also assume that the legal remedy should seek to restore the body to its prior state of productivity or compensate the individual for a loss in productivity. Contemporary bodily identity practices pose a potential challenge to these approaches.

Judith Butler and others have drawn our attention to the role of culture and performance in the construction of bodily categories, such as gender, race, and disability. Because these categories are fundamentally performative, Butler argues, they can be disrupted by performances that fail to approximate the normative expectations of the category. The increasingly widespread experimentation with bodily shape-shifting, the growing resistance to demands to adhere to the expectations of the gender binary, and the decisions of some individuals categorized as "disabled" to affirmatively select for those categorical traits in their children, are all examples of category-disrupting performances.

---

[35] Engel, *Oven Bird's Song*, 558–9.

As these category-disrupting practices go mainstream, tort law's demand for categorically productive bodies is likely to be experienced as increasingly repressive. Perhaps more troubling, contemporary bodily identity practices expose the inability of the current system to address injuries that arise under conditions that do not conform to the assumptions of the categories. What happens, for example, when a body appears to be *more* productive after a disabling injury than it was before? Does this mean that this person has not been injured? And what happens if a plaintiff undergoes a categorical shift in identity, such as a sex change, mid-injury? Under which set of categorical assumptions about productivity (e.g. male or female) should the analysis proceed? These are some of the challenges that contemporary bodily identity practices pose for tort law.

We might ask a broader set of questions about the continuing utility of a tort system grounded in assumptions about categorical productivity, especially for plaintiffs who are either unwilling or unable to participate in the processes of categorical identity assignment. Should legally sanctioned bodily categorization be part of the price of entry to the tort system? Or is it possible for an injury to be remedied without forcing plaintiffs who do not wish to be categorized to pay this psychic cost? How might tort law engage in its own shape-shifting to address these concerns? And might some of these changes already be underway?

In recent years, tort scholars have begun to pay more attention to the relationship between narratives in tort litigation and cultural understandings of bodily identity. Several scholars have noted, for example, that when legal actors in tort cases repeatedly transmit the message that the bodies of people with disabilities are "tragic," it is likely that this messaging also plays a harmful role in the construction of disability identity.[36] Similarly, Chamallas and Wriggins have noted that the practices of legal actors in tort litigation likely help to enforce and construct social hierarchies along the lines of gender and race.[37] In each of these ways, the practices of legal actors in tort litigation can be seen to help shape understandings of bodily identity outside the courthouse doors, in much the same way that Engel observed that the pursuit of legal remedies helped to construct some members of the community as "outsiders." Relatively little consideration, however, has been given to the reverse side of the equation, i.e. how changing social conceptions of identity shape legal practices, which was a question that Engel also explored.

---

[36] See Bagenstos and Schlanger, *Hedonic Damages*; Bloom and Miller, *Blindsight*.
[37] Chamallas and Wriggins, *The Measure of Injury*.

Engel found that perceptions of tort law, and the activities of legal actors engaged in personal injury litigation, were strongly influenced by the social changes around them, including the forces of globalization.[38] In the community that Engel observed, changing social conditions prompted local actors to use the legal system as a means of shoring up boundaries that they believed were disintegrating in the community. But, as Engel also noted, the world these members of the community imagined they were protecting existed only in their minds.[39]

Something similar might be said in the context of changing bodily identity practices. The assumptions about bodies on which the tort system currently relies were always a figment of our imaginations; changing bodily identity practices have simply made us more aware of their limitations. But tort law is a remarkably flexible instrument, perhaps uniquely attentive to changes in the social environment in which it operates. While the response of Engel's Sander County residents was to double down and protect existing perceptions from further erosion, tort law also has a long history of adapting to changing social conditions with new developments in the law.

Samantha Barbas' research on how privacy laws in the United States changed in response to new understandings of personal image provides an illustration of how such changes can take place, particularly as they relate to identity.[40] In the nineteenth century, Barbas reminds us, reputations and social identities were somewhat fixed. All that changed in the twentieth century, however, when urbanization seems to have prompted people to experiment more freely with fluid social identities. As "impression management" became of greater concern, so too did an interest in protecting the right to control one's image. Since the mass media were perceived as a threat to individuals' ability to control their images, existing laws were expanded. Invasion of privacy and similar claims became important new tools through which individuals could shape and control their social identities.

Might we expect similar developments in response to changing beliefs and practices concerning bodily identity? Without more research, we can only speculate about the potential implications of changing conceptions of bodily identity for tort law in the future. What seems likely is that cultural developments will push tort law in the direction of what might be characterized as "anti-foundationalism," or less reliance on categorical assumptions in legal analysis. Instead, legal actors might focus more on the experiences of the

[38] Engel, *Oven Bird's Song.*   [39] Ibid, at 53.
[40] Samantha Barbas, *Laws of Image: Privacy & Publicity in America* (Stanford University Press, 2015).

individuals involved. When confronted with plaintiffs with seemingly disabling injuries, for example, legal actors might focus on the conditions that gave rise to a particular condition becoming categorized as disabling. This, in turn, might prompt some questioning of the assumptions accompanying the categorization.

While disability may seem like an inherent, biological condition, culture plays an important role in setting the parameters of the category. As an example, at an earlier point in history, deafness was not viewed as a "disability" in the community of Martha's Vineyard but rather as a "normal" difference, so much so that when researchers asked residents to identify who was deaf, residents in the communities were not able to do so.[41] People in Geel, Belgium, which has been welcoming people with mental and emotional differences for centuries, report a similar experience.[42]

These examples expose the limitations of both "disability" as a category and the presumptions associated with it. The equation of disability with tragedy so often seen in tort law, for example, only makes sense if you assume that disability entails an inherently undesirable, and fixed, identity. But if disability identity is not fixed and only undesirable because culture makes it so, then there is the possibility of resistance to the categorization. There is also the possibility for individuals to present themselves with more complex identities, in which the cultural designation of disability may or may not play a significant role.

Under these circumstances, what may make the most sense is to simply focus on the experiences of individuals, in all their difficult-to-categorize complexity. Similar arguments can be made about the categories of gender and race, of course. In many ways, this is not a new approach so much as a return to a more evidentiary-based analysis that considers a multiplicity of views. And there are some signs that tort law is already moving in this direction, at least in certain areas. The *Restatement (Third) of Torts*, for example, now permits recovery in emotional distress cases, for a victim's "family" members, even if they are not biologically or legally related to the victim.[43] The approach acknowledges that the category of "family" is a fluid one, with diverse and changing parameters. By focusing on how individuals experience "family" rather than saddling each case with categorical

---

[41] Ray McDermott and Herve Varenne, "Culture as disability," *Anthropology and Education Quarterly*, 26 (1995), 323–48; 328–30.

[42] NPR, "The problem with the solution," *Invisibilia*, podcast audio, July 1, 2016, www.npr.org/programs/invisibilia/483855073/the-problem-with-the-solution.

[43] *Restatement (Third) of Torts: Liability for Physical and Emotional Harm*, Section 48, Comment f (2012).

expectations, tort law is both a more nimble and more relevant tool for addressing injuries.

We might take a similar approach with the category of "disability." The overreliance on categories tends to push plaintiffs in tort litigation into categorically identifying as "disabled," as if disability were a static condition that existed outside of culture. In real life, however, the experience of a physical condition varies over time. Not only do our bodies undergo continuous change, but our perceptions of the "disability" also undergo constant change in response to environmental and social conditions. A more fluid approach to the category might permit plaintiffs to express their identity, and their experience with "disability," in more complex ways.

To be clear, this not an argument that people who experience injuries that they or others categorize as "disabling" should not receive compensation. It is a plea for recognition that our current assumptions are problematic and at odds with how real people experience injuries that are categorized as "disabling." As I have argued elsewhere, it is possible for tort law to compensate individuals for injuries – including the challenges associated with a forced transition into a new identity (such as disability identity) – and to compensate them for the discrimination that they are likely to experience as a result of that forced transition, without reifying the category of "disability" and the assumptions that accompany it.[44]

Similarly, this is not an argument against the use of categories in all circumstances. It is apparent that people can take pride in a categorical identity even as they feel constrained and limited by the normative expectations with which the identity is associated. It is also apparent that categories can be very useful in other contexts, such as aggregate measures of discrimination. Rather, this is a call to recognize the limitations of the assumptions that accompany the practices of categorization, particularly when the individuals involved do not identify with the categories to which they are assigned and the corresponding assumptions, however accurate those assumptions may be (or appear to be) in the statistical aggregate. In short, it is not that categories are without utility; they are simply insufficient for a meaningful assessment of any particular individual's injuries.

Apart from the challenges to categories, some contemporary bodily identity practices also seem to pose a challenge to tort law's focus on bodily productivity as a measure of injury and remedy. As others have noted, this focus on productivity skews the discourse and overlooks important aspects of

---

[44] Bloom and Miller, *Blindsight.*

injury.[45] For example, an emphasis on bodily productivity has resulted in a failure of the tort system to fully recognize, and compensate, the injuries of those who are presumed to be inherently less productive, such as people with disabilities and older people. It also ignores other qualities of would-be claimants, such as the capacity for interpersonal caregiving that is not linked to productivity.[46] As Engel noted in "The Oven Bird's Song," narratives in American personal injury cases tend to emphasize the importance of self-sufficiency. This emphasis is particularly problematic for people with disabilities, women, and others who value their interdependence, but it also discourages claims, as those who do not wish to appear to be lacking in self-sufficiency may refrain from seeking compensation for their injuries.

What might tort law look like if the analysis of injury is untethered from the expectations of productivity and self-sufficiency? What sorts of injuries might become more compensable and how would we value the losses? Again, it seems likely that tort law in the future will move away from its current reliance on categorical assumptions, including the heavy reliance on actuarial assessments of injury. What will replace it is difficult to predict. At the very least, these developments seem to present an opportunity for a more complex of understanding of injury to be considered and for more voices in the community to have some say over when an injury has occurred and how to compensate for the loss. Perhaps, as was the case with personal image law, changing attitudes toward bodily identity will also result in the recognition of new claims that, for example, seek to protect individuals' interest in shaping and controlling their bodily identities.

Auden suggests that there is also the promise of something more, as yet (and perhaps always) undefined. Freed from the categorical demands for productivity, a more complex conception of injury law might be more attuned to the capacity of bodies for pleasure. Near death, Auden sought to embrace the flesh while eschewing attempts to define it. We see glimpses of what this might look like in the bodily identity practices of Prince, Bowie, and ORLAN. Legal actors in the future may ask us to rethink tort law to more freely allow its participants to explore these and other possibilities of becoming, what Auden might have called, irresponsible matter.

---

[45] Chamallas and Wriggins, *The Measure of Injury*.
[46] Leslie Bender, "Changing the values in tort law," *Tulsa Law Journal*, 25 (1989), 759–73.

13

Student Perceptions of (Their) Place in Relationship to "The Oven Bird's Song"

RENÉE ANN CRAMER

Now I sit on the porch and watch the lightning-bugs fly
But I can't see too good, I got tears in my eyes
I'm leaving tomorrow but I don't want to go
I love you my town, you'll always live in my soul

But I can see the sun's settin' fast
And just like they say nothing good ever lasts
Well, go on I gotta kiss you goodbye but I'll hold to my lover
'Cause my heart's 'bout to die
Go on now and say goodbye to my town, to my town
Can't you see the sun's settin' down on my town, on my town
Goodnight, goodnight

Iris Dement, "Our Town"

This chapter begins in gratitude: Gratitude to David Engel for writing a piece that is a joy to return to – for teaching, for reading, for meditating on – again and again. It begins in gratitude to my students, for their interaction with the article over the course of the years.

The chapter comes laden, too, with a less welcome emotion: nostalgia. Writing it reminds me of the nostalgia I feel for the town I grew up in, centered in Minnehaha County, South Dakota. It comes with nostalgia felt on behalf of my rural students who see the same changes that Engel chronicled thirty years ago taking place in their communities today. Nostalgia is unsettling: We remember a place and time that seems unchanging, yet we remember it from a vantage point that feels fundamentally different.

Nostalgia can also be politically dangerous, a malaise we fall into. It allows us a moment of collective mourning for changes in a mythic past that feels much more valiant than it was. Feminist theorist Mary Caputi,[1] writing about the conservative political valence of recalling the 1950s, notes that the role of nostalgia in conservative politics is to allow participants to descend into "melancholia," constructing a remembrance based on a "myth," not reality, seeking to "return" America and (some) Americans to a way of being that did not quite ever exist.

More recently, Jeffrey Dudas has noted that the underpinnings of contemporary American conservatism rest on a constructed understanding of Americans as uniquely virtuous and autonomous, "self-sufficient, and self-reliant."[2] Recent calls to "make America great again" build on a rhetoric that seeks to "return" America to a time and place that was once "better": economically, socially, culturally, and politically – without acknowledging the melancholic nostalgia that drives the expressive rage underpinning that politics.

In other words, though the article is now more than thirty years old, David Engel's Oven Bird still sings of changes that continue to unfold across rural America. His analysis provides a perspective from which to view contemporary understandings of the tensions between individualism and community, self-reliance and the rule of law, anti-professionalism and skepticism of the state. He wrote from the perspective of someone watching that change unfold. Interestingly, as my students and I engage the work, we find that we are still in the midst of the change. We are close enough to mourn something, to say goodbye with a tear in our eye – but far enough away, too, to wonder about the mythic origins of those stories, those songs.

This chapter engages my students' reactions to "The Oven Bird's Song." Those reactions center most dominantly on their relief at having the chance to read an article that acknowledges the places from which they come, and the opportunity they feel to participate in the classroom conversation from a vantage point of expertise, knowledge, and personal narrative. This chapter examines the meaning of my students finding so much to resonate with in the residents of Sander County, and how they articulate a view of law and politics that both aligns with and destabilizes those residents' views.

But first, and because Engel himself found the context of his subjects so important, I would like to introduce the reader to the layered contexts from which my students, and I, engage the work.

---

[1] Mary Caputi, *A Kinder, Gentler America: Melancholia and the Mythical 1950s* (University of Minnesota Press, 2005).

[2] Jeffrey R. Dudas, "All the rage: Clarence Thomas, parental authority, and conservative desire," *Law, Culture, and the Humanities*, 12(1) (2016), 70–105, 71, 73.

TEACHING CONTEXT: DRAKE UNIVERSITY
AND ITS STUDENTS

I teach at Drake University in an interdisciplinary undergraduate legal studies program called Law, Politics, and Society. Drake is a mid-sized regional comprehensive university in Iowa's capital city, Des Moines. Iowa – though "flyover country" – is home to politically astute and civically engaged citizens. Many of my students chose Drake in part because they wanted to experience the "first in the nation" caucuses and the tremendous political energy that surrounds presidential decision-making in Iowa. During caucus season, a good percentage of my students have internships with the campaigns; they volunteer and engage in paid employment with the major networks, and they have their own political publications. They are, by and large, a moderate population – though some have the sense of themselves as "liberal," and conservative students have a sense of themselves as "besieged"; they tend to split their votes and their political allegiances between the two major parties; and there has been, until recently, very little campus activism beyond electoral politics, toward either progressive or conservative goals.

Our major is explicitly interdisciplinary: I am trained as a political scientist; my colleagues are an anthropologist and a historian. We wear these primary disciplinary affiliations rather lightly, and focus our own work, and our courses, on questions that animate law and society/law and culture research agendas. The classes that we teach all take an interdisciplinary approach to legal studies, and students read widely: They engage journalism, ethnography, sociology, criminology, political science, literature, and many other disciplines. Through coursework in the major, our faculty hopes that students will come to have a constitutive, sociolegal perspective on law – one that understands legality itself as ideological, contingent, and contextual.

We also attend to the fact that many of our students enter the major believing that they will go to law school. And we take seriously our institutional mission, which emphasizes the role of a liberal arts education in pre-professional preparation and places significant attention on guiding our students toward an ethical and responsible "global citizenship." We design our curriculum so that students will learn to observe, analyze, and theorize about law and legality from multiple perspectives – disciplinary, identity, and (pre-) professional.

In the past ten years, I have taught "The Oven Bird's Song" several times. The first time was in our senior seminar – where I was interested in having students understand narratives of citizen engagement with law. They read

Engel in conjunction with Yngvesson and Greenhouse; Ewick and Silbey; and Haltom and McCann.[3]

Most recently, though, I have taught this article in two courses with very different goals than our senior seminar: *Introduction to Law, Politics, and Society* and our second-semester required course, *Critical Concepts in Law, Politics, and Society*. In the introductory course, I teach "The Oven Bird's Song" as part of a five-week sequence on civil litigation processes, the myths we have about our litigation explosion, the various ways that lawyers practice, the stratification of the legal profession, and the experience of legal education. Here, I teach "Oven Bird" alongside Galanter's "Why the Haves Come Out Ahead" and Jonathan Harr's *A Civil Action*, with David O. Freidrich's textbook *Law in Our Lives* as the backbone of our course.[4]

In the concepts class, I teach "The Oven Bird's Song" as part of a sequence on the constructed nature of rights and legal claims-making, as a bridge from Scheingold into the ideas of legal culture, identity, and intersectionality.[5] Here, Kitty Calavita's *Invitation to Law and Society* forms the background upon which we work.[6]

Our students come to us from a variety of places. And, though it is Iowa, there is usually much more diversity in the room than the average person might expect, and certainly more than a mere glance at the faces in front of me would suggest. We are a predominantly white enrolling institution, and we have slightly more women students than men. We have active organizations of our LGBTQ students, and students in our multicultural clubs have built a successful coalitional politics that enabled them, recently, to form their own governing body parallel to Student Senate. Drake has more students who identify as Christian than any other religion – but we have Christians from nearly all denominations. We have Muslim students and Buddhist students, atheist students – and, our campus climate survey results tell us, a fair number of "Jedi."[7]

---

3   Barbara Yngvesson, Carol J. Greenhouse, and David Engel, *Law and Community in Three American Towns* (Cornell University Press, 1994); Patricia Ewick and Susan Silbey, *The Common Place of Law: Stories from Everyday Life*. (University of Chicago Press, 1998); William Haltom and Michael McCann, *Distorting the Law: Politics, Media, and the Litigation Crisis* (University of Chicago Press, 2004).

4   Marc Galanter, "Why the haves come out ahead: speculations on the limits of legal change," 9(1) (1974), *Law & Society Review*, 95–160; Jonathan Harr, *A Civil Action* (Random House, 1995); David O. Freidrich, *Law in Our Lives: An Introduction* (Oxford University Press, 2013).

5   Stuart Scheingold, *The Politics of Rights* (University of Michigan Press, 1974).

6   Kitty Calavita, *An Invitation to Law and Society: An Introduction to the Study of Real Law* (University of Chicago Press, 2010).

7   As part of a deep desire to increase welcome and diversity on campus, we have undertaken a multi-year project on campus climate, that began with a Campus Climate Survey. On a question regarding religious affiliation, several students wrote in "Jedi," in reference to the spiritual masters and warriors found in the Star Wars films.

We draw a good half of our students from the suburbs of Chicago, St. Louis, Kansas City, Denver, and Minneapolis. Around a quarter of our students come from Des Moines and its suburbs, and the other urban areas of Iowa. These students may be white; they may also be African-American, Latinx, or Indian-American. Des Moines is the corporate home of Pioneer Hybrid, Principal Financial, and other companies with a significant transnational workforce that has moved to Iowa as part of their employment; therefore we have students who might appear to be international students, but have been educated in Iowa's excellent public schools.

A final quarter of our students are rural students. They come from Iowa, South Dakota, North Dakota, Missouri, Kansas, and Illinois. It would be a mistake to assume that these rural students are all "white"-identifying; while most are, among our rural students are also students of color. Many of our rural Latinx students come from longstanding agricultural families; others make up some of the new migrants to the area – their parents often work in the meatpacking and poultry industries, but may also be in the professional class.

Given the demographics of Drake University's student body, it is likely that in any given class I have a good number of students from places like Sander County, who represent the cultural, ethnic, and racial shifts documented by Engel in his article. Knowing this shapes how I teach the work, certainly; and their identities also shape how students receive and interact with the article. Watching my students' reactions allows me to evaluate the continued power of Engel's analysis, and the urgent relevancy it holds for contemporary political and legal life, even decades later.

OBSERVATION A: MY RURAL STUDENTS KNOW AND
RECOGNIZE SANDER COUNTY AND THE PEOPLE IN IT

When I ask my students to raise their hands if they know a place like Sander County, if they live in that kind of place, around 30 percent of them indicate that they do. I teach the article over two class sessions, and begin with this question. In that first session, we don't ever get much further. For what is sometimes the first time in their reading for a college course, the rural students feel seen and recognized by the author we are engaging. They feel like the author has visited their hometown, and they are able to discuss the reading from a new perspective, from the sense they have that the theory they are encountering is rooted in a tangible place – a place they recognize and understand.

Students point to particular people introduced in the article as folks they recognize. About the recollection of shared labor around the threshing run and dining table that Engel shares on p. 7, a student commented that "that sounds like my grandma" and read one passage in particular: "I still gotta get kind of a kick out of watching a steam engine operate."[8] Or, as one student said about the evangelical minister profiled by Engel on pp. 22 and 23, "That guy: he's just like my best friend's dad."[9] They agreed wholeheartedly that "Generally speaking, a farmer's word is good between farmers,"[10] though they worry that agribusiness conglomerates are changing that dynamic of trust and local knowledge.

I spend much time as a professor asking my students to attend to the texts we engage, asking them to cite what they are reading. With "The Oven Bird's Song," this seems to come more naturally to many of them. Students pull quotes out of the article, and read them out loud at a pace that is hard to keep up with. They bond with each other over details not in the article, but implied by the smallness of the communities Engel studies: how many students were in their graduating class, how many of their friends stayed in state for school, how many of their family members have college degrees. The article gives them a chance to talk about how they feel like fish out of water at college, coming from high schools with no AP courses, no soccer fields, no guidance counselors, and no golf teams.

We talk, in this first class session, about the stifling nature of these communities, the pressure to conform, and the closed-mindedness evinced by many of the citizens. These students come from places with more churches than gas stations or stop lights; many come from conservative religious communities where difference is viewed suspiciously.

Additionally, my students understand, immediately, the dynamic of "insider" and "outsider" that Engel's work so beautifully captures. For instance, we talk about how many generations your family has to live in the community for before you are considered an insider. I grew up in a rural South Dakota town populated by German Catholics and Norwegian Lutherans, where you had to have family in the region for about three generations before you were considered "local." I learned last semester that it takes *five* generations for a family to have that status in Pella, a rural Dutch community of just over 10,000 located forty miles southeast of Des Moines. Everyone from Iowa nodded when our Pella student told us that – Pella has a reputation for being "closed off," even though it is a college town. Iowa students agreed, in contrast, that it takes less than ten years to be an insider in Des Moines or the suburbs, which have a combined population of nearly 625,000 – but that those ten years could feel long. I have lived here a decade now, and am only now being invited to join political organizations, to subscribe to a CSA (community supported agriculture), to attend longstanding events that are community-building

---

[8] Engel, 556.   [9] Ibid, 553–4, 570–1.   [10] Ibid, 556.

staples such as the Elks lodge pancake supper or the Beaverdale Fall Festival. Everyone has been perfectly friendly here (Iowa Nice, they call it) – but as the decade mark has come and gone, I have noticed a shift: I am no longer a transplant, and almost an insider.

In class we also talk about the benefits of being in these small communities, especially if one is an insider. The benefits are not insignificant, and my students are eager to list them. They love to talk about how deeply they know the land in their communities. They have landmarks of pain: the curve that took the lives of too many high-school drivers, the farm where the cow got out and caused a horrible accident, the barb-wire fence that took out an eye when a driver couldn't stop his 3-wheeler or snowmobile in time. The communities also have landmarks of triumph: the abandoned quarry where they would go to kiss, the tree in the middle of the field where they would sit and read, the dirt road out of town they'd barrel down on their bikes. Rural students talk about how the fields are an indication of the weather, as well as the skill and timing and luck of a farmer; unlike their suburban and urban peers, these students know how high corn should be at different stages of the growing cycle, and they can tell the difference between the smells of pigs, horses, and cows. They know the politics of land use and water rights, and which families pursue which claims and which advantages.

When I visit home, and encounter people I do not know or recognize, I need merely say "I am Carolyn Drew's daughter" and folks can place me in a family. When I share that with my students, those of them from places like Sander County nod and agree. My students remind each other how well they know their neighbors, and how much they enjoy feeling close to and rooted in community. They take a lot of pleasure in telling their urban and suburban counterparts about the benefits of being recognized at home. Because they are known through their families' long-term associations with the community, my rural students know that they can pay for things "with a check" in their small towns; they explain how they can put gas or groceries "on a tab" at the local stores. That particular example – that some of us can put gas on our parents' tab at the local gas station – made my urban students' jaws drop. Which leads to my second observation:

OBSERVATION B: THOSE WHO DON'T RECOGNIZE SANDER
COUNTY AND THE PEOPLE IN IT, REALLY *DON'T*

This point barely needs elaboration. The students of mine who come from urban areas, or even the suburban areas of our regional cities, absolutely do not recognize the landscape of a place like Sander County, and they can't imagine living like the people Engel chronicles. They look at my rural students as though they are visitors from a foreign country, and pepper them with open-mouthed questions: "Don't you hate that everyone knows your business?!" "You don't even have a stop light in your town? How is that possible?" "What do you do for fun?" "You really can see for miles? Miles and miles?" "You don't have to pay for your own gas?" "Your town owns and operates the only bar in the county?" They are simultaneously indignant that they don't have some of the benefits of small-town life in the heartland and glad that they avoid some of the pitfalls of such an upbringing. Most importantly, by engaging in this conversation, my students learn that the article which many of them read as historical is in fact an ethnography of an ongoing shift in demographics, culture, and legal consciousness in the United States.

We close this first class session with a conversation that usually focuses on how we can't believe that this article is thirty years old, because our contemporary communities still feel exactly how Engel described them before my students were even born.

By the time the class session is over, we have strayed far from the text and we have talked more about ourselves than the article – but that's okay. I tell students that in class two we are going to look closely at the themes that Engel raises. I ask them to come ready to discuss those themes, and to evaluate if they – like the descriptions of the people themselves – are still visible, and relevant, today.

Self-Sufficiency and the Toughness of Insiders/Locals

My rural students feel very strongly that members of their community embody norms of self-sufficiency and toughness. They also agree with Engel that the lived experiences of citizens in places like Sander County almost mandate such a toughness. Engel tells us, "exposure to the risk of physical injury was simply an accepted part of life. In a primarily agricultural community, which depended on hard physical work and the use of dangerous implements and machinery, such risks were unavoidable."[11] My students immediately recognize this risk as part of their lived experiences. They articulate the risk in voices that also laud their own toughness and self-sufficiency. They say things like:

"Winter is hard. You have to be tough to live here."

"Ranching is lonely and dangerous. You have to be careful."

---

[11] Ibid, 558.

"My family doesn't farm, but my brother works at a factory. He stands eight to twelve hours a day on a hard concrete floor; it might not be dangerous but it is loud, and physically demanding work."

"Have you ever been in a meatpacking plant? A slaughterhouse? It's not fun work."

My students tell me that Midwesterners simply grow up learning how to "put up." To hear these students tell it, they are the original "lumpers":[12] people who understand that they have suffered a harm, but do not make a legal claim upon the person or entity who caused that harm.[13] As Engel explains, individualism, in these settings, is about self-reliance and self-sufficiency in concert with, and as an expression of, community solidarity; it is not about rights-claiming against community norms.[14]

Every single one of my rural students knows someone who hit a cow on the road, who hit a deer, who went off a curve. Everyone from these towns has a story about the homecoming king, the football captain, the sheriff's kid who crashes his car and kills himself or his girlfriend. They have stories of massive floods, of tornados, of heat indexes above 102 and wind-chills below −60.

My students nod in understanding when I mention the grain elevator explosion two towns over from mine that took the lives of many fathers in our community when I was growing up. They know about arms lost in combines, lives lost on country roads, slips and falls and broken hips of elderly people in church parking lots, the lost lives of two girls on an ATV who drove recklessly – a tragedy, yes, but mostly because, in the words of the student who told the story, "they should have known better."

Additionally, students agree with Engel that the cultural norm is one that not only mandates toughness, but also makes it an enviable character trait. Sometimes the more you endure, the more righteous you are. When conversation lags and some students aren't able to grasp this essential point, I share a story from my hometown:

> My mom has a close friend named Dorcas. Dorcas is now in her nineties, and has been widowed for decades. One day Dorcas visited while I was home for the weekend. We sat and drank (weak) coffee and played cards, and had a nice afternoon. After mom saw her to the door, she turned to me and said, "Dorcas is such a good, strong woman. Her husband beat her for years and years and she never said a word."

---

[12] Ibid, 566.   [13] Ibid, 566.   [14] Ibid, 558.

My mom would never see this statement as an endorsement of the poor treatment of women; she would certainly, though, understand Dorcas' toughness as a character trait to which we should all aspire. In my family, in my town, if you "make your bed, you lie in it," and it is the better person who can do so without complaint. When I tell my students about Dorcas, those from the Midwest nod and understand.

Don't get me wrong: students from urban areas, especially our students of color, also talk about their toughness, and the fact that they must rely on themselves, their family, and their close-knit community to survive. But there is a subtle set of differences in the ways these stories unfold. My students of color from near Ferguson, Missouri or from Minneapolis-St. Paul bring an authority to the conversations we have about policing; they speak powerfully about being insiders or outsiders when we discuss Alice Goffman's book,[15] or Nicole Van Cleve's.[16] But in these instances the very things that cause harm – the law, the state, the police – are also the site of the remedy, via reform and rights-claiming. For my rural students, a different set of enemies exists: bad husbands and dangerous weather, negligent neighbors and stupid decisions; for members of the communities these students come from, law is not necessarily the location of the remedy. There is common ground, though: Both sets of students, increasingly and dangerously, see legal institutions as suspect and perceive the rule of law to be a sham.

In Sander County, and places like it, this suspicion is worked out as part of a complex dance between individual responsibility and the role of community. While members of the community might shake their heads and say that the girls "should have known better," mutter to each other at church coffee about how Dorcas' husband treated her, or malign those who seek personal injury suit for remedy, they also feel strongly that the community should support – in substantial ways – those who fall upon hard times. Students understand hyper-individualism, the assumption of risk, and the necessity of toughness and self-sufficiency – but they articulate that self-sufficiency as against the state. The state (embodied in the courts and welfare offices), they argue, should not provide what the community can.

And they tell their classmates about how being an insider in these communities also allows rugged individuals to feel connected. One of them explained it to us in this way: "When something horrible happens, people know and

---

[15] Alice Goffman, *On the Run: Fugitive Life in an American City* (University of Chicago Press, 2014).
[16] Nicole Van Cleve, *Crook County: Racism and Injustice in America's Largest Criminal Court* (Stanford University Press, 2016).

support you." You certainly don't sue, they agree: "You don't win a major settlement – but you do get a lot of casseroles."

My students are very clear that Engel has it right – insiders in these communities do not like to sue each other. What's wrong with litigation, they tell me and their classmates, is that lawsuits aren't good things to bring to those you are connected to. Bringing a lawsuit simply isn't "nice."

In a recently published article that has made the rounds on social media, *New Yorker* contributor Paul Kix wrote about Midwesterners' restraint, specifically "the restraint from speaking ill of others, even if others should probably be ill-spoken of."[7] He continued: "What [the movie] *Fargo* nails, in other words, is Midwestern Nice, the idiosyncrasies of a steadfast populace that appear banal and maybe even bovine to the uninitiated, but in truth constitute the most sincere, malicious, enriching, and suffocating set of behaviors found in the English-speaking world.[8] In an effort to be "nice," to maintain connection, just as Engel postulates, students from these regions cannot envision lawsuits for the wrongs that occur as a part of the daily risk of living in their inhospitable environment and doing the risky jobs associated with making a living there. And they can't imagine the reception that people would get from their communities should they decide to pursue legal – rather than religious or community-based – claims to justice. Like Engel's respondents, they imagine that those who seek remedy through personal injury lawsuits are greedy, selfish, and lazy; they must also, almost by definition, be unconnected from the community that would support them in their recovery from tragedy and harm. Lawsuits, they tell me, are indeed for outsiders.

What It Means to Be an Outsider

In "The Oven Bird's Song," one clear marker of "outsider" status is the racial identity of the person holding it. Increasingly, Middle American cities are not nearly as white and homogenous as those who don't live here like to believe.[19] Nor are the rural areas. I was raised in South Dakota in the 1980s – our town was 99.9 percent "white," and diversity came either in the form of one or two American Indian families or children adopted from Korea. The city closest to my community, however (eighteen miles south), did see increasing

---

[17] www.thrillist.com/lifestyle/nation/my-life-living-midwestern-nice.   [18] Ibid.

[19] The Des Moines Independent Public School District boasts a majority-minority population, and more than 200 languages are spoken in the homes of the students attending those schools. Even the rural areas have significant diversity, with large immigrant populations from Central America and Mexico, as well as re-settled refugees from Vietnam (a generation ago) and Sudan (more recently).

diversity from Vietnamese families who had resettled there via Lutheran Social Services. David Engel would nod, I'm sure, if I told him that one of the primary political controversies of my youth was the integration of Vietnamese American laborers into union jobs at the John Morrell meatpacking plant, and a subsequent strike, use of replacement labor, and ethnically charged violent incidents. Sander County, after all, was suffering similar rifts over unions and jobs.[20]

My students also experience diversity in rural communities as a labor issue. Iowans talk about the growing Latinx population in their towns. These workers are not migrant labor working agricultural field jobs, as we would see in different parts of the United States, in large part because Iowa's crop production is primarily mechanized soy and corn production. Rather, the Latinx workforce centers on the meatpacking industry; as such, it tends to be more stable and less nomadic, which has different kinds of consequences for the towns accommodating these new populations. The same is true for my students who come from Wisconsin and Minnesota, who note their perception that the Hmong population in those states grew during their childhood.

But, while my students are interested in the dynamically shifting racial and ethnic demographics of their towns and the region, they are also insistent that they notice the outsider status of other whites as they enter into and interact with their towns. These students insist that in Engel's analysis there are people that he fails to see. They tell me, and I agree with them, that they know when particular whites in their town are not "from there." I recall that, as a teenager, we knew if we saw girls from Baltic (one town over, just three miles away) walking down our main street. A student from the city near my town nods his head; he has relatives from Baltic, and they always tell him, when he visits, that he stands out as someone from Sioux Falls. There are small – infinitesimal, really – local customs that mark even whites as insiders and outsiders.[21]

The other marker of insider and outsider that my students want to talk about is a religious one. Fifty years after my mom was called a "Cat-licker" and laughed at on the school bus, my students note that Catholics are

---

[20] Engel, 574.

[21] Other white people stand out – the poor (which Engel does attend to as part of the population of outsiders in Sander County), and members of the GLBTQ communities. It is here that I introduce students to the work of Bud Jerke, whose law review article on "queer ruralism" reminds us that gay men wear overalls as work gear, not just NYC fashion. And we talk about the work being done by Lisa Pruitt on the provision of social services in rural areas – especially focusing on domestic violence in these communities and women's access to health care, and justice in general.

marginalized in Lutheran-led communities. They talk about the splintering in the Lutheran Church between the Missouri Synod and the Evangelical Lutheran Church in America (ELCA), as well as the further splits caused by ELCA administrative rulings allowing congregations to decide if they will allow married gay clergy. One student, when pressed on religious diversity in her town, noted, "We don't have any Methodists, or Presbyterians. And we don't have any Baptists." She paused, and added: "Aren't Baptists in the South?"

It is particularly telling that my students from rural Midwestern areas are fascinated by Christian Science and Jehovah's Witnesses and their role in rights-based constitutional litigation, which they raise as distinct from the personal injury litigation avoided by residents of Sander County and their town alike. Evangelical Christians find it fascinating that a religious world-view could support using courts for justice when their religious worldviews suggest that reliance on secular authority of these kinds, for things like personal injury or an articulation of all but the most vaulted rights, is inappropriate and ill-seeming.

Finally, students in my classrooms note that they, themselves, are outsiders. Even with their whiteness, and their middle-class status, and their generations of family in town – even with their desire to return to practice law, or run a family business – by leaving town to pursue an education, they become Other. Paul Kix's essay ends with words that I like to read with and explore with my students, as they raise these issues. Kix writes:

> I grew up in Iowa but I've heard the same line repeated of people from Minnesota or Wisconsin or Nebraska, and always with the unfussy grammar of the plain-spoken: "The Midwest is a great place to be from." It is nurturing and civic-minded, maybe due to the Scandinavian and German Protestants who settled the land, living by the Golden Rule, and its history is a continuity of compassion ... The Midwest takes pride in all this; it would just rather not talk about it, you see, because that would be boasting, and boasting is not nice.

Students who leave their small Midwestern communities to go to school at Drake talk quite a bit about how they are perceived when they leave: They are boasting by leaving. They are showing off by leaving. They are entering dangerous territory full of drugs and sex work (though with the rise of crystal meth in rural communities in the past decade, they acknowledge that the risks associated with the drug trade are often right on their own doorsteps, and impacting their own families). They think they are better than their peers when they leave. They have nothing in common with their friends from high school when they leave and their friends remain.

Students, in other words, understand that they become a bit less like insiders and more like outsiders by leaving to attend college. As we discuss outsiders, and education, it becomes clear that part of what is going on with that sense of themselves as outsiders is an understanding that their peers, parents, and community members share an antipathy toward professionals and elites that extends beyond a traditional anti-legalism, and implicates the managerial class, professional workers, and those who have earned degrees through higher education.

Anti-Professionalism (It's Not Just Against Lawyers Any More)

Professionals are outsiders to my students. In fact, *they must be*. Even if these professionals are hometown kids "returning" as adults to their communities of origin, they are people who have left – who have sought other things – and come back. It doesn't matter that there are no ways to become professional without leaving – no law schools or medical schools in these towns, and often none for hundreds of miles – anti-professionalism marks lawyers and doctors, in particular, as apart/separate from others in the community. And anti-professionalism feeds into a politics of resentment and distrust that is alarming to see manifest.

Two things in particular surprise me about my students' willingness to participate in anti-intellectual and anti-professional discourses. First, the anti-professional sentiment that my students note in their towns' cultural lives goes beyond the anti-lawyer sentiment that we might expect in a society that thinks it is hyper-litigious. They evince an easy anti-medical sentiment. One student told the class, "My mom is a doctor, but she'll never take us to the doctor! She'll say: You're fine. We don't need to go in." In this instance, as in many of the stories shared in our classroom conversations and many of the stories related by Engel in "The Oven Bird's Song," self-sufficiency butts up against professionalism. Here, self-sufficiency scores an innocent victory. But there is a not-so-innocent level of distrust running through these conversations about professionals and outsiders. Sometimes it is a subtle feeling of "family knows best," or not wanting to share personal details – perhaps about reproductive decision-making, or mental illness and addiction – with local professionals who are likely to be members of your church, and parents of your best friends. But others of my students made this a more political and less social point. Some of them noted that they were not vaccinated, and that they and their parents distrusted the "medical establishment" that seemed both profit-driven and over-allied with federal government. There is a sense that the medical industry is incredibly powerful; indeed, it is a major employer in the regions from which my rural students are drawn – and an agenda-setter in terms of policy. As one student from South Dakota told the class, "the industry in many of the small cities dotting the plains is the medical industry." He added: "No one can mess with Sanford Health." It isn't mere coincidence that these states have been slow to adopt – and often hostile to – health-care exchanges mandated by the Obama administration; these are communities located in states that are hostile to alternative health practitioners, such as midwives, even though those professionals embody a self-sufficiency and tradition that should appeal to the states' populations.

The second thing that surprised me during our conversation about professionalism is that the anti-professional sentiment held true even for those students with professional parents – and even for those with lawyers for parents. In fact, those with lawyers and judges for parents sometimes most strongly shared the key attitude of Sander County citizens: Personal lawsuits are divisive, and to be avoided. They shared their opinion that the proper role for lawyers and judges is to channel disputes toward settlement. A student from Kansas summed it up perfectly when she told us, "My dad is a judge in a small town ... and he hates it when people brings these kinds of suits. He wants them to work it out. And he almost always knows the people involved."

It was this quote in particular, in the fall of 2015, that made me take notice of the deeper currents underlying our conversation. This statement – and students' views about legal and medical professionalism, elitism, and distrust of the government, science, and law – made me realize it is vitally important, as a matter of politics, that we watch how students react to "The Oven Bird's Song," and to engage them in a dialogue about whether their anti-elite sentiment is really as democratically minded as they believe.

STUDENT REACTIONS TO "THE OVEN BIRD" ILLUMINATE CONTEMPORARY POLITICAL CULTURE

I initially began assigning "The Oven Bird's Song" because it gives students an accessible foundation for future work in, and understanding of, sociolegal work, and introduces them to some key methods in our field in ways that they can replicate on a small scale. I believe that Ewick and Silbey will come more intuitively to students once they have read Engel.[22]

I also think it is useful for students – many of whom will go on to practice law – to grapple with the anti-professionalism and anti-litigious views that

---

[22] Patricia Ewick and Susan Silbey, *The Common Place of Law: Stories from Everyday Life* (University of Chicago Press, 1998).

Sander County residents share with them. How can they say they want to be lawyers, I ask them as we discuss the article, if they hold such negative views about them? How can they work with populations like those of Sander County, who value self-sufficiency and "lumping it" over claims-making? How can those who want to use their professional status and insider knowledge to help outsiders and "have-nots" gain access to justice?

But, as I indicated above, the students' reactions also show me the depth of the political and cultural shifts going on in the heartland of America. Students – liberal and moderate students, alongside their libertarian and conservative peers – articulate a distrust of authority that begins to sound like the themes of Donald Trump's presidential campaign. Their reactions to "The Oven Bird's Song" show me, and hopefully them, that their understandings of legal culture relate to their political views in complex ways – and in ways that many of them have not yet adequately acknowledged or explored. Democratic and Republican students alike espouse, in their reactions to "The Oven Bird's Song," a core contemporary conservative tenet: Law must be relied upon to maintain order.[23] However, they articulate a growing skepticism about the role of government in maintaining that law,[24] and a sympathy for more reactionary, individualistic, self-help styles of social control. Like Justice Clarence Thomas, members of the communities from which my students come despair when they see governmental and legal institutions "kowtow to . . . extravagant undeserved [rights] claims,"[25] while many of those same students are simultaneously struggling with their own outsider status and their potential need for the protective arm of a regulatory and rights-expanding state.

Student reactions to the article – which center on what is so unique about rural areas, what they recognize in the article – are nostalgic reactions. They are the discursive equivalents to Iris Dement's lament that "the sun's settin' down, on our town, on our town."[26] And their reactions evince an anxiety about what that sunset means – an uncertainty about the fate of the tight-knit communities they are part of, the rural economy which is increasingly beholden to Chinese land ownership, agri-business, and government subsidy. Their reactions articulate an anxiety about the outcome of a politics that gave them a hopeful Obama presidency followed by a campaign season of angry populism on both sides of the aisle.

Recent work on the origins and rise of American authoritarianism suggests that the paradoxes my students feel in their communities – a deep desire to be self-reliant, while enmeshed in a political economy that refuses autonomy and

---

[23] Dudas, *All the Rage*, 70.   [24] Ibid, 73.   [25] Ibid, 93.
[26] Iris Dement, "Our Town," *Infamous Angel* (Warner Brothers, 1992).

a political culture that necessitates rights claims for mundane matters like bathroom usage, breastfeeding, and falling in love – might cause an anxiety that resolves not peacefully, but with reactive politics. "Authoritarians," Amanda Taub writes, "prioritize social order and hierarchies, which bring a sense of control to a chaotic world. Challenges to that order – diversity, influx of outsiders, breakdown of the old order – are experienced as personally threatening because they risk upending the status quo order they equate with basic security." What's more, fear tends to trigger authoritarian impulses even in those who might only hold those views latently – such that "when non-authoritarians feel sufficiently scared, they also start to behave, politically, like authoritarians."[27] Nostalgic politics, coupled with anxiety and skepticism, seem ripe for authoritarianism's romance, in a time that feels increasingly unstable for many in rural and transitioning America.

So, my students are overjoyed to find their lives reflected in an academic text like David Engel's piece, but they are distraught to learn that while it feels like everything is changing, their communities are stuck in the same ruts and wearing the same grooves as Sander County was before they were even born. I, likewise, am glad to give these students a chance to reflect on where they've come from and where we all might be going – while I look, sometimes with fascinated horror and hopefully always with compassion, at the ways in which their self-reliant, anti-litigious, closed-off communities deal with outsiders, be they Latinx, professional, queer, poor, or Southern Baptist. Ultimately, this is what "The Oven Bird's Song," and indeed the totality of David Engel's work, most invites us to develop: A compassionate eye toward those who are struggling and suffering with the material consequences of injury, harm, and economic downturn, and a listening ear for the conversations we must have to understand each other's positions.

---

[27] Amanda Taub, "The rise of American authoritarianism," *Vox*, March 1, 2016, www.vox.com/2016/3/1/11127424/trump-authoritarianism.

PART IV

Conflict and Law in Other Cultures

14

The Songs of Other Birds

ANYA BERNSTEIN

"This stuff about Taipei is very interesting," David Engel told me when we first met, "but wouldn't things look roughly the same in Chicago?" We were discussing my work on Taiwanese government administrators' attitudes toward the laws they administered.[1] These attitudes were, in short, not positive. Administrators were apt to treat law and legal process as an impediment to their work, not a driver of it. When they did invoke the law, they often did so for external, non-Taiwanese audiences. Pulling law on compatriots was liable to be interpreted – by administrators and laypeople alike – as a cover-up for a bald power play.

David phrased his question in a half-joking way, with "Chicago" standing loosely for a government administration that distributed benefits on the basis of political affiliations and loyalties rather than legal entitlements. But he was, of course, posing deeper questions. Wasn't the most parsimonious explanation of

---

[1] Anya Bernstein, "The social life of regulation in Taipei City Hall: the role of legality in the administrative bureaucracy," *Law & Social Inquiry*, 33 (2008), 925–54. I spent roughly nine months working with administrators in the Taipei City Government Bureau of Urban Development, including six months as a full-time volunteer translator in the Bureau's City Hall office. During this time, I talked with administrators; sat in on their meetings with other government employees, consultants, and members of the public; and accompanied them on inspections, off-site meetings, lunch outings, weekend hikes, dinners, and other activities. I observed hundreds of meetings and less formal interactions, and had hundreds of conversations with administrators from across the Bureau, as well as from other departments. I also recorded roughly thirty hours of open-ended, semi-structured interviews with administrators at every level of the organization, from Bureau head to low-level functionary. Before working in the city government, I spent roughly one year doing ethnography with community activists in the Dali Street neighborhood, one of the oldest, poorest, and most crowded in Taipei. My ethnographic work took place in Chinese (mostly Mandarin, with some Taiwanese). I render Mandarin quotations in hanyu pinyin transliteration (without tones). Where I do not have exact wording, I give the gist of an utterance in English translation only. I use pseudonyms for all speakers.

administrators' distaste for law simply that law would obstruct their ability to wield power? And didn't my findings in Taiwan simply replicate what others had found elsewhere – that many people do not like to invoke legal process? After all, David's own research had found that people purposely avoided recourse to the law in places as different as northern Thailand and middle America.[2]

The impulse to see similarities or differences across cases is sometimes glossed as a matter of preference: lumping versus splitting. From that perspective, the decision is mostly a question of whether one attends more to what unites or what divides. Here, I want to explore a different dimension to difference and similarity. Drawing on my own work in Taiwan, I want to raise some questions about how we determine what seemingly similar phenomena mean in, and for, their surrounding social contexts. This means thinking explicitly about how we situate what we encounter in our research. It may be that lumping and splitting are not so much different ways of understanding phenomena as of contextualizing them.

When seen at higher levels of abstraction or generality, attitudes toward law among Taipei administrators, American farmers, and Thai migrants can indeed be described as similar. When viewed at a more specific and concrete level, situated within geographically, temporally, and culturally more proximate contexts, these same attitudes can appear quite distinct. Not every bird that mistrusts the law sings the same song. And any song rings in a chorus of other chirps. This suggests, as Carol Greenhouse has written, that the study of law in society is always at least implicitly comparative.[3] We compare our object of study with how we imagined it would be, with surrounding objects in the same social field, with separate objects that we know or imagine, and with what we see at other levels of generality. Here, I dive into some local contexts to unwrap the distinct significance of people's attitudes about laws and the governments that supply them, then swim back up to consider what implications this might have for the study of legal consciousness across times and places.

COMPLEXITY, COHERENCE, AND DEMOCRACY'S DISCONTENTS

Systems of governance are highly topicalized in Taiwan. Before even reaching the question of what people think about democracy, one is struck by how

---

[2] See, e.g., David M. Engel, "The oven bird's song: insiders, outsiders, and personal injuries in an American community," *Law & Society Review*, 18 (1984), 551–82; David M. Engel, "Globalization and the decline of legal consciousness: torts, ghosts, and karma in Thailand," *Law & Social Inquiry*, 30 (2005), 469–514.

[3] Carol Greenhouse, "Courting difference: issues of interpretation and comparison in the study of legal ideologies," *Law & Society Review*, 22 (1988), 687–708.

actively many people are thinking about it. It was not a topic that flared up among political junkies or during elections. In an intensely social environment, people in every class and group I encountered routinely discussed the nature of Taiwan's democracy, the quality of its political culture, and the relationship of its contemporary state to its martial law past.

This did not mean, of course, that people were satisfied with their nation, government, or legal system. On the contrary, the political conversation that suffused social life was characterized by an often gloomy dissatisfaction. Common themes were instability, incoherence, and multiplicity. Many people described Taiwan's problems as rooted in an unmanageable multifariousness that had been exacerbated with the advent of democracy.

One urban planning administrator, for instance, explained to me that, after the end of martial law and the reintroduction of city government elections to Taipei, the city's Bureau of Urban Development had ceased doing large-scale social research on the city it administered.[4] The main reason, Mr. An said, was that Taiwanese society was just too complicated (*fuza*). There were too many kinds of people doing too many kinds of things, and one simply couldn't capture it all in a survey. Indeed, the city government itself was complicated. The urban planning department was riven with conflicts between graduates of its two main feeder schools: a Marxist department that emphasized qualitative research and a systems-theoretical one that favored statistical methods. And relations among branches of government had become complicated with the introduction of elected mayors and city councils. The department head now had to please the mayor, the public, the city council, and the experts and scholars incorporated into many decision-making processes – a complicated set of demands that left little time or political capital for comprehensive planning.[5]

In contrast, Mr. An continued, America was "more *danchun* (pure, simple)." In America, he explained, warring factions would be separated, departments had stable duties that endured across administrations, elected representatives would not put pressure on administrators, and even the

---

4   Before democratization, Taipei had elected mayors from 1947 until 1967. In 1967 the central government began appointing mayors after a candidate who did not belong to the ruling party (the KMT or Chinese Nationalist Party) won a second term. See Shelley Rigger, *Politics in Taiwan: Voting for Democracy* (Routledge, 1999).

5   As Jeffrey Martin writes with respect to the police, "Taiwanese policing elevates the network-based powers of ... local elites [such as city councils] over the powers of centralized bureaucracies and the courts, even as it effectively upholds the ultimate authority of a democratically organized state. In other words, it is democratic policing without the rule of law." Jeffrey T. Martin, "Legitimate force in a particularistic democracy: street police and outlaw legislators in the Republic of China on Taiwan," *Law & Social Inquiry*, 38 (2013), 615–42, 617.

administrative leadership might stay on from mayor to mayor. In Taipei city hall, a word spoken by one person could mean something different in the mouth of someone from a competing group. In America, on the other hand, whether you read it in the *New York Times* or the *Washington Post*, a word meant the same thing. In Mr. An's America, thus, differences were clearly delineated and compartmentalized, electoral contestation did not lead to political instability, and meaning was stable throughout public discourse. This kind of contrast with an imagined "America," "the West," or "foreign countries *(guowai)*" was not unusual: many of the people with whom I spoke framed their comments about their country with their visions of mine, as a way to illuminate their ideals and disappointments.[6] The simplicity and stability attributed to America highlighted Mr. An's negative convictions about the complexity and instability of Taiwan.

Fuza, complexity, is a key term of discomfort in Taiwan. An unsolvable situation might be *fuza*, but so might social configurations and demographic arrangements. For instance, many people described the community activists I studied as living in a very *fuza* area of the city. Some people explained their use of this term with reference to the gangsters and prostitutes for which the area is famous. But most explanations had something to do with diversity. "Lower middle classes, middle classes, upper classes, it has them all," one acquaintance said.[7] Ms. Yuan used a classical idiom meaning "dragons and snakes live together there." In such a place, she explained, everything is all mixed up: Dragons and snakes are the *most* opposite creatures. One person wove both explanations together. The area's well-known sex industry, and the gangsters that go along with it, led to there being many different types of people in the neighborhood – naturally a very *fuza* situation.

As others have shown, the notion of "diversity" can serve ideological purposes beyond mere description. In the United States, it can obscure structural inequalities in circumstance and opportunity with an upbeat insistence on the value of difference.[8] The valence of multiplicity in Taiwanese political discourse is quite different. A diversity of social types or opinions is often figured as inherently problematic, almost unnatural: *fuza*, an unsolvable situation. This discomfort with multiplicity, which was prevalent both in my fieldsites and among other acquaintances, often had a distinctly historical

---

[6] I assume that many such references were made specifically for my benefit, since people knew I came from the United States. However, such contrasts were also common in conversations among administrators, for instance at meetings where I was not a central participant.

[7] "*Zhongdi jieji, zhongceng jieji, gaoceng jieji, dou you.*"

[8] Ellen Berrey, *The Enigma of Diversity* (University of Chicago Press, 2015).

implication. It brought the contemporary democratic period into sharp contrast with the long martial law era that preceded it. Martial law, with its well-controlled media and its strict limits on political participation, enforced a stability of meaning and value in political discourse. Its monopoly over the public sphere limited what could be openly asserted to be the public good.

The martial law government implemented this monopoly on legitimate ideology while also supporting a lively system of political competition. Martial law politics divided local factions, which were open to all, from national party politics, which was restricted by ethnicity, biography, and personal relations.[9] Local-level elections gave people seeking control of resources a way to organize and compete with others. Local factions were further connected to central power brokers, creating a "regime patronage system" – that is, a system in which the regime itself was a patron in a clientelist system.[10] Local elites in turn became patrons at the local level, transferring resources to local clients who lent them political support. This large-scale system kept factions balanced without disturbing centralized party control.[11]

---

[9] Joseph Bosco, "Taiwan factions: guanxi, patronage, and the state in local politics," *Ethnology*, 31 (1992), 157–84. The KMT (*Guomindang* or Chinese Nationalist Party) took control of Taiwan after World War II, when the Allies ended Japan's fifty-year colonization of the island (1895–1945). In 1949, the KMT leadership, along with many others, fled to Taiwan, away from the Communist victory in the Chinese civil war. For many years, Taiwan's national politics was reserved for those who came to island in the 1940s and their descendants, *waishengren* (outside-the-province people, or Mainlanders in English). See Steven E. Phillips, *Between Assimilation and Independence: The Taiwanese Encounter With Nationalist China, 1945–1950* (Stanford University Press, 2003). After a massive, bloody reprisal against a protest of police power, the party state instituted a martial law whose rule would last forty years: George H. Kerr, *Formosa Betrayed* (Houghton Mifflin, 1965). In the late 1970s, the government began to "localize" (*bentuhua*), increasing the number of people descended from those who had come to the island before Japanese colonization in 1895 – the *benshengren* (this-province people) or Taiwanese, who had previously been relegated to local factional politics. This process played a key role in both facilitating democratization and preserving the KMT's legitimacy: Allen Chun, "Democracy as hegemony, globalization as indigenization, or the 'culture' in Taiwanese national politics" in Wei-Chin Lee (ed.), *Taiwan in Perspective* (Brill, 2000), pp. 7–27. Taiwanese make up 84–85.5 percent of the island's population; Mainlanders 13–14 percent; and indigenous people 1.7–2 percent: Government Information Office, *Taiwan Yearbook 2003* (Government Information Office, Republic of China, 2003); Shuanfan Huang, "A sociolinguistic profile of Taipei" in Robert L. Cheng and Shuanfan Huang (eds.), *The Structure of Modern Taiwanese: A Modern Synthesis (Xiandai Taiwanhua Yanjiu Lunwenji)* (Crane, 1988), pp. 301–31. In my view, the ethnicized distinctions that fueled politics in the twentieth century are waning in importance as more young people grow up in the democratic system.

[10] Nai-teh Wu, *The Politics of a Regime Patronage System: Mobilization and Control Within an Authoritarian Regime.* Unpublished PhD diss. University of Chicago (1987).

[11] Ibid; Edwin A. Winckler, "Roles linking state and society" in Emily Martin Ahern and Hill Gates (eds.), *The Anthropology of Taiwanese Society* (Stanford University Press, 1981), pp. 50–88;

The language and forms of traditional social values helped naturalize this new political system. Political factions under martial law built on pre-existing ways of cohering social groups: real and fictive kinship, locality, educational background, occupational affiliation, and religious participation.[12] Utilizing a common social valorization of affective links and long-term relations of mutual aid and obligation, factions helped make the personal indistinguishable from the political: "As the entrepreneurs collect money, the politicians collect friends."[13] Ideological claims like assertions about the common good were reserved for the ruling KMT, or Chinese Nationalist Party, with its unified front of a tightly organized authoritarian system.[14]

External pressures from the international community's transfer of recognition to the People's Republic of China in the 1970s, and internal pressures from emergent opposition political groups in the 1980s, supported a vibrant democratization movement. That movement itself utilized the very channels that had sustained local factions under martial law: interpersonally mediated social networks based on pre-existing tropes of affiliation.[15] These personalistic networks sustained groups whose members were connected both by personal relations and by an understanding of themselves as participants in a discourse that exceeds those relations – a political faction, party, or movement. With the democratization movement, politically active participants began insinuating new ideological content into these pre-existing social networks.[16]

Many people described the rise of this ideological pluralism with mixed feelings. Democratization opened up channels of political power and allowed people to express their views freely and in their preferred languages.[17] But that

---

Hung-mao Tien (ed.), *Taiwan's Electoral Politics and Democratic Transition: Riding the Third Wave* (M. E. Sharpe, 1996).

[12] See Rigger, *Politics in Taiwan.*   [13] Wu, *Politics of a Regime Patronage System*, 265.

[14] See Bosco, *Taiwan Factions.*

[15] Ibid; Rigger, *Politics in Taiwan*; Susan Greenhalgh, "Networks and their nodes: urban society on Taiwan," *The China Quarterly*, 99 (1984), 529–52; see also David L. Wank, *Commodifying Communism: Business, Trust, and Politics in a Chinese City* (Cambridge University Press, 1999); Mayfair Mei-hui Yang, *Gifts, Favors, and Banquets: The Art of Social Relationships in China* (Cornell University Press, 1994).

[16] Pictures from the wedding of a founder of the then-opposition Democratic Progressive Party (DPP), for instance, show a veritable Orient Express of the early political underground: A group of people who all just happened to be opposition activists all just happened to gather for this happy occasion, at a time when gathering for other reasons just happened to be prohibited. Martial law strictures prohibited large gatherings of people except for certain ritual events like weddings, so opposition activists seized on the personalistic connections that gave rise to such exceptions. As the founder's ex-wife told me, "DPP history starts at my wedding."

[17] Anya Bernstein, "Bureaucratic speech: language choice and democratic identity in the Taipei bureaucracy," *PoLAR: Political and Legal Anthropology Review*, 40 (2017), 31–34.

freedom also threw the very definition of the public good into question. For many people I talked to, this discursive disarray was the undesirable underside of democracy.

Even beneficiaries of the new cacophony often expressed discomfort with the freedoms that democratization fostered. Mr. Shan was a community activist who had participated for years in protests against the city government. These activities would have landed him in jail during the martial law period. Nonetheless, he told me with disgust that the difference that democratization had made was that now, in the post-martial law era, "it is easier to be a gangster."[18] Another devoted activist, Mother Mei, had also spent years engaging in protests and other activities that were strictly prohibited under martial law. She once summed up a dinner conversation with the comment, "Taiwan is too democratic."[19] After a pause, she burst out, "[People] even cuss out the president!"[20]

Administrators, meanwhile, generally spoke favorably of the effects of democratization on relations between government employees and the populace under their purview.[21] But they consistently expressed discomfort with the unstable quality of government practice it brought about. They especially pointed to the destabilizing effects of elections. By making control of the city government unpredictable, elections had made long-term planning impossible. Elections in other cities similarly obstructed regional planning. For the first time, neighboring urban areas could be controlled by different parties, making cooperation politically unpalatable. And the new powers of the elected Taipei City Council impeded the implementation of law and policy. In Taiwan's highly personalistic electoral structure, each councilor was considered somewhat beholden to each constituent. And the City Council controlled the city government's budget. Administrators thus spent much of their time fielding elected representatives' demands to abrogate the rule of law: to protect particular constituents from the enforcement of city policies.

The newly opened stage for ideological assertions of the public good, along with election-induced turmoil in government, contributed to the destabilizing diversity of the post-martial law era. As Mr. Wei, a high-ranking administrator, told me, Taipei could be considered:

---

[18] *"Jieyan gen jieyan de butong? Jieyan hou zuo liumang bijiao hao."*
[19] *"Taiwan tai minzhu le."* Aside from some friends who self-identified as unusual – by sexual activity (e.g., gay men, women who were openly sexually active); profession (e.g., independent filmmakers, actors, writers); and upbringing or experience (e.g., people who had lived long-term in the United States, Australia, or Europe) – members of every group I came into contact with in Taiwan expressed this sentiment to me, often in these exact words.
[20] *"Dou ma zongtong ei!"*   [21] See Bernstein, *Bureaucratic Speech.*

the world's freest city . . . What I mean is, it seems like America is very free but it . . . does still have a dominant culture . . . [In] Taipei . . . if I think I have the ability, then I just do it, so it turns out [that] . . . everybody does his own thing . . . Well this is . . . also one of the origins of Taipei's . . . fun and interesting style. From the perspective of Said's *Orientalism*, of course, this is one of Asia's fascinating aspects, but it's also our predicament. Because this interesting style has been developed by different groups each acting on its own . . . This may be our particular characteristic, but we still feel that . . . this kind of characteristic isn't a good characteristic.[22]

Mr. Wei's description of social conduct could have come straight from Adam Smith: In Taipei's free society, each person pursues his or her own interests independently. But the evaluation of the result was quite different. This self-motivated pursuit of interests does not redound, willy-nilly, to the benefit of the whole society. Rather, it gives rise to something more complicated. It creates a city that is "fascinating" and "interesting" to outsiders but which suffers from a "predicament": the lack of the "dominant culture" that characterizes a hypothetical America.

Such lack of cultural coherence is commonly tied to the end of authoritarian rule. For instance, Mr. Ke, an active and enthusiastic administrator, spoke proudly of his ability to negotiate with members of the public, demonstrate his earnestness and rectitude, and forge mutually beneficial compromises.[23] But he also admitted that he sometimes missed the uncomplicated ideological commitments that had pervaded his youth. Under martial law, he told me, "it was all about 'establishing the nation.' Everyone didn't dare talk politics. We just dared to talk about 'establishing the nation.' After martial law, what did we get? We got freedom of speech. But the thing we sacrificed was even more important."[24]

These might sound like the complaints of power-hungry bureaucrats who wish people would fall in line like they used to. But as I hope I have

---

[22] "*Quanshijieshang zui ziyoude chengshi . . . Wode yisi shi kanqilai Meiguo hen ziyou keshi ta . . . you wenhua qiangshide neihanbufen cunzai. Taibei . . . wo renwei woyou zhege nengli, wo jiu zuo, suoyi hui biancheng . . . zijiqiao zijide, ah suoyi . . . zhe . . . yeshi jintian Taibei nage youqude fengmude laiyuan zhiyi . . . Zhege . . . cong Said de Dongfangzhuyi laijiang dehua dangranshi yige Yazhou de meili suozaide, danshi zhe ye shi women de kunjing. Yinwei zhezhong youqude fengmuxing you butong qunti gezi fazhan chansheng de . . . Zhe yexu shi womende tese keshi women haishi juede zhege tese . . . bushi yige haode tese.*"

[23] On the importance of compromise to government action, see Anya Bernstein, *The Social Life of Regulation.*

[24] "*Nage shihou dou shi jianguo, dajia bu gan tan zhengzhi, zhi gan tan jianguo. Jieyan ne, women dedaole shenme? Women dedaole yanlun ziyou, keshi women sunshi de dongxi geng zhongyao.*"

demonstrated, the sentiment was a common refrain among people outside the government, too. A small-scale entrepreneur in his early thirties who took me on a walk around his neighborhood, for instance, spent much of the time bemoaning the sorry state of Taiwanese culture and society. As we passed the fortune-tellers plying their trade outside a famous temple, he remarked that such old-fashioned, superstitious practices were still rampant in Taiwan. In a busy market area, he derided the Taiwanese obsession with fashion and the ephemeral nature of Taiwanese trends. Outside a movie theater, he complained that Taiwanese directors prefer incomprehensibility over relatability. Taiwan's cultural problem, he concluded, is that it *has* no culture.[25] Like administrators in the city government, my companion faulted Taiwan for its loss of a unitary, coherent identity – something one could point to and call one's own.[26] Many people posed, in their own ways, the disheartened question of the oven bird's song: "what to make of a diminished thing?"[27]

LAW IS NOT THE ANSWER

As the previous section makes clear, American academics are not the only ones who might see sociolegal analysis as inherently comparative. Many Taiwanese people that I knew used comparisons with the United States as a way to portray what an ideally functional democracy might look like. As their references to simplicity, stability, and dominant culture imply, this ideal included freedom balanced by coherence. Moreover, the strength of American democracy seemed, for many, to inhere not in things like commitments to the rule of law or procedural rights, but in cultural constraints and structural controls that could hold in check a potentially disorderly diversity. Such disorder was

---

[25] This person also brought a comparative approach to our conversation. I proposed another way to sum up the phenomena he described: As a diverse society, Taiwan supports a vibrant ritual tradition along with a cosmopolitan incorporation of foreign aesthetics and a lively arts scene. Yes, he sighed, an American *would* say that. Americans are confident. Taiwanese, he explained, are too down on themselves to ever think that way.

[26] To be sure, not everyone wishes Taiwan were more uniform. Some people I knew used the same lamentational style to bemoan Taiwanese society's *lack* of diversity. Notably, however, I only heard this relatively uncommon view of multiplicity expressed by people who described themselves as somewhat unusual in their behaviors, professions, or experiences (see n 19 of this chapter).

[27] I refer here, of course, both to the poem by Robert Frost and to David Engel's reference to it in his article "The Oven Bird's Song." Robert Frost, "The Oven Bird" in *The Poetry of Robert Frost*, ed. Edward Connery Lathem (Holt, Rinehart, Winston, 1969 [1916]); Engel, *The Oven Bird's Song*.

then figured as released in Taiwan with the fragmentation of the previously presumable cultural unity enforced under martial law.[28]

Furthermore, the transition from martial law to democracy left in place many ideas about how the general will is expressed and how the general good is fulfilled. Taiwanese education, for instance, has long emphasized appropriate behavior by model individuals as a motivating force in social development.[29] This notion continues to be prevalent in discussions of politics: People in Taiwan talk much more about the power of exemplary individuals than about the benevolence of invisible hands. As Mr. Wei's description of Taipei as an excessively free city suggests, the notion that political equilibrium could be achieved through the combination of otherwise uncoordinated activities by self-interested individuals would have seemed quite strange to most people with whom I spoke. A society in which each person acts in his own interest would result not in the fulfillment of world spirit moving through history, but in chaos.[30]

---

[28] My aim here is to explain people's understandings of their society, not to evaluate their accuracy. Still, it may be worth mentioning that Taipei was rated one of the safest cities in the world by *The Economist* magazine in 2015. See http://safecities.economist.com/whitepapers/safe-cities-index-white-paper/. In other words, perceptions of disorder likely did not refer to things like crime waves or violent unrest in the wake of democratization, but to more complex, nuanced understandings of social structure and cultural values.

[29] In his study of Taiwanese elementary schools, done around the time when a number of my informants were in school, Richard Wilson noted that children typically asserted that any group needs a leader to act as a model for its members. Richard W. Wilson, *Learning to Be Chinese: The Political Socialization of Children in Taiwan* (1970). This value can loosely be seen to derive from the Confucian tradition, although of course Confucianism itself has taken many forms over the centuries. For more on how loosely Confucian ideals permeate Taiwanese concepts of legitimate authority, see Martin, *Legitimate Force*.

[30] Taiwan's remarkable twentieth-century economic success was similarly rooted in "a system of industrial land transfer and development that was tightly controlled by the state" and largely funded by the United States. Martha Fitzpatrick Bishai, "The development of industrial land in Taiwan: a legal framework for state control," 26 (1991), *Journal of Developing Areas*, 53–64, 62. After giving the KMT about $2 billion between 1945 and 1949 to fight the Communists, the United States cut off aid, "disgusted with [the KMT's] incompetence and insatiable appetite for funds that simply vanished": Thomas B. Gold, *State and Society in the Taiwan Miracle* (M.E. Sharpe, 1986), p. 53. Then "North Korea's Kim Il-sung entered the story as the [KMT's] deus ex machina by invading South Korea," and aid resumed: ibid, 55. Taiwan's mid-century land reform, which enabled rapid industrialization by distributing farmland to small producers and encouraging large landlords to urbanize and invest, proceeded under the auspices of the US Agency for International Development (USAID) and the Sino-American Joint Council on Rural Reconstruction, a US-KMT organization. A. Y. C. Koo, *Land Reform in Taiwan*, United States Agency for International Development: Country Papers, Spring Review (1970); Alice Amsden, "The state and Taiwan's economic development" in Peter B. Evans, Dietrich Rueschemeyer, and Theda Skocpol (eds.), *Bringing the State Back In* (Cambridge University Press, 1985), pp. 78–106. These agencies provided conduits for the river of

One could imagine one way such illegitimate disorder might be tamed: through laws passed by democratically elected representatives. But in my three years of language study, fieldwork, and intensive socializing, no one ever suggested such a possibility. Law was often markedly extraneous to discussions of government practice. For instance, shortly before I started my fieldwork, agents from the Ministry of Justice raided the offices of a popular magazine that was about to publish leaked documents revealing that a former president had bypassed the national security apparatus with secret diplomacy and espionage funds. I asked the questions that seemed obvious to me: On what legal grounds was the magazine shut down? Were the secret funds illegal? The teachers and friends with whom I then spent most of my time found these questions interesting only in an ethnographic sense, as an illustration of how Americans think. They were not relevant to local discussions of the incident, which focused on whether publishing such a story actually posed a threat to national security.

The notion that law might play a central role in legitimating political action or in cohering political positions was similarly dismissed by my fieldwork participants. As one urban planning administrator explained to me, Western laws grew out of Western social norms, leading to a natural connection between legal systems and social realities. In Taiwan, in contrast, laws were imported from elsewhere – Japan, Europe, America. That led to a big "gap" – he used the English word – between law and society. In keeping with this image, administrators routinely talked about Taiwanese law as irrelevant and non-responsive to the society it purported to regulate, and as "hard (*ying*)" or unyielding in ways that amplified that irrelevance.

For instance, one administrator with whom I worked dealt with an area zoned for agricultural use whose landowners had recently built a plethora of consumer-oriented tea-houses. He blamed the laws, not the landowners, for the situation. These leisure establishments, he explained, answered a growing demand from an increasingly rich populace. The law had been too slow to acknowledge this demand; it could not keep up with social changes. Insofar as they saw their job as implementing laws at all, administrators tended to phrase it in terms of *convincing* members of the public to come around to legal strictures. But for the most part, administrators did not describe their work in

US economic aid that flowed into Taiwan with the beginning of the Korean War. They "had de facto veto power [over policy] through their control of the [KMT's] economic lifeline": Gold, *State and Society*, 68. They also probably wrote many of the Taiwanese policies on which US aid was contingent: Bruce Cumings, "The origins and development of the northeast Asian political economy: industrial sectors, product cycles and political consequences," *International Organization*, 38 (1984), 1–40, 25.

these terms in the first place. Rather, they tended to talk about it in terms of negotiation and consensus-building.[31]

Again, this attitude toward law was not limited to government administrators. When the community activist group with which I worked heard that the electric company was to break its pledge not to enlarge a local electric station without residents' agreement, my questions again revealed my own assumptions. What was the legal status of that pledge? Had anybody signed anything? The people I studied waved aside these irrelevant questions. They were busy planning to meet the electric company on the field of public values, looking for ways to emotionally connect to government administrators, demonstrate their own sincerity, and convince others of the righteousness of their cause. They did not doubt the strength of the state, but they did not speak of the state's role in terms of laws.[32]

The irrelevance of law to state-society relations emerged even on those unusual occasions when laws were invoked for political projects. The activists I studied, for instance, originally came together to protest a proposed land sale that would create a large retirement home in the already crowded neighborhood. Residents agitated for the land to be converted into a park instead. They soon discovered that Taipei's zoning law required a minimum amount of green space per capita in residential areas – a requirement that had quite obviously not been fulfilled in this crowded neighborhood. Years later, participants still chuckled over this coincidence. Administrators also commented on the creativity of invoking the law. But neither group treated it as decisive or dispositive. Activists never presented the legal stricture as a conclusive basis for a demand – a right the law conferred on them by virtue of taking them as its object. Rather, they used their adherence to other local values to demonstrate that they deserved to benefit from the application of the law.[33]

For instance, activists emphasized their earnest investment in their community, their emotional relationship with its history, and their contributions to the nation. This way of using the law to support a larger claim to desert made sense to the government administrators who were the group's primary targets. Mr. An, who would be pivotal to the group's success, shrugged: "They used the wrong law. I could have given them a better law, if they'd asked me." This was a minor objection, though. Choosing the wrong law did not affect either

---

[31] See Bernstein, *The Social life of Regulation*, Martin, *Legitimate Force*.

[32] For a fuller discussion of this process, see Anya Bernstein, "Parameters of legitimation and the environmental future of a Taipei neighborhood," in Sylvia Washington et al. (eds.), *Echoes from the Poisoned Well: Global Memories of Environmental Injustice* (Routledge, 2006), pp. 311–31.

[33] See ibid.

the legitimacy or the efficacy of the group's approach, precisely because the
law itself was not very important. Rather, it was by showing their comportment
with broader social values – community cohesion, historical attachment, and
national contribution – that they justified themselves and got the job done.[34]
What those residents were really good at, Mr. An explained with evident
approval, was moving (*gandong*) others by showing how united (*tuanjie*)
they were.

This moving unity came into play when activists wanted to go beyond the law
as well. The proposed park land held two structures built during the Japanese
colonization of Taiwan (1895–1945), when the area had grown sugar cane.[35] The
activist group wanted these buildings preserved as a tribute to the area's history
and its contribution to Taiwan's culture and economic development. Taiwan's
historical preservation law, however, did not protect structures built under
Japanese rule. As the KMT violently consolidated control over Taiwan in the
late 1940s, it discouraged even discussing – much less valorizing or preserving –
relics of the Japanese colonial era.[36] This situation reversed itself with
democratization, when Japanese colonialism became a hot topic for scholarship
and a common object of nostalgia.[37] The changing status of colonialism in
public discourse has led to movements to preserve Japanese-era structures on
grounds other than simple age, such as historical importance, architectural
quality, and local significance. The activist group I studied successfully mobilized such arguments, convincing city administrators to extend historical status to
the buildings despite the absence of a legal requirement to do so.

The invocation of law was, thus, at best icing on a cake of otherwise
appropriate social belonging. At worst, it could signal breakdown: a failure
of social engagement; of social norms; of other, more legitimate, values. For
instance, some violations of zoning ordinances in Taipei are so widespread as
to be considered standard. Owners of top-story apartments routinely build
extra living space on the roof even though zoning laws strictly prohibit it.

[34] See ibid.

[35] On the role of sugar in Taiwan's history, see Jack Williams, "Sugar: the sweetener in Taiwan's
development" in Ronald G. Knapp (ed.), *China's Island Frontier: Studies in the Historical
Geography of Taiwan* (University Press of Hawaii, 1980), pp. 219–51.

[36] Phillips, *Between Assimilation and Independence*. Tensions between the local population and
the incoming mainlanders flared with the "2-2-8 Incident (*Ererba shijian*)" of February 28,
1947, an island-wide protest or riot (depending on where one stands) that involved KMT troops
killing thousands of Taiwanese, and particularly targeting elites educated in Japanese schools.
Although the total number killed is not known, there is a "rough consensus among scholars [of]
10,000 killed and 30,000 wounded": ibid, 83.

[37] Scholars at the recently founded Institute of Taiwan History in Academia Sinica, Taiwan's
leading research institution, for instance, focus largely on the Japanese era.

(Condominium-style housing is the norm throughout urban Taiwan.) Unlicensed street stalls offering goods and services line many streets, generally acknowledged as having a claim on the space without any legal right to it. One of my informants, who ran a car wash by setting up her supplies and waiting for customers to pull into a parking space on an alley corner, once shook her head over a young man who had actually parked his car in the space: "Doesn't he know I'm running a business? Some people are really strange."[38] Occasionally, a person would object to such informal use of space with a complaint on the city government's internet complaint board. When that happened, administrators would inform the objects of complaint that someone was unhappy, so that they could figure out who the complainants might be and negotiate with them privately. What an anonymous complaint about a legal violation signaled to government administrators, in other words, was a breakdown in social relationships. A further complaint, however, pushed administrators to address the offending structure, lest the department itself became an object of complaint.[39]

The proper role for government was thus not to neutrally enforce the law, but to act as a neutral broker for private parties' social relationships. If that did not resolve the situation, administrators would find themselves unpleasantly entangled with a botched social relationship. They would then have little choice but to take recourse to law.[40] If law occupied the periphery of people's understandings of government, then, it was not so much because government was hopelessly corrupt, unresponsive, or disorganized.[41] It was because, most people agreed, legality was not the proper focal point for government concern in the first place.

WHY MARGINALIZE LAW?

I want to return to the questions I attributed to David Engel at the beginning of this chapter. First, was administrators' distaste for law not best explained by

---

[38] "*Ta buzhidao wo zaizuo shengyi ma? Youderen zhen qiguai.*" The young man, it turned out, had just returned from a year studying in England.

[39] Bernstein, *The Social Life of Regulation*, 948.

[40] Jeffrey Martin similarly explains how Taiwanese police routinely act as social peace brokers and push recalcitrants toward interpersonal negotiation even as they nominally enforce the law. Jeffrey T. Martin, "A reasonable balance of law and sentiment: social order in democratic Taiwan from the policeman's point of view," *Law & Society Review*, 41 (2007), 665–97.

[41] Taipei had its share of corruption, unresponsiveness, and disorganization, but these were not generally described in terms of legality. Rather, they too were discussed in terms of the social norms that were used to characterize other aspects of political life.

the potential restraints it imposed on their power? And second, wasn't a widespread societal distaste for law an instantiation of the same distaste we have found all over the world? The devaluation of legality in Taiwan is certainly reminiscent of the devaluation of litigation in Sander County and in northern Thailand that Engel himself has described.[42] Yet seen within its sociohistorical context, it highlights important differences as well. These differences, in turn, illuminate the way that understanding the roles of law in society depends on historically informed, culturally embedded, and locally specific research (the sort that Engel himself does).

The irrelevance of law to democratic governance in Taipei, for example, was probably exacerbated by the unpleasant associations law has in philosophy and political theory. Throughout most of Chinese philosophy, law has been presented as "punitive, coercive, and morally debased in comparison with the uplifting spiritual influence of ritual practices and human relationships."[43] No etymological link connects legality with legitimacy in the style of Indo-European languages. On the contrary, the only philosophical school to champion law as a source of governance, the Legalists, advocated for a strict, punishing government that kept people in line through "generous rewards and severe punishments" – an explicit challenge to the Confucian emphasis on modeled ethical conduct that did not garner the Legalists a good reputation.[44] In contemporary times, meanwhile, laws are often seen as foreign transplants best used for performing modernity before foreign audiences rather than for either ordering or expressing the social norms of Taiwan itself.[45]

However, this attitude toward law did not necessarily place private parties at the mercy of government agents' whims, or subject them to dependence on government agents' largesse, as one might expect if the city were run by a political machine that enforced fealty through the distribution of opportunities. On the contrary, one reason why administrators emphasized the importance of consensus may have had to do with how they were themselves constantly involved in ongoing negotiations with various sectors of the public. The apparent impossibility of simply enforcing a law did not hold just for

---

[42] See Engel, *The Oven Bird's Song*, Engel, *Globalization*.

[43] Jane Kaufman Winn, "Relational practices and the marginalization of law: informal financial practices of small businesses in Taiwan," *Law & Society Review*, 28 (1994), 193–232, 200.

[44] Wing-tsit Chan (ed. and trans.), *A Sourcebook on Chinese Philosophy* (Princeton University Press, 1963), p. 251.

[45] Winn writes that her interviewees "routinely presumed that the invocation of law involved suppression and punishment and often dismissed the idea that law could empower participants in realizing their objectives": Winn, *Relational Practices*, p. 201. See also Bernstein, *The Social Life of Regulation*.

community activists whose demands found support in a zoning ordinance. Government administrators, too, often operated by trying to convince the people under their purview that accommodating a law or policy was a good thing for them to do.[46] If law is somewhat meaningless in a number of places, then, the meaning of that meaninglessness can still be different.

The process of convincing that administrators discussed, moreover, was typically not bilateral but multinodal. It did not starkly oppose a unified body of administrators to a unified contingent of the public, but often involved multiple sets of each. A typical meeting about the neighborhood park discussed in the previous section, for instance, involved representatives from the community activist group; the electric company; the newspaper headquartered in the neighborhood, which had pledged some funding; the Taiwan Sugar Corporation, the formerly party state-owned enterprise whose status had become ambiguous with the disaggregation of party and state, and which owned the land at issue; the borough head, a neighborhood-level elected office independent of the city government bureaucracy; and several city government departments, each with its own policy orientations, personnel, and interest in the land. These groups were aligned and divergent in ways that were neither all-or-nothing nor completely predictable. Each was also deeply integrated into multiple social spheres and institutions. And each had different amounts of, and different kinds of, power.[47]

This multiplicity of personnel, positions, and powers meant that the inevitably long-term process of building consensus required flexibility and compromise on the part of all participants – both the subjects and the objects of government action. I do not mean to suggest that nobody lost out in the negotiations that characterized so much of the department's work. But there were a number of routes that could lead to political efficacy, and no one position that trumped all others. That meant that who would lose in any given instance was not necessarily predictable on the basis of easily discernable characteristics such as employment by government or control over economic resources. Government bureaucrats, in other words, were not in a strong position to simply impose whims or offer largesse; they too were negotiating parties, along with everyone else. If law was absent as an organizing force in political action in Taipei, then, it was not because some other single organizing force – such as party machinery – had muscled it out and stood in its stead. Rather, a plurality of organizing forces provided different people with different potential ways of getting things done.

---

[46] Bernstein, *The Social Life of Regulation.*   [47] Ibid.

Moreover, disinterest in the law was a widely shared attitude. It was common to government employees, activists who made demands of the government, and wide swaths of the public at large. To be sure, the law cast a shadow in which people negotiated. But it cast that shadow from the periphery of the social. Where recourse to the law was efficacious, it usually indicated a breakdown in social functioning and a breach of social norms. So when bureaucrats avoided, ignored, or maligned the law, they did not violate local values; they enacted them.

Finally, and crucially: Among the people I met, rejecting legal process did not imply that people should accept injustices or refrain from making demands of others. On the contrary. The activists with whom I worked knew that a favorable zoning ordinance would not suffice to mandate the creation of a park; they successfully pressed for the park using more acceptable strategies. They knew that historical preservation law did not extend to the neighborhood's Japanese-era buildings; they successfully demanded preservation through other means. Administrators similarly did not connect the weakness of law to a diminution of demands from the public. While administrators did not always enjoy negotiating with activists who made demands or landowners who resisted government policy, neither did they suggest that such actions were illegitimate.[48]

Forgoing recourse to the law, then, did not mean "lumping." Nor did people think it should. Engel found that his Thai participants cited religious convictions, grounded in Thai Buddhism, as a reason to refrain from making demands on others.[49] Buddhism is an important part of social life in Taiwan,[50] but the people with whom I spoke never invoked religion to suggest that someone should not be recompensed for an injury or should refrain from making a demand. In Sander County, Engel found that "insiders" cited social norms of righteous self-sufficiency to censure those who used law to seek redress for their injuries.[51] Self-sufficiency was not a strong value among the people I knew in Taiwan, who were much more likely to figure a righteous

---

[48] Moreover, when law did force the government's hand, it was likely to be at the urging of one private party who considered himself injured by another, as with the internet complaint system for zoning violations.

[49] Engel, *supra* note 2. David M. Engel, "Globalization and the decline of legal consciousness: torts, ghosts, and karma in Thailand," *Law & Social Inquiry*, 30 (2005), 469–514.

[50] Robert P. Weller, *Alternate Civilities: Democracy and Culture in China and Taiwan* (Westview Press, 1999). Taiwan is home to a syncretic mix of religious traditions, but Buddhism is sufficiently well integrated into everyday life that just about every neighborhood has at least one restaurant catering to Buddhist-style vegetarians, who refrain from eating animal flesh as well as garlic and ginger.

[51] Engel, *supra* note 2. *Oven Bird's Song.*

person as deeply embedded in ongoing relations of mutual aid and mutual obligation. Although social norms played a key part in people's distaste for law, they did not militate complacency. In fact, they often facilitated the opposite, as activists' deep connections to community, locality, and nation served to justify their demands.

Like those whom Engel studied in Sander County and Thailand, the people in my study could be both suspicious and dismissive of law. But the flavor of their distaste was different, specific to the interacting strands of their historical background, their social values, and their political experiences. Just as importantly, the effects of that distaste differed too. Engel's Sander County residents disapproved of those who made demands of others – demands that would have been legitimate within the legal system but were not legitimated by local values. In my research sites, in contrast, local social values provided more useful avenues for making demands of others than did law.

What does this suggest for the study of law in society? A range of scholarship has amply demonstrated that people everywhere have a complicated, often unhappy, relation to law. But it also suggests that, as a sociolegal Tolstoy might tell us, each unhappy relation to law is unhappy in its own way. It emerges from particular histories of social, political, and normative organization. And it fits into particular constellations of practice – that is, ways of getting things done.

Part of evaluating legal consciousness in any particular place involves evaluating broader social values and norms. But it also involves considering the other ways people have of doing things they might sometimes do through law, such as resolving disputes, pressing demands, and legitimating political claims. In a way, this recognition diminishes the centrality of law to a socio-legal study. Law turns out to be just one of numerous methods available for getting things done: one song weaving in and out of other songs, sung by other birds.

15

Imagined Community and Litigation Behavior

The Meaning of Automobile Compensation Lawsuits in Japan

YOSHITAKA WADA

David Engel's "The Oven Bird's Song"[1] clarifies the relationship between transformations in societal relationships and litigiousness through intensive participant observation and deep discussions. With local communities as subjects, the study uses analytical methodology to address the transformation of societal relationships, legal consciousness of people, and conflict behavior in a way that could be applied to any society or culture. In that sense, it is rightly regarded as a monumental work in research on law and society.

In particular, the implications of the article go beyond explanations of the relationship between social transformation and litigiousness; rather, the work focuses on the problem of consciousness of social relationships and use of litigation amid social transformations. Needless to say, when attempting to analyze the relationship between social transformation and litigiousness in a society, one must consider multi-dimensional elements such as economic factors inherent in a society and systems of law and litigation. It may be possible to conduct a macro-analysis that focuses on these elements. However, an even deeper implication of Engel's research is its understanding of the perceptions of these factors.

Of course, the analysis used by Engel in Sander County will have different results if used in, say, Manhattan or in a community with a different culture, such as in Asia. However, by focusing on the dimensions of the perceptions and narratives, Engel provides detailed differences and universal elements, which cannot be seen through an analysis of the relationship of demographic macro-factors and the results of such an analysis.

This point has the following dual meaning. First, basic concepts such as "community," "neighbor," "litigation," and "compensation" have slightly

---

[1] David Engel, "The oven bird's song: insiders, outsiders, and personal injuries in an American community," *Law & Society Review*, 18(4) (1984), 551–82.

different meanings in different communities. Superficial analyses that ignore these differences (e.g. in correlations in population mobility rates or the use of litigation) are prone to major errors by making assumptions such as simple comparability. At times, these analyses may even attempt to make comparisons despite existing differences. Second, even within communities, people's perceptions and narratives essentially capture these slight differences in meaning. Research on legal and litigation behavior in differing cultures cannot make comparisons without introducing the dimensions of perception and narrative, as Engel has shown.

At times, demographic analyses do not sufficiently cover these differences, running the risk of presenting mistaken superficial comparisons as if they were objective findings. Only a focus on the perceptions and narratives is useful for confirming various intrinsic differences and gaining exact knowledge. This shows the effectiveness of Engel's methodology and its ability to be applied to the analyses of differing cultures and communities.

Based on the implications of Engel's article, I analyze how perceptions of societal relationships, laws, and litigation and litigation-use behaviors function in Japan, which has different backgrounds as to the use of litigation and legal consciousness, by using traffic accident disputes as subjects.

This chapter begins with a logical re-summarization of Engel's methodology and findings. Second, I give an overview of Japanese society as well as Japanese law and the litigation system. I then consider discussions and analyses of litigiousness in Japan to date and present an overview of traffic accident litigation in Japanese society. After this, I clarify the meaning of the use of litigation in Japan, as shown by the perceptions and narratives of those involved in specific cases.

MEANING OF IMAGINED COMMUNITY AND LITIGATION: A SUMMARY OF ANALYTICAL CONCEPTS

A Multi-Dimensional Imagined Community Structure

In his analysis of Sander County, Engel showed that, when confronted with the circumstances of transformations in societal relationships, the perceived image of community and its normative implications differed among people depending on whether they were long-time residents, as well as on their occupations. In other words, even with similar transformations, individual responses and behaviors may present themselves differently through the interactions of complex elements. Thus, we should first ask with what meanings community changes are perceived by individuals, rather than how community changes define individual behaviors. Put simply, a "perceived community" is more significant than an "actual community."

I borrow the term "perceived community" from Benedict Anderson's concept of the "imagined community."[2] Anderson understood the formation process of a nation-state and nationalism as a process whereby the concept of a nation's people is formed even as traditional communities decline. He argued that the following factors have conditioned the formation of this concept: Advancements of capitalist economies; the broad sharing of knowledge through the development of printing; the subsequent creation of homogeneous, empty time; and human interactions via administrative organizations. For example, developments in printing technology that led to newspapers with a massive reach promote the idea of the "nation-state" as a high-dimensional community to which one may belong and which extends beyond the close community with which one is familiar. This occurs by having people share events that occurred in areas they have never seen or visited, at the same time and through the same language. Also, through the transfer of central government officials from central to rural areas, governments successfully have people identify themselves as "citizens," as members of the nation-state. It is these nation-states that are the real "imagined communities," as they extend beyond daily relationships. Almost all members of such a community have a perception of themselves as part of that community, regardless of whether all the members have met.

Anderson was interested in identifying various mechanisms through which nationalism is formed. However, a political analysis is beyond the scope of this chapter; the generally applicable concept of the imagined community is sufficient for our purposes. In communities such as Sander County, where economic development is occurring alongside the transformation of social relationships, many long-time residents experience changes and attempt to make their behavior conform to that of past community members. At the same time, new residents find themselves in conflict between conceptions of the communities to which they formerly belonged and the community configured as "Sander County" by their own perceptions, neither of which is a reflection of how the actual Sander County should be. The dynamism seen here exists as a conflict within an imagined community in one's mind, even as one is being stimulated by actual change. As Anderson himself said, "all communities larger than primordial villages" are only imaginary.[3]

---

[2] Benedict Anderson, *Imagined Communities: Reflections on the Origin and Spread of Nationalism* (Verso, 1991).

[3] Ibid, 6.

There are two critical points to this summary of the multi-dimensional imagined community structure. First, regarding the concept of the imagined community, keep in mind that a community to which one perceives a belonging is not a simple thing, but can be a complex, multi-dimensional perception. An individual is a resident of Sander County, but is also a citizen of the state of Illinois and the United States of America. At the same time, that person may be a member of a farming cooperative, a veteran's group, or a certain high-school alumni association. These diverse communities may appear to be everyday sorts of communities, but in fact they are imagined communities that subsume unknown members, both past and future, within a temporal continuum. The structure of this complex imagined community is embedded in the perceptions of individuals, which can be called multi-dimensional identities, whose awareness can easily move depending on the time and place.

Second, because the communities are imagined, they can always take on any type of norm. Whether few or many, imagined communities encapsulate behavioral norms as they should be. In fact, without them, standards for individual behavior could not be found. At the same time, these norms do not always co-exist harmoniously between the multi-dimensional imagined communities embedded within individuals; rather, there are constant dynamic conflicts between them, and these normative conflicts and dynamics surrounding the imagined communities cannot be overlooked.

The characteristics described above define behaviors of people in places with multi-dimensional and various mixed norms and are key points to understand. Setting aside routine behaviors, the imagined community, envisaged by people when confronting certain changes and acting in response to the circumstances, and the normative bases included in the imagined community sometimes contradict and cause confusion. It is not difficult to see that obligations as a resident of Sander County, as a citizen of Illinois, or as a parent may be incompatible at times. Within such contradictions, individuals subtly rewrite and adjust the meanings of these imagined communities. Undesirable behavior in an imagined community of a certain dimension may be ideal in an imagined community of a different dimension. No matter which one chooses, an individual dialectically creates a narrative for a new imagined community.[4] The narratives the residents of Sander County gave

---

[4] The construction of meaning and perception is theorized in social constructionism, which constitutes the theoretical basis of narrative therapy, narrative mediation, and so on. Criticizing essentialism and objectivism, it maintains that reality is constructed by each individual in each

Engel were not the result of a simple normative consciousness, but rather of the process of dynamically creating new community consciousness within these contradictions.

The Legal System as Constructed Meaning

When making comparisons that extend beyond cultures, it is obvious that we must focus on differences between system concepts that reflect actual differences of systems. For example, with regard to the concepts of litigation, attorneys, and so forth, if one assumes there are differences in the meaning of cultural perceptions, then superficial factors that at first may appear to be fundamental, such as the number of litigation cases and attorneys, are themselves complex narratives requiring validation for cultural differences. There are vast qualitative differences between what people in the United States perceive from the word "attorney" and what people in Japan take from it. The United States has more than one million attorneys, while Japan has approximately 30,000 after a doubling in their number in recent years. Beyond the simple numerical differences, it is quite reasonable to conclude that there are also differences in perceptions. In addition, the apparent dissimilarities in the meanings of the use of litigation in the United States and Japan make it more difficult to use and compare the concepts in each country.

The perceived meaning transforms dynamically depending on the situations in which individuals find themselves. In Japan, most individuals have no dealings with attorneys over the course of their lifetime; there is a general concept of an "imagined attorney," although individuals who have actually dealt with an attorney find it necessary to replace this conception in the course of their dealings. Litigation is much the same. Thus, when pursuing the topic of the relationship between societal transformations and the use of litigation, the validation of dynamism and the multi-dimensional meaning of key concepts in an analysis is critical.

That said, it is possible to analyze the precise significance of actions in various communities, going beyond the analysis of demographic factors, by using the analytical concept of an imagined community that individuals superficially construct within themselves and that encapsulates norms.

context applying narratives as perceptual frameworks. As those narratives can be transformed flexibly in each context, people always rewrite the story to understand the situation. Kenneth Gergen, *An Invitation to Social Construction* (Sage, 2009); John Winslade and Gerald Monk, *Narrative Mediation: New Approach to Conflict Resolution* (Jossey Bass, 2000).

In addition, by incorporating the validation of timing of the meaning of fundamental concepts of law, litigation, and attorneys, we can conduct an even more precise analysis. Prior to analyzing the significance of litigiousness between conflicting parties in Japanese traffic accidents by using these concepts and approaches, I provide an overview of the characteristics of the community in Japan as they are discussed, rather than as they are.

SOCIAL ORDERING MECHANISMS AND LITIGIOUSNESS IN JAPAN

The Structure of Japanese Societal Order

Prior to the introduction of American-style law schools in 2004, Japanese legal education was provided at the undergraduate level. Law departments were established in more than ninety universities across the country, and each year these schools generated more than 30,000 graduates. Of these, only about 500 per year passed the bar exam and became attorneys, judges, or legal practitioners, and even since the introduction of law schools, this number remains at about 2,000 per year (see Figure 15.1).

As to the path taken by many of these graduates, particularly those from Tokyo University, Kyoto University, and other top schools, civil service is one likely option. In terms of difficulty, the civil servant exam is similar to the bar exam. Many graduates end up working in an industry. In other words, bright

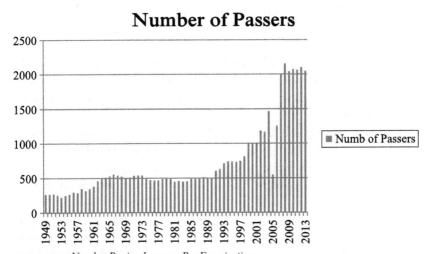

FIGURE 15.1 Number Passing Japanese Bar Examination

individuals with legal knowledge in Japan overwhelmingly take positions in the government or an industry, rather than in the legal profession.[5]

It is emblematic that the distribution of power responsible for order in Japanese society is typically managed by government and industry rather than the legal profession. In particular, each governmental agency imposes various restrictions on related industries and thereby controls their behavior. Agencies have continued to exert their informal and delicate power over various actions by the industry through licensing systems and a subsidy system, even though their power has been somewhat weakened in recent years. For example, in the airline industry, Japan Airlines and All Nippon Airways have had a monopoly up until relatively recently, gaining approval for fares with no competition. Both have been able to maintain high fares compared with those of other countries. These regulations were justified by the argument that they "protect citizens from risk that may be a threat to safety due to competition." Also, agencies have exerted their informal power over the construction industry through actual allocation of public projects in rotation. This sort of control by governmental agencies has taken the form of power disseminated throughout every type of industry.

For their part, industries actually welcome this. They are not exposed to the principles of the law of the jungle, and their activities are not impeded by excessive litigation. Existing corporate actors enjoy a peaceful coexistence, which has had a positive effect on their continuing existence. This same structure has defined the juncture between governmental agencies and not only corporations but also farmers and organizations, such as Japan Agricultural Cooperatives. Needless to say, it has been difficult for foreign or new corporations to enter such a community of industry, though the barrier experienced was formed from the inside by a community to enable mutual prosperity.

Moreover, each individual gets a stable income as they affiliate with these corporations and organizations. Though they may have small points of dissatisfaction, the system itself largely has not been a problem. Harmonious coordination between labor unions and management serves the same purpose. Apart from nominal events, Japan has had no strikes. Even within corporations, competition based on ability has been suppressed, with a seniority system and lifetime employment being the norm. Employees and their families have been

---

[5] The foundation of this system was built in the process of Meiji Restoration, succeeding the traditional idea that judicial system is just a branch of public administration from the Edo period. Benedict Anderson described nationalism led by government as official nationalism and took Japan as an example: Anderson, *Imagined Communities*, ch. 6, pp. 83–112.

the beneficiaries of welfare benefits provided by the corporations and other organizations, which gave rise to a strong sense of community.

In this manner, social order in Japan was created by communities, with companies that involve governmental agencies at the core and industry organizations as a medium. Moreover, individual companies existed as a community made up of lifetime employees. In other words, this is the idea of a broadly shared imagined community of a homogenous Japan, composed of a concentric community comprising industry, corporations, and families. Normative control and the creation of order were informally handled through community norms. From the perspective of foreign companies attempting to enter the Japanese market, it may have appeared to be an unfair system, but internally it functioned effectively in maintaining social order. Companies and industry alike were spoken of using the analogy of a home.

Another characteristic is that, from the perspective of the actual composition of communities, compared with the United States, Japan is a homogeneous environment. Other than certain mountainous regions, there are no stereotypical villages, such as those in Sander County, to be found in Japan. Even though they may not live in gigantic metropolitan areas like Tokyo or Osaka, many Japanese are tied to metropolitan areas of a certain scale by public transportation, such as railways, or live in neighboring areas. Of course, there may be cultural differences between regions, but companies typically do business throughout Japan, and lifestyles are very similar nationwide. At the same time, the neighborhood community associations that formerly were found in each community function as a formality and many communities have done away with them. Thus, regional communities similar to those perceived and lived in by residents of Sander County are on the decline, and people likely feel a strong sense of belonging to an imagined community of Japan with a high level of abstract homogeneity.

In other words, functioning groups, such as corporations or associations in Japan, have formed a sense of belonging among individuals in the form of mutual imagined communities of corporations composed of actual perceived communities, yet made up of cohesive relationships between individuals in a workplace. However, a neighboring primary group may generally decline and see its function as a community waste away. In turn, the term "homogeneous Japan," though shared in the abstract by all Japanese, may create an imagined community and function to create the basis for identity.

Figure 15.2, which is based on the Annual Statistics Report of the judicial system, shows the shift in the number of civil litigation cases nationwide in Japan, presenting the total of those handled by summary courts, for cases up to

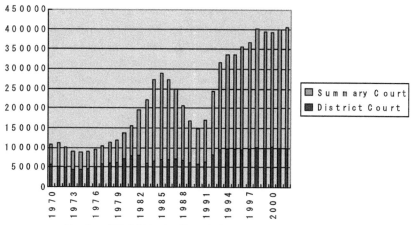

FIGURE 15.2 Number of Civil Litigation Cases in Japan

1.4 million yen, and the larger cases handled by district courts. There was a peak in cases in the late 1980s. Recently, cases have begun increasing again; however, this trend mostly indicates changes in the way cases are handled by the summary courts. In actuality, most summary court cases deal with credit loan firms and money lenders seeking repayment of relatively small debts. Only a handful of cases are brought by ordinary citizens. The extremely low appointment rate of attorneys in Japan's summary courts indicates this state of affairs.[6] The bursting of Japan's bubble economy in the late 1980s worsened the economy and caused a sudden recession, which had a major impact, with an increase and then a subsequent decrease in the number of cases. In contrast, district court cases increased only slightly, with no major fluctuations, and stayed constant at approximately 100,000 cases per year. This figure is a total of all cases and includes various corporate litigation suits. Note that there are typically fewer than 1,000 suits seeking damages because of medical accidents per year nationwide.[7]

These data show that for perhaps most Japanese, litigation is seen as existing in a different, unrelated world. Rather, in Japan, the word "court" typically evokes images of criminal cases.

For many average citizens, there is not necessarily a clear distinction between civil and criminal cases, and the first thing that comes to mind at the mention of a court is criminal proceedings. The law is perceived as a tool for vertical control of power rather than as something to manage the

---

[6]   Based on data in Japanese Federation of Bar Associations, *White Book on Lawyers* 2010.
[7]   Based on judicial statistics from the Supreme Court, www.courts.go.jp/app/sihotokei_jp/search.

horizontal rights and responsibilities shared among individuals.[8] This is because of the aforementioned mechanism creating order in Japanese society. The Japanese perceive that an upstanding individual would not have cause to become a defendant even in a civil case. Of course, this perception is changing, and there is no longer the same criticism of litigation that there was in the past. However, the view that litigation is an undesirable means to be avoided if possible is unchanged.

In such a situation, the act of litigating at any cost is extraordinarily exceptional. In concentric communities formed around governmental agencies, the judicial system and attorneys exist outside of it. In other words, normal dissatisfaction and problems go beyond complaints to the government or coordination among corporations and within regions, and can be effective for resolving problems informally. In cases where such informal methods do not work and litigation is used, there must be a compelling external factor to put things in motion. First, this occurs when the monetary value of an issue in conflict is very large. However, outside of cases where the importance of monetary value is simply and rationally demanded, monetary value is a mere formality and there are sometimes different, deeper motivations. Later in this chapter we will use traffic accident litigation to examine this point.

Second, there are cases related to issues which involve strong social justice demands that go beyond the individual. For example, this can include the following cases: instances of pollution or other environmental problems that impact many victims; the assertion of the position of different types of weak members in society, as a right; or where protestation against the powerful is an issue. In any case, litigation as a means of resolving problems corrects difficult injustices within concentric communities, and it has been perceived as a useful way to acknowledge authority. On the other hand, it has also been perceived as only an exceptional and extraordinary means of resolving conflicts.

The Image and Identity of Attorneys

This point is related to how people perceive the role of attorneys and how attorneys themselves construct their identities. In actuality, Japan has a very

---

[8]   The first legal system implanted into Japan was the Chinese Tang dynasty's "Ritsu" and "Ryo," or Criminal Code and Administrative Organization Code. There was no civil code or word "right" as a legal term. This suggests that law was traditionally a tool for domination by government in Asian culture.

positive image of attorneys. Information on how people view attorneys is mostly provided by newspapers and television. For most people who do not have opportunities for first-hand interaction with attorneys, their view comes from newspapers that show attorneys fighting against power for social issues and the weak. The reality is that attorneys manage their own offices and take on many general civil cases worth significant amounts of money, but this information is not conveyed to the average person. As a result, attorneys are seen as crusaders for social justice and people place their trust in them. This means that litigation is perceived as being a forum in which moral issues that are greater than mere legal conflicts triumph. Litigation is where rights are upheld via victory in moral issues, rather than being a process for resolving issues according to legal rights and obligations.

In contrast, the situation in the United States, with its extraordinary amount of attorneys, is very different. According to the Survey on US Views on Honesty and Ethical Standards in Professions conducted by Gallup in 2014, only 21 percent of people viewed attorneys as having high ethical standards, compared to an average of 45 percent overall, whereas 34 percent responded that attorneys have low ethical standards. A greater percentage of people feel that even corporate executives and bankers have higher ethical standards. This does not necessarily indicate actual differences between attorneys in the United States and Japan (though there may be many differences), but rather the high level of interaction and contact between ordinary individuals and attorneys in the United States, and the fact that US media does not portray attorneys as heroes of social justice. The respect given to attorneys in Japan is perhaps the result of ethical stances more than legal knowledge.

This is also related to the substantive differences between the identities of attorneys themselves and their social roles. Most attorneys in Japan have their own offices and act as individual practitioners. Many of these offices are located near courts and are not visible to the average citizen. Most of the typical work done by attorneys involves general civil cases, which may include contract disputes regarding compensation for damages as well as criminal and labor cases. So there are practically no areas of specialization for them. In addition, most work done by attorneys is litigation, and in Japan, the job of an attorney is synonymous with that of a litigator. Cases of less than one million yen do not cover the amount of labor required, and thus are not profitable. Therefore, attorneys are reluctant to work on them. Representation in summary courts has been permitted in recent years, but prior to that such cases were handled by judicial scriveners, a quasi-legal profession that only creates litigation-related documentation and has no ability to represent clients in court. The low appointment rate for attorneys in Japanese courts, including the summary court, was one direct factor in this. In an environment that limits compensation to a set amount, Japanese attorneys have gone so far as to share highly profitable litigation cases. Civil cases for small amounts were not even on attorneys' agendas.

Of course, this does not mean that attorneys in Japan only take cases that generate the highest profit in the seller's market. The Japanese Bar Association does take on a great deal of pro bono work, assigning member attorneys to represent criminal defendants with no ability to pay, dispatching them as legal advisors to remote areas where there are none, and providing counsel. Attorneys have created an identity for themselves as anti-power legal professionals, which ties into their activities as crusaders for social justice. In this way, generally, the profession of attorney in Japan is seen as one with high ethics.

Therefore, in Japan, attorneys are equivalent to litigators, and they have created an identity for themselves with overlapping characteristics of "individuals with integrity" and "crusaders for social and legal justice."

Hypotheses Explaining the Lack of Litigation

Why is there such a small amount of litigation and so few attorneys in Japan? First, let us consider the explanation of legal consciousness provided by Takeyoshi Kawashima, who was not only a scholar in the legal world of postwar Japan but also a researcher fervent in his criticism of modern Japanese society prior to the war and the modernization of Japan. Kawashima pointed to the modern West, where individual relationships are thought of in the context of legal rights and responsibilities. Kawashima had the conviction that the consciousness of the Japanese was lagging. In other words, the Japanese did not take care of mutual relationships and disputes among themselves through legal rights and litigation, but instead through vague, pre-modern standards such as the concepts of *giri* (obligation) and humanity. Having said that, Kawashima believed that, based on a growing awareness of the law and rights among Japanese, there would be increased consciousness of laws governing relationships and the resolution of disputes using litigation and the law, just as with modern-day Western society.[9] This notion assumes a comparison between two dimensions: "the concept of the modern West" and

---

9   Takeyoshi Kawashima, "Dispute Resolution in Contemporary Japan," in Arthur von Mehren (ed.), *Law in Japan: The Legal Order in a Changing Society* 1963 Harvard University Press; See also Setsuo Miyazawa, "Taking Kawashima seriously: a review of Japanese research on Japanese legal consciousness and disputing behavior," *Law & Society Review*, 21(2) (1987), 219–42.

"the current state of Japan." For example, can actual US society be one in which consciousness is regulated by norms governing relationships, despite the high level of litigation seen? In any case, Kawashima attempted to explain the small amount of litigation and the reduced presence of the judicial system as a lag in legal consciousness.

Second is the interpretation offered by Professor John Haley in his article "Myth of a Reluctant Litigant."[10] Haley asserted that there are citizens who do not like litigation, and, assuming flaws in cultural explanation, such institutional factors, including the dissemination of legal knowledge, legal access, and the ability to provide appropriate aid, serve to regulate the amount of litigation. Haley argued that the Japanese government has overall enacted policies that somewhat avoid access to litigation, though this is but a minor factor for litigation in Japan. Government, industry, and attorneys not subject to competition do not object to these points, and an institutional foundation to promote the mobilization of litigation has not been developed. An explanation similar to this one was actually raised by a Japanese researcher as a criticism of Kawashima's view.[11] One cannot fundamentally assent to Haley's view, but that leads us back to where we began, with the question: Why have these policies been used in Japan?

Third, the somewhat heterogeneous explanation put forward by Harvard professor Mark Ramseyer is the theory of predictable regulation.[12] Ramseyer states that, from the perspective of law and economics, rational decisions as to whether to mobilize or compromise on litigation depend on the predictability of the outcome of the litigation in question. Predictability in Japan, which lacks a system of juries, is very high because of the tendency of judges to decide cases in a refined and consistent fashion, based on the norms of the community of judges. If so, the rational course of action for those involved in a dispute is to come to agreement in response to the predicted outcome of a case, without ever actually bringing a case to court. This explanation

---

[10] John Haley, "The myth of the reluctant litigant," *Journal of Japanese Studies*, 4(2) (1978), 359–90.

[11] Masao Ooki pointed out that historically Japanese were not reluctant to bring their cases to a court based on historical documents. Masao Ooki, *Legal Conceptions of Japanese: Comparison with Western Legal Conceptions* (Tokyo University Press, 1983). Yoshio Sasaki also tried to explain that institutional barriers make Japanese people refrain from bringing a case to a court, based on questionnaire research. Yoshio Sasaki, *Minji Tyoutei no Kenkyu* (Research on Civil Mediation; in Japanese) (Horitsubunkasha, 1984).

[12] Mark Ramseyer, *Hou to Keizaigaku: Nihonhou no Keizaibunseki* (Law and Economics: Economic Analysis of Japanese Law; in Japanese) (Kobundo, 1990).

likely applies, in particular, to the area of compensation for damages in traffic accident litigation.

The representative examples given above are all, in some sense, correct, and yet they are insufficient. In a macro-level analysis of "litigation in Japan," one may point out the common thread of explanations only explaining things in outline and not reflecting the uniqueness of each area. Below we shall examine how imagined communities behave, based on their perception of the involved parties, using the context of traffic accidents.

RECENT CHANGES IN THE SYSTEM FOR HANDLING TRAFFIC ACCIDENT DISPUTES IN JAPAN

The System for Compensation of Damages in Traffic Accidents

Since the 1950s, economic growth has brought a dramatic increase in the number of automobiles in Japan. The number of accidents ballooned because of an undeveloped traffic control system, which caused many disputes. At first, the lack of set amounts for compensation and of a means for determining negligence caused confusion among judges, with major disparities in rulings. In addition, liability insurance was not common at the time, and even where compensation amounts were set in cases of major accidents resulting in death, defendants could not make payments sometimes, ruining the lives of both parties involved in the case.

In confronting this problem, courts at first made a comparative analysis of rulings in each region and announced standards for determining the compensation for damages in traffic accidents. This standardization has clarified factors used in determining compensation, with set amounts for payment for pain and suffering based on set levels in cases of death or complications resulting from an accident. Similarly, a method for determining lost earnings was created. Japan also recognized the concept of negligence by both parties, with compensation ratios determined by the amount of negligence by both sides. Standards for these ratios are very clear for different types of accidents. These actions have established a rationale for deciding suits for damages, and at the same time have generally made it possible for the involved parties to predict the amount of compensation.

On the other hand, providing relief for accident victims requires payment of compensation, based on the aforementioned standards. The Automobile Liability Security Act was created to ensure that there is no variability in payments because of the resources of wrongdoers, and car owners are obligated by law to have automobile insurance. Cars are inspected every two years in Japan, and those which do not pass the inspection cannot be driven. Insurance premiums are collected at the time of these inspections, which means that as long as a car is not stolen, all cars must have the obligatory liability insurance. However, liability amounts are set with a 30 million yen limit, and thus about 70 percent of cars are insured with optional insurance, the amount of which is unlimited. So, if necessary, owners can pay high amounts of compensation. Thus, even in major accidents, victims can receive aid up to a certain amount.

Another important reform is the addition of private settlement services for personal injury accidents in the optional insurance just mentioned. In the event of an accident, employees of insurance companies will represent the wrongdoer in negotiations for compensation. This enables negotiations between both parties to proceed without either side having to directly face the other. When this service was introduced, there was some criticism from attorneys that it constituted unauthorized practice of law. However, attorneys did not have the capacity to respond to such a broad range of needs, and thus the practice was accepted under the oversight of insurance company attorneys. Even in these cases, no one opined that more attorneys were necessary to respond to this issue. The implementation of the private settlement services led to 95 percent of disputes over car accidents not ending in litigation or alternative dispute resolution (ADR). In addition to this, the Bar Association and others have established ADRs for use in the case that the insurance company and victims do not reach an agreement. Along with court-annexed mediation, the use of ADR for traffic accident compensation is robust.

These reforms have had a clear impact, with litigation over traffic accidents being kept relatively low. Tokyo District Court (which handles cases of 1.4 million yen or more) dealt with a peak 2,185 cases in 1960, and the number gradually decreased to several hundred per year until relatively recently. There was a slight increase in the late 1980s, with cases numbering more than 1,000 once again in 2000 and increasing to 1,485 in 2010.

There were even more dramatic changes in summary courts, which handle cases of less than 1.4 million yen. Cases dealing with compensation for damages in traffic accidents that were brought to summary courts nationally numbered 958 in 1988. This number has continued to increase, hitting 16,954 in 2013, seventeen times higher than that seen in 1988. However, there were 952,709 traffic accidents in 2004 and only 573,842 in 2014. Fatal accidents have also been halved, and currently stand at about 4,000 per year.[13]

---

[13] Cabinet Secretariat, Material No. 2-2, The 15th meeting of Council for Legal Profession Training System Reform, 2015.

Despite that, litigation has dramatically increased in the summary courts and has seen some increase in district courts. What does this mean? Perhaps the perception of litigation has changed for some Japanese.

The following section explains how reforms of Japan's traffic accident dispute resolution system have influenced the perceptions of those involved in accidents and how the reforms have been organized, leading us to our current situation.

Private Settlement Services and Imagined Communities

Private settlement services for liability insurance were used because of the norms of imagined communities in Japan, and those services resulted in changes to decidedly important perceptions. In particular, for accidents with severe damages, such as complications or death, disputes between wrongdoers and victims are perceived as moral conflicts involving great amounts of emotion, even where there are legal negotiations for damages. A direct apology from the wrongdoer is required, and settlement negotiations around compensation place considerable stress on both parties. For the wrongdoer, monetary negotiations themselves may, based on the norms of Japan's homogeneous imagined community, be heavily criticized by society as "trying to solve things with money." Similarly, when victims broach the issue of compensation, they are criticized for "replacing the misfortune of family with money." Thus, the topic of monetary compensation is, for both parties, an issue that demands resolution, but one where negotiations must be handled carefully because of the norms of the imagined community. The private settlement system involves insurance company employees proposing compensatory amounts and handling negotiations as an insurance policy service. This is important as it frees both the wrongdoer and the victim from these moral dilemmas and prevents conflicts with imagined community norms. Since the introduction of private settlement services by insurance companies, the parties involved in an accident often never meet. In small accidents, insurance companies mediate directly after the accident, which means that victims and wrongdoers never come face to face.

In addition, accidents between vehicles where fault is unclear cause emotions to erupt when attempting to determine facts, and often result in personal attacks. Even private settlement services avoid direct contact with the parties involved and minimize direct conflict. For the involved parties, private settlement services are saviors, removing the risk of conflict with the fundamental norms of the homogeneous imagined community – which require a calm approach to events, even where there is an excessive emotional response to a conflict.

As far as can be seen, the system of private settlement services helps parties involved in an accident by removing the risk of running afoul of norms in a homogeneous imagined community, and was created out of real needs. These services change the meaning of disputes over car accidents. Through the use of private settlement services, moral conflicts between individuals that go hand in hand with highly emotional conflicts which are difficult to solve and can easily become intense morph into monetary compensation issues that do not impinge on the norms of the imagined community. Of course, conflicts in which both parties are highly emotional are not resolved through private settlement services, but it is a fact that parties in such cases, for the most part, never meet. From a monetary compensation perspective, a certain amount of work is being done, which, in turn, takes away any motivation to litigate. The ability of private settlement services to change the meaning of a dispute has, in a manner of speaking, the effect of maintaining the entire homogeneous imagined community in the midst of extraordinary risk for the parties involved.

Attorney Fee Insurance and the Increase in Summary Court Cases

However, as we have already seen, traffic accident cases in summary courts have dramatically increased, despite the fact that traffic accidents have almost halved in the past ten years. How is this to be explained? The monetary jurisdiction of summary courts is kept at 1.4 million yen and below, with most cases involving physical accidents with property damage. There are no private settlement services for such property damage cases. So long as there is no dispute over the levels of negligence or other facts, insurance company representatives will propose compensation amounts, and the involved parties typically never meet, thereby avoiding disputes. However, when facts are in dispute and questions of negligence arise, cases can turn into personal attacks, with emotional conflicts coming from a fixation on correctness. In addition, when there is irreparable damage, such as in some personal injury cases, wrongdoers have less room to make strong arguments based on the norms of the imagined community; therefore, they are suppressed in a way that does not occur in property damage accidents. Conflicts may escalate because of the nature of property damage cases, and disputes are reimagined to be about morality and justice, rather than money. Even in these cases, litigating a case over such small amounts does not make monetary sense, and in light of attorneys' costs, rational decisions over money are probably the greatest reason for avoiding litigation.

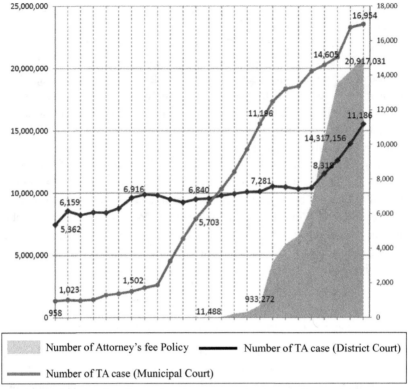

FIGURE 15.3 Number of Traffic Accident Compensation Litigation and Lawyers' Service
Policies from 1988 to 2013

Despite the above, we must still understand the reason for the increase in
traffic accident litigation. Let us look at Figure 15.3.[14]

The line connecting the black dots represents changes in the number of
traffic accident cases in district courts, and that connecting the gray dots
represents the number of cases in summary courts. The gray portion on the
right shows the number of liability insurance policies that cover attorneys' fees.
Foreign insurance companies began offering such riders in 2001, with other
insurance companies following suit. Their numbers increased yearly, reaching
20,917,031 in 2013. Such a rider is now considered *de rigueur* for liability
insurance, which has led to the removal of attorneys' fees as a threshold for
avoiding litigation. As noted above, in moral conflict cases where disputes over
facts turn into attacks on character, parties will turn to litigation, increasing the

[14] Ibid.

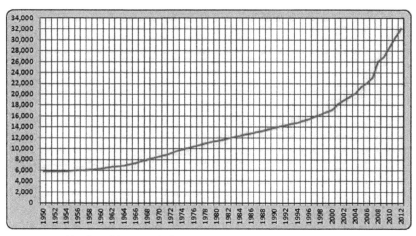

FIGURE 15.4 Number of Attorneys in Japan

number of court cases. Because imagined community norms are being main-
tained through private settlement services at the district court level, though not
at the level of summary courts, the litigation threshold is dropping here as
well. The greater increase in the number of cases at the summary court level
in comparison to the district court level can perhaps be explained by whether
imagined community norms are suppressed in personal injury cases or
whether private settlement services are used.

Moreover, the growing number of attorneys (see Figure 15.4) might also be
related to this. There were about 16,000 attorneys in 1988 and 20,000 in 2004,
when law schools were introduced. By 2012, the number had hit 32,000.[15] One
attorney candidly noted that this increase has brought attempts to earn more
money through litigating cases that previously would have been resolved by
attorney-led negotiations, because of the competitive environment.[16] Regardless, the increase in the number of attorneys and the growing competition
have caused attorneys to be more aggressive about taking on summary court
cases and accepting cases that they previously would not have considered.

The real issue is how this trend has been explained. Newspaper coverage
provided the first opportunity for discussions regarding this issue. Though
some viewed the growing use of litigation as a positive development, it was
more common to criticize attorneys and to imply that it was a problem.
Insurance companies obligated customers to consult with them prior to hiring

---

[15] Based on the Japan Federation of Bar Associations (ed.) *White Book of Lawyers*, 2012.
[16] Nikkei News Paper 23/05, 2015.

an attorney and moved to make no payments to those who did not consult with them. The Japanese Federation of Bar Associations had to create arbitration procedures to deal with disputes between attorneys and insurance companies. All these activities imply a negative evaluation of the increase in the number of attorneys and the expansion of their job field. Increased litigation is not necessarily a welcome phenomenon. There is a hidden pressure that does not welcome increased intrusion by the judiciary. Even attorneys themselves often criticize the increase in their number, as it imposes upon them the burden of competition.

Moral Hopes and the Reconstruction of Norms in an Imagined Community

A certain number of people bring personal injury cases to district courts despite imagined community norms or systemic controls such as private settlement services. As we consider what sorts of perceptions these individuals work under in litigation, the example of one such case is instructive.

In 1999, there was a tragic incident near the Tokyo interchange on the Tomei Expressway. A car carrying a family returning home from a day of fun slowed to go through the expressway's toll gates and was rear-ended by a truck operated by a drunk driver. The car caught fire, and although the wife was able to escape, the husband was severely burned and the couple's one- and three-year old daughters were trapped in the flames. They died screaming "Burning!" and the image brought to mind the parents' unbearable pain as they heard the final words of their children crying out over the intense heat. The truck driver had consumed a bottle of whiskey and a Chuhai alcoholic beverage before the accident and could not even stand up straight. A cameraman from a TV station happened to be driving by and caught the incident on film, which brought an enormous amount of attention because the lives of the small children had been cut short.

The parents sued the driver and his company for damages. Critical to the case was the fact that the parents sought regular payments to be made for fifteen years starting from the date of each child's death until the year that each child would have turned nineteen. In regard to compensation, it is typical for courts to order a single payment with no interest. The parents' demand for split payments was itself unusual, and there was no precedent for payments to be made on the day of death. Also, in the case of deaths of small children in Japan, parents receive any lost earnings.[17] From the parents'

---

[17] In Japanese law, the right to seek damages is inherited by parents when a baby, a child, or a single person is killed negligently. In most European countries, it is not inherited, probably

perspective, having the defendant make payments on the date of death does not allow the defendant or company to forget the incident. Moreover, it was likely felt that payments of a certain amount each year would feel as if the children were bringing home a portion of their earnings, which they would do once they become adults. It was likely felt that these payments would bring comfort to and assuage the parents' pain due to the loss of their children. However, legal professionals who share a common legalistic perspective feel the role of civil courts is to compensate for damages and not to comfort parents or penalize wrongdoers (there is no punitive damage in Japan). The parents' demands in this case were, in a certain sense, a challenge to the conventional wisdom of legal professionals and the legal community. These issues generated significant interest in the decision in this case.

Ultimately, the court handed down a ruling that recognized almost all of the parents' demands. Critical to the case was the fact that the parents sought a part of payments to be made on every anniversary of death for fifteen years, starting from the year that each child would have turned nineteen.

The defendants were ordered to make equal payments for compensation for lost earnings totaling 49,795,756 yen each year for fifteen years. As it happens, the amount of compensation for payment for pain and suffering previously recognized by a court was 34,000,000 yen per child, making this the highest payment awarded at that time. The ruling did not stop there. The judge also had the president of the driver's company testify in court in response to the parents' demand, in addition to the defendant's submittal of an opinion statement. On this point, the family commented as follows:

> Out of consideration for the surviving family, it was our fervent desire to have Shigehisa Nomura, the president of the defendant's company, testify in the public setting of the court, and not merely provide an opinion in the first and second oral statements during the plaintiff questioning. The judge in the end allowed this, despite the distress it caused. Through the president's testimony, new facts came to light regarding the management of the transportation company. Thus, we feel our decision to ensure a thorough civil court case was a good one.[18]

---

because parents do not depend on support from a baby or a child. Lost income is not the loss of parents' income, but of the victim's income. In Japan, historically, family is an important mechanism to perform social security functions for elder parents. Sons and daughters are expected to financially support and take care of elder parents after they become adults, though this is changing. This suggests that for Japanese parents, the death of their baby or child means the loss of future income.

[18] Yasutaka Inoue, *Judgement and Voice of Parents: Civil Law Suit by Yasutaka & Ikumi Inoue*, 2003, www.ask.or.jp/ddd_inoue3.html.

Many victims in personal injury cases note their dissatisfaction with criminal trials in which victims have no direct involvement. At the same time, in civil trials, victims sue the other side out of grief and expect that the other party will be made to testify. Civil cases in Japan are not where legal professionals think about compensation for damages in a legalistic fashion, but rather where expressions of moral conflicts are made. Thus, there is an expectation with regard to responsibility. In this case, by demanding split payments, those expectations were met from the perspective of resolution. The judge in this case commented as follows:

> The two sisters were left unable to move in the back seat of the car, and died from the heat of the flames without losing consciousness, amid screams of pain. Their death was extraordinarily miserable and cruel, and exceeds the scope of a traffic accident ... the plaintiff's recollection of regret and feelings of helplessness at the level of flames, leaving them with nothing to do but watch as their beloved daughters died by fire in front of them, is unimaginable.[19]

In this ruling, one can safely say that the judge is showing concern for the moral conflict of the parents, both procedurally and practically. From a legal perspective, there is considerable criticism about the judgment going beyond the function of civil cases in handing down a penalty to the wrongdoer. When law-school students in Japan were asked to evaluate the ruling, about half were in agreement and half opposed. Outside of law departments, most students were in agreement with the decision. There were actually several rulings around this time for similar payments to be made on the date of death, though these were criticized and subsequently vanished.

In the criminal trial in this case, the defendant received a prison term of four years. At the time, the maximum sentence for professional negligence resulting in death was five years. The parents afterward participated in a movement supporting stricter punishment of traffic accidents, resulting in maximum sentences of fifteen years for dangerous driving resulting in death.

What are the implications of this case? As heretofore discussed, in the case of personal injury, monetary compensation is not often the victim's goal. In an objective sense, personal injury cases are not about money and the acquisition thereof, but rather about expressing a level of grief in monetary form and making a strong statement in a moral conflict, regardless of the amount of compensation being sought. In this case, drunk driving was involved in addition to negligence, which is not morally acceptable. The norms of a homogeneous imagined community were seen in the suppression of excessive

---

[19] *Inoue v. Kochi Transport Co., Ltd*, Tokyo District Court Judgment July 24, 2003, WA 22987, www.courts.go.jp/app/files/hanrei_jp/641/005641_hanrei.pdf.

antagonism. However, where there is drunk and reckless driving (as in this case), a lack of remorse after an accident, or the presence of malice, circumstances may be different. In those cases, norms shared within an imagined community reinforce moral assertions and powerful expressions of grief and will allow monetary demands as a means of expressing these emotions. The parents' demand that payments be made on the date of death is, from the perspective of legal professionals, difficult to acknowledge in civil litigation cases, though from the perspective of citizens in a shared imagined community it is effective in changing normative perceptions that promote the suppression of litigation to perceptions that accept and support litigation based on shared grief. The narrative of grieving parents who witnessed the deaths of their daughters in flames reverses the meaning of the burden of litigiousness, and works as a means of engendering empathy and acceptance in an imagined community. In the eyes of plaintiffs and ordinary people as the audience, courts themselves are not simply a place for legal resolution, but are reconciled as places where these moral narratives are expressed and accepted.

The case of Sander County is perhaps similar. Imagined communities do not impose objective, static norms on their members, but rather change norms flexibly based on circumstances. This allows imagined communities to reconstruct themselves and should be thought of as a type of dynamism.

As can be seen in the case of property damage cases in summary courts, personal injury cases with functioning private settlement services, or moral conflicts that go beyond these into the use of litigation, imagined communities and their norms sometimes act to suppress and sometimes to promote depending on the impact of various circumstances.

CONCLUSION

In this chapter, by using the approach of David Engel and borrowing the concepts of Benedict Anderson, I have examined the meaning of the structure of the imagined community in Japanese society and, based on that structure, the behavior of parties involved in traffic accident disputes.

The structure of Japan's imagined community is weakening at the local level, and the crumbling cohesiveness of companies and other secondary institutions has consequently strengthened the homogeneous perception of Japan as the most fundamental imagined community. Likewise, the citizens of Sander County lived in a concentric imagined community structure, not only a local community but also with secondary associations, such as agricultural cooperatives, the state of Illinois, and the United States itself. Major differences are likely to exist in the actual characteristics of the local community and with the permeation of daily actions and perceptions as US citizens. In Japan, the more actual communities become diluted, the more Japan as an imagined community – abstract yet foundational – takes its place. The impact of Japan's public nationalism during the Meiji era, as analyzed by Benedict Anderson, still remains strong.[20]

However, the dynamic changes to the imagined community are more import-ant, based on personal action rather than the imagined community's mainten-ance of static stability. In many cases, litigation is far from being an everyday occurrence and is perceived as a means of managing disputes that should be avoided, if not entirely rejected. Here, we find an awareness that cannot be explained by policies simply causing a higher threshold for litigation. The system of private settlement services has had the effect of keeping cases from evolving into moral conflicts as victims and wrongdoers confront each other in antagon-istic relationships. Through the use of private settlement services, issues are bound by monetary compensation, which reduces moral conflict and an escal-ation of feelings by keeping both parties apart from one another. The private settlement services offered by insurance companies are truly a result of imagined communities and have even strengthened them. In addition, private settlement services perform a valuable function because they standardize methods for calculating compensation and make the outcomes of the Japanese judicial system highly predictable, as was noted by Ramseyer.[21]

At the same time, summary courts do not handle many property damage cases, where there are no private settlement services, which have caused a steady increase in litigation and a dramatic increase in insurance that covers attorneys' fees. Property damage cases do not involve private settlement ser-vices, such as those found in personal injury cases. Thus, disputes over facts can often leave both parties fighting, moving these cases away from issues over monetary compensation and transforming them into moral conflicts. This does not mean that this happens in all property damage cases. Certainly, insurance coverage of attorneys' fees has reduced the burden of paying those fees, which acted as a barrier to litigation in the past, and this has promoted the use of litigation. However, in this case litigation is much more likely to be perceived as part of a system for processing compensation for damages from traffic accidents rather than as a process for resolving disputes in a new dimension. In other words, there is a significant difference between the act of victims taking wrongdoers to court and that of litigating with insurance that covers attorneys' fees, as an extension of the process for demanding

[20] Anderson, *Imagined Communities*, ch. 6, pp. 83–112.   [21] Ramseyer, *Hou to Keizaigaku*.

compensation from insurance. On this point, if the institutionalization of litigation avoidance through policy is reduced, as was noted by Haley, then the Japanese will use litigation. This view, although somewhat applicable, cannot be generalized because of the peculiarities of the system for traffic accident compensation being only part of the overall system, and because of the fact that the system suppresses the use of litigation in Japan.

People using litigation in cases of personal injury, despite the aforementioned, are really important here. Of course, strong conflicts around the facts on the same level of summary courts can be analyzed, as we have done, though there are diverse types of cases such as those where a defendant is uninsured and unable to pay the awarded compensation. The problem is with cases such as the Tomei Expressway accident discussed above.

In such cases, the change in the meaning of the term "litigation" must be noted. In general, Japan as an imagined community takes a dim view of litigation, equating it to a forum for people with problems. This general image of litigation is changing in the particular case of personal injury accidents. The grief that comes from death, through drunk and reckless driving or through other condemnable acts, is shared by all people, and a demand for split payments on the date of death acts as an allegory in bringing this to mind. In such a case, litigation is not so much a place for determining legal rights and responsibilities; rather, it is becoming a forum where sympathy for grief is shown, and for overcoming moral issues and punishing wrongdoers. An imagined community supports this narrative of grief and accepts litigation as an expression of these feelings. Accordingly, the use of litigation is changing people's perceptions of litigation, resulting in changes to the traditional imagined community structure through the flexible transformation or reconstruction of imagined community norms. This is a process of re-strengthening.

As I have noted, the significance of the use of litigation cannot be understood merely in terms of demographics. The process flowing from various elements, such as the resilient flexibility of imagined communities, the diversity of lawsuits, and individual strategies stemming from system characteristics, as well as changes in perception, must be examined. David Engel's text provides us with the opportunity to develop such an analysis.

16

Can "The Oven Bird" Migrate North of the Border?

ANNIE BUNTING

INTRODUCTION: INSIDERS AND OUTSIDERS

In David Engel's elegant 1984 piece "The Oven Bird's Song: Insiders, Out-siders, and Personal Injuries in an American Community," he documents legal perceptions of residents of the pseudonymous Sander County, Illinois that were disconnected from the legal realities he measured, and concluded that these perceptions were reactions to social change that produced greater pluralism in the community.[1] This gave rise to "symbolic efforts . . . to preserve a sense of meaning and coherence in the face of social changes that they found threatening and confusing."[2] Residents sought to "recall and reaffirm an untainted world that existed nowhere but in their imaginations."[3] These conclusions are fascinating and prescient, and have led many of us since then to probe legal perceptions in the face of growing normative pluralism.

Much like the study of residents of Sander County in Engel's "Oven Bird's Song," Carole Greenhouse writes about perceptions of disputes and litigation in a small town she calls Hopewell in *Praying for Justice: Faith, Order, and Community in an American Town* (1986).[4] In Greenhouse's preface, she discusses her own assumptions going into her study. She writes:

> I went to Hopewell in September 1973 to study dispute settlement in an American community, and my assumption, or hope, was that the role of the

---

[1] David M. Engel, "The oven bird's song: insiders, outsiders, and personal injuries in an American community," *Law & Society Review*, 18(4) (1984), 551–82.

[2] Ibid, 580.   [3] Ibid, 581.

[4] Carol J. Greenhouse, *Praying for Justice: Faith, Order, and Community in an American Town* (Cornell University Press, 1986). Marc Galanter noted in his remarks at our "Oven Bird" conference on October 23, 2015, that Sander County is not like Hopewell, however, since there was not a general objection to litigation in Sander County, such as Greenhouse found in Hopewell.

court in the social fabric of a town would be thrown into relief if the community was in the process of change. The rest of the book should make it clear why such a legal study was not possible in this community and also how it is that one can begin a study of an American community by looking for conflict and end by considering a person's relationship to God.[5]

I am often reminded of Engel's and Greenhouse's words as I embark on a study in a community not my own. We have to be mindful of the researcher's distance from the community in which the research takes place and the assumptions that are brought to bear on our research design and analysis. By "laying bare" and interrogating these assumptions, as Marilyn Strathern suggests,[6] we can go some way toward mitigating our bias and expectations in interpreting what we see. This mirrors what David Engel discovers in terms of litigation and physical and social distance between members of the same community. Engel finds that residents of Sander County have their own assumptions about their neighbors' litigation behavior – notions and perceptions that may not be well founded. He also argues that litigants' distance from each other determines, in many cases, whether their personal injury matter will end up in court: The farther the physical or social distance, the more likely it is that the matter will be litigated. Engel explains:

> Among the relative handful of personal injury cases filed in the Sander County Court, almost all shared a common feature: the parties were separated by either geographic or social "distance" that could not be bridged by any conflict resolution process short of litigation. In at least half of the fifteen personal injury cases in the sample, the plaintiff and the defendant resided in different counties or states.[7]

Given the subject of Engel's article, his title is mysterious at first, until you read the asterisked footnote. He says nothing about the significance of the "Oven Bird" poem after that footnote. There is no mention of it in the text of his article. Engel invoked Robert Frost's poem "The Oven Bird" because he sees the poem as describing "a response to a perception of disintegration and decay" like that expressed by some of the residents of Sander County he interviewed, and as expressed by the opponents of arbitration on religious principles that I observed in my own work.[8] The oven bird's song is a response to the changing of seasons, so it is a lament about the loss of the fresh blooms

---

[5] Ibid, 9.

[6] Marilyn Strathern, *The Gender of the Gift: Problems with Women and Problems with Society in Melanesia* (University of California Press, 1990).

[7] Engel, *The Oven Bird*, 567.   [8] Ibid, 551.

of spring. Or, at least, that's what Frost heard in it. As the closing line in Frost's poem puts it, the bird is trying to figure out "what to make of a diminished thing."[9] But, of course, the coming of summer and fall need not be a "diminished thing." Change and renewal is constant. Summer, fall, and winter all have their own distinct beauty and each brings us closer to another spring rebirth. But the oven bird in Frost's account seems fixated on the perception of loss, as are many of Engel's community interviewees in Sander County – as were many of the opponents of religious arbitration in Ontario in my study of the importance of culture and religion in family law disputes in the early 2000s. While religion seemed to be an implicit factor shaping the fundamental norms that informed litigation choices, or reactions to those choices by others, in Engel's study of Sander County it was not addressed explicitly. My research builds on Engel's and reveals that religion is an important consideration that can impact a person's dispute resolution decisions and perceptions.

I too came to my reading of "The Oven Bird's Song" as a neighbor to the north. In this chapter, I want to share two reflections on how sociolegal research travels in scholarship and in the classroom. From my position as a law and society scholar on the other side of the United States-Canada border, there is a certain social distance with which I engage with "The Oven Bird's Song" and other American law and society scholarship on disputing, legal consciousness, and legal pluralism. This social distance allows, one might assume, some issues of justice to be thrown into relief. But physical distance also comes with presumptions and stereotypes about our differences from our neighbo(u)rs to the south, American litigiousness, and legal behavior.

My first observation in this chapter is about the ease with which we find resonance and application in Canada of sociolegal scholarship such as that found in David Engel's "The Oven Bird's Song." Engel and others in the field of disputing explore how citizens define and resolve disputes and why they choose certain venues and not others. This rich scholarship has been taken up by disputing and conflict resolution scholars in Canada. I read this piece as much as a study in legal pluralism, as we see that other normative systems and social relationships determine how residents of Sander County define and resolve personal injury disputes. Further, Engel documents community perceptions, and how they reflect traditional norms, power, and status and stigmatize some dispute resolution choices. Engel's study of self-sufficient individualism versus rights-based individualism, and the impact of these

---

[9] Ibid.

different notions of individualism on disputing, adds to our understanding of both disputing behavior and critical legal pluralism.

Second, and paradoxically, I argue that there is a persistent parochialism in law and society research on both sides of the border. From my scan of undergraduate syllabi in Canadian law and society programs, for example, it appears that "The Oven Bird's Song" is rarely taught. Thus, at first glance, the answer to my question is that "The Oven Bird" is not migrating north of the border. We also know, however, how influential this piece is for sociolegal scholars all over North America. The methodologies employed by Engel in "The Oven Bird's Song" have inspired generations of Canadian scholars, and Engel's ideas and analysis resonate with our own contemporary community responses to pluralism. The perception of change as loss that Frost heard in the oven bird's song, and that Engel heard in his "community observers," seems to be a feature of human thinking that transcends borders. In this chapter, I explore these two seemingly contradictory reactions to "The Oven Bird's Song" – migration and parochialism.

DISPUTES, RELIGION, AND LEGAL PLURALISM

In reflecting on Engel's "The Oven Bird's Song" as a study in normative and social change, I was taken back to research I had conducted in the early 2000s on cross-cultural issues in Canadian family law, including how courts evaluate culture and cultural identity in child-placement decisions, childrearing practices, religious and polygamous marriage practices, community-based mediation of family disputes, and the now infamous religious arbitration debates in Ontario (2003–6).[10] I was taken to questions of religion, dispute resolution, and legal pluralism. My interest in exploring attitudes to dispute resolution in a minority community through interviews with participants was inspired by pioneering work done by sociolegal scholars such as Engel. This interest was provoked also by widespread perceptions that displayed little understanding of dominant legal traditions or the realities of dispute resolution within Muslim communities.

[10] Annie Bunting, "Complicating culture in child placements decisions," *Canadian Journal of Women & the Law*, 16(1) (2004), 137–64; Annie Bunting and Shadi Mokhtari, "Migrant Muslim women's interests and the case of 'Shari'a tribunals' in Ontario" in Vijay Agnew (ed.), *Racialized Migrant Women in Canada: Essays on Health, Violence, and Equity* (University of Toronto Press, 2009), pp. 233–64; Annie Bunting, "Family law's legal pluralism: private opting-out in Canada and South Africa" in Albert Breton, Anne Des Ormeaux, Katharina Pistor, and Pierre Salmon (eds.), *Multijuralism: Manifestations, Causes and Consequences* (Ashgate Press, 2009), pp. 77–98.

The controversy over faith-based arbitration of family disputes ended with the provincial government in Ontario pronouncing "one law for all" (2006 law reform) and forbidding the judicial enforcement of any religious arbitration decision. This "one law for all" was a fantasy that never existed, an imagined past like that in Sander County. The "Shari'a debates" led to public outcry which was often racist or Islamophobic. As Engel writes,

> there are times when the invocation of formal law is viewed as an anti-social act and as a contravention of established cultural norms. Criticism of what is seen as an overuse of law and legal institutions often reveals less about the quantity of litigation at any given time than about the interests being asserted or protected through litigation and the kinds of individuals or groups involved in cases that courts are asked to resolve.[11]

I would argue that this piece can guide us today in our explorations of community dispute resolution, especially within communities seen as "outsiders" by mainstream society in Ontario – migrant farm workers, ortho-dox religious communities, and refugees. While Toronto is a large, multicul-tural city in southern Ontario – quite unlike Sander County, Illinois – at the time of the religious arbitration debate there was a general fear of social change brought about by migration, a particular fear of Islamic religious arbitration in the post-9/11 context, and a lack of empirical understanding of the dispute resolution processes at the center of the debates (including both Jewish and Muslim mediation and arbitration). Thus, like the residents of Sander County, residents in Ontario in the early 2000s were in the midst of what they perceived to be a demographic and normative shift in the province, without much information about the legal processes at the heart of the debates. In this case, in Ontario, it was the invocation of religious law rather than formal law that provoked loud public outcry about the antisocial charac-ter of Shari'a law and Muslims who would avoid secular dispute resolution. Related to this was the request that "secular" courts uphold decisions from religious arbitrators that incensed some members of the public in a climate of fear over the spread of "fundamentalism." Thus, like in Sander County,

> the entry of the stranger produced a new awareness (or perhaps a reconstruc-tion) of the traditional normative order at the very moment when that order was subjected to its strongest and most devastating challenges. This process triggered a complex response by the community – a nostalgic yearning for the older world view now shattered beyond repair, a rearguard attempt to shore up the boundaries of the community against alien persons and ideas

[11] Engel, *The Oven Bird*, 552.

(compare Erikson, 1966), and a bitter acceptance of the fact that the "stranger" was in reality no longer outside the community but a necessary element brought in to preserve the community, and therefore a part of it.[12]

In 2003, the Islamic Arbitration Board made public its intention to arbitrate separation and divorce matters in Ontario according to Islamic law. Up until this time, both Muslim and Jewish mediation of family matters had been taking place informally and formally. There was an active Beit Din (Rabbinical Court) operating in Ontario which decided matters of religious law, including divorce matters. Rarely were those decisions reviewed by or challenged in the secular courts. Domestic contracts abiding by religious law were enforceable in the province under the Family Law Act, whereas religiously mediated or arbitrated separation agreements rarely went before the Ontario courts. Religious minority communities, therefore, were resolving some of their family disputes (and making decisions about kosher or halal meats, etc.) for themselves. Unlike Engel's study of Sander County, then, I was interested in this project in the disputes *within* outsider communities and when those disputes might spill over into the mainstream. My work shares with Engel's an exploration of how social change leading to increased normative pluralism can produce nostalgic yearning, rearguard actions, stigmatization of some legal processes, and demands for assimilation to norms asserted with new vigor.[13]

Following the 2003 announcement by the Islamic Arbitration Board, the provincial Attorney-General appointed Marion Boyd to review the Arbitration Act; the Boyd report was released on December 20, 2004, under the title *Dispute Resolution in Family Law: Protecting Choice, Promoting Inclusion.* Following this logic of "inclusion,"[14] the report recommended the continuation of religious arbitration of family matters subject to numerous safeguards.[15] These safeguards are grouped under the headings of legislative and regulatory changes, independent legal advice, training for professions, oversight of arbitrators, public legal education, community development, and further policy developments.

The province took a different approach and in September 2006 announced that there would be "one law for all," denying direct legal effects to the outcomes

---

[12] Ibid, 579–80.   [13] Ibid (and see Jamie Longazel's chapter in this collection.)

[14] For an excellent critique of the logic of inclusion, see Pascale Fournier, "Sharia Court in Canada and Global Civil Society: from *Protecting Choice, Promoting Inclusion* to Producing Choice, Promoting Exclusion," paper for "A World for All? The Ethics of Global Civil Society," September 4–7, 2005 (on file with author).

[15] Marion Boyd, *Dispute Resolution in Family Law: Protecting Choice, Promoting Inclusion* (Ministry of the Attorney General, 2004), p. 133.

of religious arbitration in family matters. The result of the 2006 amendments is that family arbitration decisions are brought within the complex set of provisions in the Family Law Act that seek to respect private autonomy and secure some basic civic entitlements. Family arbitrations that are not based on Canadian law – for example, those based on religious principles or foreign law – have no direct legal effect.[16]

Couples may still arrange their affairs after separation on the basis of religious principles by entering into a separation agreement that may or may not be based on an arbitration decision. In such a separation agreement, they may choose, for example, not to abide by the provisions for equal division of family property found in the statute or the spousal support obligations set out therein. Separation agreements are not affected by the new law. They may be based on any laws or principles the parties choose, and are legally binding subject to the general limitations described above.

The arbitral door to creating binding agreements based on religious principles has been firmly shut by the 2006 amendments. But parties determined to settle their family rights and obligations on the basis of religious principles in a legally binding manner have other options open to them. They can create separation agreements by any means other than binding arbitration. Negotiated separation agreements, even those concluded with the assistance of informal advisors, mediators, or arbitrators (so long as the latter's awards are "advisory" only or not legally binding), can be based on religious principles and are legally binding under the Family Law Act. Thus, the government's denial of legally binding force to family arbitration based on religious principles is, it turns out, a matter of legal form rather than normative substance. The formal obstacle to binding religious arbitration of family matters is easily evaded, if the parties so desire, by embodying the results of advisory religious arbitration decisions in negotiated separation agreements.

In my study with Shadi Mokhtari, we found that Muslim women preferred to resolve their separation and divorce matters within their extended families, in their communities, or with the help of their mosque rather than take the matter to the secular courts.[17] While few women knew about the exact rights found in the Family Law Act and the Divorce Act, even those who knew they might get more in the secular courts said they would still choose the resolution that conformed to religious law. In our interviews, we found that this choice was influenced by a number of factors including their relationship to their faith, their desire to keep their children, and their sense of fairness. Like the

---

[16] Family Law Act, R.S.O. 1990 c.F.3.
[17] See Bunting and Mokhtari, *Migrant Muslim women* for full discussion.

migrant laborers in Engel's study, Muslim women in Toronto were marginalized minorities in a predominantly Judeo-Christian city. And like some participants in Engel's article, they knew they might be forfeiting some of their rights.

One theme that arose in our focus group was the importance of religion for migrant Muslim woman in the diaspora. While in Somalia or India or Egypt women need not organize around religion, in Canada religion becomes an important shared marker of identity. One woman stated that we "are becoming more faithful in the diaspora ... restarting our identities in this country."[18] Fazia reiterated that "in diaspora we are getting closer to the religion because it is some commonality."[19] She added that since in Somalia "everyone was Muslim ... culture was more important in many ways than the religion itself. But as we came out and they ask for ... we are learning more about religion, we keep getting closer to religion because we have the opportunity now to see ourselves."[20]

In "The Oven Bird's Song," religion is not a distinct subject of analysis, except as part of the move from a sense of settled norms to conditions of normative pluralism. In the past few decades, the increased importance of religion in shaping community norms and perceptions has made it a prominent focus of study in contemporary sociolegal scholarship. In one interview in which we see the relationship between litigation and faith, Engel writes of his discussion with a Christian minister. In the minister's mind, faith trumps rights:

> For this minister, born-again Christianity offered socially marginal people a form of contentment and stability that was denied them by their lack of a recognized position in the local society. He argued that external problems such as personal injuries were secondary to primary questions of religious faith. He told me, "[I]f we first of all get first things straightened out and that is our relationship with God and is our help from God, all of these other things will fall into order."[21]

Some critics in Ontario argued that there was potential for women to be coerced into religious proceedings and that this risk had increased in recent years with the rise of political Islam, combined with new dynamics associated with many Muslims' sense of being targeted and under siege in the post-9/11 era.[22]

---

[18] H1, interview, June 24, 2005, Toronto.   [19] Fazia, interview, June 24, 2005, Toronto.
[20] Ibid.   [21] Engel, *The Oven Bird*, 571.
[22] For a study of how a diasporic Muslim community's marginalization fosters identity politics that disempower women within that community, see Robina Mohammad, "Marginalization, Islamism and the production of the others' other," *Gender, Place and Culture: A Journal of Feminist Geography*, 6(3) (1999), 221–41.

Accordingly, in addition to being seen as a religious obligation, participating in religious arbitration may take on a political significance as a form of resistance to the racism and Islamophobia Muslims currently experience. Added pressure to use religious tribunals can be presented by a prevailing sentiment that seeking gender equality in a Canadian court when a Shari'a tribunal is available is tantamount to confirming Western stereotypes of Islam's misogyny and inferiority. Finally, some opponents of religious arbitration have argued that migrant Muslim women may be more susceptible to such pressures than non-immigrant Muslim women due to the presence of language barriers and their lack of familiarity with the Canadian legal system and norms.[23]

One key theme that arose in our interviews *prior to* the change in the law was the perception among participants that an arbitrated decision would not be binding and enforceable in a "Canadian court."[24] One woman stated that she would use Shari'a tribunals if they were available in her area "because I am a Muslim and Shari'a is my Koran book. If I am not happy about the Shari'a decision I have the right to choose Canadian law."[25] Another woman said she would use religious tribunals "only as a last resort before going to family law."[26] A third woman, Fazia, described arbitration as "counselling, the step before going to court."[27] Interestingly, after the 2006 amendments to the law, religious arbitrations conducted according to an Islamic legal code would indeed just be "counselling," and not binding in an Ontario court. Generally, we found there was a lack of legal literacy, or understanding, about the nature of mediation and arbitration in our interviews and in public discussion about the issue.

It is important to document and analyze the complex nature of domestic relations in Muslim families in Canada, in order to undermine the simplistic presumptions about Muslim men and women's roles in the family and in society.[28] Common stereotypes and misunderstandings see Muslim women's

---

[23] Ziba Mir Hosseini, lecture at Noor Cultural Centre, Toronto (April 10, 2005). While no doubt language and cultural barriers result in some Muslim women being pushed in the direction of religious arbitration, there are also a number of countervailing considerations. Foremost among these is that to varying degrees, Muslim migrant women in Canada will have far greater exposure to social norms surrounding women's rights and gender equality than the average Muslim woman living in a Muslim-world context, where prevailing social norms are more inclined toward gender inequality.

[24] On the other hand, a few women commented that it would be desirable to have decisions enforced by the family courts, sanctioned by government.

[25] Interview, June 16, 2005, Toronto.   [26] Interview, June 16, 2005, Toronto.

[27] Interview, June 24, 2005, Toronto.

[28] Shahnaz Khan, *Aversion and Desire: Negotiating Female Muslim Identity in the Diaspora* (Women's Press, 2002).

roles as emblematic of the oppressive character of Islamic law and Muslim social norms. This type of public perception has echoes in Engel's findings of mainstream community members' perceptions of newer residents in Sander County. Such views leave little room for nuanced discussion of the importance of religion for women in the diaspora, negotiations of cultural and religious gender identity, deficiencies in the provincial family court processes, and dynamics of private ordering and political Islam. At the same time, issues in Islamic family law, such as the marriage of minors and custody dispositions, pose some of the most profound challenges to cross-cultural judgement in a diverse society. While some Muslim community leaders have expressed a desire for greater deference to and accommodation of Islamic family codes in the family courts, feminists and other critics have identified problems with this proposal.[29]

"The Oven Bird's Song" enters this multicultural space to help us understand when people turn to law and the courts and when they turn to other dispute resolution mechanisms, including religion. Couples from the same socioreligious community may have adequate resources to resolves their matters at separation with the help of their mosque, community center, or extended family. If they have a socially marginal status,[30] they may not have faith in the Ontario courts to respect their wishes. Or, as we found, one party may use the court as a way of levelling the power in their relationship with their spouse. In Sander County, one's "socially marginal status in the community precluded any significant form of nonjudicial conflict resolution" with someone who was socially distant from them.[31] Engel's study invites us to be open to the various routes to and *understandings of* justice in times of social change. Further, thinking about "The Oven Bird's Song" in the context of legal pluralism reminds us that not going to court does not necessarily indicate "lumping it." People may be finding alternative ways to settle their disputes. As Shadi Mokhtari and I argued, Muslim women who opt out of the minimum guarantees contained in Ontario family law may do so not because of oppressive controlling community norms, but on account of their faith or for a host of other reasons, including power and social location.

Like the oven bird's response to the changing of the seasons (or Frost's account of that response), the residents of Sander County's response (or Engel's account of that response) to the social change brought on by the arrival of newcomers in their midst manifested itself in a lament for things lost.

---

[29] Anna C. Korteweg and Jennifer A. Selby (eds.), *Debating Sharia: Islam, Gender Politics, and Family Law Arbitration* (University of Toronto Press, 2012).
[30] Engel, *The Oven Bird's Song*, 569.   [31] Ibid.

Certain legal discourses and rights were stigmatized in a way that reflected status and power relations in the community as a whole (as was the case with the religious arbitration debate). The entry of the "stranger" produced a new awareness and a new articulation of the traditional normative order – as was the case with the "one law for all" conception of the rule of law articulated by the opponents of religious arbitration – even though privatized legal pluralism through domestic contract was a well-established feature of Ontario family law.

SOCIAL DISTANCE IN SCHOLARSHIP

Let me turn now to the second theme: the challenges of teaching "The Oven Bird's Song" in the Canadian law and society classroom. My scan of introductory law and society courses in Canada indicated that Engel's article is rarely assigned. Surprisingly, it is also rarely cited by authors published in the *Canadian Journal of Law and Society* and other sociolegal and law journals in the country. A (not) random sample of colleagues and graduate students told me they found the article on their own or were recommended it by supervisors or peers. Unlike Renée Cramer's students reading this article,[32] some graduate students in Toronto reported not being able to relate to the residents of Sander County. Why might that be? While the thesis of Engel's article is that one has to be cautious about what we think we know about our neighbo(u)rs and, in particular, their litigious culture, we in Canada continue think of American legal culture on personal injury as very distinct from our own. It is the case that contingency fees in civil suits were introduced in Canada much more recently than in the United States and, therefore, personal injury law holds a different place north of the border in legal culture and practice and in the national imaginary. Nonetheless, the broader themes of Engel's piece resonate strongly.

With so many law and society scholars in Canada having trained in the United States, and working in regional and international research networks, one might not expect a persistent parochialism in Canadian classrooms and scholarship. Harry Arthurs and I recently found, however, that the Canadian field is not as comparative or international as one might think.[33] Looking back to the late 1970s and early 1980s when Engel published this piece, we see that Canadian law and society scholars were overwhelmingly working in law

---

[32] Renée Cramer, *This Collection*.

[33] Harry Arthurs and Annie Bunting, "Socio-legal scholarship in Canada: a review of the field," *Journal of Law & Society*, 41(4) (2014), 487–99.

schools and the majority of articles published in legal journals were doctrinal (71 percent in English-language legal journals in 1983) and not comparative (only 2 percent) or empirical (only one article in 1983). Further, only 8 percent of articles published in leading social science journals in 1983 were sociolegal. These factors have changed over time, along with changes in law schools and the growth of interdisciplinary law and society programs in social science and humanities departments across the country. In terms of sociolegal articles published in the thirty years since Engel's "The Oven Bird's Song," there has been a steady increase in the number and proportion of non-doctrinal pieces (to 47 percent of the English articles and 46 percent of the French law journals in 2012). Notably for our purposes, however, the proportion of those non-doctrinal articles which we coded as comparative or transnational was fairly steady between 1983 and 2012 at only 2–3 percent of the total number of articles published in any of our given sample years.

Outside the consideration of international or comparative work by Canadian law and society researchers, one might expect scholars to be relying on Engel and his peers more often than was the case. Here we did find that law and society authors who were exploring Canadian topics were increasingly influenced by the broader developments in the field. As we wrote in our 2014 article:

> Some sense of the significance of this growing body of scholarship can be gained by reviewing the themes of special issues of the *Canadian Journal of Law and Society*. Perusal of the 22 themes of the special issues of the Journal since 1992 shows abiding attention to a number of important preoccupations in socio-legal research in Canada: Aboriginal law and Indigenous peoples' engagement with law; gender and sexuality; *legal pluralism*; rights discourse; policing and security; and social exclusion on the basis of race, ethnicity and citizenship. Articles in political science, to cite another example, focus on group politics and Charter litigation and on *"naming, blaming and claiming"* in the controversies surrounding HIV, Hepatitis C and Canada's tainted blood supplies. Some of these themes, of course, represent distinctive Canadian preoccupations or idiosyncrasies while others correspond to broader theoretical developments in the field of law and society. For example, over the past thirty years, socio-legal research has become increasingly international and interdisciplinary. Major influences and challenges to the field have come from cultural studies, geography, psychoanalysis, and economics to name few.[34]

---

[34] Ibid, 495–6 (emphasis added).

Legal consciousness has been discussed in twenty-one articles in the *Canadian Journal of Law and Society* since 1986, with many leading American scholars cited. Legal pluralism has a deeper tradition in Canada, I would argue, which can crudely be demonstrated by the fact that more than double the number of articles (fifty-five) have been published on the topic in the journal since 1986. Perhaps this explains why I teach "The Oven Bird's Song" in the context of legal pluralism in our introductory course.

In terms of law and society teaching and research in Canada, we may not ask the same questions as our American colleagues. With different legal cultures in terms of breach of contract and personal injury claims and litigation in general, and no-fault approaches in some areas, Canadian researchers do not approach the field of disputing from the perspective of personal injury in the same way. Engel describes how in the early 1980s in the United States, "perhaps no category of litigation has produced greater public criticism than personal injuries."[35] While we may find good scholarly research in Canada that follows a similar methodology to the disputing and conflict resolution literature in the United States of the 1970s and 1980s, I hazard a guess that it would land on different disputes.

As the next generation of law and society scholars are working their way through graduate programs, I expect the parochialism of scholarship will further subside. This next generation is more robustly interdisciplinary and global in their outlook than those of us "trained in" disciplines and "made in" interdisciplinary research. Some new scholars may be the product of socio-legal doctoral programs where debates about the canon of the field – or about whether an interdisciplinary field should even have a canon or boundaries – have animated their transgressing of borders and boundaries of fields.

So as not to leave the wrong impression of Canadian law and society classrooms and research, I would note in closing that many Canadian socio-legal students and scholars read David Engel and Frank Munger's more recent book, *Rights of Inclusion: Law and Identity in the Life Stories of Americans with Disabilities* – another rich study of the legal consciousness of marginalized outsiders and their choice to litigate (or not) or bring forward formal complaints for discrimination to their employer or school.[36] As others explore in this collection, in *Rights of Inclusion* Engel and Munger analyse many of the important themes that we see in "The Oven Bird's Song," including issues of subjectivity and identity formation in relation to legal change.

---

[35] Engel, *The Oven Bird's Song*, 552.
[36] David M. Engel and Frank W. Munger, *Rights of Inclusion: Law and Identity in the Life Stories of American with Disabilities* (University of Chicago, 2003).

CONCLUSIONS

Engel finds that, even more than physical distance, a more elusive but no less significant form of distance was suggested by interviews with the parties as well as by the court documents in several personal injury cases. In these cases, it became apparent that "social distance," which was less tangible but just as hard to bridge as geographic distance, separated the parties even when they were neighbors.[37]

As we think of our own national identity formation, scholarship, and pedagogy, it is wise to remember David Engel's invitation to use moments of legal debate to expose "important underlying conflicts in cultural values and changes or tensions in the structure of social relations."[38] Whether regarding the residents of Sander County, Americans living with disabilities, or Muslim women in southern Ontario, David Engel asks us to empirically assess the assumptions on which legal stories are told. By understanding those stories of non-litigation, we might better understand the diversity of normative orders.

But it would be a mistake to think of "The Oven Bird's Song" as an article only about personal injury claims, rather than one documenting legal perceptions and legal realities and measuring, explaining, and critically evaluating the gap between them. Here it has a resonance that should continue to influence sociolegal scholarship in Canada and elsewhere. In the current political climate, we have been reminded of the power and persistence of nostalgic longing for a return to imaginary worlds untainted by pluralism. Engel's article is admirable in using a combination of social science techniques – data collection and analysis, interviews with participants and observers of legal phenomena – both to record and to challenge dominant wisdom. "The Oven Bird's Song" will continue to inspire us to document and challenge ceremonies of regret, and to construct alternative legal visions that herald the arrival of new springs.

---

[37] Engel, *The Oven Bird's Song*, 568.   [38] Ibid, 552.

PART V

Afterword

17

Looking Backward, Looking Forward
Past and Future Lives of "The Oven Bird's Song"

DAVID M. ENGEL

ORIGINS AND INFLUENCES

Out walking in the frozen swamp one gray day,
I paused and said, "I will turn back from here.
No, I will go on farther – and we shall see."
Robert Frost, "The Wood Pile"

Looking back at an article written some years ago by a younger version of
oneself, it becomes possible to see more clearly the influences that shaped
both the text and the author. As we conduct our scholarly work, we tend to
imagine that we are freely choosing the ideas we pursue and the methods we
employ. We are the agents of our own destiny – or so we tell ourselves as we
move forward in time. But, viewed retrospectively, there is ample evidence to
support a much more contingent, even deterministic, view. The author as
auteur seems less plausible. The text is also – perhaps more significantly –
written by its intellectual environment, by contemporaneous minds and
scholarly works, by the events of the day, and by the quirks and happenstance
of life. That is how it now appears when I reflect on the origins and influences
of "The Oven Bird's Song"[1] more than thirty years later.

In the late 1970s, I found myself driving through the streets of what I called
"Sander County," a small, predominantly agricultural community in Illinois.

My profound thanks to Mary Nell Trautner for her tireless work in editing this collection of essays.
Thanks for their comments on this chapter go as well to Fred Konefsky and Lynn Mather. Indeed,
the concept for the conference itself was Fred's, one of the countless acts of generosity and
friendship for which he is so well known and appreciated by his colleagues. Thanks to Samantha
Barbas and Anya Bernstein for working with Mary Nell, Fred, and Lynn to make the event
unforgettable. And my profound thanks to all the contributors to this volume for their thoughtful
and provocative observations.
[1] David M. Engel, "The oven bird's song: insiders, outsiders, and personal injuries in an
    American community," *Law & Society Review*, 18(4) (1984), 551–82.

I had begun to understand that Sander County was undergoing major social and economic changes, largely as the result of a new factory that had opened the county to global flows of people, capital, and economic influence. In the course of my fieldwork, I identified former litigants who had been involved in different types of civil cases. I knocked on their doors and tried to learn from them how they had traveled the path to litigation in the local court and what the results had been. Later, I also identified and interviewed dozens of "community observers" –ministers, youth leaders, beauticians, farmers, teachers, funeral parlor operators, social workers, town council members, insurance adjusters, lawyers, judges, and many others. I asked them about their perspectives on the transformations underway in their community, and I solicited examples of trouble cases that had not necessarily entered the legal system. At the same time, I spent what seemed like endless days sitting quietly in the back room of the Sander County courthouse, where I read hundreds of old case files, extracted from them their stories of local conflict, and constructed a quantitative portrait of the flow of litigation over an extended period of time.

How did all of this happen, and why? What sequence of events led me to attempt this kind of fieldwork in a small, out-of-the-way American community? I was not alone. I would soon discover that other colleagues who were then unknown to me – people such as Barbara Yngvesson,[2] Carol Greenhouse,[3] Frank Munger,[4] and Sally Merry[5] – were doing similar research in other parts of the country. Our community-based legal ethnographies were a product of their time – researchers attempt them less often nowadays. In retrospect, it seems quite clear that scholarship of this kind is not merely the result of our conscious choices and decisions. It grows out of the soil in which it's rooted. It pokes its head above the ground and responds to the intellectual climate that surrounds it. It turns toward the light that happens to shine at a particular time and place.

This opportunity to look back at the writing of "The Oven Bird's Song" has helped me to situate it at the confluence of four particularly important influences. First, the field of law and society was emerging as a discipline in its own right, with an institutional structure and a "canon" that made the study of

---

[2] Barbara Yngvesson, "Making law at the doorway: the clerk, the court, and the construction of community in a New England town," *Law & Society Review*, 22(3) (1988), 409–48.

[3] Carol J. Greenhouse, *Praying for Justice: Faith, Order, and Community in an American Town* (Cornell University Press, 1986).

[4] Frank W. Munger, "Social change and tort litigation: industrialization, accidents, and trial courts in Southern West Virginia, 1872 to 1940," *Buffalo Law Review*, 36(1) (1988), 75–118.

[5] Sally Engle Merry, *Getting Justice and Getting Even: Legal Consciousness among Working-Class Americans* (University of Chicago Press, 1990).

disputes and dispute-processing a central concern. Second, the times being what they were in the 1960s and 1970s, many American law and society scholars had acquired experience in other countries and cultures. They were subsequently drawn to studies of their own society that would apply the same methods and cultural interpretive frameworks that they had developed in non-Western settings. Third, law and society research had begun to reflect broader intellectual trends that challenged exclusively positivist interpretations of social behavior and encouraged interpretivist and social constructionist perspectives. Fourth, when it comes to scholarly work, the personal is the professional. We as scholars like to pretend that our ideas, our interests, and our methods are somehow divorced from events in our private lives – the places we have been, the people we have befriended, our likes, our dislikes, our personal styles, and our values. But the writing of "The Oven Bird's Song," like the production of much scholarship, reflects the intersection of the author's autobiography with the ideas and intellectual influences of the day.

As I try now to explain the origins of this article, I find myself attempting to weave these four influences together into a plausible account. No doubt, the narrative I offer here is itself a product of the same four influences even as I write it down. Our explanations and self-justifications become part of an endless regression, frames within frames. But this is the best I can do at this time and at this stage in my own life, offering a version of events that occurred many years ago, seen now through the eyes of a person closer to the end than the beginning of his scholarly career.

In college and, briefly, in graduate school, I had been an American Studies student. In that sense, it is completely unsurprising that I would later join the small cohort of law and society scholars in the 1970s who decided to explore law and conflict in American communities. But in another sense, it was highly improbable that events in my life should have taken me in this direction. Circumstances had actually led me to *drop out* of my graduate program in American Studies at Yale at the height of the Vietnam war, travel to Thailand in the Peace Corps, and then, after coming back and finishing law school, return a second time to Thailand to conduct research on a court and community there. In other words, my first scholarly undertakings had everything to do with Asia and very little to do with American Studies or, for that matter, with America. After writing two monographs on Thai law, culture, and history, however, a somewhat random chain of events led to my first job at the American Bar Foundation (ABF), where it was assumed that I would focus primarily on US topics. I felt fortunate indeed to be employed by an institution that expected nothing more of me than fulltime research and writing – and which provided substantial resources to carry out my work. I had ample time to design my Sander County study, obtain additional funding from the National Science Foundation, and then launch a multi-year ethnographic study of an American court and community. But what now seems obvious in retrospect is that the Sander County study was heavily influenced by my work in Thailand. I was both surprised and delighted to discover that, in their aversion to litigiousness and in their nostalgic evocation of a conflict-free community, the residents of Sander County talked and behaved in so many respects like the residents of Chiangmai. It is only a slight exaggeration to say that, in my mind, the farmers of Sander County were Thai villagers in overalls.

As I have said, I was not alone in this circuitous journey. World and national events had led other law and society scholars of my generation to spend time abroad and then return home. We came back to see our own society through new eyes. The familiar really had become strange to many of us, and we were eager to rediscover American law and culture, drawing on our experiences in Sweden (Barbara Yngvesson), India (Marc Galanter and Robert Kidder), Chile (Stewart Macaulay), Kenya (Richard Abel), Brazil (David Trubek), Israel (Richard Schwartz), Lebanon (Laura Nader), Tanzania (Sally Falk Moore), and elsewhere. It is unlikely that such large numbers of sociolegal scholars working on American topics had undergone a prior immersion in a non-US culture in previous eras. Our outlook on American law and society reflected the shared experience of an entire generation.

But it is also worth asking why so many of us were drawn to "law and society" as the lens for viewing our culture. What was the unique attraction of this emerging interdisciplinary field as opposed to the more traditional disciplines of sociology, anthropology, political science, or law? In the 1970s, the US-based Law & Society Association (LSA) was taking shape. LSA had been incorporated in 1964, and the first issue of the *Law & Society Review* (*LSR*) had been published in 1966 under the editorship of Richard D. (Red) Schwartz. But the first standalone meeting of LSA, not held in conjunction with the annual meeting of another disciplinary organization, occurred a decade later – in Buffalo in 1975 – and regular annual meetings of the LSA did not commence until 1978. Thus, LSA attained its formal organizational identity at the very time that my research in Sander County was underway. LSA's influence on my work cannot be overstated, and I am quite sure that other colleagues conducting fieldwork on law in American communities would say the same thing about their own research.

Sociolegal scholarship had, of course, been around long before the 1970s, and sociolegal centers and associations had arisen elsewhere in the world – the Japanese Association of the Sociology of Law, for example, was founded in 1947. But for US-based scholars in the 1970s, LSA had a unique attraction.

It was not only interdisciplinary – fostering highly productive conversations among researchers from many different scholarly backgrounds – but also comparative. The founding figures included North Americans with extensive experience abroad and also a group of non-North Americans whose work was highly influential in the development of LSA – scholars such as Upendra Baxi, Boaventura de Sousa Santos, Neelan Tiruchelvam, and others.

The most prominent sociolegal research paradigm in the 1970s was "dispute processing." LSA scholars of that era, regardless of their home disciplines, shared the assumption that disputes were a universal unit of analysis whose study would be valid in any place, time, and legal context. In a very significant way, dispute processing became the foundation on which LSA was built. From the individual dispute, one could extend the analysis as necessary to every other aspect of law and culture in order to explain how conflict arose and was handled, whether within the formal legal system or outside it. Influenced by Llewellyn and Hoebel's classic study of the "trouble case" among the Cheyenne,[6] research on dispute processing in the 1960s and 1970s fostered a vibrant body of theoretical and empirical literature, much of it published in the pages of *LSR*.[7] This literature shaped the field, and the field shaped those of us who entered it.

When I first embarked on my own scholarly career, I had no knowledge of LSA as an organization or the research literature associated with it. If anything, I fancied myself a historian of Southeast Asia with an interest in the advent of legal modernity in Thailand. Sheer happenstance led me to the law and society field. After graduating from law school, I received a fellowship to return to Thailand, where I had lived for three years as a Peace Corps volunteer. I planned to spend a postgraduate year in Chiangmai, the historic northern capital, to document the establishment of Thailand's European-style court system under King Chulalongkorn in the late nineteenth and early twentieth centuries. Before leaving for Thailand, I happened to visit my

---

[6] Karl N. Llewellyn and E. Adamson Hoebel, *The Cheyenne Way: Conflict and Case Law in Primitive Jurisprudence* (University of Oklahoma Press, 1941).

[7] See, e.g., Richard L. Abel, "A comparative theory of dispute institutions in society," *Law & Society Review*, 8(2) (1973), 217–348; Sally Falk Moore, "Law and social change: the semi-autonomous social field as an appropriate subject of study," *Law & Society Review*, 7(4) (1973), 719–46; Marc Galanter, "Why the 'haves' come out ahead: speculations on the limits of legal change," *Law & Society Review*, 9(1) (1974), 95–160; Laura Nader and Harry F. Todd Jr. (eds.), *The Disputing Process – Law in Ten Societies* (Columbia University Press, 1978); Lynn Mather and Barbara Yngvesson, "Language, audience, and the transformation of disputes," *Law & Society Review*, 15(3–4) (1980–1), 775–821; William L. F. Felstiner, Richard L. Abel, and Austin Sarat, "The emergence and transformation of disputes: naming, blaming, claiming...," *Law & Society Review*, 15(3–4) (1980–1), 631–54.

cousins, Robin and Jim Magavern, in Buffalo. They shared my love of Southeast Asia, had lived and worked there themselves, and had even slept on the floor of my little Peace Corps house in southern Thailand. Jim, a valued mentor, told me about a colleague at the UB law school I should meet. An hour later, I was sitting in the Magaverns' living room talking with a young law professor named Marc Galanter, and a new field opened up for me. Marc rattled off the names of a dozen people I should read and correspond with – people such as Dan Lev, Rick Abel, Bob Kidder, June Starr, Dave Trubek, and Barry Hooker. To my amazement, all of them answered my letters – this was before the age of email, of course. I quickly found myself part of the emerging law and society network, and there I discovered a set of theories and methods that helped to explain Thai law and culture much better than anything I had learned in law school. When I arrived back in Chiangmai and learned that the historical records I sought did not exist, my grounding in law and society research prepared me to change my project into a contemporary study of dispute processing centered in the local court but situated in its cultural and historical setting – and to combine the analysis of hundreds of case files with fieldwork interviews.

By the time I began work at the American Bar Foundation, I considered myself as much a law and society scholar as a Thailand specialist. The transition from research based in Chiangmai to research based in Sander County seemed quite natural. As the LSA began to hold annual meetings on a regular basis, I met other like-minded colleagues with similar personal stories. In particular, I found myself on panels with two young anthropologists named Barbara Yngvesson and Carol Greenhouse. All three of us had independently conducted our own studies of American courts and communities. We soon realized we were completing one another's sentences and influencing one another's ideas. Later we decided to write a single book about our three communities, combining our insights from different regions of the country.[8] Sheer happenstance, but also the result of intellectual and institutional developments beyond our control. Free will or determinism? I'm not sure.

As I began to write about the Sander County research, the intellectual climate had changed within LSA and in the related disciplines. Originally, I had thought my aim was to map disputes in Sander County as they emerged from the social milieu and traveled to different forums, in some cases all the way to the court. That is what the first draft of "The Oven Bird's Song" looked like. But this paradigm felt less and less satisfactory as time went on. In the late 1970s and early

---

[8]   Carol J. Greenhouse, Barbara Yngvesson, and David M. Engel, *Law and Community in Three American Towns* (Cornell University Press, 1994).

1980s, the so-called "interpretive turn" began to change the thinking of many in the law and society field. The writings of Clifford Geertz have become overly familiar to us today, and some of his most felicitous turns of phrase have become clichés – nowadays, who doesn't claim to do "thick description"? But in the 1970s, Geertz had a liberating impact on law and society research and encouraged us to see behavior and practice as inseparable from meaning. As he wrote, the analysis of culture is "not an experimental science in search of law but an interpretive one in search of meaning. It is explication I am after, construing social expressions on their surface enigmatical."[9]

Reading Geertz and other interpretivist theorists and responding to the paradigm shift underway in our field, I identified myself with a group of LSA scholars who struggled against the constraints of the conventional dispute-processing framework. I tried to ask different kinds of questions about the community where I had conducted my fieldwork. What was the meaning of the narratives offered by the longtime residents of Sander County? Why were they so often filled with anguish, anxiety, and loss? Why were the interviewees so concerned about the problem of litigiousness when law actually played such a negligible role in local injury cases? What were the words behind the words that the interviewees spoke?

A later draft of the article became my job talk at SUNY Buffalo, and I kept working on it after I moved to Buffalo in 1981. Once again, the institutional context proved crucially important. I doubt that any other law school in the country would have hired me on the basis of that presentation! But the UB law school, with its unique mix of critical legal scholars and law and society specialists, stood for something different. It had even hired as its dean a sociologist, Red Schwartz, who was an LSA founder and president. By the time I got there, both Red and Marc Galanter had left, but a group of remarkable colleagues were still determined to challenge traditional legal and social scientific ideas. Thomas Headrick's deanship was an exciting time, before the long shadow of the *US News and World Report* rankings made legal academics afraid to defy convention. Settling for conventional scholarship in my new law-school setting almost felt like letting the team down. It was in this institutional climate that "The Oven Bird's Song" took its final form, in conversation with my new colleagues – Fred Konefsky, Jim Atleson, Jack Schlegel, Rob Steinfeld, Guyora Binder, Virginia Leary, and others.

I should add that the title of the article, taken from a Robert Frost poem about the call of a woodland bird during a time of change and decay, was itself

---

[9] Clifford Geertz, *The Interpretation of Cultures* (Basic Books, 1973), p. 5.

a bit unconventional and caused some difficulty. Frost's poem depicted the bird's loud and inharmonious song as a response to a post-lapsarian world, when springtime is long past, "the highway dust is over all," and one is left to ask "what to make of a diminished thing." This poem seemed an apt expression of the worldview I found in Sander County, where the denunciation of litigation by longtime residents became part of what I called "a ceremony of regret" to mourn the loss of "an untainted world that existed nowhere but in their imaginations." During the publication process, however, I was told to change the title, not just because it was unconventional, but also because potential readers would have no idea what the article was about. I consulted a number of colleagues, particularly Felice Levine, who had been a close colleague at the ABF and tends to have excellent judgment about this sort of thing. Felice thought for a moment and then advised me to keep the title. "This might be an article," she said, "that people will read ten years from now, and they will see the title as part of its identity." That's why it's still called "The Oven Bird's Song."

CORE THEMES, PAST AND FUTURE

It is this backward motion toward the source,
Against the stream, that most we see ourselves in,
The tribute of the current to the source.
It is from this in nature we are from.
It is most us.

Robert Frost, "West-Running Brook"

After publishing "The Oven Bird's Song," I became, in Isaiah Berlin's terms, a hedgehog not a fox. I found myself returning again and again to the article's central theme: the radical disparity between "the mythology of modern law"[10] and the actual tendency of rights holders to avoid lawyers, frame important issues in non-legal terms, and forgo claims when they suffered harm. Although law seemed to offer remedies for the problems facing many residents in Sander County, they viewed legal recourse in injury cases as a Catch 22. To make a legal claim was to identify themselves as uncultured – as outsiders to the community in which they sought acceptance. For those at the margins who lacked power and were most likely to suffer injustice, this posed a painful dilemma. Invoking the law seemed to deny them the very things it purported to offer: dignity, respect, and status.

---

[10] See Peter Fitzpatrick, *The Mythology of Modern Law* (Routledge, 1992).

Something similar was true of the men and women with disabilities whom Frank Munger and I interviewed in the 1990s. Many felt they had been treated unfairly and excluded, but they also worried that asserting their rights under the Americans with Disabilities Act to gain access to mainstream settings would simply reaffirm their identities as dependent and abnormal outsiders. Claiming legal rights took them through the looking glass – the faster they ran toward social justice, the farther they fell behind.[11]

When I returned to Thailand to explore changes in litigation and legal consciousness a quarter of a century after my initial research there, I expected to find at least modest growth in the invocation of legal rights among injury victims. After all, globalization is said to heighten people's awareness of the rule of law as a resource to redress social wrongs. Much to my surprise, however, I found that the central theme of "The Oven Bird's Song" – the avoidance of law and the positive value accorded to "lumping" – was even more evident than before. In Chiangmai Provincial Court I found fewer tort cases litigated per injury than was the case in the 1970s. Among injury victims, a new philosophy of karmic acceptance had replaced a centuries-old view that village-based wrongs demanded village-based remedies for the good of the entire community. Litigation now seemed selfish and anti-communitarian. For an injury victim to mobilize the law was to oppose fundamental cultural and religious values. Interviewees feared that legal claims would ultimately work to the disadvantage of the claimant and offer little in return. In short, economic development had disrupted longstanding customary law traditions, and "modern" legal institutions had failed to replace them in the minds of our interviewees.[12]

Pursuing the core themes of "The Oven Bird's Song" has thus been a recurring preoccupation. My latest book, *The Myth of the Litigious Society: Why We Don't Sue*,[13] returns even more explicitly to the questions that animated "The Oven Bird's Song" and illustrates my current perspective on tort law, culture, and legal consciousness in contemporary American society. Ample research over the past three decades has documented again and again that the vast majority of injury victims never make a claim of any kind against those who harm them. When injured, only a tiny percentage of Americans consult lawyers, file lawsuits, or even approach the injurers or their insurance

---

[11] David M. Engel and Frank W. Munger, *Rights of Inclusion: Law and Identity in the Life Stories of Americans with Disabilities* (University of Chicago Press, 2003).

[12] David M. Engel and Jaruwan S. Engel, *Tort, Custom, and Karma: Globalization and Legal Consciousness in Thailand* (Stanford University Press, 2010).

[13] David M. Engel, *The Myth of the Litigious Society: Why We Don't Sue* (University of Chicago Press, 2016).

companies extrajudicially to request compensation. Lumping as default in injury cases has been confirmed in so many studies that its predominance is beyond dispute – although this fact conflicts directly with what most Americans believe about their own supposedly litigious society. In fact, most injury victims – more than 90 percent, at a conservative estimate – simply absorb the sometimes devastating costs and consequences of their mishaps and rely on their own resources, on friends and family, or on government benefits.

But what we don't understand very well is *why* lumping is the predominant response to injuries in American society. My new book offers the results of a broad-ranging search for answers, not only in the law and society literature, but also in books and journal articles from rehabilitation science, nursing, anesthesiology, neuroscience, psychology, behavioral economics, anthropology, cultural studies, and other disciplines that study injury and pain, mind and body, human decision-making, law, and culture. These findings can be summarized in four general explanations of the tendency to lump injuries.

First, many injury victims are actively coping with trauma and pain, which disrupts their ability to make rational choices about the value of pursuing a claim as compared to lumping. Injury victims are not cool and dispassionate rational actors, pausing in the aisle of a grocery store to choose between two different brands of toothpaste. Physical injuries are exhausting and debilitating. It becomes difficult to think clearly. Injuries' effects and treatment – including the use of powerful pain medications – can lead to social isolation and confusion. Furthermore, as Elaine Scarry has made clear, pain is difficult to communicate.[14] The person in pain feels he or she has entered a new world impossible to describe to others. Injuries quite literally impair the use of language and thus make it exceedingly difficult to voice a claim. "Physical pain," Scarry writes, "does not simply resist language but actively destroys it."[15] Cognitive scientists tell us that "we think with our bodies," not just with our brains.[16] But what happens when the bodies with which we think are damaged and in agony? Pain promotes lumping because it obstructs rational decision-making and makes it difficult to articulate and pursue a remedy.

Second, researchers in many disciplines have discovered that people who suffer pain and trauma have a baffling tendency to blame themselves above all else. They believe that somehow they must have caused their own misfortune, through carelessness or through some moral failure. Pain is punishment – not

---

[14] Elaine Scarry, *The Body in Pain: The Making and Unmaking of the World* (Oxford University Press, 1985).

[15] Ibid, 4.

[16] Daniel Kahneman, *Thinking, Fast and Slow* (Farrar, Straus and Giroux, 2011), p. 51.

just etymologically ("pain" derives from the Latin *poena*, meaning punishment) but also psychologically and even theologically. Victims are not the only ones who feel intuitively that injuries must be their own fault; studies show that outside observers have the same perception. They tend to think that if someone has experienced injury, disability, or disfigurement, that person must somehow have deserved it. It follows that blaming the victim becomes a reason not to blame the injurer, no matter how culpable he or she may have been. The claimant's supposed responsibility for the harm displaces and preempts the injurer's responsibility. Lumping becomes the only appropriate response, even if the victim is only partly at fault – and even if tort law doctrine would allocate some of the blame to both parties.

Third, cultural practices and framing make many injuries appear "natural" even when they can be foreseen and easily prevented. Injuries are not objective facts; they are social constructs. Our culturally conditioned perceptions of injuries can make them appear a normal part of life and not at all an appropriate occasion for bringing a claim against anyone. For example, it took quite a while for people to see anything wrong with cars that lacked seat belts and air bags, since it seemed natural for passengers in a violent collision to be thrown from the car or through the windshield. And it is only in the past few years that people have begun to view vehicles without rearview cameras as defective, despite the thousands of children who were killed or injured each year by cars backing up. As Sarah Lochlann Jain has observed, every product, every activity, is encoded with a certain quantum of acceptable injury.[17] But those codes are not necessarily legible to injury victims or to others. The suffering of individual victims appears inevitable until a consensus develops that their injuries are worth avoiding by the adoption of different, safer ways of doing things. Moreover, the machinery of cultural production that constructs injuries as natural or unnatural is more accessible to the Haves than the Have-Nots, for all the reasons Marc Galanter first explained in "Why the Haves Come Out Ahead."[18] Repeat players and potential tort defendants have a much greater capacity to persuade the public that injuries are unavoidable. When an injury is naturalized, lumping by the victim appears to many Americans to be the only sensible response, and claiming appears absurd.

Fourth, the infrequency of claims also results from the social stigma that attaches to those who challenge their injurers directly. Tort litigation has acquired a very bad name, and tort litigants are belittled. Social stereotypes

---

[17] Sarah S. Lochlann Jain, *Injury: The Politics of Product Design and Safety Law in the United States* (Princeton University Press, 2006).

[18] Galanter, *Why the Haves Come Out Ahead*.

portray injury claimants and their lawyers as greedy, whining, dishonest, and dishonorable. Think of Saul Goodman in *Breaking Bad*, who keeps a box of neck braces in his office to help his clients exaggerate (or fabricate) their injuries. Think of Walter Matthau as lawyer "Whiplash Willie" in *The Fortune Cookie*, encouraging Jack Lemmon to fake partial paralysis after a Cleveland Browns football player runs over him at a game. Longstanding negative images of tort plaintiffs and their lawyers have been magnified by a highly effective PR campaign waged by tort reform advocates since the 1980s with ample funding from tobacco companies, other large corporations, and insurance companies. William Haltom and Michael McCann have documented how the tort reform campaign permeated the mass media and shaped societal understandings of tort litigation.[19] Our culture is saturated with negative perceptions of injury victims who bring claims. These stereotypes influence potential claimants as well as the family and friends who advise them. Lumping is the predictable result in a culture that stigmatizes people who bring claims instead of the people who cause them harm.

These are the explanations for lumping that I offer in my latest book. My interest in the problem has roots extending back to "The Oven Bird's Song." Since my article was published in 1984, we have learned that Sander County was not a unique cultural throwback or a quaint rural exception to the general rule of American litigiousness. Sander County spoke more broadly to American culture and to our legal consciousness as a society – a point that Carol Greenhouse, Barbara Yngvesson, and I tried to make in our combined study of communities in three different parts of the country, whose residents shared an aversion to litigation and explained their reasons in similar words.

Despite the obvious continuities between "The Oven Bird's Song" and my latest book, there are some differences that reflect changes in the field and in my own thinking about the problem of legal culture and consciousness. For example, the first explanation of lumping described above – the alienating and disabling effects of trauma on potential claimants – was not apparent to me thirty years ago. Indeed, I taught torts and wrote about legal consciousness for many years without properly appreciating the significance of the fact that tort plaintiffs tended to be persons in physical pain. Even worse, after conducting research among persons with disabilities, I utterly failed to put two and two together and recognize that disability was a common result of tortious injuries. A number of the people with disabilities whom Frank Munger and I interviewed in the 1990s were former injury victims. Their ambivalence

---

[19] William Haltom and Michael McCann, *Distorting the Law: Politics, Media, and the Litigation Crisis* (University of Chicago Press, 2004).

about law was very closely connected to the ambivalence I had previously encountered in Sander County, although I didn't see the relationship at the time.

On the other hand, the second explanation for lumping – victim-blaming and self-blame – was at least partially apparent to me at the time of my Sander County research. As described in "The Oven Bird's Song," when I told one of the community observers about the little girl in Sander County who had been seriously harmed by an "attractive nuisance," he rather coldly blamed the child by commenting that he would "figure that the kid ought to be sharp enough to stay away" from the hazard.[20] And sure enough, the mother in that case eventually came around to the view that she herself was to blame for not watching her daughter closely enough. I was not prepared at that point to generalize about the significance of self-blaming and victim-blaming, but in my new book, drawing on additional research from a variety of disciplines, I was ready to conclude that blaming the victim is one of the most powerful explanations for lumping in injury cases.

The third explanation for lumping – the naturalization of injury – was also partially evident to me at the time of "The Oven Bird's Song." From my discussions with farming families, I learned that these stoic and admirable oldtimers considered injuries a part of life. Farming was hard work, and it involved dangerous machinery. Injuries and pain were familiar hazards, though risks could be reduced if one was careful (again, the importance of self-blame!). But it was "normal" to experience painful accidents, and what was "abnormal" was to view those mishaps as potential windfalls and to convert them into demands for compensation from someone else. As I wrote in "The Oven Bird's Song," "money was viewed as something one acquired through long hours of hard work, not by exhibiting one's misfortunes to a judge or jury or other third party, even when the injuries were clearly caused by the wrongful behavior of another."[21] Unless injuries were perceived as an exception, as contrary to the natural order, they would not be viewed as an occasion to assert a claim. My new book presents numerous examples of the naturalization of injury, but the original insight is rooted in my experience in Sander County.

The fourth explanation for lumping – the stigmatization of claiming in a culture that disvalues tort litigation – owes everything to my research in Sander County. The light bulb that went on as I was reading Geertz while struggling to write "The Oven Bird's Song" was the realization that so-called

---

[20] Engel, *The Oven Bird's Song*, p. 570. [21] Ibid, 559.

American litigiousness was not an objective fact but a symbolically important myth. This was the meaning of the song that the oven bird sang – it expressed nostalgia for an imagined world before the economy shifted away from agriculture, before "strangers" entered the community, before racial and ethnic diversity became visible on the main street of the town. It extolled lumping because claiming was a sign of cultural decline.

Surely this deep connection between the myth of litigiousness and the resentment of a modern, globalized, multicultural society is even more evident today than it was thirty years ago in rural Illinois. Today, the discourse of social decay is everywhere. The stigmatization of tort claimants makes injury victims even more fearful of demanding their rights. In Sander County, the norms opposing tort claims created a symbolic wall to separate insiders from outsiders in a changing community. Today, the call for moral rectitude has taken on even greater urgency in the face of social changes many Americans find confusing and threatening. One might think that moral rectitude would mean invoking the law and conforming to it, but for personal injury victims it means just the opposite. The morally upright person is one who *abstains*. He or she refuses to mobilize the law when injured by another. The paradox is compounded when we realize that people who oppose invoking the law against tort defendants tend to be the same people who applaud using the law against criminal defendants who injure others. Using the law to sanction injurious behavior is not in itself a signifier of moral depravity or societal decline; it is the use of law by the wrong people against the wrong defendants in the wrong kinds of cases. Those whose lives are transformed by pain and trauma are told to endure their misfortune and not to challenge those who harm them. In 2016 there is much less tort litigation in state courts and more lumping than there was thirty years ago, when "The Oven Bird's Song" was published. In this sense, America has become Sander County writ large.

The question remains as important and complex as ever – can or should the law play a role when pain disrupts the relationship between self and community? Pain isolates its victims from society, it destroys their relationships with others and their ability to communicate, and too often it leaves them destitute or with a greatly reduced capacity to earn and to thrive. And the pain of accidental injuries does not fall equally on the rich and the poor alike. Statistically speaking, risk flows down the social hierarchy and pools among the least privileged. Have-nots are exposed to more accidental injuries than the haves, yet they are the ones least able to bear the after-effects of serious harm. What a terrible irony, then, that the effort to seek a legal remedy frequently reinforces the injury victim's identity as socially marginal, as inferior, and as culturally alien. It remains an urgent task for law and society scholars to understand the cultural meaning and social consequences of painful and damaged bodies – for individuals, for entire communities, and for justice.

Research on tort law and society has advanced considerably in the past thirty years, but there is so much left to discover. My research growing out of "The Oven Bird's Song" has focused primarily on physical injuries, despite our growing recognition of non-physical harms to reputation, privacy, and emotional well-being. In my next project, I hope to remedy this shortcoming, but other law and society scholars are already leading the way.[22] It is always useful and gratifying to revisit the past, but the future of law and society scholarship is full of promise, as exemplified by the scholars who have contributed to this volume. Law and society researchers will continue to explore the most important sociolegal myths that prevail in our society. But, equally important, they will expand our theories about law and deepen our understanding of when and how law actually matters. What is true of tort law is equally true of other fields – the human side has been largely neglected in favor of explicating theories and rules that often have little practical relevance to the individuals whom law is meant to serve. If it is true that the vast majority of injury victims simply lump their misfortunes, if they never bring a claim of any kind against their injurers, then we must reconsider both the value and the efficacy of a great deal of tort law doctrine. Law and society research at its best forces us to question the obvious, to reassess prevailing legal practices in the light of actual behavior, and to remember that the law concerns real human actors, not fictional beings such as the reasonable person or the rational actor.

Too seldom do we hear the real voices of injury victims. What do pain and trauma mean for their lives? What are their anxieties, feelings, and concerns? How do power relationships affect the risks they face and their responses to harm when it occurs? I am confident that the next generation of law and society scholars will continue to take full advantage of the countless opportunities for research on injuries and on other pressing issues relevant to law in the lives of ordinary people. In the last analysis, "The Oven Bird's Song" was no more than a single response to this wealth of topics awaiting the attention of law and society researchers. It was shaped by the inspiring work of contemporaries and forebears and it was given meaning by the scores of imaginative studies that followed. It offered the portrait of a community, but it was also the product of a community of colleagues to whom I remain forever grateful.

---

[22] See, for example, Samantha Barbas, *Laws of Image: Privacy and Publicity in America* (Stanford University Press, 2015).

Index

Bowie, David, 188–91, 198
Bruner, Jerome, 40, 48, 50–1, 53

contracts, 4, 5, 30–4, 77, 113–20, 149, 154
critical race theory, 6, 164, 167, 179–80

disability, 6, 40–1, 50, 182–3, 185–6, 190, 192–4,
    196–7, 289–90
disputing process, 4, 6, 22, 40, 144–5, 156,
    264–5, 274

Frost, Robert, 3, 8, 51, 56, 82, 123, 181, 182, 227,
    263–5, 271, 279, 285–6

Galanter, Marc, 11, 62–3, 145, 202, 262, 282,
    284–5, 289
Geertz, Clifford, 39, 64, 150, 285, 291
gender, 6, 66, 76, 91–3, 95–7, 140, 145, 152–4,
    159, 182–5, 187–8, 190–4, 196, 270–1, 273
globalization, 40, 43, 46, 182, 195, 287
Greenhouse, Carol, 54–5, 139, 202, 220,
    262–3, 280, 284, 290

haves and have nots, 4, 65, 143, 145, 149, 289,
    292
hyperlexis, 11, 40, 141, 155–8

immigrants/immigration, 4, 6, 24, 74, 76,
    92–3, 131, 144, 152–5, 158, 161–80,
    209, 270
individualism, 15, 29, 33, 148, 183, 193, 200,
    207, 208, 264, 265
interpretive turn, 5, 7, 39, 44, 46, 64, 139, 281,
    285

Japan, 6, 28–9, 118, 149, 223, 229, 231, 237–61,
    282
juries, 4, 5, 17, 20–1, 87–8, 91, 98–112, 146, 148,
    157–8

legal consciousness, 4, 5, 7, 38, 40, 43,
    46, 54, 71–80, 124, 134, 143, 149, 155,
    206, 220, 236–7, 248–9, 264, 274,
    287, 290
legal profession, 4, 9, 21, 26, 82–4, 92–3, 95, 97,
    202, 243, 257–9
Llellewyn, Karl, 57–61, 64–8, 283

McDonald's hot coffee case, 102–3, 156–8
Munger, Frank, 41, 274, 280, 287, 290

nostalgia, 4, 12, 35, 124, 133, 134, 138, 140, 149,
    153, 159, 199, 200, 214, 215, 231, 266, 267,
    275, 282, 292

ORLAN, 191, 198
outsiders, 6–7, 11–12, 25, 27, 33–5, 51,
    65, 74, 77, 83, 94, 124, 131–3, 137,
    140–1, 147, 150–2, 154, 160, 163–4,
    182–3, 187

parochialism, 7, 33, 265, 272, 274
populism, 4, 214
Prince (artist), 188–91, 198

race, 6, 12, 29, 54, 66, 91–2, 119, 131, 141,
    143–4, 147, 151–2, 154, 159, 164–70,
    173–5, 179–80, 184–5, 187, 194,
    203, 273

religion, 27, 40, 73, 75, 78, 91, 95, 152, 202,
210–11, 235, 264, 265, 269, 271
rights mobilization, 4, 6, 72, 144–5, 158, 163

Scheingold, Stuart, 140–1, 143–5, 148, 150–1,
154, 202
social change, 3, 4, 11, 13, 15, 29, 33, 35, 59, 73,
78, 79, 82, 84, 94, 152, 179, 195, 229, 262,
265–7, 271, 292

social distance, 23–5, 27, 133, 151, 263, 264, 272,
275

Thailand, 38–47, 220, 233, 235, 236,
281–4, 287
tort reform, 6, 53, 87, 101, 156, 158, 290

Yngvesson, Barbara, 5, 38, 139, 202, 280, 282,
284, 290

Books in the Series

Diseases of the Will
Mariana Valverde

The Politics of Truth and Reconciliation in South Africa: Legitimizing the Post-Apartheid State
Richard A. Wilson

Modernism and the Grounds of Law
Peter Fitzpatrick

Unemployment and Government: Genealogies of the Social
William Walters

Autonomy and Ethnicity: Negotiating Competing Claims in Multi-Ethnic States
Yash Ghai

Constituting Democracy: Law, Globalism and South Africa's Political Reconstruction
Heinz Klug

The Ritual of Rights in Japan: Law, Society, and Health Policy
Eric A. Feldman

The Invention of the Passport: Surveillance, Citizenship and the State
John Torpey

Governing Morals: A Social History of Moral Regulation
Alan Hunt

The Colonies of Law: Colonialism, Zionism and Law in Early Mandate Palestine
Ronen Shamir

Law and Nature
David Delaney

Social Citizenship and Workfare in the United States and Western Europe: The Paradox of Inclusion
Joel F. Handler

Law, Anthropology and the Constitution of the Social: Making Persons and Things
Edited by Alain Pottage and Martha Mundy

Judicial Review and Bureaucratic Impact: International and Interdisciplinary Perspectives
Edited by Marc Hertogh and Simon Halliday

Immigrants at the Margins: Law, Race, and Exclusion in Southern Europe
Kitty Calavita

Lawyers and Regulation: The Politics of the Administrative Process
Patrick Schmidt

Law and Globalization from Below: Toward a Cosmopolitan Legality
Edited by Boaventura de Sousa Santos and Cesar A. Rodriguez-Garavito

Public Accountability: Designs, Dilemmas and Experiences
Edited by Michael W. Dowdle

Law, Violence and Sovereignty among West Bank Palestinians
Tobias Kelly

Legal Reform and Administrative Detention Powers in China
Sarah Biddulph

The Practice of Human Rights: Tracking Law Between the Global and the Local
Edited by Mark Goodale and Sally Engle Merry

Judges Beyond Politics in Democracy and Dictatorship: Lessons from Chile
Lisa Hilbink

Paths to International Justice: Social and Legal Perspectives
Edited by Marie-Bénédicte Dembour and Tobias Kelly

Law and Society in Vietnam: The Transition from Socialism in Comparative Perspective
Mark Sidel

Constitutionalizing Economic Globalization: Investment Rules and Democracy's Promise
David Schneiderman

The New World Trade Organization KnowledgeAgreements: 2nd Edition
Christopher Arup

Justice and Reconciliation in Post-Apartheid South Africa
Edited by François du Bois and Antje du Bois-Pedain

Militarization and Violence against Women in Conflict Zones in the Middle East: A Palestinian Case-Study
Nadera Shalhoub-Kevorkian

Child Pornography and Sexual Grooming: Legal and Societal Responses
Suzanne Ost

Darfur and the Crime of Genocide
John Hagan and Wenona Rymond-Richmond

Fictions of Justice: The International Criminal Court and the Challenge of Legal Pluralism in Sub-Saharan Africa
Kamari Maxine Clarke

Conducting Law and Society Research: Reflections on Methods and Practices
Simon Halliday and Patrick Schmidt

Planted Flags: Trees, Land, and Law in Israel/Palestine
Irus Braverman

Culture under Cross-Examination: International Justice and the Special Court for Sierra Leone
Tim Kelsall

Cultures of Legality: Judicialization and Political Activism in Latin America
Javier Couso, Alexandra Huneeus, Rachel Sieder

Courting Democracy in Bosnia and Herzegovina: The Hague Tribunal's Impact in a Postwar State
Lara J. Nettelfield

The Gacaca Courts and Post-Genocide Justice and Reconciliation in Rwanda: Justice without Lawyers
Phil Clark

Law, Society, and History: Themes in the Legal Sociology and Legal History of Lawrence M. Friedman
Robert W. Gordon and Morton J. Horwitz

After Abu Ghraib: Exploring Human Rights in America and the Middle East
Shadi Mokhtari

Adjudication in Religious Family Laws: Cultural Accommodation: Legal Pluralism, and Gender Equality in India
Gopika Solanki

Water on Tap: Rights and Regulation in the Transnational Governance of Urban Water Services
Bronwen Morgan

Elements of Moral Cognition: Rawls' Linguistic Analogy and the Cognitive Science of Moral and Legal Judgment
John Mikhail

A Sociology of Transnational Constitutions: Social Foundations of the Post-National Legal Structure
Chris Thornhill

Mitigation and Aggravation at Sentencing
Edited by Julian Roberts

Institutional Inequality and the Mobilization of the Family and Medical Leave Act: Rights on Leave
Catherine R. Albiston

Authoritarian Rule of Law: Legislation, Discourse and Legitimacy in Singapore
Jothie Rajah

Law and Development and the Global Discourses of Legal Transfers
Edited by John Gillespie and Pip Nicholson

Law against the State: Ethnographic Forays into Law's Transformations
Edited by Julia Eckert, Brian Donahoe, Christian Strümpell and Zerrin Özlem Biner

Transnational Legal Process and State Change
Edited by Gregory C. Shaffer

Legal Mobilization under Authoritarianism: The Case of Post-Colonial Hong Kong
Edited by Waikeung Tam

Complementarity in the Line of Fire: The Catalysing Effect of the International Criminal Court in Uganda and Sudan
Sarah M. H. Nouwen

Political and Legal Transformations of an Indonesian Polity: The Nagari from Colonisation to Decentralisation
Franz von Benda-Beckmann and Keebet von Benda-Beckmann

Pakistan's Experience with Formal Law: An Alien Justice
Osama Siddique

Human Rights under State-Enforced Religious Family Laws in Israel, Egypt, and India
Yüksel Sezgin

Why Prison?
Edited by David Scott

Law's Fragile State: Colonial, Authoritarian, and Humanitarian Legacies in Sudan
Mark Fathi Massoud

Rights for Others: The Slow Home-Coming of Human Rights in the Netherlands
Barbara Oomen

European States and their Muslim Citizens: The Impact of Institutions on Perceptions and Boundaries
Edited by John R. Bowen, Christophe Bertossi, Jan Willem Duyvendak and Mona Lena Krook

Environmental Litigation in China
Rachel E. Stern

Indigeneity and Legal Pluralism in India: Claims, Histories, Meanings
Pooja Parmar

Paper Tiger: Law, Bureaucracy and the Developmental State in Himalayan India
Nayanika Mathur

Religion, Law and Society
Russell Sandberg

The Experiences of Face Veil Wearers in Europe and the Law
Edited by Eva Brems

The Contentious History of the International Bill of Human Rights
Christopher N. J. Roberts

Transnational Legal Orders
Edited by Terence C. Halliday and Gregory Shaffer

Lost in China?, Law, Culture and Society in Post-1997 Hong Kong
Carol A. G. Jones

Security Theology, Surveillance and the Politics of Fear
Nadera Shalhoub-Kevorkian

Opposing the Rule of Law: How Myanmar's Courts Make Law and Order
Nick Cheesman

The Ironies of Colonial Governance: Law, Custom and Justice in Colonial India
James Jaffe

The Clinic and the Court: Law, Medicine and Anthropology
Edited by Tobias Kelly, Ian Harper and Akshay Khanna

A *World of Indicators: The Making of Government Knowledge Through Quantification*
Edited by Richard Rottenburg, Sally E. Merry, Sung-Joon Park and Johanna Mugler

Contesting Immigration Policy in Court: Legal Activism and its Radiating Effects in the United States and France
Leila Kawar

The Quiet Power of Indicators: Measuring Governance, Corruption, and Rule of Law
Edited by Sally Engle Merry, Kevin Davis, and Benedict Kingsbury

Investing in Authoritarian Rule: Punishment and Patronage in Rwanda's Gacaca Courts for Genocide Crimes
Anuradha Chakravarty

Contractual Knowledge: One Hundred Years of Legal Experimentation in Global Markets
Edited by Grégoire Mallard and Jérôme Sgard

Iraq and the Crimes of Aggressive War: The Legal Cynicism of Criminal Militarism
John Hagan, Joshua Kaiser, and Anna Hanson

Culture in the Domains of Law
Edited by René Provost

China and Islam: The Prophet, the Party, and Law
Matthew S. Erie

Diversity in Practice: Race, Gender, and Class in Legal and Professional Careers
Edited by Spencer Headworth and Robert Nelson

A Sociology of Transnational Constitutions: Social Foundations of the Post-National Legal Structure
Chris Thornhill

Shifting Legal Visions: Judicial Change and Human Rights Trials in Latin America
Ezequiel A. González Ocantos

The Demographic Transformations of Citizenship
Heli Askola

Criminal Defense in China: The Politics of Lawyers at Work
Sida Liu and Terence C. Halliday

Contesting Economic and Social Rights in Ireland: Constitution, State and Society, 1848–2016
Thomas Murray

Buried in the Heart: Women, Complex Victimhood and the War in Northern Uganda
Erin Baines

Palaces of Hope: The Anthropology of Global Organizations
Edited by Ronald Niezen and Maria Sapignoli

The Politics of Bureaucratic Corruption in Post-Transitional Eastern Europe
Marina Zaloznaya

Revisiting the Law and Governance of Trafficking, Forced Labor and Modern Slavery
Prabha Kotiswaran

Incitement on Trial: Prosecuting International Speech Crimes
Richard Ashby Wilson

Criminalizing Children: A History of Welfare and the State in Australia
David McCallum

Global Legislators: How International Organizations Make Trade Law for the World
Terrence C. Halliday and Susan Block-Lieb

Duties to Care: Dementia, Relationality and Law
Rosie Harding